Fuel pumps

Also including Gunson Colortune tuning

SU.4.1.

ISBN 0-85113-113-1

First impression . . . . April 1968
Second . . . . July 1970
2nd Edition . . . . June 1972
3rd Edition . . . . February 1975
4th Edition revised & enlarged Feb 1981

Technical Collation G. R. Wade C. Eng.,
F.I. Mech. E., F. Inst. F.

Typesetting and
layout by. . . . . . HGA Printing Co Ltd.

Published by. . . . Speedsport Motobooks

Printed in Brentford, England
by . . . . HGA Printing Co. Ltd.

Acknowledements

We should like to acknowledge the invaluable assistance given by the British Leyland Motor Corporation and SU Carburetter Company in providing so much of the literature forming the basis of this manual.

Our thanks are also due to Gunson's Color plugs limited for permission to reproduce information on their color-tune system of engine tuning.

We hope that this manual will serve as a beneficial guide to millions of motorists running cars with SU Carburation and/or fuel supply equipment.

Contents

	Introduction	vii
	In Retrospect	ix
Chapter 1	Basic Design and Function	1
Chapter 2	Overhauling and Fault Finding	7
Chapter 3	Mixtures and Tuning	9
Chapter 4	Burning Characteristics of different mixtures	25
Chapter 5	Size selection	27
Chapter 6	The use of special racing fuels	31
Chapter 7	Dismantling & Assembly	33
Chapter 8	Auxilliary Enrichment	88
Chapter 9	Automatic Enrichment Device	92
Chapter 10	Electric Fuel Pumps	94
Chapter 11	Mechanical Fuel Pumps	140
	Appendix 1	150
	Appendix 2 Jet Identification	182
	Appendix 3 Jet Needle Identification	183
	Appendix 4 Gunsons Colortune Device	188

Introduction

The SU carburetter has been with us for many decades, in fact since the First World War era. Since it's introduction it has undergone many subtle changes in design which have brought it to it's present day standard of high efficiency and reliability, coupled with basic simplicity and versatility.

Although it has been subjected to continuous development over the years, the operation of the SU has remained basically unchanged for virtually half a century. Such was the soundness of the basic design. Over the years, the SU has been in service in virtually every type of engine from agricultural engines to racing engines; from buses to limousines. Because of it's simplicity, versatility and effectiveness, the SU has found widespread use, not the least important of these is it's application to high performance engines, both for road and competition use. For road use, the SU is expected to give both good power and good economy. This it can do when correctly tuned. On the track it is expected to give the sort of power necessary for winning performances. This, the SU also achieves, and in a manner which is surpassed only by the most sophisticated and expensive types of carburetters or even fuel injection.

Once in a while, one hears of carburetter troubles manifesting themselves. Such maladies as rich mixtures, flat spots, misfiring, etc., are often lumped together under one heading of 'going out of tune'. The SU carburetter, simple though it may be, is often blamed for faults which are, in fact, none of it's doing. This is not to say that it is faultless, but it can be said that many carburation troubles stem from a lack of understanding of the carburetter concerned. The SU, like any other carburetter, has to perform a delicate function, that of mixing the correct amount of petrol with the air passing through it. To do so, it must be in proper working order, and correctly set within relatively fine limits. To achieve this, one must understand the working of this carburetter. Then, and only then can it's true potential in any given situation be fully realized. Both from the performance and economy aspect, the correct setting up and use of an SU carburetter cannot be over-emphasized. With the aid of this book, it is hoped that all those using SU carburetters will benefit, whether it be from the aspect of economy or power.

Following a brief historical note this manual informs on the principles generally applicable to the use of SU carburetters and fuel pumps, and details the constructional features of specific unit types. The tuning details given in Chapter 3 apply generally to H, HD and HS units when read in conjunction with the specific carburetter text. The somewhat different construction and control features of the integral float chamber emission control carburetter (HIF) however require separate description and this is given in the HIF unit section.

With the assistance of this manual it is hoped that all those using SU carburetters and fuel pumps will benefit in obtaining optimum performance from either a power or fuel economy point of view.

If, despite 'working to the book' a satisfactory result is not obtained the Technical Service Department of SU will be pleased to advise. State your problem simply and clearly, giving carburetter specification (on aluminium tag attached to suction chamber cover) or fuel pump specification (stamped on top flange).

If these numbers cannot be found or identified, then state vehicle year, model and engine size.

Address enquiry to:—

    SU.BUTEC
    Technical Services Department,
    Dormer Road,
    Thame,
    Oxon.
    OX9 3UB

In retrospect

In 1905 Mr. George H. Skinner took out a patent for a carburetter in which both the air and fuel passages varied in accordance with the requirements of the engine. The original design was a clean and simple layout in marked contrast to the multi-jet fixed choke carburetters and it provided a standard of flexibility and economy of operation hitherto unknown.

George Skinner together with brothers John and Carl formed the S.U. Carburetter Company in 1910, setting up business in a small workshop in London. The initials S.U. stand for Skinners Union.

From these beginnings the S.U. Company grew into one of the major manufacturers of car fuel systems and components in Europe, its carburetters being widely used on both touring and competition vehicles.

SU carburetters are to be found on such widely differing types of vehicles as the British Leyland Mini, Swedish Volvo and the Rolls-Royce Silver Shadow. Although the basic design has altered little, the SU carburetter is one of the most renowned and reliable on the market.

The scope of the company was widened by the introduction of its now well-known range of electrical and mechanical fuel pumps and Automatic Enrichment. Device (AED). More recently the sophisticated Horizontal Integral Floatchamber (HIF) carburetter has been introduced to meet demanding pollution control requirements.

The company has further expanded its manufacturing and development facilities in order to maintain the unique reputation that SU has acquired in the field of carburation and fuel delivery pump equipment.

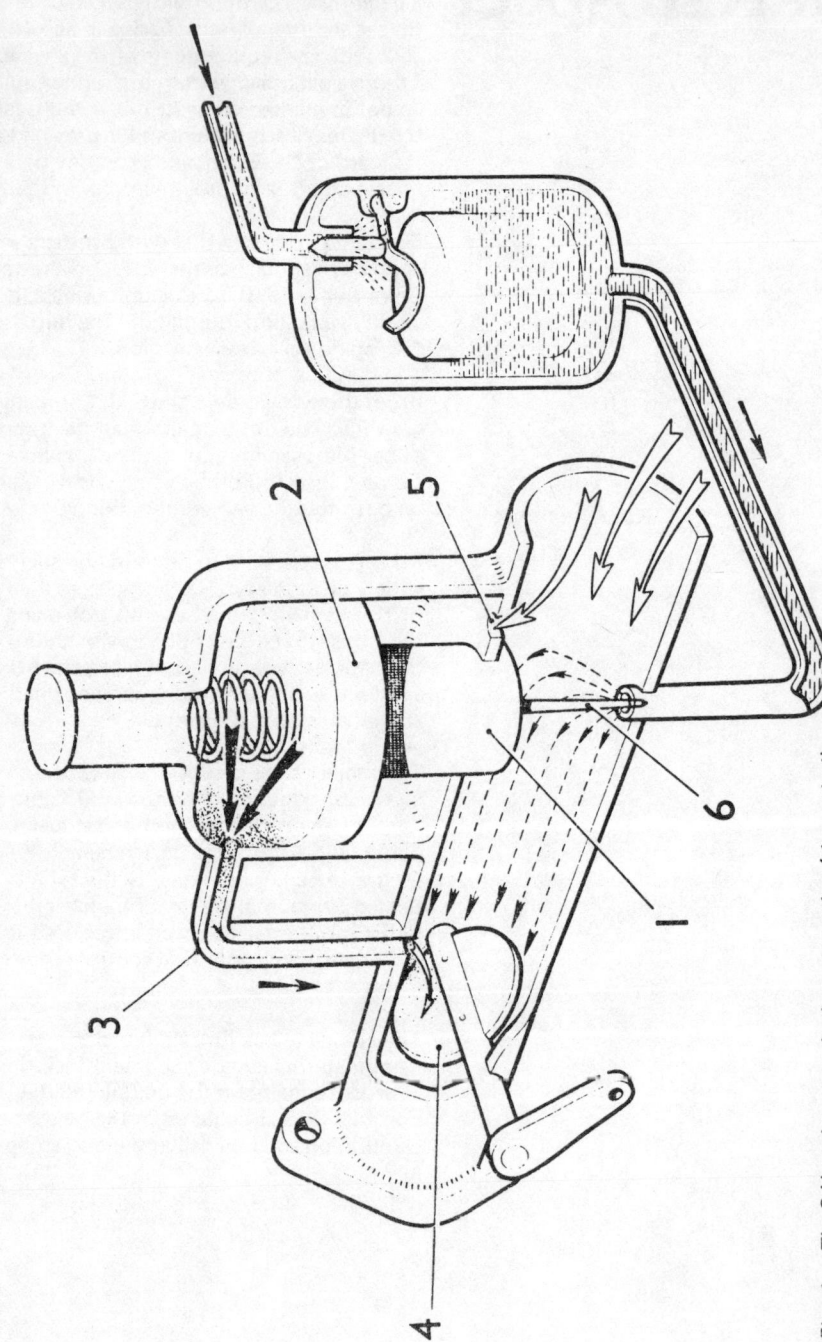

Fig. 1 — The S.U. carburetter—basic construction (theoretical)

Chapter 1

Basic design & function

The SU carburetter falls into a class of instrument commonly known as a constant depression or variable choke. The reason for so doing stems from the fact that the depression, vacuum or suction, call it what you will, over the jet orifice, remains relatively constant, throughout the range of airflow requirements of an engine. To see how this is achieved, let us look at the basic principles of operation of the SU carburetter.

Take a look at Fig. 1. Here we have the basic layout of the SU carburetter. The engine is situated to the left of the butterfly. When the engine is running, there will be a large depression existing on the left hand side of the butterfly simply because the butterfly is restricting the flow of air to the engine as it would do under idling conditions. Because the butterfly is slightly open (it will have to be to supply the engine with air to idle) part of this depression is connected to the right hand side of the butterfly. From the drawing, it can also be seen that a hole in the suction chamber (3) connects the right hand side of the butterfly with the suction chamber above the body of the carburetter. The underside of the large diameter of the piston (2) is connected to normal atmospheric pressure by a hole 5. Now, when we open the throttle slightly (4), the depression on the left hand side of the butterfly, will be allowed to communicate to a greater degree with the slight vacuum existing on the right hand side of it. This, in turn, will draw air out of the bell chamber from above the piston. We now have an unequal pressure existing across the piston. Underneath the large piston diameter is normal air pressure, whilst above it, it is lower than normal air pressure. Hence this pressure differential will cause the piston to rise. In so doing, it will pull the tapered needle (6) out of the jet, thus allowing more air and more petrol to pass into the carburetter and thus to the engine. If we open the throttle still further and, via (3) suck even more air out of the bell chamber, then the piston will rise even further. This will allow more air into the engine and also, since the needle comes out of the jet further, allow more petrol, thus keeping the mixture ratio in correct proportion. If the throttle is opened fully while the engine is at low rpm, the suction will not be particularly large, due to the fact that the engines air requirement will be low while it is at low rpm. This means that the piston will only open far enough to satisfy the engines demand for air and no more. As revs rise, so the piston will rise. By this system, it can be seen that not only does the carburetter adjust itself for throttle demand, i.e. how much rpm a driver requires at the particular instant, but also, it adjusts itself to engine load condition. To look at it another way, we could say that whatever the throttle butterfly does, the piston in the carburetter lifts only sufficiently to supply the air required by the engine for it's particular needs of the moment.

This, then, is the basic mode of operation of the SU carburetter. We can say that as there is a constant depression or suction over the jet, then the mixture is governed by the taper of the needle and this is why this component is all important.

Fuel Levels and Float Chambers

Again, looking at Fig. 1, we can see that the further the needle comes out of the jet, the greater the area that is available for fuel to pass. Now, although this is the means of governing the rate of fuel introduced into the air, it does depend on one other factor, this being the initial level of the fuel in the jet. If the fuel is a long way down the jet before we start the engine, we can see that quite a bit of suction will be needed just to draw the fuel up to the top of the jet before it starts being emitted into the air. On the other hand, if the fuel is only just below the jet before the engine is started, then when it is started, only a small amount of suction will cause fuel to flow out of the jet. From this, then, we can see that at least in the initial stages, the level of the fuel in the jet is important, as it will effect the mixture ratio that the carburetter delivers.

In practice the fuel in a carburetter main jet is set such that it is between an eighth and a quarter of an inch below it's point of discharge. The pressure drop needed to draw the fuel up to the lip of the jet under these circumstances will be between two-thirds and one and a third ounces per square inch.

From the straightforward carburation point of view, the fuel level is best set dead level with the top of the jet. However, under these conditions, braking, accelerating and cornering forces would cause the fuel to spill out of the jet, thus grossly enriching the mixture. It is for this reason that the fuel level needs to be set some distance below the top of the jet so that the mixture is not too badly effected by various accelerations that the car is subjected to. Now that we can see why the fuel level must be set a certain distance below the edge of the jet, we can consider the means for setting this level. The fuel supplied to the jet is drawn from the float chamber. The float chamber has two principle functions, the first of these being to set the fuel level. This is achieved by allowing so much fuel into the chamber before the float rises, operates a valve, and prevents further fuel entering the float chamber. The float should cut off the supply of fuel into the float chamber such that it leaves a fuel level in the jet in it's correct position.

The second function of the float chamber (which is related in part to the first) is to regulate the supply of fuel to the engine. The amount of petrol supplied by the fuel pump is always more than the engine needs. If some form of regulation were not present, then the fuel pump would flood the engine with petrol. The float chamber then, apart from setting the fuel level, regulates the flow such that the main jet has a steady source from which to draw it's supply or needs.

Choke and Mixture Control

When an engine is cold, it needs a richer mixture than when it is warm. This stems

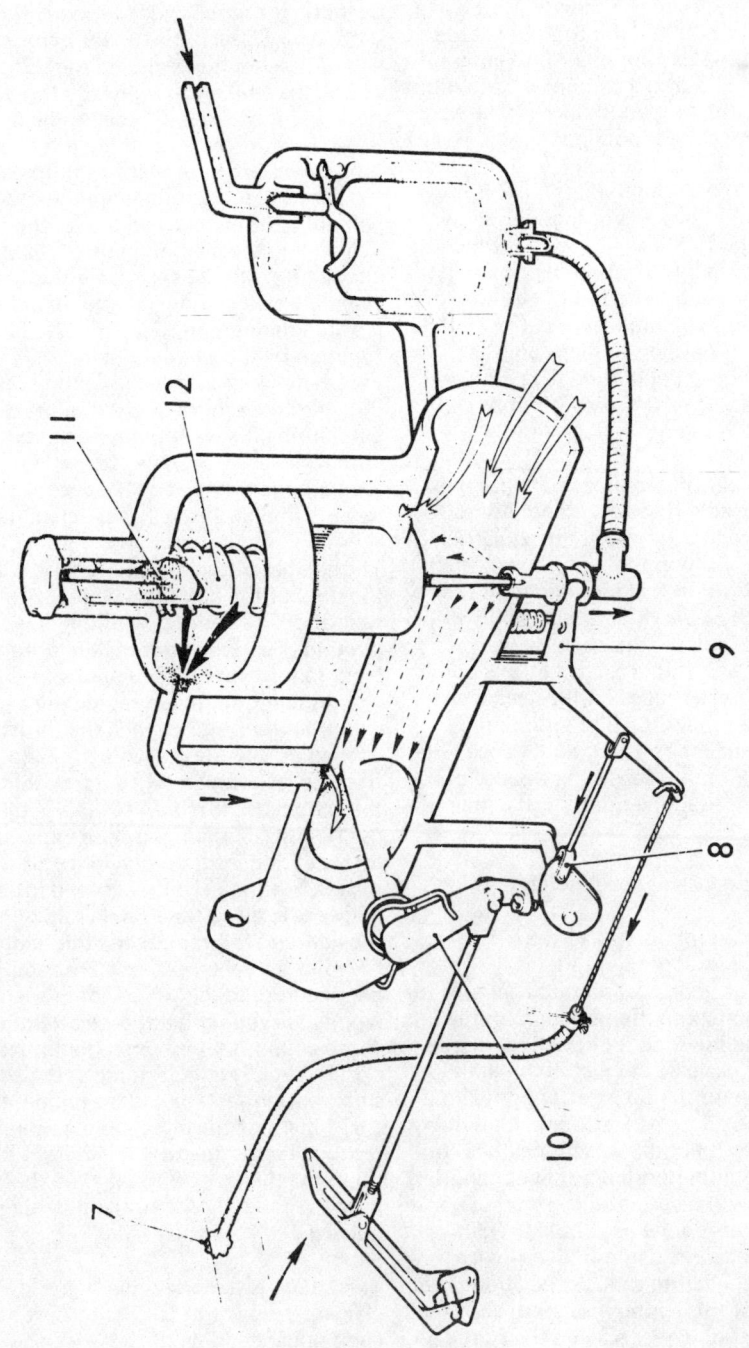

Fig. 2 — Addition to the basic design (theoretical)

from the fact that at low temperatures the petrol does not vapourise so easily to form a combustible mixture. Hence we have to use a lot more petrol to get a sufficiently vapourized amount of gas within the cylinder to ignite properly. The rich starting mixture is obtained on the H, HD and HS types, but not on the HIF type, by simply lowering the jet, Fig.2 (9). Inspection of relevant drawings will show that the jet is in a carrier within which it can slide Fig.3 (15). By bringing this jet down, the needle fills less of the bore of the jet, thus allowing more petrol to flow through it. As soon as the engine has reached normal operating temperature, the jet can be returned to it's normal position.

Mixture control (assuming one has the correct needle fitted) is accomplished in a similar manner, a nut on the jet carrier Fig.3 (14), allows the jet to be adjusted up and down in fine increments until the mixture is correctly set. Such adjustment, of course, will set the mixture only at tickover, and if it is correct at this point the carburetter relies on the needle profile alone to give the correct mixture throughout the rest of the rev range. The adjustment nut, then, in all essence can be termed an idling mixture adjustment nut.

The Suction Chamber Assembly

We have already looked at the basic function of the dashpot, and that is it's ability to lift the piston to a required amount for a given pressure differential across the upper and lower face of the large piston diameter. Raising the piston to admit more air into the carburetter body, however, is not it's sole function. It has many secondary functions which together are of significant importance. Let us consider, first of all, the spring within the suction chamber assembly, Fig. 2 (13). This spring loads the piston in a downward direction, i.e. into a closed position. The tension of this spring is selected such that the piston only just reaches the fully open position when the engine has it's maximum air demand (i.e.. it's peak bhp output). If the spring is too weak, the dashpot will reach it's full lift before the engine reaches it's peak bhp rpm. This means that the metering of the fuel will not be as it should be, because the needle is fully out of the jet and there is no more movement left for metering purposes. If the spring is too strong, then the dashpot will not lift fully even when the engine is demanding the maximum throughput of air. Apart from the spring, the dashpot assembly also contains the guide rod and a piston damper Fig. 2 (11 & 12). The function of the guide rod is virtually self explanatory - it guides the piston accurately within the bore of the suction chamber. During it's up and down motion within the chamber, the outer edges of the dashpot piston should not contact the inner diameter of the suction chamber.

The damper piston which is housed within the bore of the guide rod works within a well of oil. The function of the damper is twofold. Firstly it prevents the piston from following the fluctuations of the air flow at low rpm, thus keeping the piston steady and secondly, when the throttle is opened quickly, it prevents the piston from rising in unison with the opening of the throttle. The reason for this is that air has less inertia than petrol, so when the throttle is opened rapidly, extra air will rush in but the petrol will take a little longer before it's flow catches up with the new air flow rate. When this happens, the mixture becomes weak. By damping the piston such that if cannot move too rapidly we get in effect, an accelerator pump action, that is, when the throttle is opened rapidly, the piston is retarded, sufficient, in fact, to cause a momentary enrichment of the mixture to give a sharp pickup. This is due to the increased suction over the jet during the time the piston lags behind when the throttle is opened.

This, then, is the basic function of the elementary parts of the SU carburetter. A good understanding of the working of this type of carburetter will greatly simplify it's use and setting up.

It will also serve in providing a better understanding for the need and manner of effect of the various adjustments necessary for best performance and which are described in following chapters.

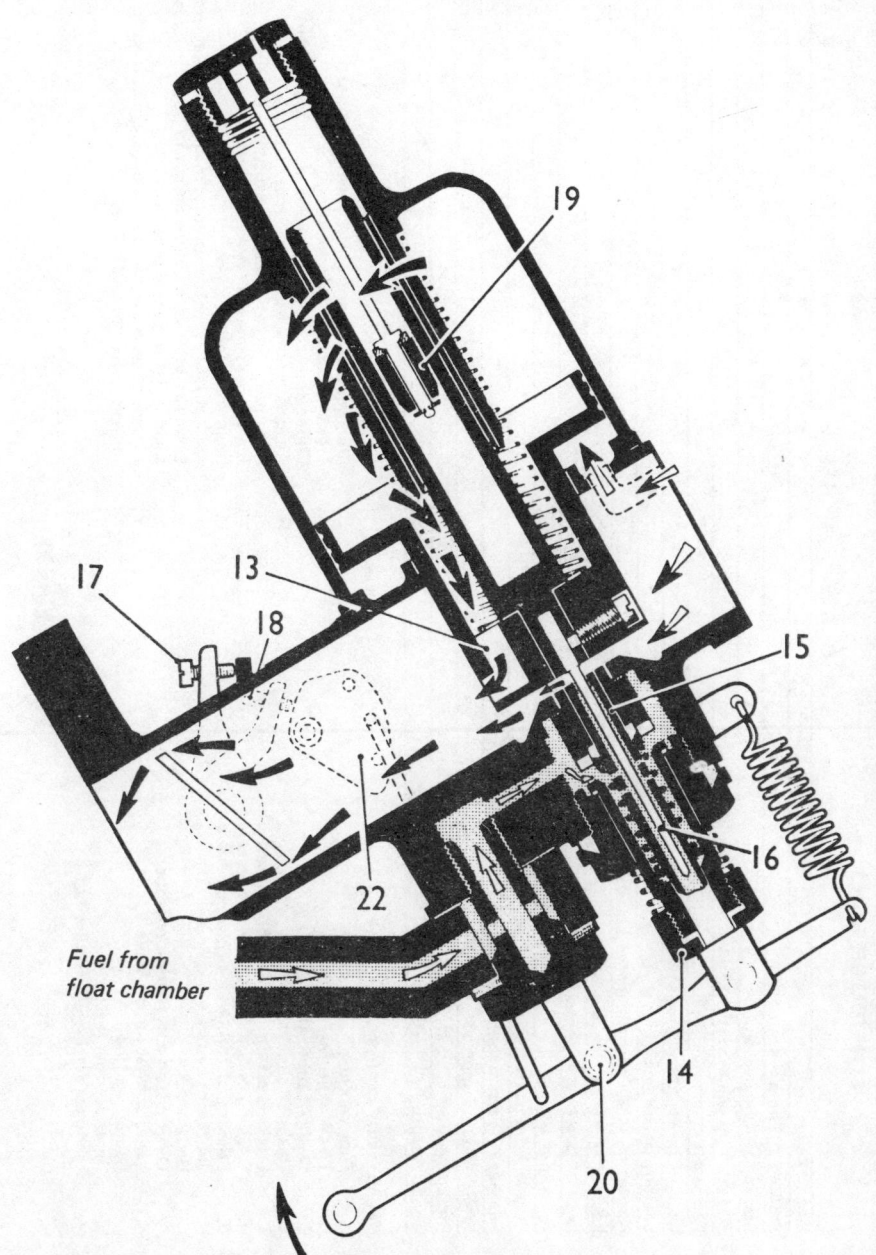

Fuel from float chamber

Fig 3 Basic arrangement showing jet & piston functions.

SYMPTOM OR FAULT

'CAUSE'

	A	B	C	D	E	F	G	H	I	J	K	L	M	N	O	P	Q	R	S	T	U	V	W	X	Y
Bad tickover	*														*	*	*	*	*	*	*	*			*
Stalling at idling when cold		*															*								*
Stalling at idling when hot			*												*										
Bad starting when cold	*				*	*	*	*	*	*	*	*	*	*	*		*								
Bad starting when hot	*				*	*	*	*	*	*	*	*	*	*	*			*	*						
Lack of power throughout rev range	*				*	*	*	*	*	*	*	*	*	*	*	*	*	*			*				
Lack of power at certain revs							*	*																	
Hesitation when throttle opened quickly					*	*																			
Lack of power at low revs	*	*			*					*	*	*	*	*											
Lack of power at high revs	*	*				*					*	*	*	*				*	*						
Flooding	*						*				*	*	*	*											
Fuel leaking from underside of jet											*	*	*										*		
Fuel leaking from float chamber											*	*												*	
High fuel consumption	*						*				*	*	*	*				*				*			
Rich mixture											*	*	*	*				*	*	*		*			
Weak mixture											*	*	*	*				*	*	*		*			

Key to 'cause' section.

A. Rich mixture
B. Weak mixture
C. Dashpot oil to thin
D. Dashpot oil level to low
E. Sticking piston (won't drop properly)
F. Sticking piston (won't rise properly)
G. Sticking piston (won't go up or down)
H. Jet out of centre
I. Bent needle
J. Dirty piston and suction chamber
K. Leaking float needle valve
L. Punctured float
M. Incorrect fuel level
N. Incorrect setting of mixture nut
O. Sticking choke control (in down position)
P. Tickover screw needs resetting
Q. Choke controlled fast tickover needs adjustment
R. Air cleaner clogged needs replacing
S. Fuel pump giving inadequate supply
T. Air cleaner removal weakening mixture
U. Incorrect needle fitted
V. Air leaks, i.e. throttle spindle, manifold gasket etc.
W. Chamber joint face and/or gasket to body at fault
X. Leaking jet or petrol pipe seals
Y. In case of twin carburetter balance is incorrect in terms of mixture or air flow

Fault tracing chart

Chapter 2

Overhauling & fault finding

Before we can expect a carburetter to deliver the correct fuel/air ratio, we must make sure that it is in proper working order. To determine whether or not the carburetter is fit for service, one should remove it from the car and thoroughly clean it. Petrol makes a reasonable solvent for cleaning carburetters, or if it is obvious that the carburetter is going to have to be stripped completely, then one can wash the carburetter in neat washing up liquid and then rinse it off with hot water.

Immediately after this it should be dipped in petrol to prevent any corrosion. If the carburetter is really being cleaned to check for suspect wear, then the best carburetter cleaner to use is one of the proprietory carburetter cleaning fluids, as these will remove carbon and petrol stains, and leave the carburetter looking like new.

Once the carburetter has been thoroughly cleaned, we can check for various points where wear may occur. First of all, wear of the throttle spindle can easily be detected by a sloppy fit of the spindle in the throttle body. When this spindle wears, it admits air into the carburetter, thus weakening the mixture. If it is badly worn at this point, it may be found impossible to get the engine to idle smoothly. Wear of the butterfly spindle effects the initial setting and this can in turn effect the top end performance.

The next step is to remove the bell chamber and piston assembly and check the needle for wear. If there are any apparent signs of scratching or wear on the needle, then this indicates that the jet is out of centre. This should be remedied as detailed in the relevant sections, later on in this book.

Next, thoroughly clean out the piston and inside of the suction chamber, using petrol. Check that the piston rod slides freely in the suction chamber and that there is no oil on the stem. With the damper in place, relocate the piston into the suction chamber, and push it in to the limits of it's travel. Then seal off the transfer holes (this can sometimes be done with a thumb on carburetters having only one transfer hole), with plasticine or something similar. (The transfer hole is the aperture which communicates the engine vacuum with the space above the piston.) With the suction chamber inverted, allow it to drop off of the piston. The time taken for it to fall should be between three and five seconds on carburetters up to 1¼ inches and five to seven seconds for larger carburetters. If it takes longer than this, then try to establish why. It could be that there is still some dirt left on the inside of the suction chamber or on the periphery of the piston or maybe needle drag. If the carburetter has been maltreated at any time it could be that the suction chamber is distorted. Whatever the cause, it should be remedied such that the drop time of the suction chamber falls within the period quoted.

Now let us come back to this business of the jet and jet centreing. If the needle showed any signs of wear then it has obviously been touching the sides of the jet, in which case one should replace not only the needle but also the jet, for obviously the jet would be worn. On some carburetters, sealing the main jet is done by glands. If these appear at all in bad order, they should be replaced, otherwise leakage will occur. The relevant overhaul kit for the carburetter will contain all the parts needed for this aspect of maintaining the carburetter.

The piston should fall freely on to the carburetter bridge with a 'click' when the lifting pin is released with the jet in the fully up position. If it will only do this with the jet lowered then the jet unit requires re-centreing.

Jet centreing should be carried out as described for the appropriate carburetter detailed in Chapter 7.

Float Chamber

Bearing in mind the importance of ensuring a correct fuel level in the jet at all times we must make sure that the float and inlet needle valve are operating correctly. With the float and needle valve assembly inverted, correct float level is set dimensionally (as indicated in the individual carburetter dismantling and assembly sections) and sealing of the valve is checked by sucking through the petrol inlet pipe; the valve should seal with very little pressure applied to the float. Even a small leak past the valve will be apparent when testing in this manner. If a leak is detected the valve and seating must be replaced.

As the needle valve is operated by a float of which a certain amount of buoyancy is required, we should check the float to see that it is not leaking, otherwise it will not operate the needle valve properly and incorrect fuel level will result. (Test metal floats by immersing in hot water — air bubbles will emerge if leaks are present.) Replace if defective.

In its working life, even well maintained equipment may develop problems arising from one or perhaps several causes. Reference to the Fault Tracing Chart will enable you to quickly pinpoint these and determine the corrective line of action necessary to restore performance.

Chapter 3

Mixtures and tuning

The whole point of a carburetter is to deliver and mix the correct amount of fuel with the air going into the engine. The proportions of air and fuel going into an engine is known as the air/fuel ratio. For the burning of petrol (the fuel) in air, the mixture of air and petrol must fall within certain limits. These limits are called the limits of inflammability and, for a fuel like petrol they fall within 20/1 to 7½/1. What this means is that 20 lbs. of air mixed with 1 lb. of petrol will just burn. Such a mixture is a weak mixture for the simple reason that there is very little petrol for a large amount of air. At the other end of the scale we find that if 1 lb. of petrol is mixed with 7½ lbs. of air, the mixture will again only just burn because there is an excess of petrol, i.e. it is a rich mixture. In the first instance, the weak mixture, we find that when the petrol is burnt there is a great deal of oxygen left over after combustion. In the second instance, the rich mixture, when the mixture is burnt all the oxygen is consumed and there is petrol left over which is still unburnt. Falling between these two extremes is the chemically correct mixture. For a fuel such as petrol, the extremes is the chemically correct mixture. For a fuel such as petrol, the chemically correct mixture is about 14.8/1 i.e. 14.8 lbs. of air for 1 lb. of petrol. When a mixture such as this is burnt all the petrol and all the oxygen are used up in combustion.

At first thought, one would assume that the best performance would be given when the air/fuel ratio was that of the chemically correct mixture. Although a car would perform well on such a mixture, it is not quite the ultimate for either power or economy, although it must be said that it does represent a good compromise. Experiments with engines have shown that the best economy is achieved when the mixture is set slightly weak, i.e. with mixtures in the order of 16/1. There are, however, problems which can arise from setting an engine this weak. Firstly, unless the distribution between cylinders is good, one can get some cylinders running weaker than others and hence misfiring can result. Secondly, without making alterations to the distributor, one can find that such weak mixtures cause higher exhaust valve temperatures which can lead to a failure in this quarter. For maximum power, the mixture requirement is again different. Most engines give their maximum power when the air/fuel ratio is about 12:1. This, it will be noticed, is quite appreciably on the rich side of a chemically correct mixture. The reason that such a rich mixture gives best power is that the excess petrol in the air cools the incoming charge, therefore allowing a denser charge to enter the cylinders, the result of which is more power. Also an excess of fuel ensures that all air is burnt.

A well designed carburetter is able to vary the mixture it delivers to the engine so that it is able to cater for varying requirements. For instance, if you are cruising along at a speed reasonable below the top speed of the car there is no need for the carburetter to deliver a rich mixture for maximum power. Under these conditions it should be delivering a slightly weak mixture for maximum economy. However, when the throttle is opened fully, it is obvious that the driver will be wanting maximum power and under these conditions, the carburetter should deliver a slightly rich mixture so as to give the best performance. This change in mixture ratio for varying conditions, is known as mixture spread. The SU carburetter, by virtue of it's design, automatically spreads the mixture between the ratios required for cruising, and economy, and the ratio required for maximum power. The mixture spread of the SU, however, is not so great that it goes to the extreme of each requirement, for as stated before, unless distribution is good, running at the most economical mixture may lead to misfiring. At the other end of the scale, running at the very richest mixture for the rich mixture for maximum power, fuel consumption is quite excessive. What the SU does is to strike a reasonable compromise between these two extremes, and in so doing, gives a very acceptable performance.

Before we leave the rather more theoretical side of things, one more point may be well worth noting. The mixture ratios just quoted for economy and power are those required when the throttle is reasonably well open. When throttle openings are very small, we find that under a given set of circumstances, the mixture required is richer. The reason for this is that as the throttle is closed, so the amount of air going into the engine is less. This means that as the fresh charge enters the cylinder, it undergoes greater dilution with the residual gas from the last combustion phase. When it comes to the time to ignite this new charge, then because of it's dilution with exhaust gases, the chances of an ignitable mixture being close to the spark plug is reduced. To overcome this, more fuel must be introduced into the incoming air to ensure an ignitable charge at the plug. For this reason we find that at tickover, the mixture ratio required is a lot richer than one would expect, and it is because the engine is running at virtually no load and the amount of air drawn is very small, that the dilution with burnt gases is very large. With SU carburetters, a smooth tickover is usually achieved when the mixture is about 13.2:1, but this varies considerably from engine to engine.

As we have seen in the previous paragraph, the mixture strength greatly effects power and the amount it effects power can be seen by the graph Fig. 4. From this graph it can be seen that the power very rapidly drops off as the mixture becomes weaker, but that there is not such a rapid drop off in power on the rich side. In setting our carburetter, we should aim to get the mixture under normal driving conditions, somewhere between the chemically correct mixture and the maximum power mixture. It should be borne in mind however that maximum power mixture ratios are on the rich side and will produce carbon monoxide (CO) and unburnt fuel (hydrocarbons, HC) in the exhaust gases. Apart from being wasteful,

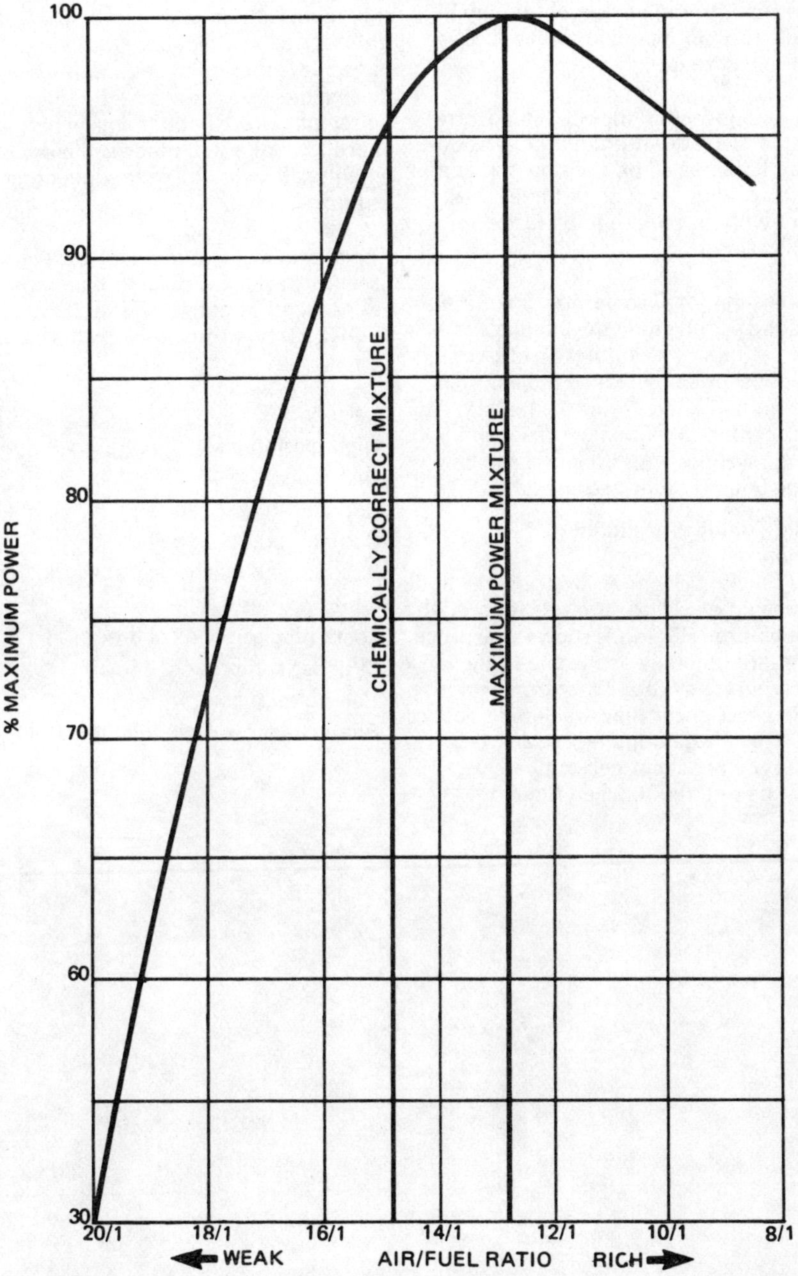

Fig. 4 —

these emissions are atmospheric pollutants, possibly subject to control in some countries; in this event it may be illegal to change certain carburetter and ignition settings.

In consequence of the emission control regulations current production carburetters will be sealed on the slow run and/or mixture adjusters. The fast idle adjustment will not require to be sealed for any application.

The sealing (or 'Tamperproofing') is a means of controlling the idling and mixture settings of a carburetter in service and is achieved by sealing the adjusters before the vehicle leaves the factory. The seals consist of aluminium plugs and plastic shrouds which damage and become unusable when removed.

Basic Tuning Procedures

The general principles governing the basic setting up of SU carburetters follow. Although type HS unit is shown, the procedures are generally applicable to the range of carburetter types. Where important differences occur, they are noted as appropriate in the descriptive section of each unit type (which of necessity anyway, must be referred to when tuning).

Pre-Tuning Engine Check.

Certain electrical and mechanical features of the engine affect combustion performance. It is important therefore, before servicing or tuning a carburetter in an attempt to rectify poor engine performance, to make sure that the maladjustment or fault is not from some other source.

The following features should be checked against the engine maker's recommendations, and be corrected if necessary BEFORE carrying out work on the carburetter.

Battery
High tension coil
Distributor
Contact breaker gap
Contact breaker dwell angle
Vacuum and mechanical advance operation
Ignition timing
Spark plug gap and condition
Cylinder compresion
Valve clearances
Eliminate air leaks in inlet manifold

Standard Engine, Single Carburetter Setting Up

Having considered what the engine needs in the way of mixture requirements, we can think about setting the carburetter up to deliver such a mixture. We will deal first of all with single carburetters on an engine which is in every way standard, i.e. completely unmodified. Assuming that the carburetter is in perfect condition, then we set up the carburetter as follows:

1. (a) Warm up the engine to it's normal working temperature.
   (b) Switch it off.
   (c) Unscrew the throttle adjusting screw until it is clear of it's stop and the throttle is fully closed.
   (d) Set the throttle adjusting screw 1½ turns open.

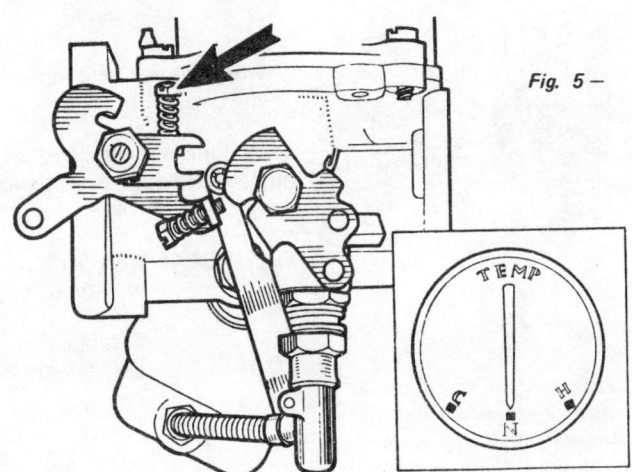

Fig. 5 –

2. (a) Mark for reassembly and remove the piston/suction chamber unit.
   (b) Disconnect the mixture control wire, i.e. the choke cable.
   (c) Screw the jet adjusting nut (1) until the jet is flush with the bridge of the carburetter, or fully up if this position cannot be obtained.

Fig. 6

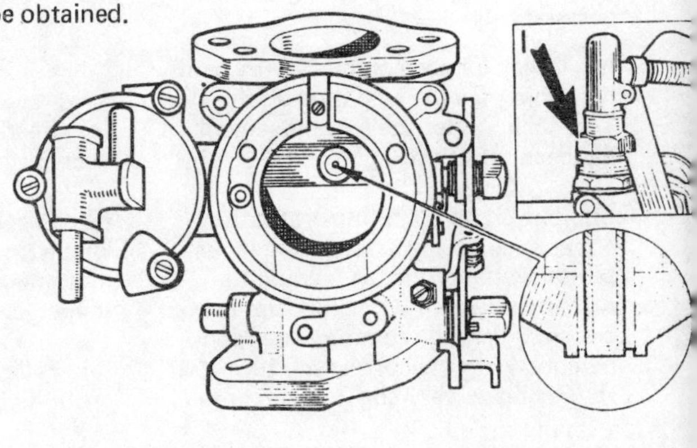

13

3. Replace the piston/suction chamber unit as marked. Check that the piston falls freely onto the bridge when the lifting pin (6) is released. If it does not do this, then the jet needs centreing, so turn to the relevant page on centreing in the appropriate carburetter section. Then turn down the jet adjusting nut (1) by two complete turns.

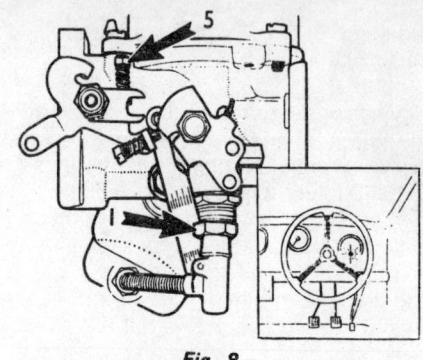

Fig. 8 —

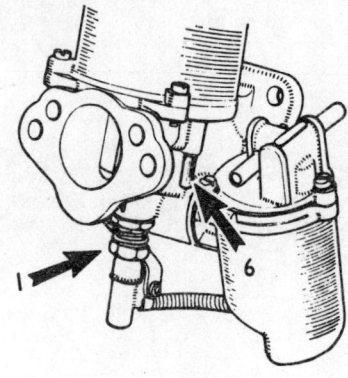

Fig. 7 —

weak mixture, the rpm will drop and the engine will stall.

An audible and visual indication of mixture strength may be observed from the exhaust as follows:—

TOO WEAK: Irregular note, 'splashy' misfire, colourless.
TOO RICH: Regular or rhythmical misfire, blackish.
CORRECT: Regular and even note.

4. (a) Restart the engine and adjust the throttle adjusting screw (5) to give the desired idling as indicated by the rev counter or by the ignition warning glow.

   (b) Turn the jet adjusting nut (1) up to weaken or down to richen until the fastest idling speed consistent with even running is obtained.

   (c) Readjust the throttle adjusting screw (5) to give the correct idling if necessary.

5. (a) Check for correct mixture by gently pushing the lifting pin up about 1/32 inch after the free movement has been taken up.

   (b) The graph Fig. 9 illustrates the effect on engine rpm when the lifting pin raises the piston, indicating the mixture strength. If the mixture is excessively rich, the rpm increases considerably. With the correct mixture, the rpm increases very slightly, and with a

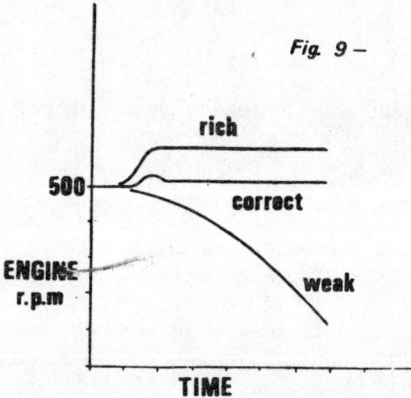

Fig. 9 —

(c) Readjust the mixture strength as necessary.

(d) Reconnect the mixture control wire with about 1/16 in (1.6 mm) free movement before it starts to pull on the jet lever.

(e) Pull the mixture control knob until the linkage is about to move the

carburetter jet and adjust the fast-idle screw to give an engine speed of about 1.000 r.p.m. when hot.

(f) Finally top up the piston damper with the recommended engine oil until the level is ½ in (13 mm) below the top of the hollow piston rod.

NOTE: On non-dust-proofed units (identified by a vent hole in the piston damper cap) the oil level should be ½ in (13 mm) **above** the top of the hollow piston rod.

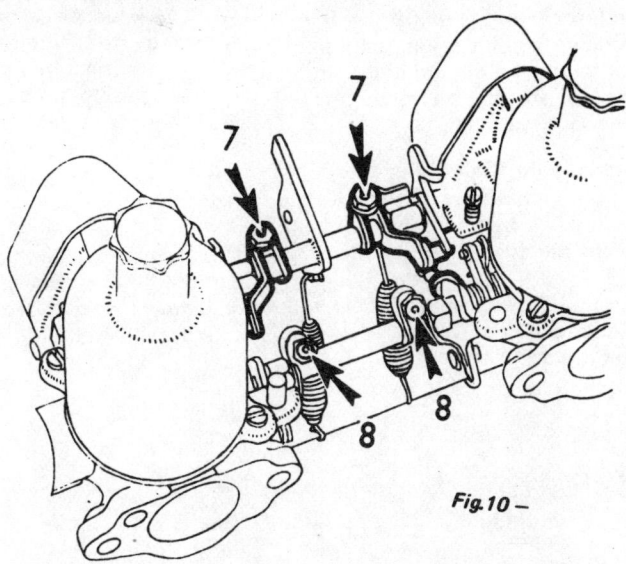

Fig. 10 –

Tuning Multi-Carburetter Set Ups

Remove the air cleaners and carry out item 1 as for single on all carburetters then:

2. (a) Slacken both the clamping bolts (7) on the throttle spindle interconnections.

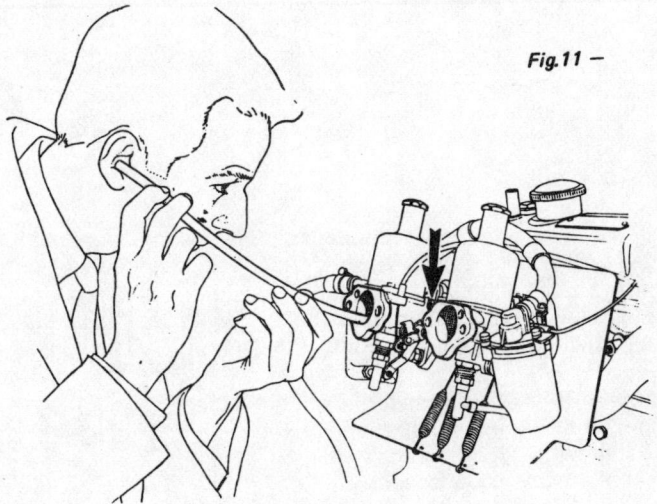

Fig. 11 –

15

(b) Disconnect the jet control interconnection by slackening the clamping bolts (8).

(c) Carry out items 2 and 3 as for single carburetters, then additionally:

3. (a) Restart the engine and adjust the throttle adjusting screws on each carburetter to give the desired idling speed as indicated by the rev counter or the ignition warning glow.

(b) Compare the intensity of the intake 'hiss' on all carburetters and alter the throttle adjusting screws until the 'hiss' is the same.

4. (a) Turn the jet adjusting nuts (1) on all carburetters up to weaken or down to richen the same amount until the fastest idling speed consistent with even running is obtained.

(b) Readjust the throttle adjusting screws (5) to give correct idling if necessary.

5. (a) Check for correct mixture by gently pushing the lifting pin of the front carburetter (right hand in the case of transverse engines) up by 1/32 inches after free movement has been taken up. The graph illustrates the possible effect on engine rpm. Readjust the mixture strength as necessary.

(b) Repeat the operation on the other carburetter or carburetters and after adjustment, re-check since they are all interdependant.

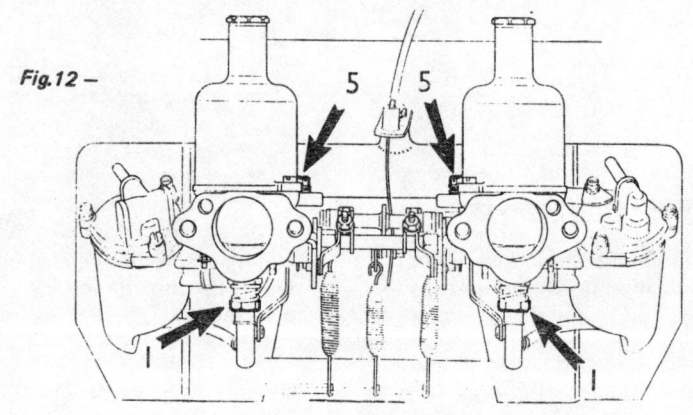

Fig. 12 —

6 (a) Set the throttle interconnection clamping levers (7) (if applicable) so that the link pin is 0.006 inches away from the lower edge of the fork (see inset fig 14). Tighten the clamp bolts.

(b) With both jet levers at their lowest position, set the jet interconnection lever clamp bolts (8) so that both jets commence to move simultaneously.

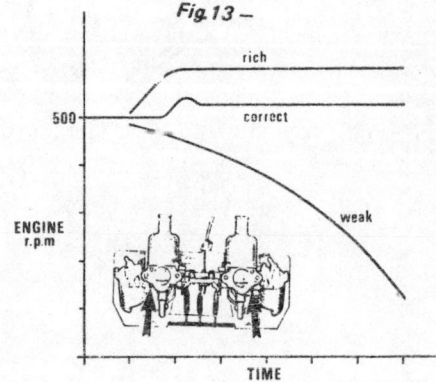

Fig. 13 —

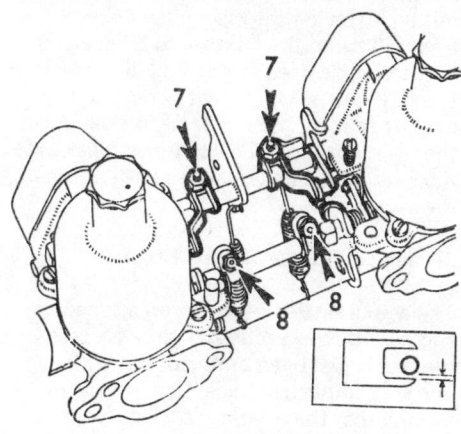

Fig. 14 —

7. (a) Reconnect the mixture control wire with about 1/16 inch free movement before it starts to pull on the jet levers.

   (b) Pull the mixture control knob until the linkage is about to move the carburetter jets, and adjust the fast idle screws, comparing the intensity of the air intake 'hiss' to give an engine speed of about 1,000 rpm when hot.

   (c) Refit the air cleaners after checking that they are clean and unclogged. Recheck the mixture strength as described in item 5, as the air cleaner can cause a slight enrichment of the mixture.

Variations on Basic Setting Up

To get the best by setting the carburetter in the foregoing manner one does, strictly speaking, need a little experience, but even then it is possible, still to achieve less than the ultimate. There are, however, numerous other ways of varying degrees of sophistication which can make the setting of these carburetters simpler.

Let us first consider adjusting the mixture. Basically, when adjusting the tickover mixture, we must consider that the manufacturer has selected the optimum needle for the job and by adjusting our tickover mixture we are hoping to achieve the right mixture throughout the rev range of the engine. The needle size is determined during engine development and will provide the correct mixture strength except under extremes of temperature, humidity or altitude; e.g. a weaker needle will be necessary at altitudes exceeding 1800 m. If modifications are made to the engine (e.g. camshaft, compression ratio, air inlet or exhaust system etc.) a different needle may be necessary to maintain performance.

Adjusting the mixture as has just been described is going to depend a little on how you interpret the instructions. However, if one can use a piece of equipment which will measure the mixture strength, then this considerably reduces the room for error. One way of getting the tickover mixture correct is to have the engine exhaust analysed on an electronic engine tuner. A typical example of such an engine tuner is the Sun and Crypton engine tuner, so there should be no problem in locating a garage to set your tickover mixture. Just out of interest, these electronic engine tuners measure the air/fuel ratio by taking a sample of the exhaust, passing it through the meter, and then the air/fuel ratio is shown on a dial as 12/1, 13/1, 14/1 or whatever it may be. When set up on one of these machines, the tickover mixture should be as has been said before, about 13.0:1. It can't be stressed too often at this stage that setting up the mixture as described while the engine is idling only sets the mixture at tickover, and we are relying on the fact that the manufacturer has selected the correct needle to give us the correct mixture throughout the rest of the rev range, however, any error in setting the tickover mixture will cause a corresponding error throughout the rev range.

As an alternative to getting a garage to set up your mixture on an engine tuner, you can use a little device known as a Colortune. This device is essentially a spark plug with a transparent end to it which enables one to see into the cylinder and thus see the colour of the combustion flame. During combustion, the mixture strengths either side of the chemically correct one, burn at different colours. For instance, a mixture with an excess of petrol (rich) will burn with a bright orange colour, whereas a mixture which is just chemically correct or slightly weak will burn with a blue flame. Excessively weak mixtures burn with a bluish white flame. The Colortune makes use of the fact that different mixtures burn at different colours, and by seeing into the cylinder, we can set the mixture pretty accurately. Fuel consumption improvements in the range 4 to 17% have been authenticated on a sample of cars tuned according to the Colortune technique. Appendix 4 gives details of this system.

Setting up the mixture on twin carburetters is just a little more difficult than setting up a single, and it is at times like this that using a Colortune really pays dividends for it allows the carburetters to be set very accurately indeed especially as far as mixture balance is concerned.

Balancing the tickover airflow of twin carburetters is another job which can prove to be a good patience trier unless one has had a little experience. In the procedure just described on setting up twin carburetters, the method of using the pipe and listening to the intake hiss is quite satisfactory once you get the hang of it. However, in many cases a superior job can be done by using a carburetter balancing tool. There are many carburetter balancing tools on the market, and one need only pay a visit to the local accessory shop to acquire such an item. There is often a mistaken belief that balancing the carburetter at tickove will give more power. In fact, all that balancing the carburetters at tickover will give more smoother tickover. The difference that it is likely to make in top speed and power output is so small as to be almost unmeasurable. Of the two adjustments available on an SU carburetter, the tickover air flow balance and the mixture adjustment, the most important is definitely the mixture. Having the mixture out at tickover will cause the mixture to be in error by varying degrees throughout the rev range. If the mixture is set rich at tickover, then it can be richer all the way up the rev range, and likewise if it is weak at tickover, it can be weaker all the way up the rev. range.

Setting Up SU's on Tuned Engines

The actual setting of an SU on a tuned engine follows exactly the same proceedure as has just been outlined, but with one very important exception. We cannot assume that the needle is correct for the particular state of tune of the engine. It needs only minor modifications to the engine to warrant a different needle. This is because the airflow characteristics of the engine will be changed and they no longer suit the standard needle. The question now arises, how do we go about establishing a needle to use for the particular engine.

The first step is to understand that the thinner the needle is, the richer the mixture will be. Now, SU needles are calibrated by their diameter every 1/8 inch as is shown in Fig.15. The further the needle emerges from the jet the more petrol will flow, we have to select a needle whose form will give us the correct mixture. Under a given set of driving conditions, the needle will be a certain distance out from the jet. For instance, at tickover the piston will only be just off it's seat, hence the needle will be only just out of the jet and only a small amount of petrol will flow. As more power is required, so the piston will rise further, bringing a different portion of the needle into operation.

When we up rate an engine we do, if we are successful in tuning it, increase it's consumption of air. Therefore, inevitably we need a needle which will pass more petrol than a standard one so as to keep the air/fuel ratio at it's correct level.

When we select a needle which will allow

more petrol into the engine, we have to select one which has a smaller diameter at any given point along it's length. However, it is unlikely that the tickover part of the needle will need to be any different on a tuned engine to a standard one, since the amount of horsepower needed to make the engine idle will virtually remain unchanged, therefore it's airflow requirement at this point will be unchanged and, it follows, so will it's fuel consumption. Where the needle needs to deliver more fuel is from around a quarter of an inch from the shoulder upwards, this means from the position the engine would be under light throttle openings on upwards to the position it would assume under full throttle. The question now arises as to how we can best select an appropriate needle, for the state of tune of the engine. The first thing to do is to look through the appendix of this book and find a car which has a similar carburation set up and a similar power output to the car you are tuning. At this point we can use the needles of the particular car you have selected as a starting point for your own car. A jet needle part number identification cross reference chart is given in Appendix 2.

Fit the needles into the carburetter and set up the carburetter or carburetters as you would for a standard engine. If you have done this properly, we will now have the mixture correct at tickover, and this we can use as a datum from which to work. Next, take the car out on the road and see if it falters at any particular rpm in the rev range. If it does falter, drive along at the point at which it falters for a little while, just sufficient enough to colour the plugs and then stop and inspect the plugs. If the plugs are a light brown colour, then the mixture is too weak; if on the other hand the plugs are black and sooty, then the mixture is too rich. Bearing in mind which part of the needle operates over which part of the rev range (see Fig.15) select a needle from the charts at the back of this book that you think will overcome the mixture problem.

Fig 15

Needle diameter Calibration

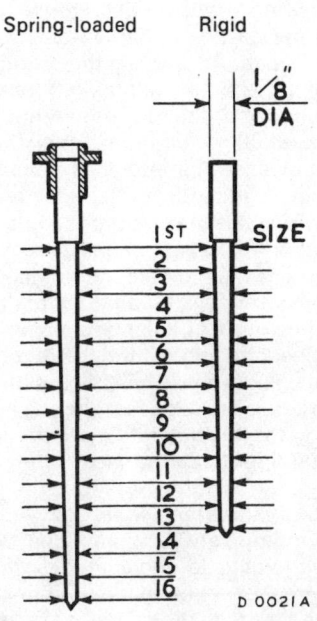

Sizes taken every $\frac{1}{8}$" from top shoulder

When doing this, it is essential to remember that the thinner the needle is, the richer the mixture will be at any given point, and conversely, the thicker the needle is, the weaker the mixture will be at any given point. The easiest way to determine just how different one needle is to another is to draw a graph of their profile. Such a graph is shown in Fig.16. By drawing a graph, it is much easier to see where one needle differs from another and this does make selection easier.

Once you have found a needle on which the engine fires regularly, then we can get down to some serious needle selection to get the mixture as near spot on as possible.

For most people, the most important aspect of a tuned engine is that it gives the performance that it should, so first we will deal with setting up the mixture in wide open throttle conditions. As has been said before, having the throttle pedal to the floor with an SU carburetter does not mean that the carburetter itself is fully open. At low rpm the piston need only be less than half it's full travel from the bridge of the carburetter, hence the needle will not be too far out of the jet. What we now have to do is make the engine work against a load so that we may evaluate the mixture at any particular rpm, or at least at reasonable rpm intervals. The most simple way to make an engine work against a load is to drive it up hills. To test the mixture at various engine rpms under full throttle conditions, you will obviously need slopes of varying degrees so as to load up the engine to bring the revs down to a particular level. Let us look at an instance:

Let us assume that we are going to correct the mixture at 2,000 rpm. What we now need to do is to find a hill of sufficient length that we can drive up it in, say, top gear such that the car will hold a steady speed equivalent to 2,000 revs when the throttle is wide open. The slope of the hill need not be exact for this. If, for instance, we find that the car pulls 2,500 rpm up the hill in top gear, then we can simply pull the revs down a little more by applying just a shade of hand brake until the revs are at the point at which we require to check the mixture (it obviously won't do to make too much use of the hand brake or it will overheat). After having kept the engine under these conditions for at least a minute we then cut the engine and inspect the plug. When the mixture is right for road use, i.e. one which provides good power output without an astronomical fuel consumption the plug will be coloured approximately as follows: the shell of the plug will be black without being sooty, whilst the electrode will be a very dark brown or almost black, again, without any sign of sootiness. Should the mixture be a shade weak, the plug shell will appear dark brown with the electrode a slightly lighter brown. If the mixture is very weak, then the shell will appear a light brown and the centre electrode may be a very light brown, almost white in colour. If the mixture is too rich, then the plug will appear black with a sign of sootiness. Excessively rich mixtures will be detected by the presence of lots of soot. From these low revs, it will obviously be the lower part of the needle which will want correcting if the mixture should be out. At 2,000 revs the average SU will, under full throttle conditions, be about ½ inch open but this figure will, of course, vary depending on the size of engine you have, the number of carburetters and the size of the carburetters fitted to this engine.

Having ascertained what the mixture is like at 2,000 revs, one should then try at 3,000 revs to determine the mixture ratio at this point. Again this will mean loading up the engine against a suitable hill to give full throttle conditions while holding steady rpm. Having maintained these conditions for a while we do, again, in a similar manner check the colour of the plugs and note the state of the mixture. This procedure is repeated at 4,000 revs and 5,000, on up until peak rpm.

Having noted the discrepancy between the mixture the needle presently fitted is giving, and that required, we can then refer to the needle charts in the back of this book and attempt to select one which will bring us nearer the required mixture. When selecting another needle, we must remember that a change of only a few thousandths of an inch in needle diameter significantly effects the strength of the mixture. For instance, if our mixture should prove only a little weak or a little rich, then we should only select a needle, at most, two thou different to the

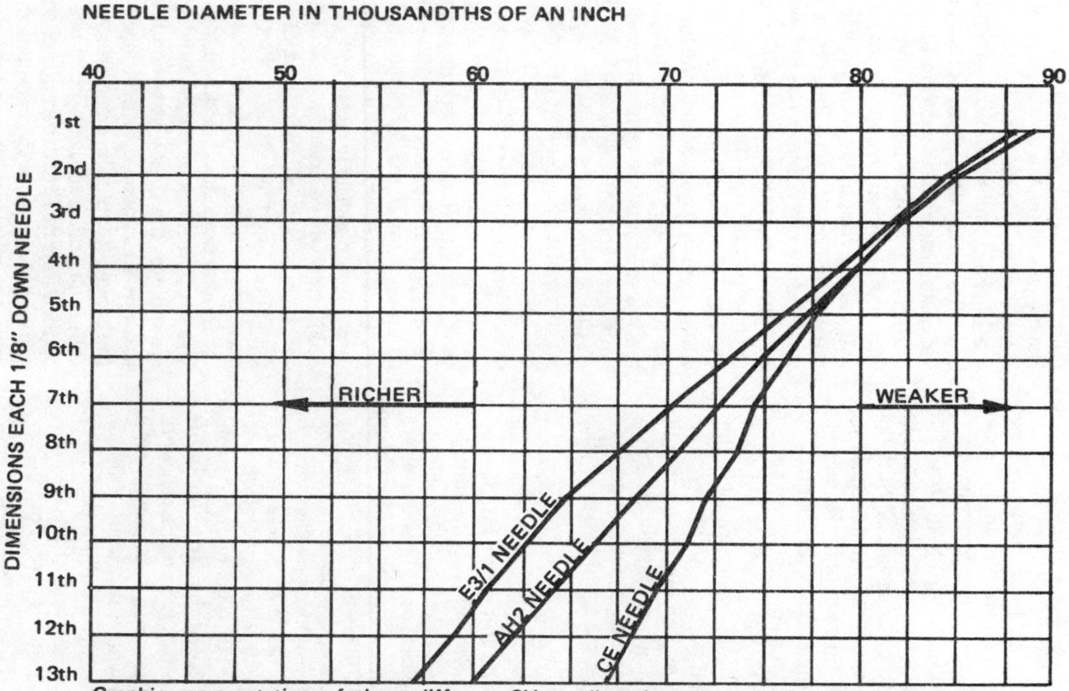
NEEDLE DIAMETER IN THOUSANDTHS OF AN INCH
40
50
60
70
80
90
DIMENSIONS EACH 1/8" DOWN NEEDLE
1st
2nd
3rd
4th
5th
6th
7th
8th
9th
10th
11th
12th
13th
RICHER
WEAKER
E3/1 NEEDLE
AH2 NEEDLE
CE NEEDLE

Graphic representation of three different SU needles, those towards the left of the graph are richer than those towards the right. The graph also illustrates that the needles are not plain tapers but a much more complex tapering form the steepness of which can vary down the length of the needle.

Fig.16 – Needle profile comparison

one fitted at the particular point that the error in mixture is occuring. If the mixture should prove to be wildly out, then a needle which has four or five thou difference at the point the error occurs may be well worth trying. But take care not to go to weak.

Once we have selected a needle which gives us the correct mixture for all power requirements, then we find that in most cases, the offload or cruising mixture will look after itself, merely by virtue of the design of the carburetter. Having selected a needle which gives us virtually the right full power mixture requirements, we can make minor adjustments to the mixture by virtue of the idle mixture control nut. Such adjustments are likely, however, to upset the mixture at tickover, but for performance purposes this is probably the least important part of the rev range so we need not concern ourselves too much with a slightly rich or slightly weak mixture at tickover, but it should be stressed at this point that it should be only slight.

The selecting of a needle in the fashion just described sounds like rather a long winded job, and if it is to be done properly, it is a long winded job. The time taken to select a needle for a tuned engine, or needles in the case of twin carburetters, can be considerably reduced if we bring a little more sophistication to the technique. If you want to do the job of selecting your own needle or needles then there is a method which is relatively simple, which involves the use of a Colortune. (See appendix IV). This method involves using the brakes of the car to apply the load against which the engine can work (revving up the car in neutral will in no way indicate what the mixture will be like in steady state conditions). To utilize this technique, we first of all jack the driving wheels of the car up off the ground. This is best done in such a manner (a) that it is impossible for the car to fall off the jacks, and (b) that the driving wheels assume reasonably normal angles, i.e. angles which are achieved whilst on the road. This last statement, of course, only applies to cars having independant suspensions. A normal rear wheel drive car with a solid axle will, of course, have the right angles irrespective of where the car is jacked up. However, it is best to jack up on the axle so that the drive shaft assumes a normal angle.

Having jacked up the car, on suitably located safety stands, fit a Colortune into one of the cylinders in place of a plug. Start the car up and get an accomplice to 'drive' the car as if he were on the road. The 'driving' will be done as normal, but with one important exception; the 'driver' will use the foot-brake of the car to pull the engine revs down to the revs at which the mixture is required to be known at. Say we are starting again at 2,000 revs to analyse the mixture, then the 'driver' of the car will gradually open the throttle whilst applying greater and greater amounts of footbrake pressure until he reaches the state where the throttle is wide open and the footbrake is hard enough on to keep the revs at, say, 2,000. At this point you can note: (a) how far the carburetter is open, and (b) whether or not the mixture is rich or weak at the particular revs concerned by looking at the Colortune. This procedure can now be repeated at 3,000 revs, 4,000 revs and so on up through the rev range until the rev limit is achieved. (With high revving cars it is not advisable to exceed about 5,000 rpm with a Colortune). When using this technique it is important that (a) the person reading the colour of the Colortune and noting the distance the carburetter is open does so as quickly as possible, and (b) that the accomplice 'driving' the car achieves the steady state conditions as quickly as possible, as prolonged use of the brakes to hold the engine down, will cause the brakes to overheat. However, applications of fifteen seconds or so are well within order, and in practice this proves to be plenty of time to make the reading required.

By utilizing this technique with the Colortune it is possible to get the needle pretty well sorted out in a very short space of

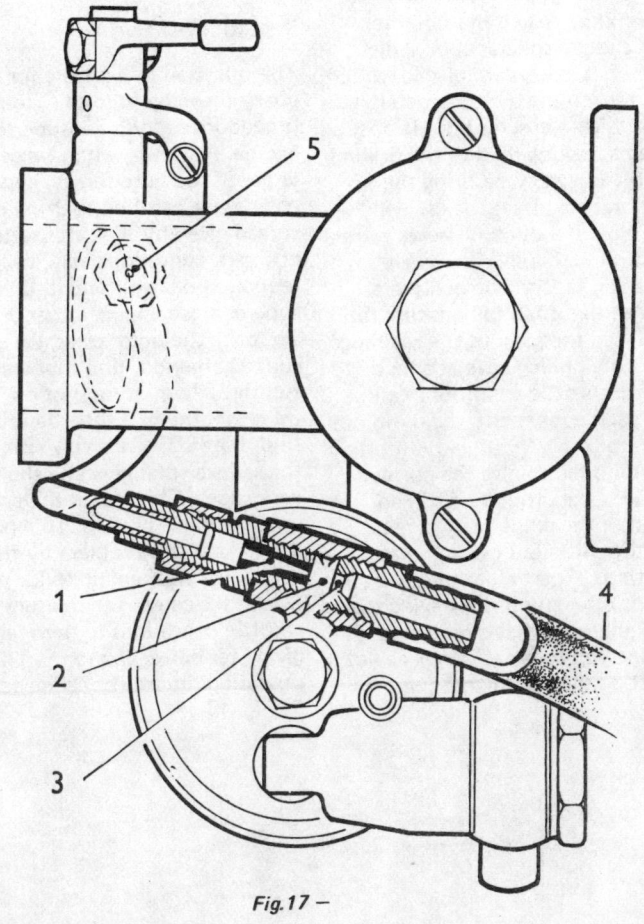

Fig. 17 –

Weakening device - part throttle (S/C engines).

time. For instance, starting from scratch it is possible to have a carburetter correctly needled within an hour, providing you and your accomplice work well as a team.

The best method for getting carburation as accurate as possible is to utilize the services of a rolling road dynomometer. Basically a rolling road dynomometer consists of a set of rollers, upon which the car's driving wheels are placed, which are coupled up to the dynomometer. This is a device which measures bhp. It does so by applying a braking load to the driving wheels of the car and measuring the amount of braking affect the car will overcome. Now if a dynomometer is used in conjunction with a mixture analyser such as the Sun or Crypton analysers mentioned earlier, then the mixture ratio can be analysed throughout the rev range with the engine pulling against a load such that full throttle conditions can be held. With such equipment, the dynomometer operator can very quickly ascertain the needle required to give the correct fuel/air ratio. Apart from this he can, with the aid of the equipment at hand spot any other little fault which may have gone unnoticed. Apart from this you will also have the opportunity of having the hp curve at the rear wheels measured, thus enabling you to see whether or not you are getting the power that you should be.

Although they are for the performance enthusiast an extremely useful device to be able to get the use of, dynomometers are not found in every garage. However, unless you live in the remotest parts of the country, you are sure to find a dynomometer within twenty miles of your home.

Supercharged Engines

The selection of a needle for a supercharged engine follows virtually the same procedure as for an unsupercharged engine. However, when we get to the larger SU carburetters on supercharged engines we can find that the mixture spread given by the carburetter under ordinary conditions may, because of a reduction be insufficient, thus making the supercharged engine rather uneconomical. To make the point clear, we can, with a supercharger on, find that we can get our full throttle mixture spot on, yet when we check the part throttle mixture, we find that it is excessively rich, i.e. about the same as that given by the full load conditions. This makes the engine rather uneconomical on fuel. To a point we can get around this problem by fitting the additional weakening device produced by SU's. This causes the mixture at part throttle conditions to be weakened, thus giving far better economy. The method of operating the additional device is shown in Fig. 17.

Chapter 4

Burning characteristics of different mixtures

To sum up this chapter it would be wise to say a few things about the way different mixtures burn. A weak mixture, for instance, burns relatively slowly compared with a chemically correct mixture. A slightly rich mixture burns slightly quicker than a chemically correct mixture, and an excessively rich mixture burns, again, like a weak mixture, more slowly.

Now the rate at which a mixture burns is important, for it effects the setting of our optimum ignition timing. By this, it is not meant that altering your mixture alters your timing - what it does mean is that if you have a weak mixture, then you will need different ignition timing for the best performance than the ignition timing required for a rich mixture. This means that, having set up your carburetter, you must then set the ignition to make the best use of the potential power available. It may also be wise at this point, to look into the effects of running an engine with the mixture either too weak or too rich.

Let us first of all consider the weak mixture. Because the mixture burns slowly, much of the combustion has not taken place by the time the exhaust valve opens. Consequently the exhaust valve can be subjected to far more heat than it would normally be called upon to do. Also because the mixture is weak we do not have the same degree of cooling from the petrol that we would normally have if more petrol was present. The result of this is that a weak mixture can result in burnt out valves, and in some instances, burnt pistons. The degree of weakness that we are talking about in this context is a noticeably weak one. The slightly weak mixtures used for economy purposes are quite safe to use, providing the engine is set up properly to cater for them.

The use of excessively rich mixtures can also bring about its problems. Petrol is very good at washing oil from cylinder bores and the use of an excessive amount of petrol within the incoming charge will do just that. Consequently, bore wear can be very high which will mean early replacement of rings, and possibly a rebore as well as heavy fuel consumption bills. Apart from this, dilution of the oil by the petrol can cause bearings to suffer.

Mixtures which are just slightly rich, however, are not necessarily harmful to the engine. Again, these things have to be done in moderation.

To avoid any of the aforementioned maladies, it pays to make sure that the mixture is correct within reasonably close limits.

Chapter 5

Size selection

One of the problems which often confronts the amateur tuner is the dilemma brought about as to which size of carburetter to use or indeed, how many to use. Given a perfect carburetter, an engine in any given state of tune can only consume so much air. Now if we are to choose carburation for such an engine, then there is no point in choosing carburetters which can pass more air than the engine can consume. All it means if we do choose too big carburetters, is that we shall not be using the full potential of the carburetters and we will have had to spend more money on the instruments than would otherwise have been necessary. Apart from this, a carburetter which does not work to within just it's full capacity invariably is not metering the fuel quite as accurately as it could be.

Apart from sizing the carburetters, we also have the question as to what number of carburetters to use. Do we use one large single carburetter or two smaller ones, or even three smaller ones still? The answer to this can be very difficult and in many cases must inevitably be a compromise.

Let us firstly consider a single carburetter setup. In terms of the amount of air passed, one large SU will produce just as much power as two smaller ones with the same venturi area, providing all else is equal. However, it is not always possible to conform to the all else being equal bit of that last statement. Inevitably, a single carburetter gives less effective distribution of the petrol within the airstream than a twin carburetter setup. If we have one carburetter feeding, say, four or six cylinders, then in most cases we can find the centre cylinders rich and the outer cylinders weak. By substituting twin carbs, we find that the mixture distribution is far better, hence we can usually achieve slightly more power or economy, depending on how the carburetters are set in terms of mixture ratio with a multiple carburetter setup than a single carburetter setup. However, the difference in power and economy between a single carburetter

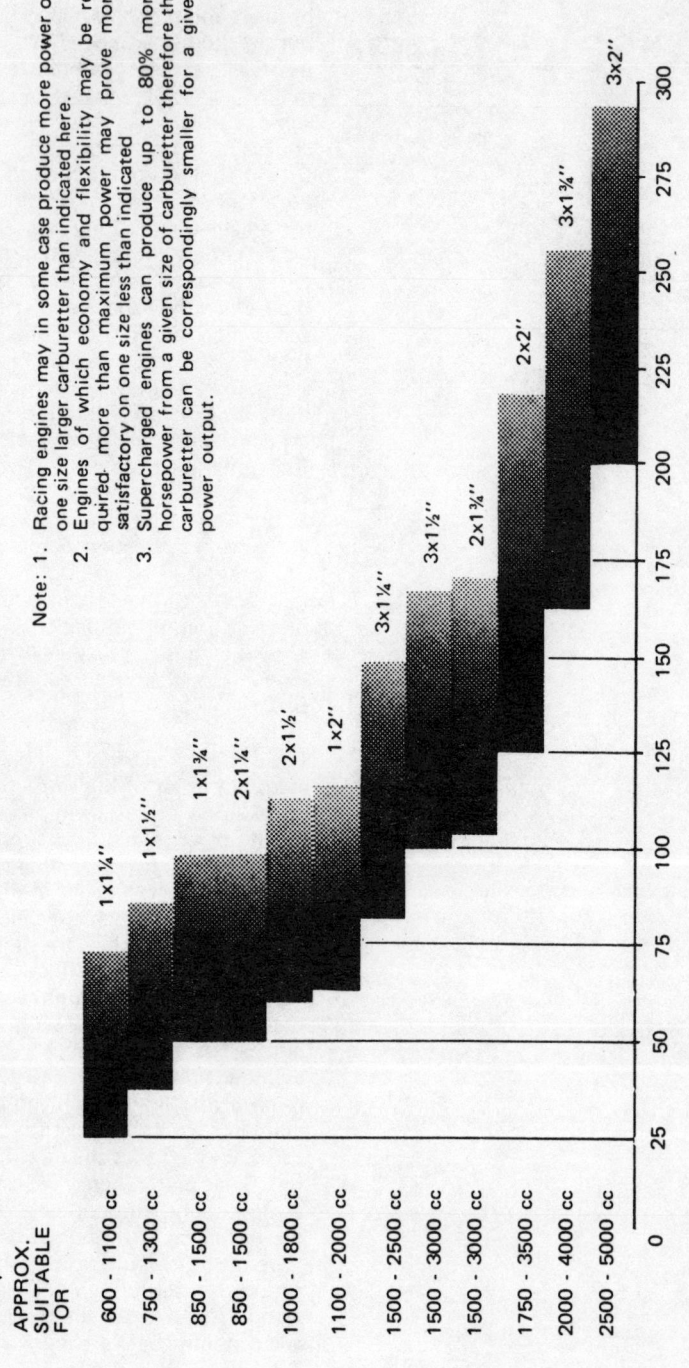

Fig. 18 — Carburetter Selection.

and twin carburetter on a four cylinder engine can be fairly small when the comparable venturi areas are similar. Let us look at an example: A pair of 1¼ inch SU's has a very similar venturi area to a single 1¾ inch SU. In terms of power, the 1¾ inch SU will give a performance very near that of the twin carburetter setup. However, it does inevitably give less power and its fuel consumption in terms of fuel consumed for a given power output is usually slightly more than the twin carburetters.

Talking of fuel consumption of twin carburetters, it is often mistakenly thought that twin carburetters will always put up the fuel consumption simply because there are two carburetters delivering fuel instead of one. However, this is not so. Under perfect conditions, twin carburetters will give an identical fuel consumption to a single carburetter. Under less than perfect conditions, they will probably give better fuel consumption than a single carburetter. Let us assume that we have an engine whose horsepower is x amount. If, at this power output the engine consumes 100 cu. ft. of air, then that 100 cu. ft. of air will have to be mixed with a certain amount of petrol. That amount of petrol will be the same whether it gets it all from one carburetter or half from one carburetter and half from another carburetter, as it would in the case of twin carburetters. So, for a given power output the fuel consumption should be identical. Now, as we said earlier, the distribution with twin carburetters is probably better and therefore all cylinders can run at nearer the ideal mixture instead of some running rich and the others weak. Therefore, it will be quite obvious that twin carburetters can, when correctly set, give better consumption figures than a single carburetter. When we consider six cylinder engines which have the single carburetter replaced by triple carburetters, we find that the difference in fuel consumption with the triple carburetters can be quite noticeable. Indeed, it can be as much as four or five mpg when the mean mixture ratio is the same in both cases. The reason for this vast difference is, of course, the inequality of the mixture when a single carburetter is used, the centre cylinders being noticeably rich while the end cylinders are quite noticeably weak.

Bearing this last statement in mind, we should not run away with the idea that fitting twin carburetters will necessarily reduce consumption. If fitting a multiple carburetter setup gives a vast increase in power, then it is obvious that the engine was being starved of air on the original carburation. Now we don't get power for nothing; if we are to use all this extra power that the engine is giving, then it will obviously consume more petrol, since to get the extra power it is being allowed to draw in more air, therefore more fuel must be given to the engine to keep the mixture ratio correct. What it all boils down to is that if you drive the same speed on both the single and multiple carburetter setup, then if the mixture is set the same in both cases, the multiple carburetter setup will give better fuel consumption figures. If however you continually use the extra power available you will inevitably use more fuel.

To enable the selection of the size and number of carburetters, the chart of Fig. 18 has been included. Now this chart should be taken as a reasonable guide and not as a hard and fast law as to what in needed. The chart tends to be biased in favour of performance engines. Now if you were using an SU carburetter merely to gain better economy, then you may well find that the performance is satisfactory on carburetter sizes of one less than indicated by the chart.

Effect of Air Filters and Ram Pipes

Air filters are fitted to carburetters with two functions in mind. Firstly, they cut down carburetter noise and secondly, and by far the most important factor, is that they stop the induction of dirt into the engine. However, even the best design of air filter tends to restrict the airflow into

29

the engine. How much the airflow is restricted depends very largely on the design of the filter. The best filters are capable of passing large amounts of air without causing a noticeable restriction. Indeed they may only loose the engine as little as 1 bhp. However, when performance is the prime consideration, it is necessary to let the carburetters breathe as well as possible, and providing that one is not too much worried about the length of time between engine re-builds, the air filters can be removed to give a little more performance. Removing the air filters, however, weakens the mixture by virtue of the fact that the air filter was causing a choking effect on the main jet, so removing this choking effect, drops down the amount of petrol being introduced into the airstream. Apart from this, removing the filter increases the amount of air going in, so when an air filter is removed, the mixture must be richened to compensate. If we attempt to further increase the flow by adding a ram pipe to the carburetter, then it will be necessary to richen up the mixture even further to compensate for the effect of the ram pipe.

Chapter 6

The use of special racing fuels

Very often, for use in competition such as drag strip racing, sprinting or hill-climbing, the SU carburetter is called upon to pass a fuel other than petrol. Probably the most popular alternative fuel, other than petrol, is methanol. If an engine is to be fed on methanol via an SU carburetter, then there are certain points of which we should take note.

Firstly, the amount of methanol required to complete combustion with 1 lb. of air is twice as much as petrol. Therefore, if we are to get the mixture to the chemically correct ratio, the carburetter is going to be called upon to pass twice as much fuel as it would be if it were running on petrol. Apart from this, methanol gives it's best power when it is running very rich, much richer in fact than a normal petrol mixture. This adds further loads to the amount of fuel the carburetter has to contend with.

The first job when running on methanol is to make sure that adequate supply of fuel can be given to the engine and secondly, that the float chamber needle valve is capable of passing this vastly increased amount of fuel. In most cases, this will mean fitting a larger float chamber to allow a greater throughput of fuel and in some cases it may well mean using twin float chambers to supply enough fuel to the jet. Having made sure that an adequate supply of fuel can be given to the engine, then we can turn our attention to metering the fuel into the engine.

If we are converting an engine to run on methanol, and we know from previous experience the needling of the carburetter for use on petrol then we can, within reason calculate what this will need to be when the engine is run on methanol. With fixed jet carburetters the calculation is very easy. All we do to get the chemically correct mixture, if we know what it is on petrol, is to multiply the main jet size by 1.41 or to get maximum power we multiply the main jet size by about 1.6 to 1.65. With an SU

31

carburetter the calculation is, however, a little more complex because the fuel flow is not governed by the jet size but by the effective jet area. This is the area given when the amount the jet is blocked by the needle is taken account. The effective jet area is given by the formula $\frac{\pi}{4}(j^2 - n^2)$ where j = the jet size in thou and n = the needle diameter in thou at the orifice of the jet. Having calculated what this is on petrol, we then multiply it by 1.6 to give us the effective jet area required for methanol.

It is best to start at the top end of the needle (the thin end), as in some cases we may find that with the needle fully out of the jet, the area is still insufficient for a great enough throughflow of methanol. If this is the case, then we have to increase the jet size. SU jets are made in three sizes 90 thou, 100 thou and 125 thou. If, as you would be with a 2 inch SU you are already on the biggest jet, then you will have to resort to making your own jet and needle to suit. However, let us assume at the moment that we are merely calculating the needle required. Having found the maximum effective jet area for methanol, we can work our way down the needle profile, multiplying the effective jet area by the factor of 1.6 at each 1/8 inch increment.

Having determined the effective jet area all the way down the needle for use on methanol, we must then calculate the needle diameter to give us this effective jet area. Now the new needle diameter will be given by the following formula:

New needle diameter =

$$\sqrt{\frac{(\text{Maximum jet area} - \text{Effective jet area}) \times 4}{\pi}}$$

Using these two formulas mentioned we can calculate the needle diameter throughout the movement of the piston and needle in the jet and this, since methanol is less fussy about mixture strength when it is rich it is likely more often than not, to give us almost perfect results straight off.

These calculations may seem a bit lengthy, but it is certainly a lot quicker and cheaper to do it this way than it is to do it by trial and error. Also, the results obtained are likely to be far better.

Methanol is not the only fuel which is likely to be used. Mixtures of methanol and nitro methane are popular for use on drag strips. Adding nitro methane brings about a further complication in selecting the jet sizes. The most popular blend of fuel is to use a nitro methane methanol mixture and where this is so, the best plan is to increase the effective jet area by 1% for every 1% content mixture of nitro methane within the methanol mixture. For instance if we are running a 55% nitro methane content with the remaining 45% methanol then the main jet effective area needs to be increased by 55% over that used on straight methanol. With nitro methane, as with methanol, the best plan is to err on the rich side if anything, as nitro methane mixtures can stand being exceedingly rich. However, if you calculate the effective jet area and needle sizes from these figures just given you will be pretty near the mark from scratch.

While on the subject of these fuels it should be remembered that both nitro methane and methanol burn relatively slowly compared with petrol, therefore the ignition advance needed will be far greater.

Chapter 7
Dismantling & assembly

DISMANTLING & ASSEMBLY OF SU CARBURETTERS.

TYPE H. TYPE HD.

TYPE HS & VARIANTS

TYPE HS 4 HS 6

TYPE HS 8

TYPE HIF (EMISSION CONTROL)

TYPE H CARBURETTER

Dismantling.

1.

Thoroughly clean the outside of the carburetter. Remove the banjo bolt, banjo union and fibre washers. Extract the filter and spring assembly from inside the inlet of the float-chamber lid.

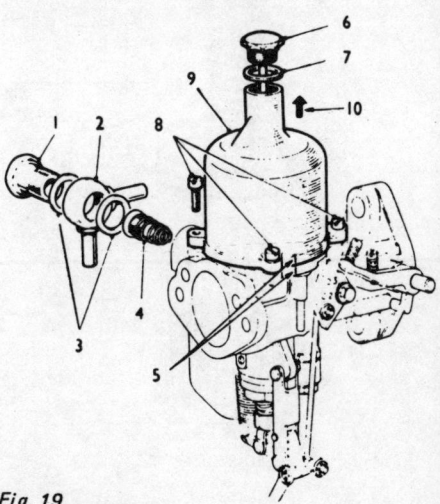

Fig. 19

1. Banjo bolt
2. Banjo union
3. Fibre washers
4. Filter assembly
5. Marks for replacement
6. Damper
7. Washer for damper
8. Suction chamber retaining screws

33

9. Suction chamber
10. Direction of removal.

Mark the relative positions of the suction chamber and the body.

Remove the damper and its washer. Unscrew the chamber retaining screws. Lift off the chamber without tilting it.

2.

Remove the piston spring and washer (when fitted) and carefully lift out the piston assembly and empty the damper oil from the piston rod.

Remove the needle locking screw and the needle. If the needle cannot be easily removed, first tap it inwards and then pull it out; do not bend it.

3.

Unhook the lever return spring. Remove the split pins and clevis pins. Remove the fast-idle cam pivot bolt. Note the positions of the double-coil spring washer and the aluminium spacing washer.

Detach the linkage assembly. Press up the piston lifting pin, extract the circlip from its groove and withdraw the pin and its spring downwards.

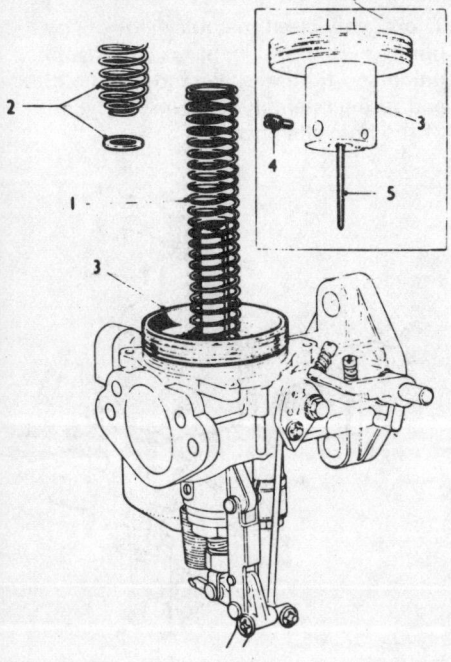

Fig. 20

1. Piston spring
2. Alternative spring and washer
3. Piston assembly
4. Needle locking screw
5. Needle

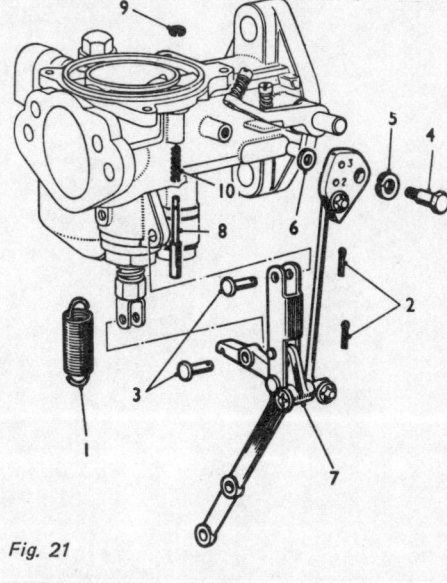

Fig. 21

1. Lever return spring
2. Split pins
3. Clevis pins
4. Cam plate pivot bolt
5. Spring washer
6. Spacing washer
7. Lever assembly
8. Piston lifting pin
9. Circlip for pin
10. Spring for pin

Withdraw the jet downwards and detach the jet adjusting nut and spring.

bearing. Do not disturb the jet locking nut cork washer.

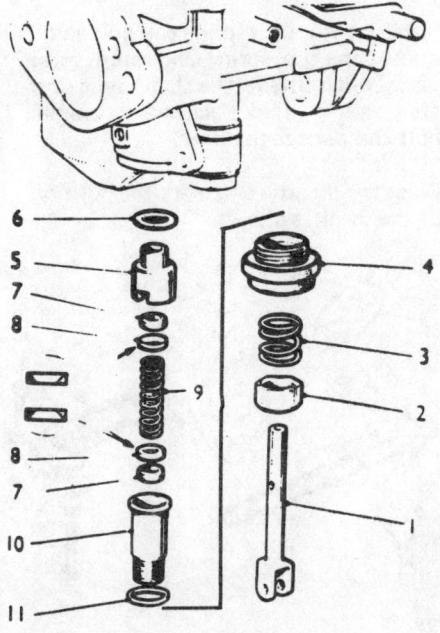

Fig. 22

1. Jet
2. Jet adjusting nut
3. Spring for nut
4. Jet locking nut
5. Upper jet bearing
6. Copper washer for upper bearing
7. Gland packing
8. Gland washer
9. Gland spring
10. Lower jet bearing
11. Brass washer for lower bearing

Unscrew the jet locking nut and withdraw the assembly carefully. Lift off the upper jet bearing and copper washer. From inside the bearing extract the gland and brass gland washer.

Remove the gland spring and withdraw the lower jet bearing from the jet locking nut. Note the brass washer under the shoulder of the bearing. Extract the gland and brass gland washer from inside the

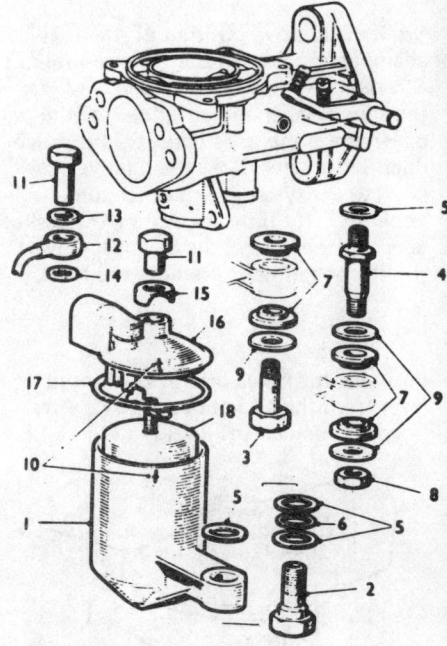

Fig. 23

1. Float-chamber
2. Float-chamber retaining bolt
3. Float-chamber retaining
4. Bolts (alternative)
5. Fibre washer
6. Brass washer
7. Rubber grommet (alternative)
8. Nut (alternative)
9. Steel washer (alternative)
10. Marks for replacement
11. Central nut
12. Drain pipe
13. Washer for nut
14. Fibre washer
15. Cover cap
16. Float-chamber lid
17. Lid gasket
18. Float

5 Fig 23
Remove the screw retaining the stay to the carburetter body (when fitted). Remove the bolt or nut retaining the float-

chamber to the body. Note the positions of the three fibre washers and the brass washer, or alternatively, the position of the rubber grommets and steel washers.

Mark the relative position of the float-chamber and lid. Unscrew the central nut and remove the drain pipe and washers; the stay, washer and cover cap, or the cover cap alone, as is fitted to the individual carburetter. Note the relative positions of the washers and other components. Lift off the lid, noting the gasket between the lid and the chamber. Invert the float-chamber to remove the float.

6.

Push out the hinge pin for the hinged lever from the end opposite to its serrations and detach the lever.

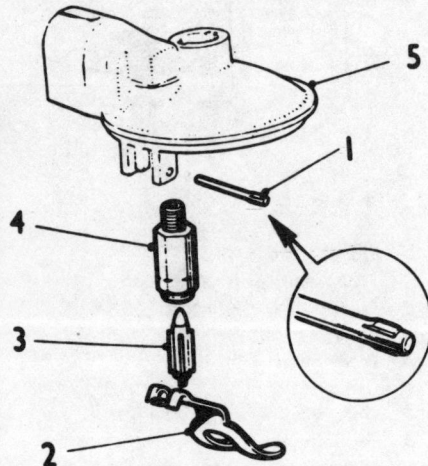

Fig. 24

1. Hinge pin
2. Hinged lever
3. Needle
4. Seating
5. Float-chamber lid

Lift out the needle from its seating and unscrew the seating from the lid using a box spanner 0.338 in. (8.58 mm) across the flats. Take great care not to distort the seating.

7.

Slacken the return spring clip bolt and remove the clip, spring, and return spring plate (when fitted). If a clamp type operating lever is fitted, slacken the clamping bolt and remove the lever.

Close the throttle and mark the position of the throttle disc.

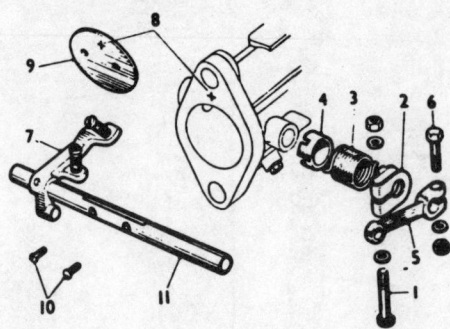

Fig. 25

1. Return spring clip bolt
2. Clip
3. Return spring
4. Plate for spring
5. Operating lever
6. Lever clamping bolt
7. Fixed lever
8. Marks for replacement
9. Throttle disc
10. Retaining screws
11. Throttle spindle

Unscrew the two disc retaining screws. Open the throttle and ease out the disc from its slot in the throttle spindle. The disc is oval and will jam if not withdrawn carefully. Withdraw the spindle from the carburetter body.

Assembly

1.

Check the throttle spindle and its bearings in the carburetter body for wear or scoring. Renew any part as necessary.

Refit the spindle to the body, ensuring that the fixed operating arm is in its correct position. Slide the throttle disc into its slot in the spindle until the two securing screws can be entered. Use two new screws. Manoeuvre the disc until it is a snug fit in the body with the throttle closed. Check the fit visually, and tighten the screws fully. Spread the split ends of the screws just sufficient to prevent turning.

2.

Examine the gland packings for compression and wear. Check the jet for ovality and security of its fork. Renew parts as necessary. Reassemble the jet assembly in the reverse order to dismantling. Ensure that the washer is under the shoulder of the lower jet bearing, that the coned faces of the gland washers face towards the gland packing, and that the copper washer (6, Fig.22) is fitted with its sharp edge towards the upper jet bearing.

Refit the assembly to the carburetter body but leave the jet locking nut slack. When the jet is correctly centred, (see Fig.26) it may appear offset from the centre of the jet bearing drilling.

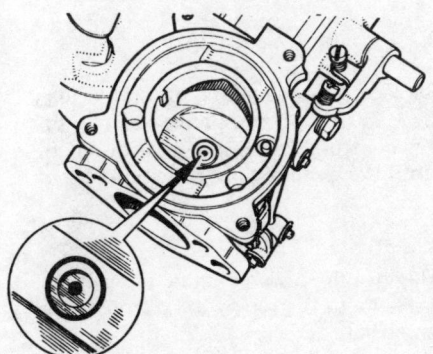

Fig. 26

3.

Examine the piston assembly for damage to the piston rod and the outside surfaces of the piston. Check the piston key for security in the carburetter body. The piston must be scrupulously clean. Use petrol or methylated spirits. Do not use abrasives.

Examine the needle for damage or signs of wear. Refit the needle to the piston. The shoulder should be level with the face of the piston rod. Fit and tighten the locking screw. Fit the piston assembly to the suction chamber, invert the complete assembly and spin the piston to check for concentricity of the needle.

Refit the piston assembly to the carburetter body, taking care not to damage the needle. Replace the washer (when fitted) and piston spring in position over the piston rod.

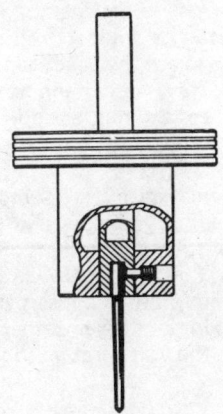

Fig. 27

The shoulder must be flush with the bottom face of the piston rod

4.

Clean inside the suction chamber and the piston rod guide using petrol or methylated spirit.

Lightly oil the outside of the piston rod, and refit the suction chamber in its original position as marked on dismantling. Fit and tighten the securing screws.

Centralize the jet and refit the damper and washer. Do not fill with oil at this stage.

5.

Examine the float needle and seating; renew if faulty. Refit the seating to the float-chamber lid, taking care not to distort or overtighten. Put the needle into the seating, coned end first. Test for leakage with air pressure. Refit the hinged lever and hinge pin and check the float level.

6.

Examine the float-chamber lid gasket; renew if necessary. Check the float for damage or puncturing; renew if necessary. Refit the float to the chamber. Fit the lid and gasket in its original position as marked. Replace the cover cap and nut cover cap, stay, washer and nut; or drain pipe, washers and nut, as appropriate to the carburetter. Do not overtighten.

Refit the float-chamber assembly to the carburetter body. Ensure that the fibre washers or rubber grommets are in good condition. Check that the washers are in their correct positions. Insert the rubber grommets in the float-chamber banjo and then push the bolt through them (when fitted).

Insert the filter assembly, spring end first, and refit the banjo and bolt together with the fibre washers. Note that the recessed face of the banjo fits towards the hexagon end of the bolt.

7.

Refit the return spring plate, return spring and return spring clip to the throttle spindle. Tension the spring by turning the clip on the spindle and tighten the clip

pinch-bolt. Refit the operating lever, and tighten the clamping bolt.

Refit the linkage assembly; use new split pins. Ensure that the distance washer and double-coil spring washer are in their correct positions in relation to the fast-idle cam.

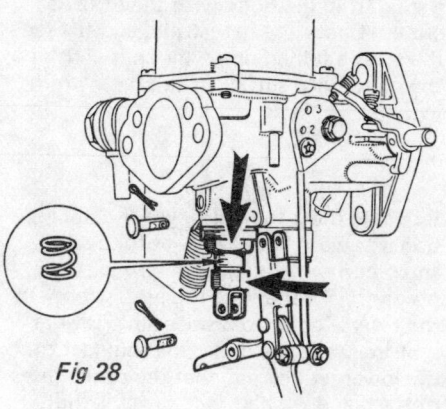

Fig 28

Jet centreing

1.

Remove the jet control linkage and swing it to one side. Mark for reassembly and withdraw the jet, remove the jet locking spring, replace the adjusting nut and screw it up as far as it will go.

2.

Replace the jet, keeping the slot in the jet head in the correct relative position to the control. Slacken the jet locking nut until the assembly is free to rotate.

3.

Remove the piston damper and apply pressure to the top of the piston rod with a pencil.

Tighten the jet locking nut keeping the slot in the jet head in the correct position and the jet hard up against the adjusting nut.

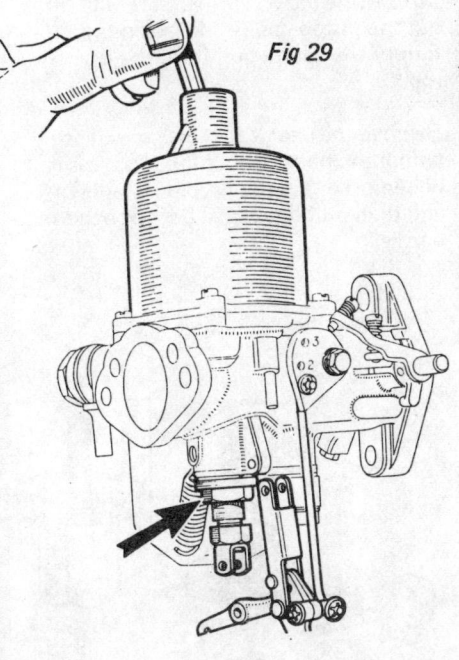

Fig 29

reassembly and carefully remove the piston/suction chamber unit.

Using a petrol-moistened cloth, clean the inside bore of the suction chamber and the two diameters of the piston. Lightly oil the piston rod only and reassemble as marked.

Float Chamber Fuel Level

Remove the float chamber lid and invert it. With the needle on its seating insert a 7/16 in. (11 mm) diameter round bar between the forked lever and the lip of the float chamber lid.

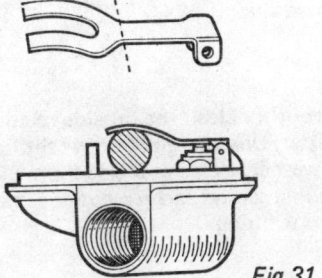

Fig 31

4.

Make final check for piston free fall onto carburetter bridge.

Refill the piston damper with engine oil.

Re-assemble the controls.

Cleaning

At the recommended intervals mark for

The prongs of the lever should just rest on the bar; if not, carefully bend the lever until they do.

Needle Size and Position

To check the needle fitted, remove the piston/suction chamber unit. Slacken the needle clamping screw, extract the needle, and check its identifying mark against the recommendation.

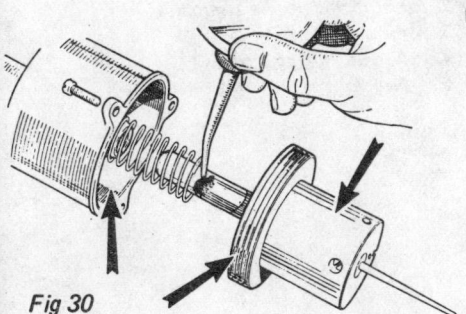

Fig 30

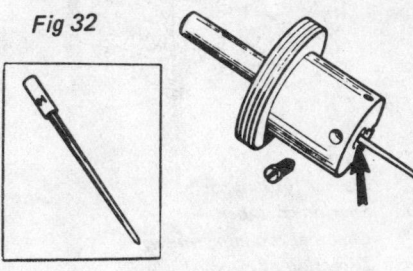

Fig 32

39

Fit the correct needle and lock it in position so that the shoulder on the shank is flush with the piston base. Reassemble the piston/suction chamber unit.

Tuning And Adjusting

For general principles on carburetter setting and mixture control adjustments for best performance see Chapter 3.

2.

Lift off the piston spring. Carefully lift out the piston and needle assembly. Empty the damper oil from the piston rod.

Remove the needle locking screw and withdraw the needle. If it cannot easily be removed, tap the needle inwards first and then pull outwards. Do not bend the needle.

TYPE HD CARBURETTER

Dismantling

1.

Thoroughly clean the outside of the carburetter. Unscrew and remove the damper and washer. Remove the suction chamber retaining screws and remove the chamber without tilting it.

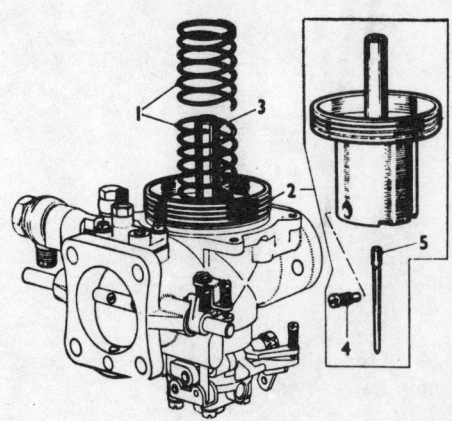

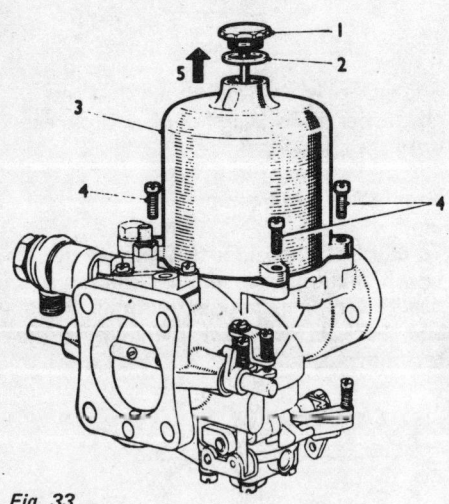

Fig. 34

1. Piston spring
2. Piston and needle assembly
3. Piston rod
4. Needle locking screw
5. Needle

Fig. 33

1. Damper
2. Washer for damper
3. Suction chamber
4. Chamber retaining screws
5. Direction of removal

3.

Remove the plate retaining screw and lift off the plate and spring. Note the shakeproof washer either side of the place. Withdraw the cam rod assembly.

Mark the relative position of the float-chamber, jet housing, and carburetter body. Unscrew the float-chamber screws, holding the float-chamber against the pressure of the jet spring. Detach the float-chamber carefully.

10. Float-chamber screws
11. Jet spring
12. Jet diaphragm
13. Jet assembly
14. Jet locking nut
15. Jet bearing

Lift out the jet spring. Mark the jet diaphragm opposite one of the screw holes in the jet housing and withdraw the jet assembly. Lift off the jet housing.

Using a ring spanner slacken and remove the jet locking nut together with the jet bearing.

4.

Unscrew the banjo bolt and remove the bolt, banjo, and fibre washers. Extract the filter and spring assembly from inside the float-chamber lid inlet.

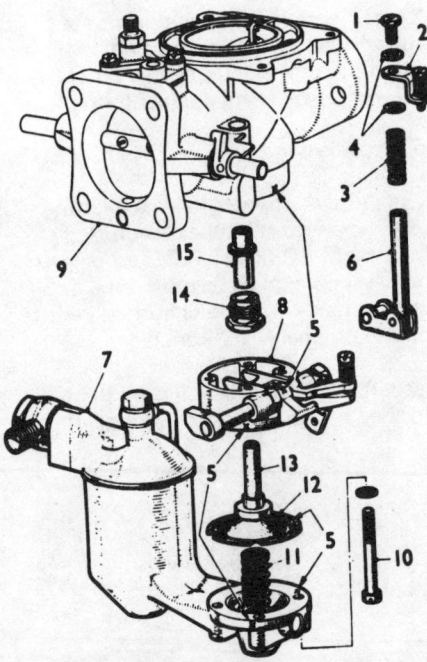

Fig. 35

1. Plate retaining screw
2. Plate
3. Spring
4. Shakeproof washer
5. Marks for replacement
6. Cam rod assembly
7. Float-chamber
8. Jet housing
9. Carburetter body

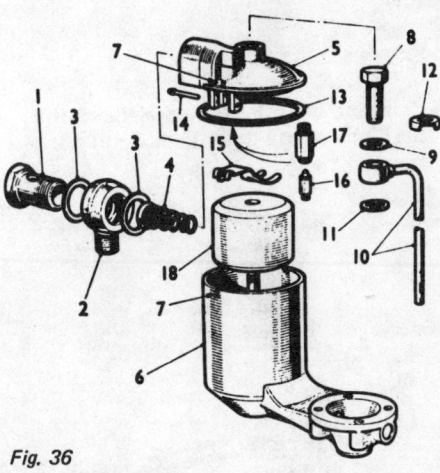

Fig. 36

1. Banjo bolt
2. Banjo
3. Fibre washer
4. Filter assembly
5. Float-chamber lid
6. Float-chamber
7. Marks for replacement
8. Central nut
9. Washer for nut
10. Drain tube and banjo

11. Fibre washer
12. Cover cap (alternative)
13. Lid gasket
14. Float lever hinge pin
15. Float lever
16. Float needle
17. Needle seating
18. Float

3. Carburetter flange
4. Disc retaining screws
5. Throttle spindle
6. Spindle sealing glands
7. Piston key

Mark the relative positions of the float-chamber and lid. Remove the central nut retaining the float-chamber lid together with the drain-tube banjo and fibre washer, or cover cap, as fitted.

Detach the lid and gasket. Push out the float lever hinge pin from the end opposite to the serrations. Detach the lever.

Extract the float needle from its seating and unscrew the seating from the lid using a box spanner 0.338 in. (8.58 mm) across the flats. Do not distort the seating. Invert the chamber to remove the float.

5.

Close the throttle and mark the relative positions of the throttle disc and the carburetter flange.

Slacken and remove the disc retaining screws. Withdraw the disc from its slot in the throttle spindle. The disc is oval and will jam if care is not taken.

Slide out the spindle from its bearings. The throttle spindle sealing glands should not be removed as they require no servicing.

Note:- Some H.D.8 carburetters are fitted with plastic spindle bushes and have no spindle sealing glands. In this case refer below for replacement of the bushes.

6. Replacement of PTFE Spindle Bushes

The illustrations and clearance setting given apply to HD type carburetters, the method of fitting P.T.F.E. bushes may however be applied to other type of S.U. carburetter, where these bushes are fitted on the original specifications.

New P.T.F.E. bushes will need to be formed by hand into a cylindrical shape.

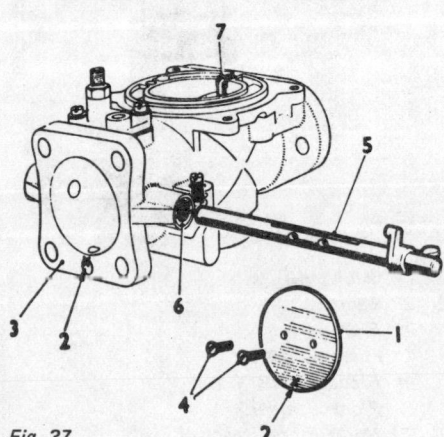

Fig. 37

1. Throttle disc
2. Marks for replacement

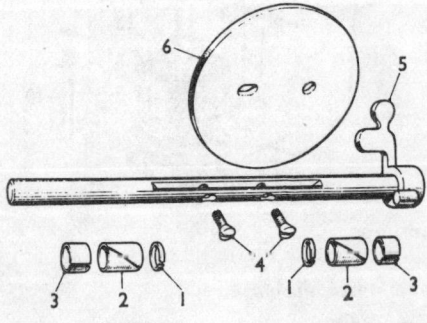

Fig. 38
The component parts of the throttle spindle assembly

Slide one of the large spring clips (3) (Fig. 38) along the throttle spindle until it is approximately 1/4 in. (6 mm) from the throttle stop (5) (Fig.39). Insert a P.T.F.E. bush (2) into each spindle aperture from inside the carburetter bore and then feed the throttle spindle through from the throttle stop side, rotating the spindle gently and keeping the bush within the body (Fig.39).

Place the two smaller spring clips (1) (Fig. 40) on the inserted end of the spindle into the opposite bush. This must be done gently so as to prevent the bushes from being pushed out of position (a piece of tubing that will just fit over the spindle will help to keep the second bush in place). When the disc slot in the spindle is central, separate the smaller clips (1) (Fig. 40) and position them so that their gaps are at 90° to the disc slot, then slide the clips outwards until they are concealed in the body casting, one each side. Slide the remaining large clip (3) over the throttle spindle end.

(Fig.41), fully tighten the disc screws and spread their ends. Finally check that the gaps in the inner spring clips (1) are not likely to foul the throttle disc and that the outer spring clips (3) are hard against the P.T.F.E. bushes.

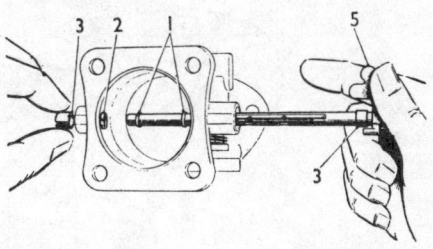

Fig. 40
The small clips (1) fitted to the throttle spindle

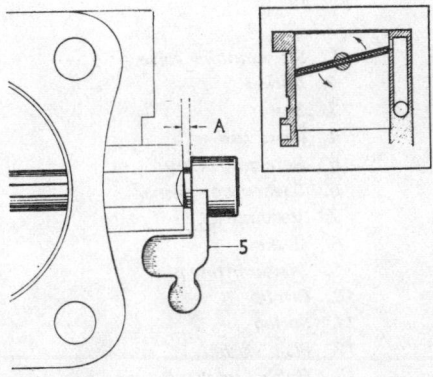

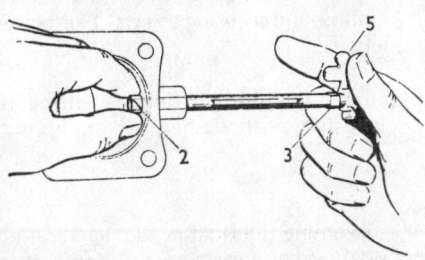

Fig. 39
Inserting the throttle spindle into the P.T.F.E. bush

Rotate the throttle spindle to the fully open position and insert the throttle disc (6) (Fig.38), ensuring that the chamfered edges slope in the correct direction (Fig. 41). Close the throttle and screw in the two disc securing screws (4) (Fig.38) just tight enough to prevent the disc from moving.

Centralize the disc by snapping the throttle shut several times, then, allowing 0.015 to 0.030 in. (0.4 to 0.8 mm) clearance between the stop lever and body (A)

Fig. 41

Setting the clearance between the stop lever and carburetter body before tightening the disc screws. (Inset) the correct throttle disc position. A = 0.015 to 0.030 in. (0.4 to 0.8 mm).

7.

Unscrew and remove the slow-running valve complete with spring, seal, and brass washer.

Remove the two screws and shakeproof washers retaining the vacuum ignition take-off plate and union. Lift off the plate and gasket.

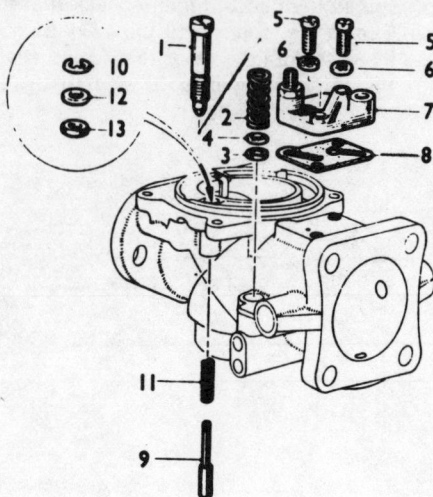

Fig. 42

1. Slow running valve
2. Spring
3. Seal
4. Brass washer
5. Retaining screw
6. Shakeproof washer
7. Vacuum take-off plate
8. Gasket
9. Piston lifting pin
10. Circlip
11. Spring
12. Plain washer
13. Rubber washer

Remove the piston lifting pin by extracting the circlip from its groove with the pin pressed upwards. Withdraw the pin downwards.

Assembly

Note:- Before reassembling, examine all components for damage and/or wear. Unserviceable components must be renewed.

1.

Examine the throttle spindle for scoring or signs of wear. Refit the spindle in its bearings and check for slack in the bearings and freedom of operation.

Refit the throttle disc to the slot in th throttle spindle in the position marke dismantling. The countersunk ends of screw holes in the spindle must face o wards towards the flange of the carbu ter body. Insert two new retaining scr but do not tighten.

Adjust the disc until it closes fully. Ch this visually, then tighten the screws. Spread the split ends of the screws jus enough to prevent turning.

2.

Examine the slow-running valve seal fc serviceability. Check that the concave face of the brass washer is towards the seal. Refit the valve assembly.

Check that the passages in the carbure body and the vacuum ignition take-of plate are not obstructed. Examine the gasket for re-use and refit the gasket, plate, and securing screws. Tighten sec ly.

Refit the piston lifting pin, spring, rut washer, plain washer, and circlip.

3.

Examine the float needle and seating f damage or wear. Screw the seating int the float-chamber lid but do not overtighten. Refit the needle to the seating coned end first. Test the assembly for leakage with air pressure.

Refit the float lever and insert the hin pin. Check the float level as later described.

Examine the float for damage or punc ures. Refit the float to the float-cham

Examine the lid gasket for re-use. Fit t gasket to the lid and replace the lid on the chamber as marked on dismantling Fit the fibre washer, drain-tube banjo, plain washer, and nut or cover cap and nut, as applicable. Do not overtighten the nut.

Clean the filter assembly and examine for damage. Refit the filter to the lid inlet, spring end first. Refit the banjo, fibre washers, and banjo bolt. The recessed face of the banjo must be towards the hexagon of the bolt.

4.

Examine the piston assembly for damage on the piston rod and the outside surface of the piston. The piston assembly must be scrupulously clean. Use petrol or methylated spirits as a cleaning agent. Do not use abrasives. Lightly oil the outside of the piston rod.

Clean inside the suction chamber and piston rod guide using petrol or methylated spirits. Refit the damper assembly and washer. Check that the piston slides freely in the suction chamber as described in Chapter 3.

Refit the needle to the piston assembly. The shoulder or lower edge of the groove must be level with the lower face of the piston rod. Fit a new needle locking screw and tighten. Invert the suction chamber and spin the piston assembly inside it to check for concentricity of the needle.

Check the piston key for security in the carburetter body. Refit the piston assembly to the body and replace the piston spring over the piston rod. Fit the suction chamber and retaining screws. Tighten the screws evenly.

5.

Refit the jet bearing and jet locking nut. Leave the nut sufficiently slack to allow the bearing to be moved from side to side.

Fit the jet assembly to the bearing in the same position as marked on dismantling and centralize the jet.

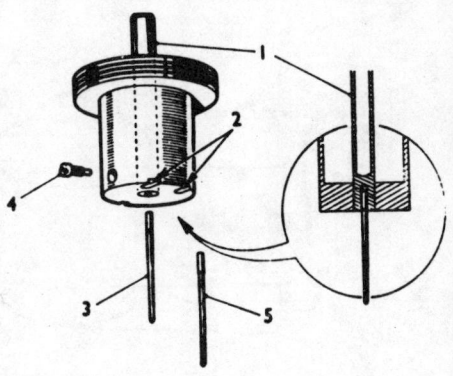

Fig. 43

1. Piston rod
2. Transfer holes
3. Needle
4. Needle locking screw
5. Alternative needle

Replace the jet and refit the jet housing, jet, jet spring, and float-chamber in the same relative positions as marked on dismantling. Fit and tighten the securing screws evenly.

Replace the cam rod assembly and refit the spring, plate, and plate retaining screw with a shakeproof washer either side of the plate. Ensure the plate is positioned so that its adjustment screw strikes squarely on the lug of the throttle spindle operating arm.

Jet centreing

1.

Mark the position of the jet housing and float-chamber in relation to the carburetter body for reassembly.

Remove the plate retaining screw and withdraw the cam rod assembly (14).

Unscrew and remove the float-chamber securing screws.

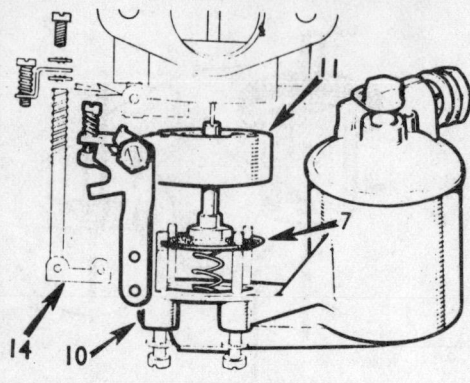

Fig. 44

Remove the float-chamber (10) and the jet housing (11) and release the jet assembly (7).

2.

Slacken the jet locking nut (12), using a ring spanner, until the jet bearing (13) is just free to move.

Remove the piston damper, hold the jet (7) in the 'fully up' position, and apply light pressure to the top of the piston rod. Tighten the jet locking nut (12).

Check that the piston falls freely and also ensure that the jet moves down the bearing freely.

Reassemble, ensuring that the jet and diaphragm are kept to the same angular position and the beaded edge of the diaphragm is located in the housing groove.

Refill the piston damper with oil.

Cleaning

Remove the piston/suction chamber unit.

Using a petrol-moistened cloth, clean the inside bore of the suction chamber and

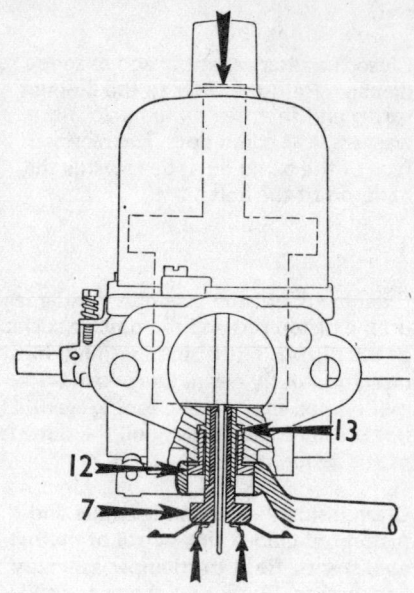

Fig. 45

the two diameters of the piston.

Lightly oil the piston rod only and re-assemble.

Float-chamber fuel level

Remove and invert the float-chamber lid.

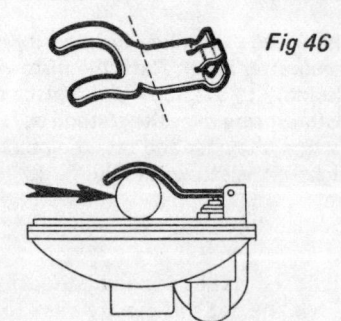

Fig 46

With the needle on its seating, insert a 7/16 in. (11 mm.) diameter bar between the forked lever and the lip of the float-chamber lid.

The prongs of the lever should just rest on the bar, if they do not, carefully bend at the start of the pronged section until they do.

Needle size and position.

To check the needle fitted, remove the piston/suction chamber unit.

Slacken the needle clamping screw, extract the needle, and check its identifying mark against the recommendation.

Fit the correct needle and lock it in position so that the shoulder on the shank, or the lower edge of the groove, is flush with the piston base.

Reassemble the piston/suction chamber unit.

Tuning and Adjusting

For general principles on carburetter setting and mixture control adjustments for best performance see Chapter 3.

Note that whenever throttle adjusting screws are fitted it is they, and not the slow-running valves, which must be used to adjust the idling speed.

Screw down the slow-running valves (which must remain closed) and set the throttle adjusting screw 1½ turns open — adjust to give the required idling speed.

TYPE HS CARBURETTER AND VARIANTS

The HS (i.e. Horizontal Short body) is the latest side-mounted float chamber SU carburetter. The jet is fed by a flexible nylon tube from the base of the float-chamber and vertical movement of the jet provides cold start enrichment.

On the basic HS model, jet movement for mixture adjustment purposes is provided by an adjustment nut located in the underside of the carburetter body. On the HS4C and HS8 variants jet movement is obtained by means of a lever push rod assembly and an adjusting screw accessible from above the unit. The basic type and variants may be readily identified by suction chamber and control linkage style as shown in Fig.47.

Optional features contributing to exhaust emission control include crankcase ventilation control, overrun limiting valve and temperature compensated jet movement.

Subsequent sections show typical constructional features of the HS range of units. The procedures for single carburetter and multi-carburetter setting, and general principles governing mixture control adjustment for best performance (i.e. 'Tuning and Adjusting') are given in Chapter 3.

HS TYPE CARBURETTERS:

(HS2 Typical Shown)

Dismantling

1

Remove the baffle plate from the inlet nozzle.

Thoroughly clean the outside of the carburetter.

Mark the relative positions of the suction chamber and the carburetter body.

Remove the damper and its washer. Unscrew the chamber retaining screws.

Fig 47 HS Type carburetter Variants

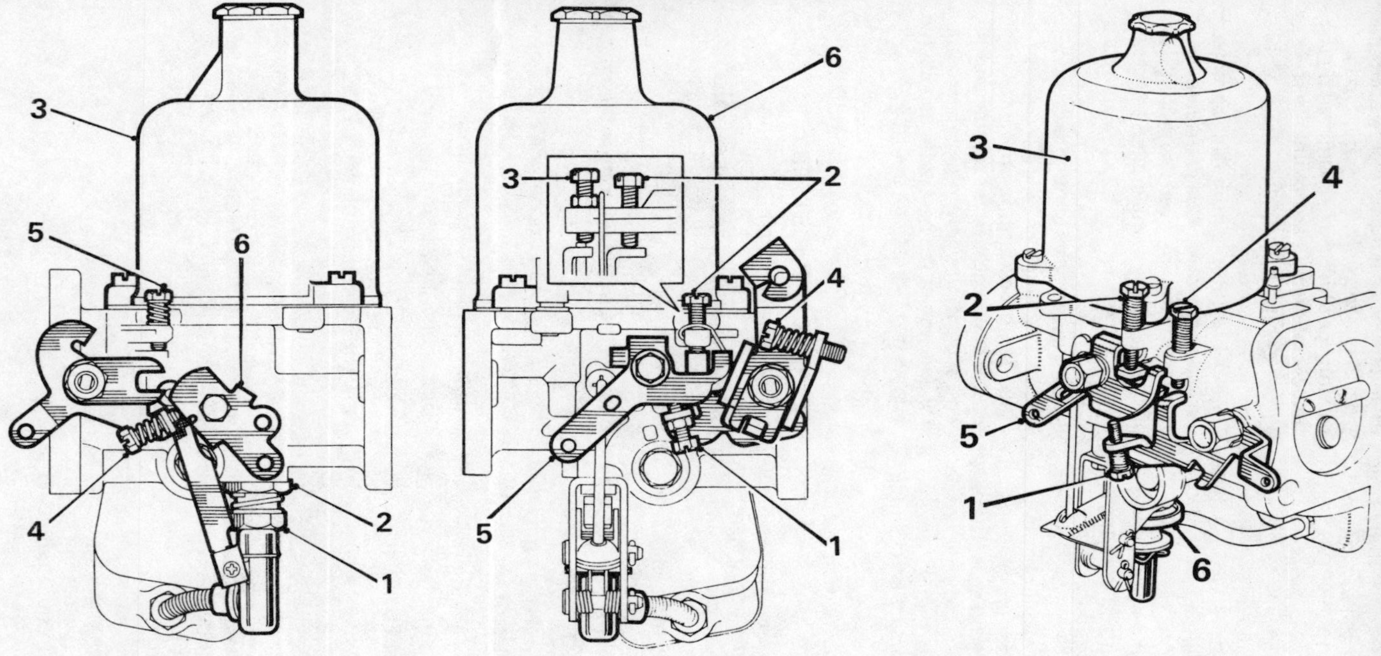

HS8
1. Fast-idle adjusting screw
2. Jet adjusting screw
3. Suction chamber assembly
4. Throttle adjusting screw
5. Cam lever
6. Temperature compensator (bi-metallic)

HS4C
1. Fast-idle adjusting screw
2. Throttle adjusting screw
3. Jet adjusting screw
4. Lost motion adjusting screw
5. Cam lever
6. Suction chamber assembly

HS2 – HS4 – HS6
1. Jet adjusting nut
2. Jet locking nut
3. Suction chamber assembly
4. Fast-idle adjusting screw
5. Throttle adjusting screw
6. Cam lever

2.

Remove the piston spring and washer (when fitted).

Carefully lift out the piston assembly and empty the damper oil from the piston rod.

Remove the needle locking screw and withdraw the needle. If it cannot be removed, tap the needle inwards first and then pull outwards. Do not bend the needle.

If a piston lifting pin with an external spring is fitted, remove the spring retaining circlip and spring, then push the lifting pin upwards to remove it from its guide. With the concealed spring type, press the pin upwards, detach the circlip from its upper end, and withdraw the pin and spring downwards.

3

Support the moulded base of the jet and slacken the screw retaining the jet pick-up link.

Relieve the tension of the pick-up lever return spring from the screw and remove screw and brass bush (when fitted).

Unscrew the brass sleeve nut retaining the flexible jet tube to the float-chamber and withdraw the jet assembly from the carburetter body. Note the gland, washer, and ferrule, at the end of the jet tube.

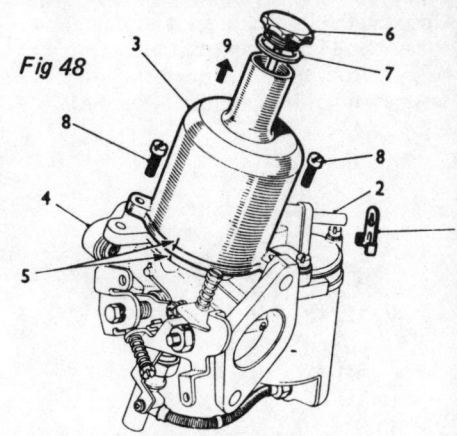

Fig 48

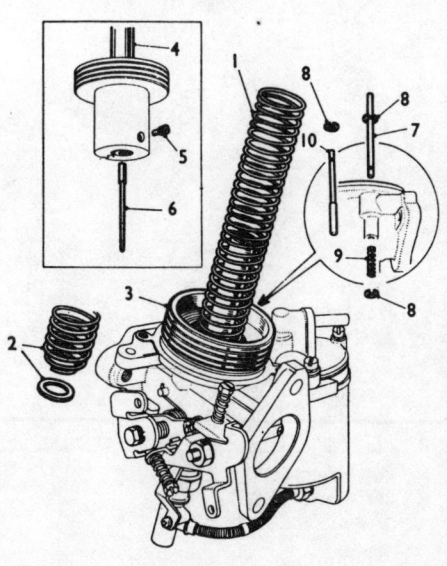

Fig. 49

Fig. 48

1. Baffle plate
2. Inlet nozzle.
3. Suction chamber
4. Carburetter body
5. Marks of replacement
6. Damper
7. Damper washer
8. Chamber retaining screws
9. Direction of removal

Fig. 49

1. Piston spring
2. Alternative spring with washer
3. Piston assembly
4. Piston rod
5. Needle locking screw
6. Needle
7. Piston lifting pin
8. Circlip for pin
9. Spring for pin
10. Alternative lifting pin

Remove the jet adjusting nut and screw. Unscrew the jet locking nut and detach the nut and jet bearing. Withdraw the bearing from the nut, noting the brass washer under the shoulder of the bearing.

its double-coil spring washer, or spacer. Detach the lever assembly and return spring.

Note the location of the two ends of the cam lever spring and push out the pivot bolt tube or tubes, taking care not to lose the spring. Lift off the cam lever, noting the skid washer between the two levers.

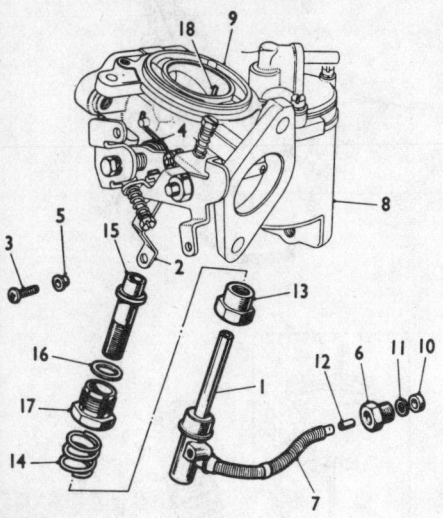

Fig. 50

1. Jet assembly
2. Pick-up link
3. Link retaining screw
4. Pick-up lever return spring
5. Brass bush
6. Sleeve nut
7. Flexible jet tube
8. Float-chamber
9. Carburetter body
10. Gland
11. Washer
12. Ferrule
13. Jet adjusting nut
14. Spring for nut
15. Jet bearing
16. Brass washer
17. Jet locking nut
18. Piston key

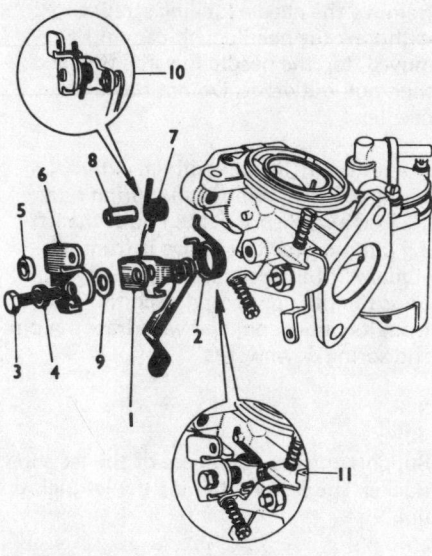

Fig. 51

1. Pick-up lever
2. Lever return spring
3. Lever pivot bolt
4. Double-coil spring washer.
5. Space (alternative)
6. Cam lever
7. Lever spring
8. Pivot bolt tube
9. Skid washer
10. Cam lever spring location
11. Pick-up lever spring location

4.

Note the location points of the two ends of the pick-up lever return spring. Unscrew the lever pivot bolt together with

5

Slacken and remove the bolt retaining the float-chamber to the carburetter body. Note the component sequence with flexibly mounted chambers.

Close the throttle and mark the relative positions of the throttle disc and the carburetter flange.

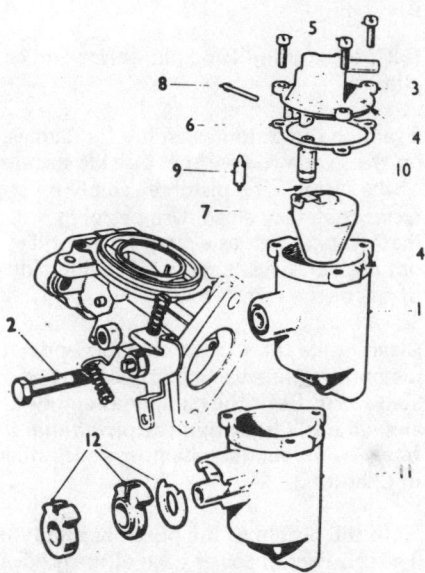

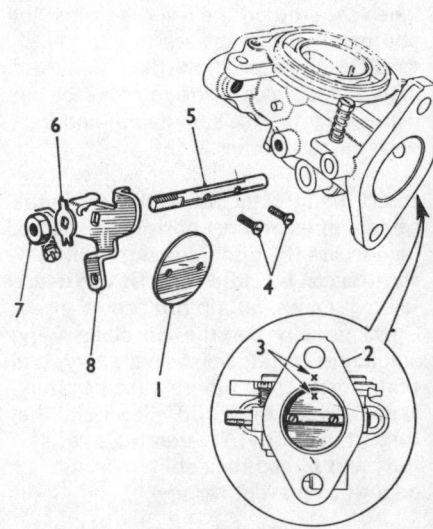

Fig. 52

1. Float-chamber
2. Retaining bolt
3. Float-chamber lid
4. Marks for replacement
5. Lid retaining screws
6. Lid gasket
7. Float assembly
8. Float hinge pin
9. Float needle
10. Needle seating
11. Alternative float-chamber
12. Alternative spacers

Fig. 53

1. Throttle disc
2. Carburetter flange
3. Marks for replacement
4. Disc retaining screws
5. Throttle spindle
6. Tab washer
7. Spindle nut
8. Lever arm

Mark the location of the float-chamber lid. Unscrew the lid retaining screws and detach the lid and its gasket, complete with float assembly.

Push out the float hinge pin from the end opposite its serrations and detach the float.

Extract the float needle from its seating and unscrew the seating from the lid, using a box spanner 0.338 in. (8.58 mm.) across the flats. Do not distort the seating.

Unscrew the two disc retaining screws. Open the throttle and ease out the disc from its slot in the throttle spindle. The disc is oval and will jam if care is not taken.

Tap back the tabs of the tab washer securing the spindle nut. Note the location of the lever arm in relation to the spindle and carburetter body; remove the nut and detach the arm.

Assembly

Examine the throttle spindle and its bearings in the carburetter body. Check for excessive play. Renew parts as necessary.

Refit the spindle to the body. Assemble the operating lever with tab washer and spindle nut, to the spindle. Ensure that when the stop on the lever is against the abutment on the carburetter body; i.e. throttle closed position, the countersunk ends of the holes in the spindle face outwards. Tighten the spindle nut and lock with the tab washer.

Insert the throttle disc in the slot in the spindle in its original position as marked. Manoeuvre the disc in its slot until the throttle can be closed and fit two new retaining screws, but do not fully tighten. Check visually that the disc closes fully, and adjust its position as necessary. With the throttle closed there must be clearance between the throttle lever and the carburetter body. Tighten the screws fully and spread their split ends just enough to prevent turning.

2

Examine the float needle and seating for damage. Check that the spring-loaded plunger in the end of the plastic-bodied needle operates freely.

Screw the seating into the float-chamber carefully. Do not overtighten. Replace the needle in the seating, coned end first. Test the assembly for leakage with air pressure.

Refit the float and lever to the lid and insert the hinge pin. Check the float level as later described.

Examine the lid gasket for re-use. Assemble the gasket on the lid and refit the lid to the float-chamber in the position marked on dismantling. Tighten the securing screws evenly.

Refit the float-chamber assembly to the carburetter body and tighten the retaining bolt fully, making sure that the registers on the body and the chamber engage correctly.

3

Refit the piston lifting pin, spring and circlip.

Examine the piston assembly for damage on the piston rod and the outside surface of the piston. The piston assembly must be scrupulously clean. Use petrol or methylated spirit as a cleaning agent. Do not use abrasives. Lightly oil the outside of the piston rod.

Clean inside the suction chamber and piston rod guide using petrol or methylated spirit. Refit the damper assembly and washer. Check that the piston slides freely in the suction chamber as described in Chapter 3.

Refit the needle to the piston assembly. The shoulder or lower edge of the groove must be level with the bottom face of the piston rod. Fit a new needle locking screw and tighten. Invert the suction chamber and spin the piston assembly inside it to check for concentricity of the needle.

Check the piston key for security in the carburetter body. Refit the piston assembly to the body and replace the piston spring over the piston rod. Fit the suction chamber and retaining screws. Tighten the screws evenly.

4

Refit the jet bearing, washer, and locking nut; do not tighten the nut. Refit the jet in its bearing and the flexible tube to the base of the float-chamber without the gland and washer.

Centralize the jet as later described.

Withdraw the jet and tube; refit the spring and jet adjusting nut. Fit the gland washer and ferrule to the flexible tube. The end of the tube should project a minimum of 3/16 in. (4.8 mm.) beyond the

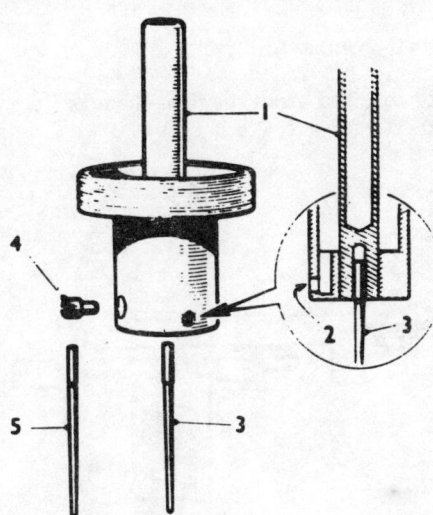

Fig. 54

1. Piston rod
2. Transfer holes
3. Needle
4. Needle locking screw
5. Alternative needle

gland. Refit the jet and tube. Tighten the sleeve nut until the neoprene gland is compressed. Overtightening can cause leakage.

Refit the damper and washer.

5

Reassemble the pick-up lever, cam lever, cam lever spring, skid washer, and pivot bolt tube or tubes in the positions noted on dismantling.

Place the pick-up lever return spring in position over its boss and secure the lever assembly to the carburetter body with the pivot bolt. Ensure that the double-coil spring washer or spacer fits over the projecting end of the pivot bolt tube.

Register the angled end of the return spring in the groove in the pick-up lever,

and hook the other end of the spring around the moulded peg on the carburetter body.

Fitt the brass ferrule to the hole in the end of the pick-up link. Relieve the tension of the return spring and fit the link to the jet with its retaining screw. When finally tightening the screw, support the moulded end of the jet.

Refit the baffle plate to the float-chamber lid nozzle.

Jet centreing

1

Remove the jet head screw to release the control linkage.

Withdraw the jet, disconnecting the fuel pipe union in the float-chamber, and removing the rubber sealing washer. Remove the jet locking spring and adjusting nut.

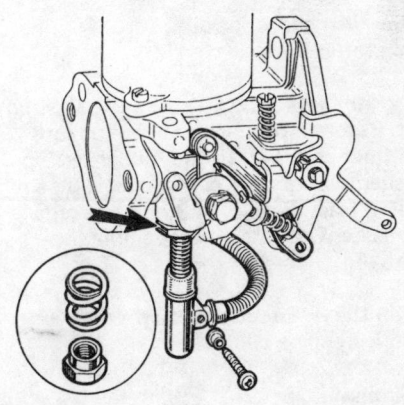

Fig. 55

Replace the jet and insert the fuel feed pipe connection into the float-chamber.

Slacken the jet locking nut until the assembly is free to rotate.

2

Remove the piston damper and apply

pressure to the top of the piston rod with a pencil.

Tighten the jet locking nut keeping the jet hard up against the jet bearing.

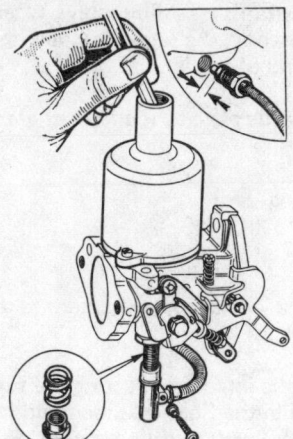

Fig. 56

Make final check for piston free fall onto carburetter bridge.

Re-fit the jet locking spring and adjusting nut. Before replacing the fuel pipe into the float-chamber, fit the rubber sealing washer over the end of the plastic pipe so that at least 3/16 in. (4.8 mm.) of pipe protrudes (see inset). Reassemble the controls.

Refill the piston dampers with the recommended engine oil.

Cleaning

At the recommended intervals mark for reassembly and carefully remove the piston/suction chamber unit.

Using a petrol-moistened cloth, clean the inside bore of the suction chamber and the two diameters of the piston.

Lightly oil the piston rod only and reassemble.

Refill piston damper.

Float-chamber fuel level.

Remove and invert the float-chamber lid.

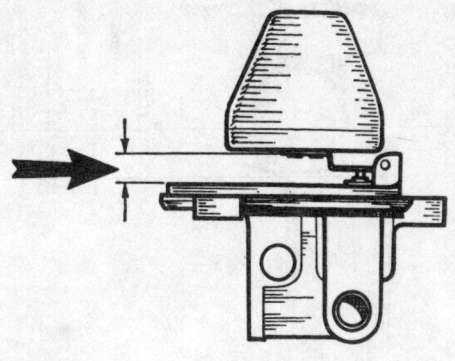

Fig. 57

With the needle valve held in the shut-off position by the weight of the float only, there should be a 1/8 to 3/16 in. (3.2 to 4.8 mm.) gap between the float lever and the rim of the float-chamber lid.

The float may be set by bending at the crank.

Needle size and position

To check that the correct needle is fitted: mark for reassembly and remove the piston/suction chamber unit.

Slacken the needle clamping screw, extract the needle, and check its identifying mark against the recommendation.

Replace the correct needle and lock it in position so that the shoulder on the shank is flush with the piston base.

Reassemble the piston/suction chamber unit as marked.

Tuning and adjusting

For general principles on carburetter setting and mixture control adjustments for best performance, see Chapter 3.

TYPE HS4, HS6 CARBURETTERS.

Component parts typical of later HS4, 6, and 8 types and variants are illustrated in Figs. 58 and 59. Note that a spring loaded jet needle is shown; this feature is as fully described in the HIF type Emission Control Carburetter section.

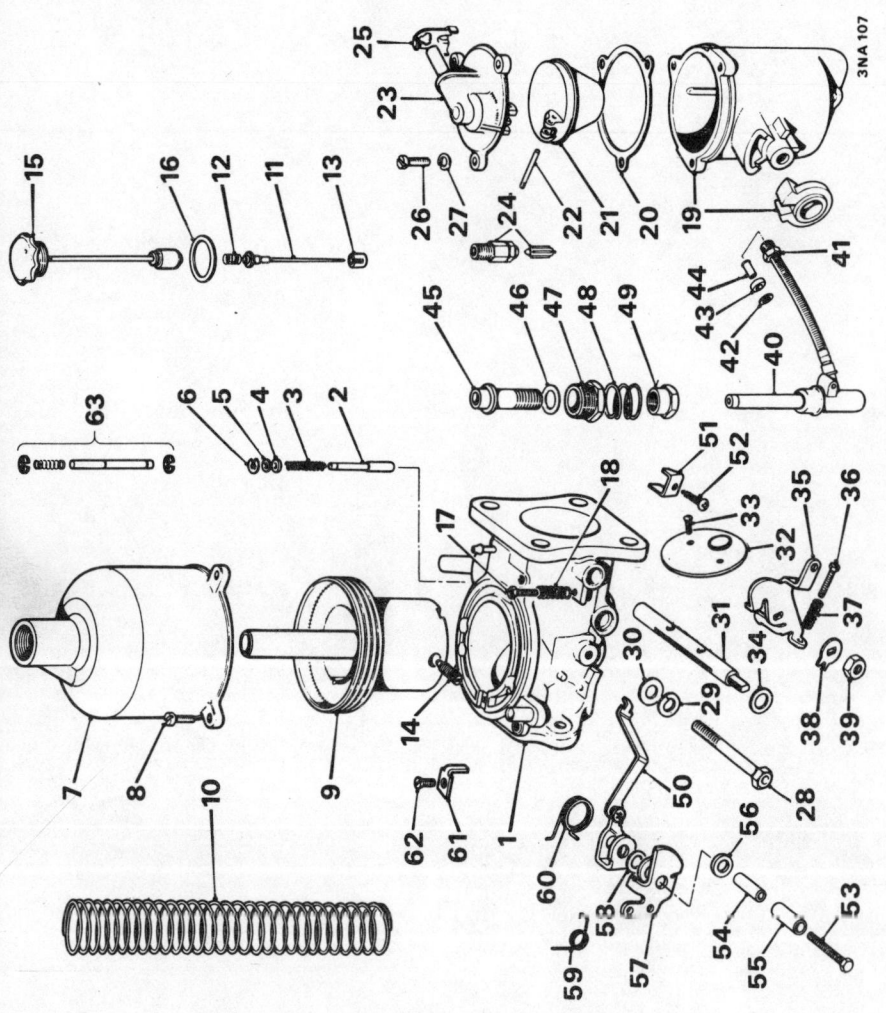

Fig 58

THE TYPE HS CARBURETTER COMPONENTS

1. Body
2. Piston lifting pin
3. Spring for pin
4. Sealing washer
5. Plain washer
6. Circlip
7. Suction chamber
8. Suction chamber screw
9. Piston
10. Spring
11. Jet needle with collar
12. Needle spring
13. Needle guide
14. Needle guide—locking screw
15. Piston damper
16. Damper sealing washer
17. Throttle adjusting screw
18. Spring for screw
19. Float-chamber and spacer
20. Chamber joint washer
21. Float
22. Float hinge pin
23. Float-chamber lid
24. Float needle and seat
25. Baffle plate
26. Float-chamber lid screw
27. Spring washer
28. Float-chamber securing bolt
29. Spring washer
30. Plain washer
31. Throttle spindle
32. Throttle disc assembly
33. Throttle disc securing screw
34. Throttle spindle washer
35. Throttle return lever
36. Fast-idle screw
37. Spring
38. Throttle spindle nut lock washer
39. Throttle spindle nut
40. Jet assembly
41. Jet assembly sleeve nut
42. Washer
43. Gland
44. Ferrule
45. Jet bearing
46. Skid washer
47. Jet locking nut
48. Spring
49. Jet adjusting nut
50. Pick-up lever assembly
51. Pick-up lever link
52. Lever to jet securing screw
53. Pivot bolt
54. Pivot bolt tube—inner
55. Pivot bolt tube—outer
56. Distance washer
57. Cam lever
58. Washer
59. Cam lever spring
60. Pick-up lever spring
61. Piston guide key
62. Key securing screw
63. Piston lifting pin—alternative

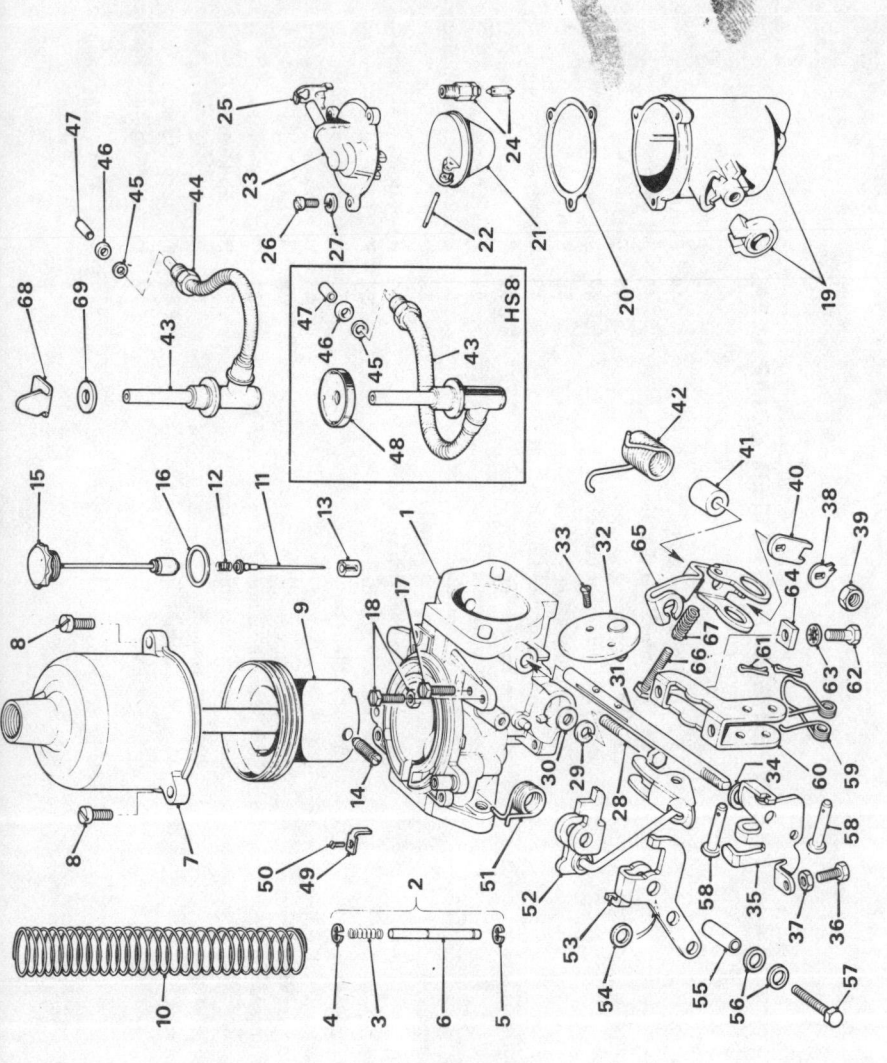

Fig 59

The type HS4C & HS8 carburetter components

1. Body
2. Piston lifting pin assembly
3. Lifting pin spring
4. Circlip
5. Circlip
6. Lifting pin
7. Suction chamber
8. Suction chamber screw
9. Piston
10. Spring
11. Jet needle with collar
12. Needle spring
13. Needle guide
14. Needle guide locking screw
15. Piston damper
16. Damper sealing washer
17. Throttle adjusting screw
18. Jet adjusting screw and locknut
19. Float-chamber and spacer
20. Chamber joint washer
21. Float
22. Float hinge pin
23. Float-chamber lid
24. Float needle and seat
25. Baffle plate
26. Float-chamber lid screw
27. Spring washer
28. Float-chamber securing bolt
29. Spring washer
30. Plain washer
31. Throttle spindle
32. Throttle disc assembly
33. Throttle disc securing screw
34. Throttle spindle washer
35. Throttle return lever
36. Fast-idle screw
37. Fast-idle screw locknut
38. Throttle spindle nut lock washer
39. Throttle spindle nut
40. Lost motion lever
41. Spacer
42. Throttle return spring
43. Jet assembly
44. Jet assembly sleeve nut
45. Washer
46. Gland
47. Ferrule
48. Temperature compensator
49. Piston guide key
50. Key securing screw
51. Pick-up lever spring
52. Jet fork assembly pick-up lever
53. Cam lever
54. Skid washer
55. Pivot bolt tube
56. Washers
57. Pivot bolt
58. Clevis pin
59. Jet return spring
60. Jet assembly securing bracket
61. Split pins
62. Securing bracket bolt
63. Starlock washer
64. Spacer
65. Throttle actuating lever
66. Lost motion adjusting screw
67. Spring
68. Jet fork centering washer
69. Washer

59

HS4C AND HS8 VARIANTS

The HS4C and HS8 carburetters differ from others in the design of the jet assembly, the means of mixture adjustment, and in the use of a common body casting for right and left hand versions.

Cold starting jet control

Jet actuation for cold starting purposes and for mixture setting is affected by a rocking lever mounted on the side of the carburetter body; movement of this lever being transmitted via a push rod to a fork acting on the jet head. The rocking lever is moved down either by a cam lever for starting purposes or by a screw for mixture setting. A jet return spring is mounted below the jet fork and bears upon a disc moulded into the jet head.

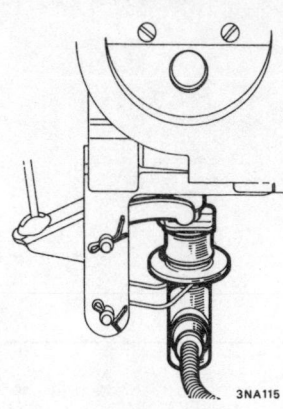

Fig 60 HS4C Jet Assembly

This arrangement provides access to the mixture adjustment from above the carburetter and allows provision for temperature compensation.

Mixure control tempreture compensation

Changes in mixture strength will occur in a jet control position as set, due to variations in fuel and air temperature. Temperature sensitive devices have been introduced for the HS series whereby the jet is automatically re-positioned with temperature change.

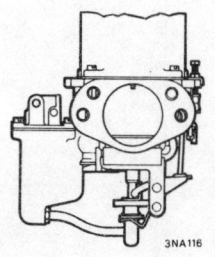

Jet lowered for cold start enrichment

Two types of compensator arrangements are shown in Fig. 62; one form employs a wax filled capsule, the other bi-metallic discs. These elements are so arranged that their expansion and contraction resulting from temperature changes, is transmitted to the jet, so re-positioning it to compensate for the changes in mixture strength which could otherwise occur.

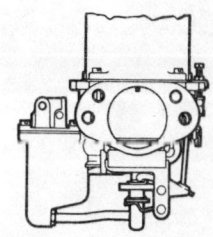

Jet in normal position

Crankcase emission control

With this control system engine crankcase fumes are fed to the air inlet manifold by carburetter depression. Details are given

Fig 61 HS8 Jet Operation

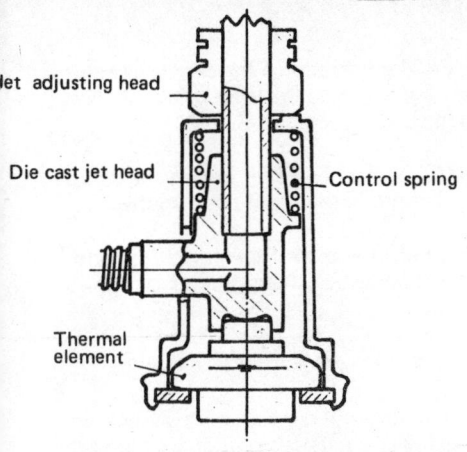

CAPSTAT TEMPERATURE COMPENSATION

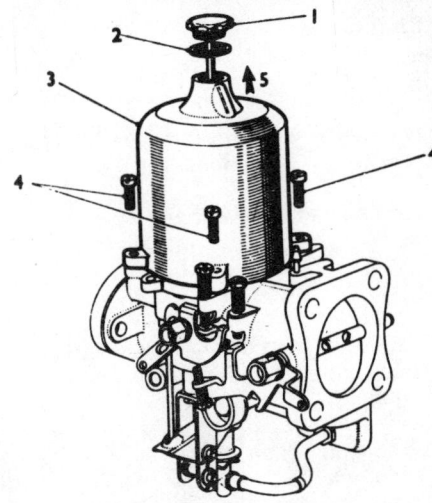

in the HIF Emission Control Carburetter section.

The Overrun Valve

This valve improves combustion during overrun/closed throttle conditions. Refer HIF Emission Control Carburetter section for details.

Fig. 63

1. Damper assembly
2. Washer for damper
3. Suction chamber
4. Chamber securing screws
5. Direction of Removal

TEMPERATURE COMPENSATION

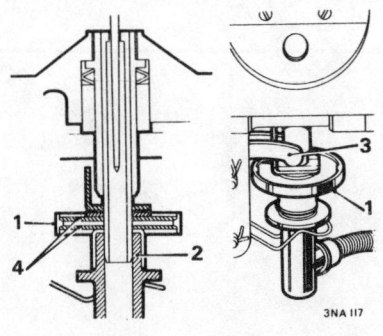

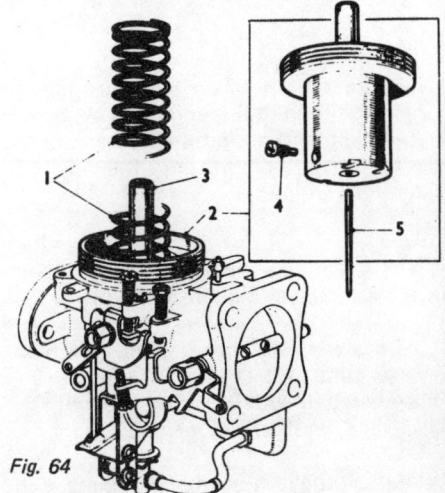

Fig. 64

1. Temperature compensator
2. Jet head
3. Jet fork lever
4. Bi-metal discs

1. Piston spring
2. Piston and needle assembly
3. Piston rod
4. Needle locking screw
5. Needle

TYPE HS8 CARBURETTER

Dismantling

1

Thoroughly clean the outside of the carburetter.

Unscrew and remove the damper and washer.

2

Remove the suction chamber securing screws and detach the chamber without tilting it.

Lift off the piston spring.

Carefully lift out the piston and needle assembly and empty the oil from inside the piston rod.

Remove the needle locking screw and withdraw the needle. If it cannot be removed, tap the needle inwards first and then pull outwards. Do not bend the needle.

3

Note the location of the jet return spring. Remove the split pins and plain washers retaining the jet spring anchor pin and the jet fork pivot pin. Withdraw the pins and jet return spring.

Withdraw the jet fork from the fork bracket, unscrew the bracket retaining screw and detach the brackets.

Unscrew the sleeve nut retaining the flexible jet tube to the base of the floatchamber, and withdraw the tube, noting the gland, washer, and ferrule.

Withdraw the jet assembly complete with copper washer from the jet bearing.

Unscrew the jet locking nut and withdraw the nut and bearing. Note the brass washer under the shoulder of the bearing.

4

Note the position of the cam lever return spring. Unscrew the lever pivot bolt and detach the assembly.

Remove the pivot bolt noting the double coil spring washer and plain washer.

Push out the pivot tube noting the skid washer between the cam lever and link arm.

Detach the cam lever return spring.

To remove the piston lifting pin extract the lower circlip from its groove, detach the spring and push the pin upwards.

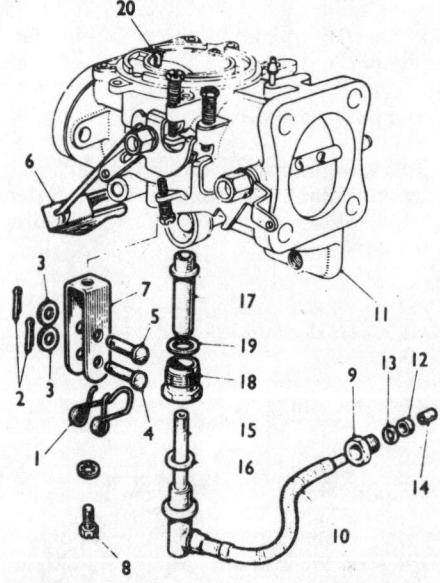

Fig. 65

1. Jet return spring
2. Split pin
3. Plain washer
4. Jet spring anchor pin
5. Jet fork pivot pin
6. Jet fork
7. Fork bracket
8. Bracket retaining screw
9. Sleeve nut

10. Flexible jet tube
11. Float-chamber
12. Gland
13. Washer
14. Ferrule
15. Jet assembly
16. Copper washer
17. Jet bearing
18. Jet locking nut
19. Brass washer
20. Piston key

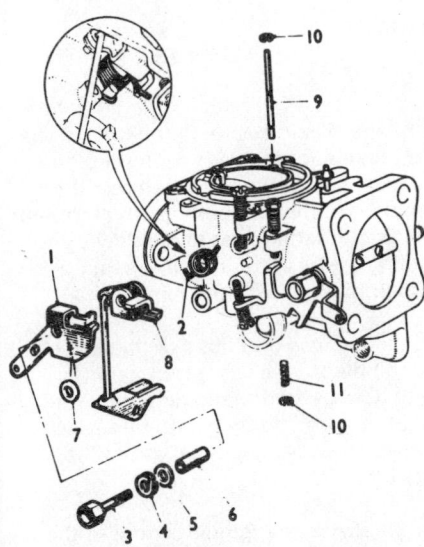

Fig. 66

1. Cam lever
2. Lever return spring
3. Lever pivot bolt
4. Spring washer
5. Plain washer
6. Pivot tube
7. Skid washer
8. Link arm
9. Piston lifting pin
10. Circlip
11. Spring

5

Mark the location of the float-chamber lid. Remove the float-chamber lid retaining screws and lift off the lid and float assembly together with the lid gasket.

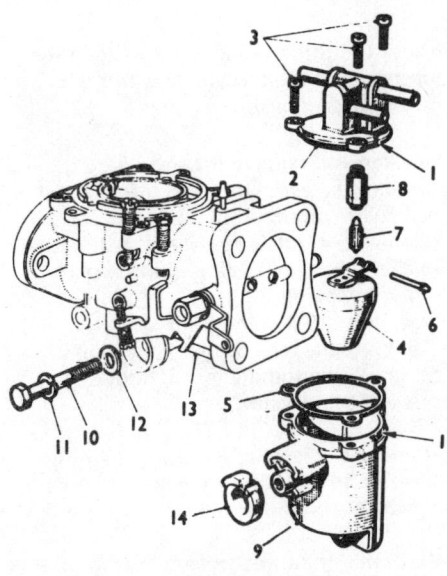

Fig. 67

1. Marks for replacement
2. Float-chamber lid
3. Lid retaining screws
4. Float assembly
5. Lid gasket
6. Float hinge pin
7. Float needle
8. Needle seating
9. Float-chamber
10. Retaining bolt
11. Spring washer
12. Plain washer
13. Carburetter body
14. Distance piece

Push out the float hinge pin from the end opposite to its serrations and detach the float.

Extract the float needle from its seating and unscrew the seating from the lid using a box spanner ·338 in. (8·58 mm.) across the flats. Do not distort the seating.

Slacken and remove the bolt retaining the

float-chamber to the carburetter body.

6

Close the throttle and mark the relative positions of the throttle disc and the carburetter flange.

Slacken and remove the two disc retaining screws. Open the throttle and carefully withdraw the disc from its slot in the throttle spindle. The disc is oval and will jam if care is not taken when removing.

Tap back the tabs of the tab washer retaining the spindle nut. Remove the nut and tab washer.

Remove the lever arm, noting its position in relation to the spindle. Lift off the brass washer.

Withdraw the throttle spindle from the body, noting the plastic bush in each side of the carburetter body, the two narrow clips, one on the inside of each bush, and the wide clip on the plain end of the spindle.

Note

Before reassembling, examine all components for damage and/or wear. Unserviceable components must be renewed.

1. Throttle disc
2. Carburetter flange
3. Marks for replacement
4. Disc retaining screws
5. Throttle spindle
6. Tab washer
7. Spindle nut
8. Lever arm
9. Brass washer
10. Plastic bush
11. Narrow clip
12. Wide clip

Assembly

1

Refit the plastic bushes to the carburetter body and place the wide spring clip on the plain end of the spindle. Insert the spindle into the first bush gently, screwed end first, rotating the spindle slowly and holding the bush to prevent it being pushed through with the spindle.

Fit the two narrow clips over the end of the spindle from inside the carburetter body. Gently feed the spindle through the other bush, holding both bushes to prevent them being pushed out of position.

Set the slot in the spindle central in the body, with the gaps in the narrow clips at 90 degrees to the slot. Slide the clips outwards until they are concealed in the carburetter body at either side.

Fit the brass washer, lever arm, tab washer, and spindle nut in their original locations. The countersunk ends of the screw holes must face outwards when the lever arm is in the closed throttle position. Tighten the spindle nut and lock it with the tab washer.

Insert the throttle disc in the spindle slot as marked on dismantling. Fit two new securing screws but do not tighten. Adjust the position of the disc until it closes fully. Check this visually, then tighten the securing screws, at the same time ensuring that there is clearance

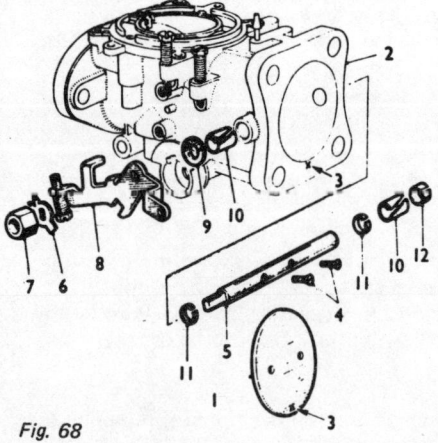

Fig. 68

between the throttle lever and the carburetter body. Spread the split ends of the screws just enough to prevent turning, and push the wide clip hard up against the plastic bush.

2

Examine the float needle and seating for damage. Check that the spring-loaded plunger in the end of the plastic bodied needle operates freely.

Screw the seating into the float-chamber lid carefully. Do not overtighten. Replace the needle in the seating, coned end first. Test the assembly for leakage with air pressure.

Refit the float assembly to the lid and insert the hinge pin. Check the float level as later described.

Examine the lid gasket for re-use. Assemble the gasket to the lid and refit the lid to the float-chamber in the position marked on dismantling. Tighten the securing screws evenly.

Refit the float-chamber and distance piece to the carburetter body. The stepped face of the distance piece must face towards the body. The lugs on the distance piece must engage in the radiused casting on the float-chamber, and the lug on the carburetter body must register in the slot in the distance piece. Refit the retaining bolt, plain washer, and spring washer. Tighten securely.

3

Refit the piston lifting pin, spring, and circlip to the carburetter body.

Clean and examine the piston and section chamber for damage. Reassemble with damper and carry out the free fall time check as described in Chapter 3.

Refit the needle to the piston assembly. The shoulder or lower edge of the groove must be level with the bottom face of the piston rod. Fit a new needle locking screw and tighten. Invert the suction chamber and spin the piston assembly inside it to check for concentricity of the needle.

Check the piston key for security in the carburetter body. Refit the piston assembly to the body and replace the piston spring over the piston rod. Fit the suction chamber and retaining screws. Tighten the screws evenly.

4

Refit the jet bearing, washer, and locknut. Leave the locknut slack enough to enable the bearing to be moved sideways by hand. Refit the jet in its bearing and the flexible tube to the base of the float-chamber without the gland, spring, washer, and ferrule.

Centralize the jet as later described.

Withdraw the jet and tube. Fit the spring, gland, washer, and ferrule to the end of the tube. The end of the tube should project a minimum of 3/16 in. (4·76 mm.) beyond the gland. Refit the jet, copper washer, and flexible tube. Tighten the sleeve nut until the gland is compressed. Overtightening can cause leakage.

5

Refit the fork bracket and retaining screws. Replace the cam lever spring over its boss on the carburetter body. Refit the pivot bolt tube to the lever assembly, with the skid washer between the cam lever and link arm.

Refit the lever assembly to the carburetter body with the pivot bolt, spacing washer, and double coil spring washer.

Insert the jet fork in the fork bracket with the fork ends resting on the copper jet washer. Refit the fork pivot pin, washer, and split pin. Position the jet return spring and refit the jet spring anchor pin, washer, and split pin.

Jet Centreing

1

Remove the jet spring anchor pin and the jet fork pivot pin.

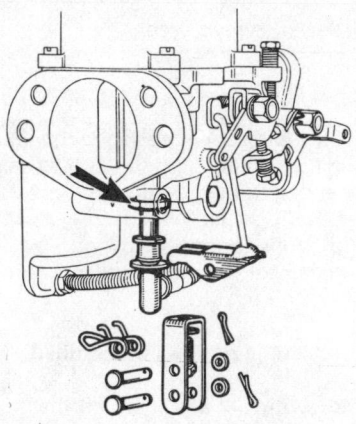

Fig 69

Remove the fork bracket and allow the linkage to swing to one side.

Slacken the jet locking nut until the jet bearing is free to rotate by hand.

2

Remove the piston damper and apply light pressure to the top of the piston rod with a pencil.

Ensuring that the jet is pressed fully home, tighten the jet locking nut.

Make final check for piston free fall onto carburetter bridge.

Refill the piston damper with engine oil.

·Reassemble the controls.

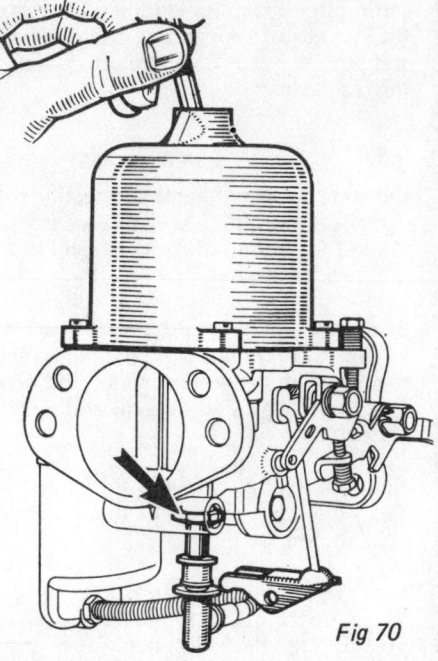

Fig 70

Cleaning

At the recommended intervals mark for reassembly and carefully remove the piston/suction chamber unit.

Using a petrol-moistened cloth, clean the inside bore of the suction chamber and the two diameters of the piston.

Lightly oil the piston rod only and reassemble as marked.

Refill piston damper with engine oil.

Float-chamber fuel level.

Remove and invert the float-chamber lid.

With the needle valve held in the shut-off position by the weight of the float only, there should be $\frac{1}{8}$ to $\frac{3}{16}$ in. gap (3·2 to 4·8 mm.) between the float lever and the rim of the float-chamber lid.

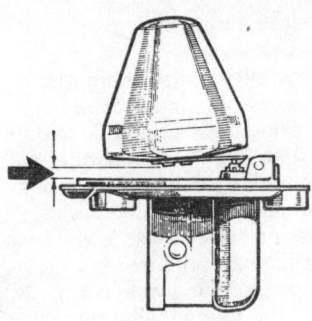

Fig 71

The float-lever may be set by bending at the crank.

Needle Size and Position

To check the needle fitted, remove the piston/suction chamber unit.

Slacken the needle clamping screw, extract the needle and check its identifying mark against the recommendation.

Fit the correct needle and lock it in position so that the lower edge of the groove is just visible at the piston base.

Reassemble the piston/suction chamber unit.

Tuning and Adjusting

For general principles on carburetter setting and mixture control adjustments for best performance see Chapter 3.

TYPE HIF
EMISSION CONTROL CARBURETTER

The HIF (i.e. Horizontal Integral Float-Chamber) carburetter was developed primarily to meet the requirements of exhaust emission control carburation systems.

As the need for such systems arose from the introduction of pollution control regulations some early remarks in this respect are thought appropriate; the text therefore commences with brief background information on automotive pollution, exhaust emission standards and control system development.

Exhaust Emission Control Development

Automotive Pollution

Atmospheric pollution from various sources has necessitated official action being taken in many countries to prevent danger to health and property. For example, in some domestic and industrial situations legislation may limit the nature and quantity of chimney emissions, or allow specific fuels only to be used.

With regard to motor vehicles atmospheric pollution is caused by the presence of carbon monoxide (CO) and unburnt fuel (hydrocarbon, HC) discharged in the exhaust gases. This form of pollution is particularly objectionable since it occurs at street level and cannot be avoided by the public.

Legislation has been introduced in the US, some European countries and others, to control the proportions of CO and HC emitted, as measured under specified test procedures. Depending on the effective date of such legislation IT MAY THUS BE ILLEGAL to change certain carburetter and ignition settings, most probably, a statement will appear in the vehicle handbook if this applies. In the US there are also limits for nitrogen oxides — NO_x. The regulations are subject to change and will become more restrictive if US Federal proposals as indicated below materialise:

TENTATIVE EXHAUST EMISSION STANDARDS

	grams/mile		
	HC	CO	NO_x
1973	3.00	28.0	3.1
1976	0.41	3.4	0.4

Control Systems Development

In the development of exhaust emission control systems two distinct methods have evolved; these consist of 'destructive' and 'preventive' measures respectively.

'Destructive' measures usually consist of the location within the exhaust system of a thermal reactor, or a catalytic afterburner; both devices operate to reduce the pollutants to acceptable levels. 'Preventive' measures, in contrast, take place on the induction side of an engine.

Preventive measures consist of fuel/air metering devices designed and manufactured to control the mixture ratio within a very close limit of the optimum requirement. These devices comprise petrol injection and low emission carburation systems; additional equipment may control crankcase vapour emission and fuel system evaporative loss. In the context of this manual however we are concerned only with a low emission carburation system.

The interaction of fuel properties during the induction, combustion, and exhaust cycles is a complex process varying widely throughout the performance range and with different engine makes. In consequence no common solution can be applied, and each type of engine has to be separately assessed for an appropriate form of control. In some instances a 'standard' design of unit may be adequate, in others a carburetter of 'e.e.c.' performance specific to the engine may be necessary.

Carburation Control

The problems arising from exhaust emissions occur principally during engine deceleration and when idling. Fuel temperature/viscosity compensation, throttle controllers and modifications to jet circuits have been developed whereby the fuel to air mixture ratio is automatically adjusted to ensure complete combustion and hence satisfactory exhaust quality during these periods.

Throttle controllers usually comprise overide devices which operate automatically during the deceleration and overrun period. They may consist of a simple closure delay damper, electric or induction depression operated device, or throttle overrun valve. These operate to allow more air to be admitted during the critical period than would otherwise be the case, so improving cylinder scavenging and combustion.

Control methods may be adopted singly or in combination and vary with make, type and application of the unit.

Crankcase and Fuel Vapour Loss Control

Other sources of automobile pollution arise from the emission of crankcase and fuel tank vapours. Detailed discussion on methods of control of such emissions is outside the scope of this manual except to say that they may often depend upon carburetter depression for their operation, a suitable connection in the carburetter body being provided for the purpose.

The Horizontal Integral Floatchamber (HIF) Carburetter — Operating Principles

The HIF exhaust emission control (e.e.c.) carburetters are designated HIF 4, HIF 6, and HIF 7, having 1.5", 1.75" and 1.875" throttle bore diameters respectively. The units, Fig. 72 operates on the well established SU variable choke/constant depression principle of mixture control and have the following specific features:

Overrun depression limiting valve
Spring-loaded jet needle assembly
Part throttle by-pass emission system
Rotary valve cold start enrichment system
Easy accessible mixture adjustment with sealing facility
Integral float chamber
Float concentric to jet
Fuel viscosity compensator

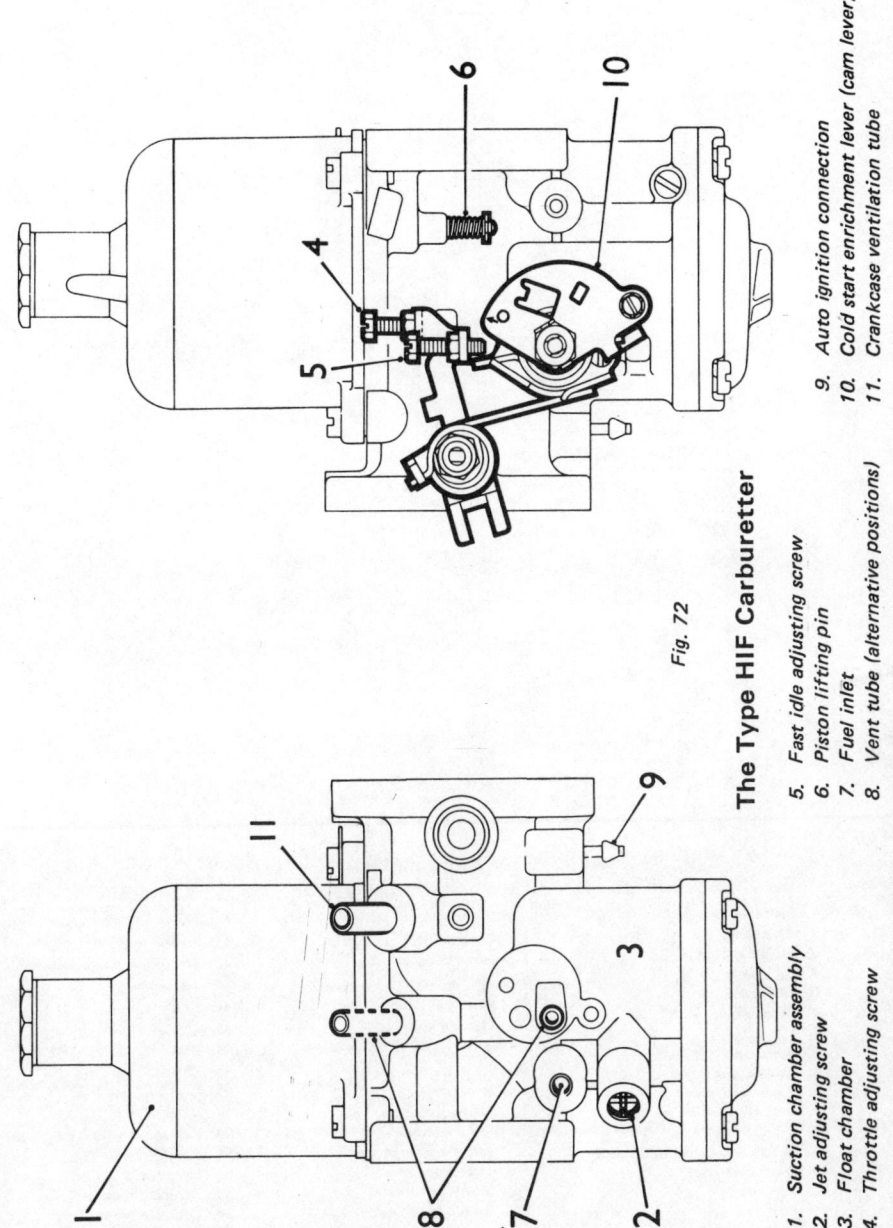

Fig. 72

The Type HIF Carburetter

1. Suction chamber assembly
2. Jet adjusting screw
3. Float chamber
4. Throttle adjusting screw
5. Fast idle adjusting screw
6. Piston lifting pin
7. Fuel inlet
8. Vent tube (alternative positions)
9. Auto ignition connection
10. Cold start enrichment lever (cam lever)
11. Crankcase ventilation tube

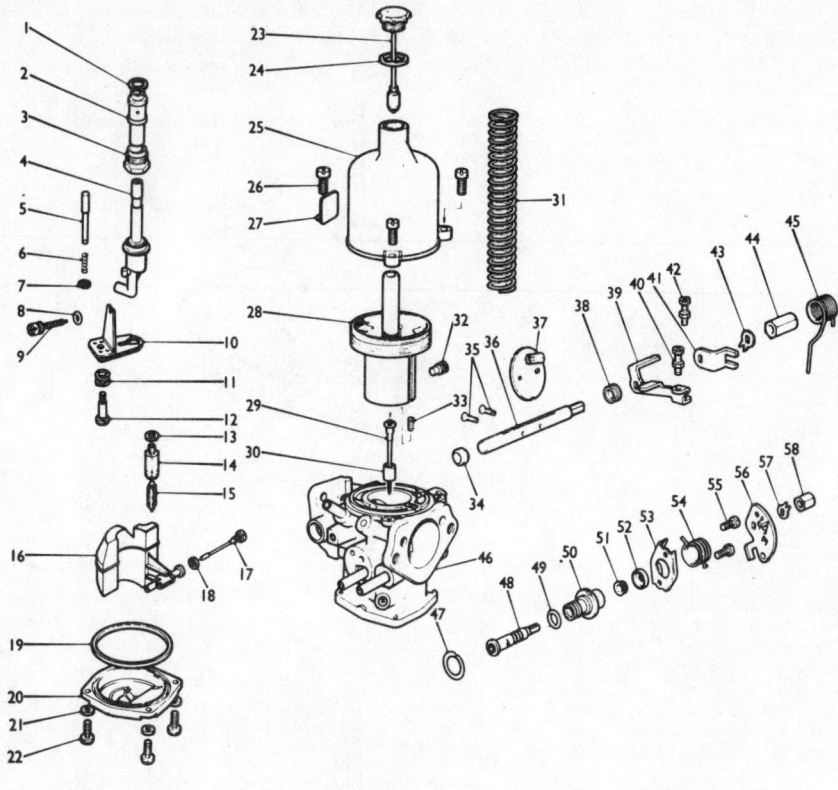

Fig. 73. **THE TYPE HIF CARBURETTER COMPONENTS**

1. Jet bearing washer
2. Jet bearing
3. Jet bearing nut
4. Jet assembly
5. Lifting pin
6. Lifting pin spring
7. Circlip
8. Adjusting screw seal
9. Jet adjusting screw
10. Bi-metal jet lever
11. Jet spring
12. Jet retaining screw
13. Needle seat washer (if required)
14. Float needle seat
15. Float needle
16. Float
17. Float pivot
18. Pivot seal
19. Float chamber cover seal
20. Float chamber cover
21. Spring washer
22. Cover screw
23. Piston damper
24. Damper washer
25. Suction chamber
26. Chamber screw
27. Identity tag
28. Piston
29. Jet needle
30. Needle guide
31. Piston spring
32. Needle retaining screw
33. Needle spring
34. Throttle spindle seal
35. Throttle disc screws
36. Throttle spindle
37. Throttle disc
38. Throttle spindle seal
39. Throttle actuating lever
40. Fast idle screw and nut
41. Throttle lever
42. Throttle adjusting screw and nut
43. Tab washer
44. Retaining nut
45. Throttle spring
46. Body
47. Cold start seal
48. Cold start spindle
49. 'O' ring
50. Cold start body
51. Spindle seal
52. End cover
53. Retaining plate
54. Cold start spring
55. Retaining screw
56. Fast idle cam
57. Tab washer
58. Retaining nut

Crankcase ventilation control

The e.e.c. carburetters are readily distinguished from standard units by absence of the externally mounted float-chamber and cold-start jet positioning lever.

An 'exploded' view of HIF type carburetter components is shown in Fig. 73. The assembly of parts will be self evident from this and later illustrations.

Variable Choke

The effective choke area at any time is determined by the amount of induction passage obstruction by the lower part of the spring loaded piston (28). The piston carries tapered jet needle (29) which rides in jet assembly (4) and so determines the corresponding effective jet area. Vertical movements of the piston (and hence variations in effective choke and jet area) occur in response to changes in induction air flow.

The space below the suction disc of the piston is in communication with the air supply upstream of the choke, whereas the space above the disc communicates with the induction passage downstream of the choke. This passage is at a depression under fuel jet and choke, and hence across the piston, causing this to rise or fall to a position of balance determined by the spring in opposition to the differential force.

The amount of the differential force (and therefore extent of piston and jet needle movement) is determined by the air mass flow required by the engine at any time, together with the corresponding throttle position controlling the passage depression. As the tapered needle is withdrawn from the jet, the increasing effective area allows more fuel to glow. The fuel/air requirements throughout the engine load/speed range are thus automatically controlled.

Jet Needles

Each size of jet needle is specific to the carburetter/engine duty. For some carburetter applications variations from the standard needle are available to give alternatively richer or weaker mixtures. For HIF units however — whatever the application — standard needles only are available.

A feature of the HIF units is that they are already pre-set on the weak side and sealed before a vehicle is delivered (to help meet the exhaust emission regulations) and no overall weaker setting is recommended. Alteration of mixture strength is therefore limited to adjustment of the jet tube height, which is later described.

Spring-loaded Jet Needle

The amount of fluid flow in a pneumatic or hydraulic system is affected by the shape, position, and effective area of the metering orifices. To obtain repeatability of emission control performance in carburetters of the same specification it is essential that the geometry of the flow passages is identical. This is achieved in type HIF carburetters by using a spring-loaded jet needle arrangement, Fig.74.

The shoulder of the needle (3) abuts a protusion formed on the face of the needle guide (5), so that when held in place by spring (4) the needle adopts a biased position (7) in the fuel jet orifice. The direction of the bias is either to the inlet, or the outlet side of the carburetter as indicated by etched location marks on needle guide and piston.

As the needle is retained in a predetermined position no jet centreing is required and a non-centreable jet bearing is fitted.

Mixture Adjustment

Whereas on the standard type of SU carburetter the jet tube is lowered down the jet needle to provide cold start enrichment, its vertical movement on HIF types

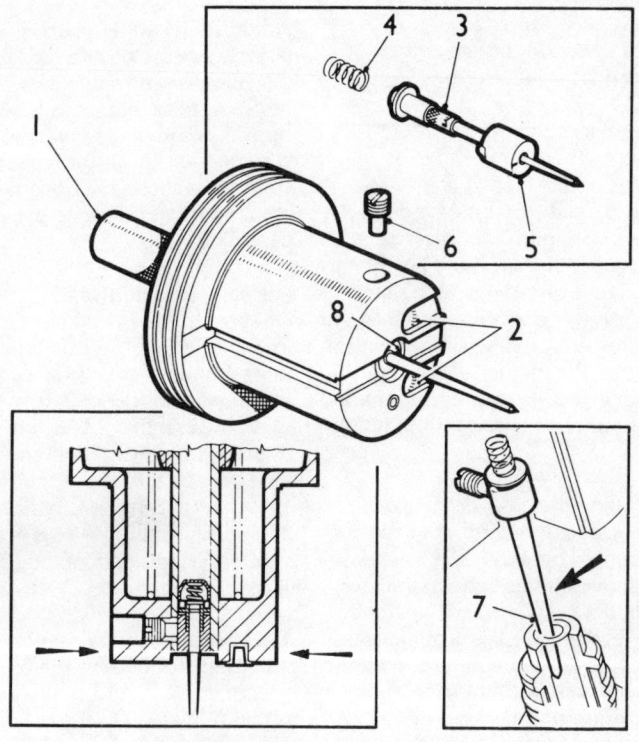

Fig. 74 — The spring-loaded jet needle

1. Piston rod
2. Transfer holes
3. Jet Needle
4. Needle spring
5. Needle guide
6. Needle locking screw
7. Needle biased in jet
8. Etch mark

is used for mixture adjustment only. Cold start enrichment is obtained from a separate starting device.

An enlarged view of the floatchamber arrangement showing the jet assembly is given in Fig.75. The adjustment device consists of an adjusting screw (4) and combined adjusting lever/bi-metallic blade (1). The lever element of the assembly reacts to mechanical adjustment of the screw; the bi-metallic element compensates for fuel temperature changes as described in section 2.6. The effect of these actions is to move the jet vertically within the jet bearing and relative to the tapered jet needle, so altering the effective jet area and hence mixture strength.

The lever is located in the carburetter body by spring-loaded retaining screw (5); this arrangement constrains the lever to pivot on the outer edge of its short end and keep its upper, longer end in contact with the adjusting screw (4). Turning adjusting screw inwards will cause the jet to be lowered so enriching the mixture; turning the screw outwards will have opposing effects.

The inner end of the bi-metallic blade is cut out to accept the jet head (3). The shape of the head is formed so that any movement of the blade is transmitted to the jet head, moving it in the vertical plane within the jet bearing.

Fuel Temperature/Viscosity Compensation

The rate of fluid flow in a system is affected by (among other things) its viscosity, and this changes with temperature. Thus when the temperature of a liquid fuel rises its viscosity is lowered and there is less resistance to flow. In an uncompensated carburetter assembly this would allow more fuel to flow for a given needle/jet relationship, and so change the mixture strength.

In the HIF carburetter, fuel temperature compensation is achieved by means of a bi-metallic blade submerged in the fuel in the floatchamber, see Fig.75. The blade (1), is an integral feature of the lever assembly used for mechanical jet height adjustment already described. Changes in fuel temperature cause the blade to deflect in the vertical plane such that the jet is raised or lowered.

When the fuel temperature increases, the jet is raised to a relatively weaker position on the jet needle. Conversely, when the fuel temperature decreases, the jet is lowered to a relatively richer position. From this it will be seen that once the jet has been positioned by adjusting screw (4), viscosity effects arising from fuel temperature changes will be automatically compensated for.

The advantages of the fuel temperature compensation device are that driveability is improved over a wide range of temperature, and exhaust emissions can be kept within closer limits during the cold start and warm-up period. Also, it allows carburetters to have the mixture setting preset and sealed before a vehicle is delivered.

Float Chamber

The float-chamber is incorporated in the main body casting, see Fig.73; access to the chamber is obtained by removing the bottom cover plate (9). The moulded float (2) is shaped so that is surrounds the jet tube and is pivoted along a line parallel to the inlet flange. The float is retained by a spindle (6) which screws into the body casting.

Entry of fuel into the float chamber is via a brass tube (7) in the side of the carburetter body to a needle valve assembly (8). The needle assembly is of a spring-loaded design to prevent engine vibration affecting seating of the valve. The jet is pressed into the top of an aluminium tube which in turn is pressed into the jet head (3). The jet head is a hollow plastic moulding with a right-angled stub pipe at its base for fuel entry.

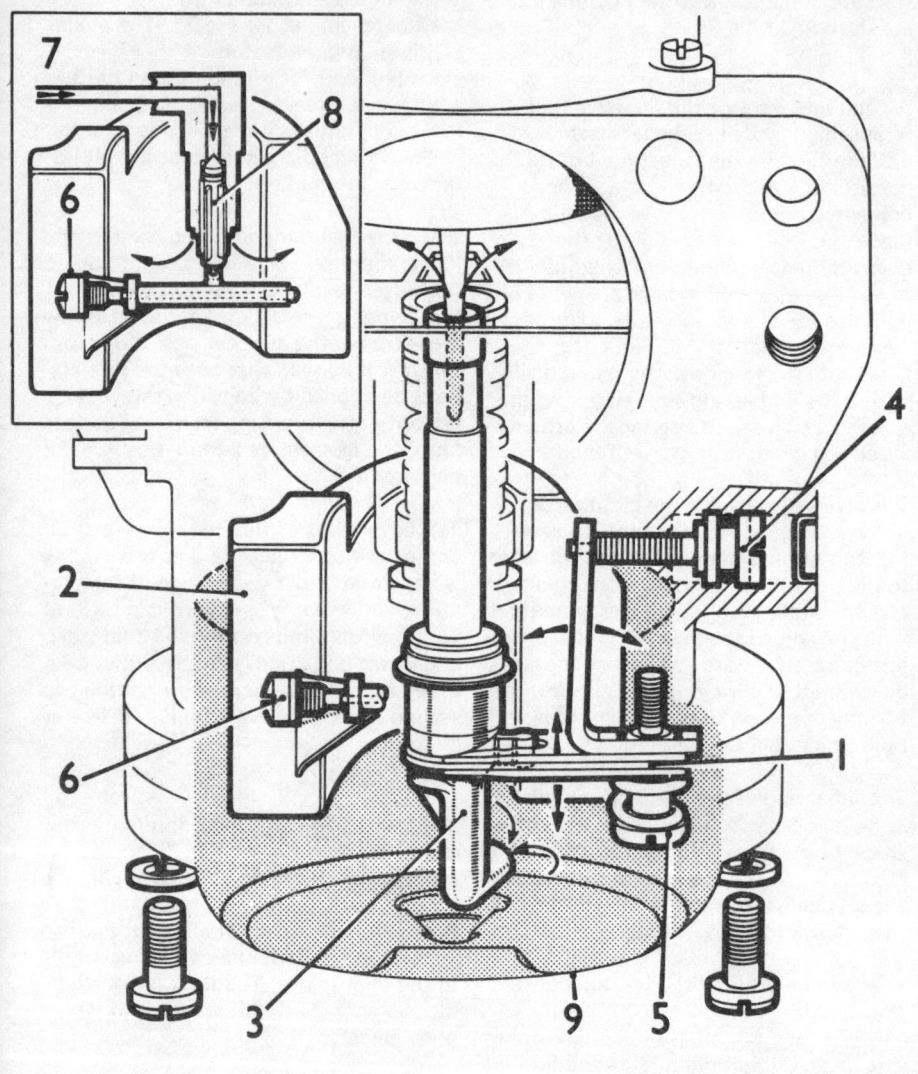

Fig. 75 — An enlargement of the float-chamber layout

1. Bi-metal assembly
2. Concentric float
3. Jet head
4. Jet adjusting screw
5. Bi-metal pivot screw
6. Float fulcrum screw
7. Fuel inlet
8. Needle valve
9. Bottom cover-plate

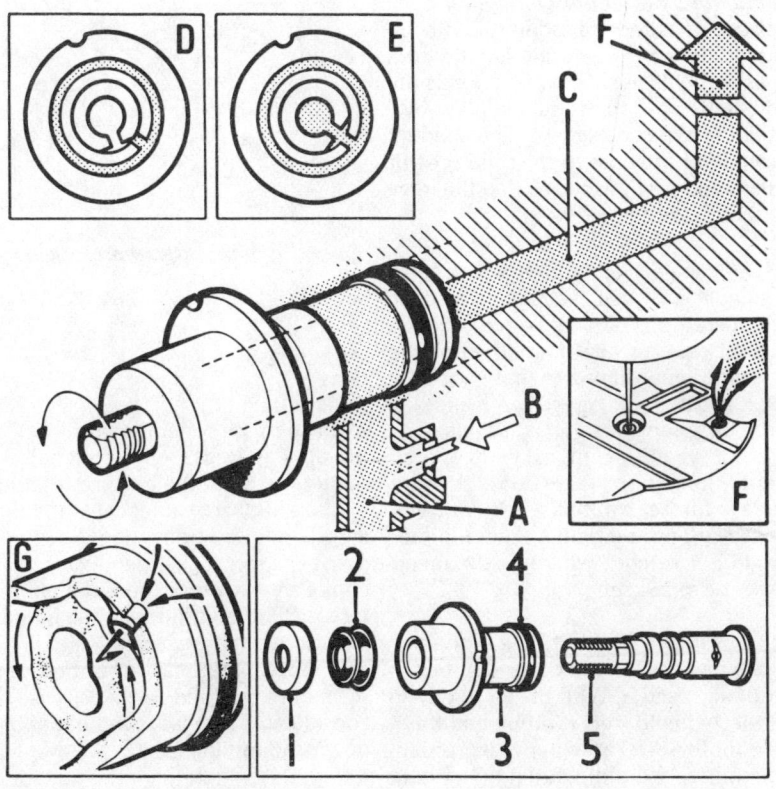

Fig. 76 — Cold start enrichment device

1. End seal cover
2. End seal
3. Starter valve body
4. 'O' ring
5. Valve spindle

A. Fuel supply
B. Air bleed
C. Fuel delivery to jet bridge
D. Commencement of enrichment
E. Maximum enrichment
F. Enrichment outlet
G. Fuel flow through valve

Cold Start Enrichment Device

In HIF carburetters the additional mixture for cold start enrichment is supplied separately to that from the main jet. The starting device is in the form of a rotary valve, Fig.76, which allows the flow of additional fuel from passage A located in the side of the floatchamber to an outlet F adjacent to the jet bridge. The valve consists of a cylindrical body (3) with internally locating operating spindle (5). The assembly is positioned in the side of the floatchamber and is held in place by a retaining plate and screws. The operating cam lever attaches to the solid protruding threaded part of the spindle; the inner part is bored out.

Fuel ports are drilled radially in the body and spindle such that they are coincident when operative (E and G). A 'vee' section groove of tapering depth, intersecting the hole in the spindle ensures that enrichment is progressive. At the commencement D of spindle rotation the beginning of the groove (nil depth and width) meets the entry hole in the valve body; as the spindle is further rotated, a progressively larger vee groove section is exposed until position E is reached where maximum enrichment is provided.

When the engine is at rest, fuel is present to floatchamber level in passage A, but clear of air bleed B. With the valve turned to a selected cold start position and the engine motored for starting, a depression is transmitted from the outlet hole F to the passage A and air bleed B by way of the spindle bore, fuel ports and fuel feed annulus around the valve body. This results in a discharge of emulsified enriched starting mixture as indicated at F.

Part Throttle By-pass Emulsion System

At part throttle operation, the air velocity in the main bore of the carburetter is relatively low and hence not conducive to efficient atomisation and mixing of fuel introduced in the normal way. In HIF units conditions are improved by the introduction of a part throttle mixture by-pass system, Fig.77.

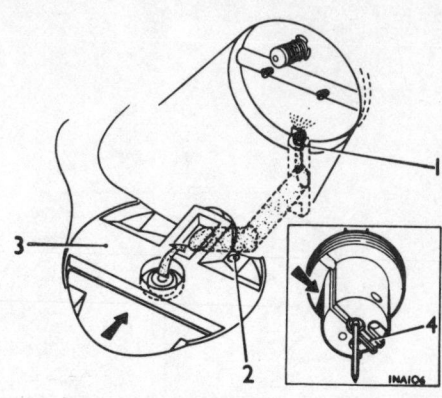

Fig. 77 — Part throttle by-pass emulsion system

1. By-pass emulsion outlet
2. Cold start enrichment outlet
3. Carburetter bridge
4. Slot in piston

In the by-pass system, a small-bore passageway leads from a duct adjacent to the jet orifice in the carburetter bridge (3), to a discharge point (1) at the throttle edge. Under part-throttle conditions this point is under higher depression than the choke area and mixture is therefore preferentially drawn through the by-pass passage. As the passageway and final discharge areas are small in relation to the main bore the mixture velocity is considerably increased and better breakdown and mixing result.

A slot (4) in the piston base corresponds with and shrouds the rectangular duct opening in the carburetter bridge (3), so guiding the mixture to the by-pass passage.

Overrun Throttle Valve

When 'closed-throttle overrun' occurs a high manifold depression results; combustion is incomplete and high values of hydrocarbon emissions are produced.

This problem is overcome on HIF units

by the operation of an overrun valve. The valve arrangement, shown in Fig.78, consists of a precisely set spring-loaded plate valve (1) located in the upper half of the throttle butterfly disc (2).

The valve opens at overrun conditions; the manifold depression is slightly reduced and a quantity of correct fuel/air mixture supplied. Combustion is thereby improved and hydrocarbon emission minimised.

Crankcase Emission Control

A typical crankcase emission control arrangement is shown in Fig.79. With this system the engine breather outlet is connected by hoses to the constant depression area between the piston and the throttle disc valve of the carburetter(s). Engine fumes and blow-by gases are drawn from the crankcase by the depression in this area, through an oil separator incorporated in the engine outlet connection and from there to the inlet manifold. Fresh air is supplied to the engine through the combined oil filler cap and filter, or on cars fitted with fuel evaporative loss control systems through the breather hose of the adsorption canister.

Tuning Type HIF Carburetters

It is important to realise that HIF carburetters are precision flow-metering devices that have been rigorously checked and set to meet the performance requirements for their specific application. This is more particularly so in the case of units designed to meet exhaust emission control standards, where special instrumentation is required to check carburetter performance. Attempts to 'improve' performance therefore should not be lightly undertaken! Tuning must be carried out in accordance with the vehicle manufacturer's tuning data. A reliable engine rpm counter, carburetter balancing meter, and exhaust gas analysis equipment (to measure carbon monoxide, nitrogen oxides and unburnt fuel) **are essential**.

To complete a servicing or tuning operation efficiently it is essential that the instructions are carried out progressively as given. This is supported by sequential action/component numbering in appropriate illustrations.

Pre-tuning Procedure. Single and Multi-carburetter Installations (refer to Fig.80)

Remove air cleaner(s) and check that throttle(s) operate freely and do not stick.

Unscrew the throttle adjusting screw (3) (each screw, multi-carburetters) until it is just clear of the throttle lever with the throttle closed, then turn the screw(s) one and a half full turns on single carburetters; one turn on each multi-carburetters.

Raise the piston of each carburetter with lifting pin (4) and check that it falls freely on to the bridge when the pin is released. If the piston shows any tendency to stick, the carburetter must be serviced. Lift and support the piston clear of the bridge so that the jet is visible. (If this is not possible due to the installed position of the carburetter, remove the suction chamber assembly).*

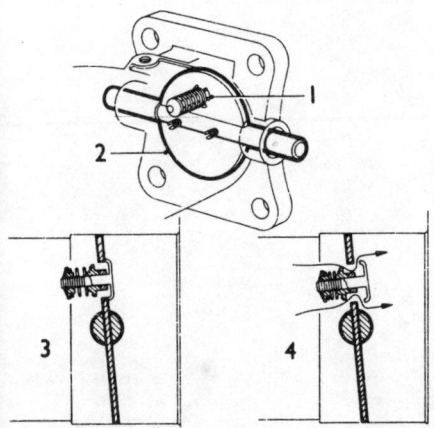

Fig. 78 — The overrun valve

1. Throttle butterfly disc
2. Overrun valve
3. Overrun valve closed
4. Overrun valve open

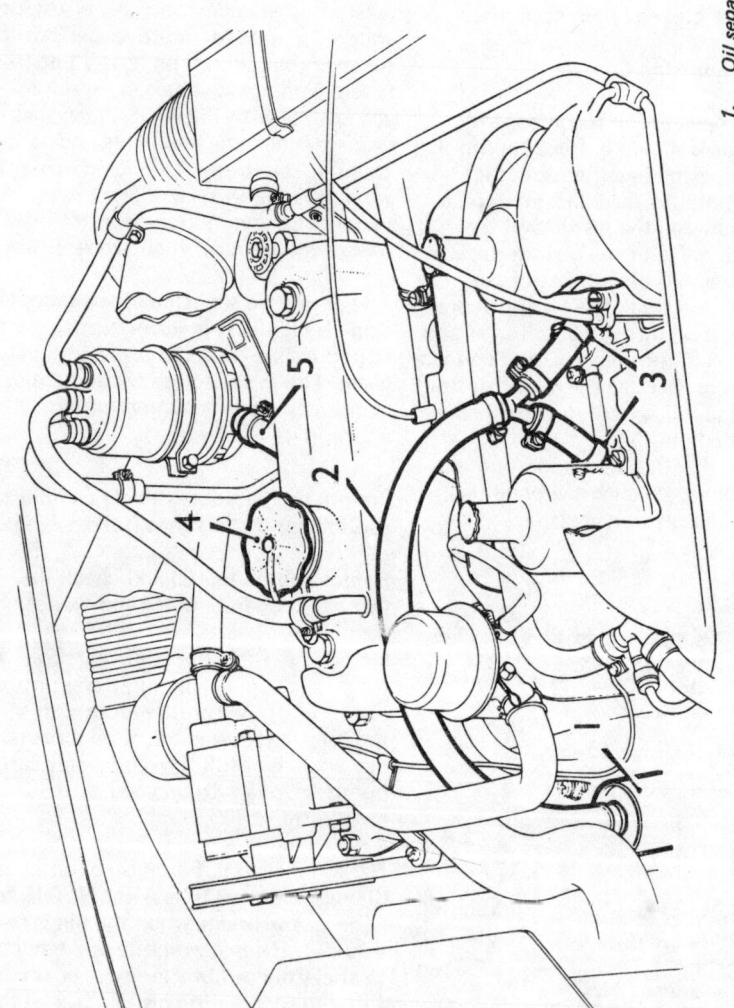

1. Oil separator
2. Breather hose
3. Carburetter chamber connection
4. Filtered filler cap
5. Adsorption canister breather hose

Fig. 79 – Crankcase emission control

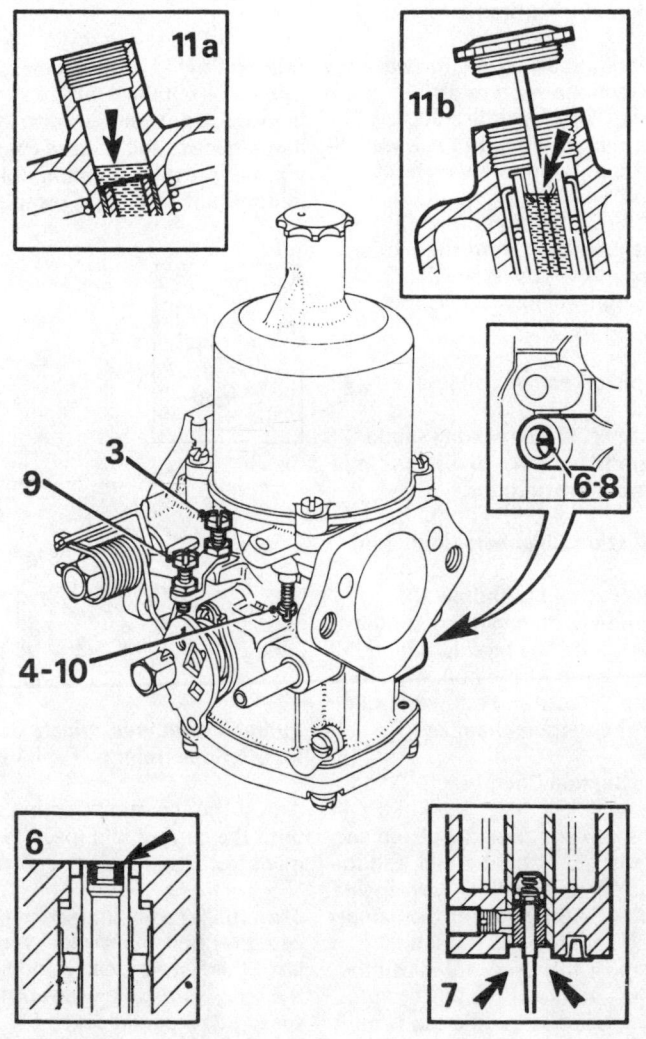

Fig 80
Pre - tuning procedures.

Turn the jet adjusting screw (6) anti-clockwise until the jet is flush with the bridge (inset 6), or as high as possible without exceeding the bridge height. On multi-carburetters ensure that the jets are all in the same position relative to their respective bridges.

Check that the needle shank is flush with the underside of the piston (inset 7).

Turn the jet adjusting screw (8) two turns clockwise (each screw on multi-carburetters). Turn fast idle adjusting screw (9) anti-clockwise until it is well clear of the cam (each screw on multi-carburetters).

If it has been removed, refit the suction chamber assembly*, using the lifting pin (10), check that the piston falls freely on the bridge.

Check the piston damper oil level.

* IMPORTANT. If ball bearing suction chambers are fitted refer to dismantling and reassembly instructions.

Standard Suction Chambers (inset 11a)

Unscrew the cap and withdraw the damper. Top up with engine oil (preferably SAE 20) until the level is ½ inch (13 mm) above the top of the hollow piston rod, refit the damper and screw the cap firmly into the suction chamber.

Ball Bearing Suction Chambers (inset 11b)

Unscrew the cap and raise the piston and damper to the top of their travel. Fill the recess in the damper retainer with engine oil (preferably SAE 20), lower the damper until the cap contacts the suction chamber, repeat this procedure until the oil level is just visible at the bottom of the retainer recess. Screw the cap firmly into the suction chamber.

Connect a reliable rpm counter and exhaust gas analyser to the engine in accordance with the instrument manufact-urer's instructions.

Start the engine and run it at a fast idling speed until normal running temperature is reached, then run for a further five minutes.

Increase the engine speed to 2500 rpm for 30 seconds; tuning can now commence.

IMPORTANT. If the correct setting cannot be obtained within three minutes, increase the engine speed to 2500 rpm for half a minute and then re-commence tuning. Repeat this operation every three minutes until tuning is completed.

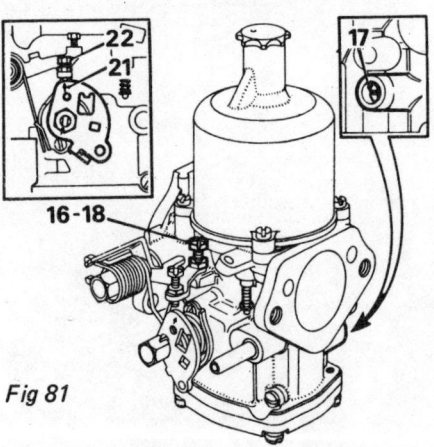

Fig 81

Tuning Procedures - Single Carburetter Installations (refer to Fig.81 and 82)

Adjust the throttle adjusting screw (16) until the correct idle speed (see vehicle manufacturer's tuning data) is obtained.

Turn the jet adjusting screw (17) clockwise to enrich or anti-clockwise to weaken until the fastest speed is indicated; turn the screw anti-clockwise until the engine speed just commences to fall. Turn the screw clockwise very slowly the minimum amount until the maximum speed is regained. From this setting adjust the mixture screw according to the vehicle manufacturer's recommendations.

Check the idle speed, and re-adjust it as necessary with the throttle adjusting screw (18) to obtain the correct setting.

Using the exhaust gas analyser, check the percentage CO reading is within the limits given by the vehicle manufacturer. If the reading falls outside the limits given, reset the jet adjusting screw by the minimum amount necessary to bring the reading just within the limits. If an adjustment exceeding half a turn of the adjusting screw is required to achieve this, the carburetter must be removed and serviced.

With the fast idle cam against its return stop, check that 0.06 in (1.5 mm) free movement of the mixture control (choke) cable exists before the cable moves the cam.

Pull out the mixture control (choke) until the arrow (21) marked on the cam is positioned under the fast idle adjusting screw.

Turn the fast idle adjusting screw (22) clockwise until the correct fast idle speed (see vehicle manufacturer's recommendations) is obtained.

Refit the air cleaner.

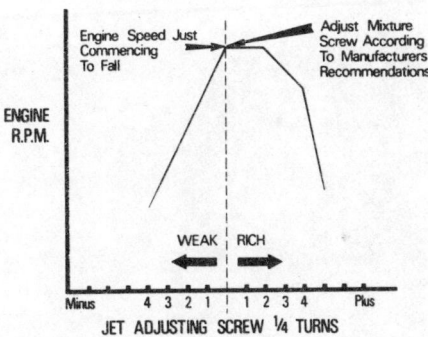

Mixture change - Engine RPM response

Fig 82

Tuning Procedure — Multi-Carburetter Installations (refer to Figs. 83-86)

Slacken throttle spindle and cold start interconnection clamps (24 and 25), Fig. 83

Using a vacuum balance meter, Fig.84, or 'listening tube', Fig. 85, alter throttle adjusting screws (26) to obtain correct idling speed and balance. (The listening tube is used to compare the intensity of the intake 'hiss' on each carburetter - adjust the throttle until the 'hiss' is the same).

Turn each jet adjusting screw the same amount clockwise to enrich, or anti-clockwise to weaken, until the fastest rpm is indicated then turn each screw anti-clockwise until the engine speed just begins to fall. Turn each screw very slowly clockwise by the minimum amount until the maximum speed is regained. From this setting adjust the mixture screws in accordance with the vehicle maker's recommendations (see Fig.82).

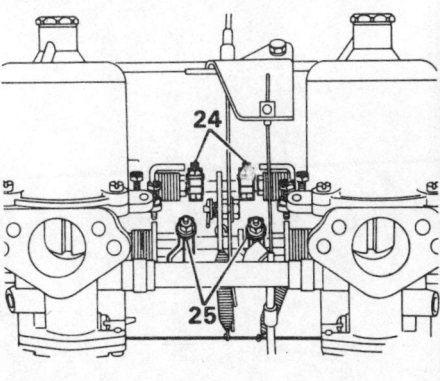

Fig 83

Check the idling speed and re-adjust as necessary, turning each throttle adjusting screw by the same amount.

Check that the exhaust gas analysis is within the limits given in the vehicle manufacturer's tuning data. If the readings are outside the limits given, re-set

81

Carburetter balancing

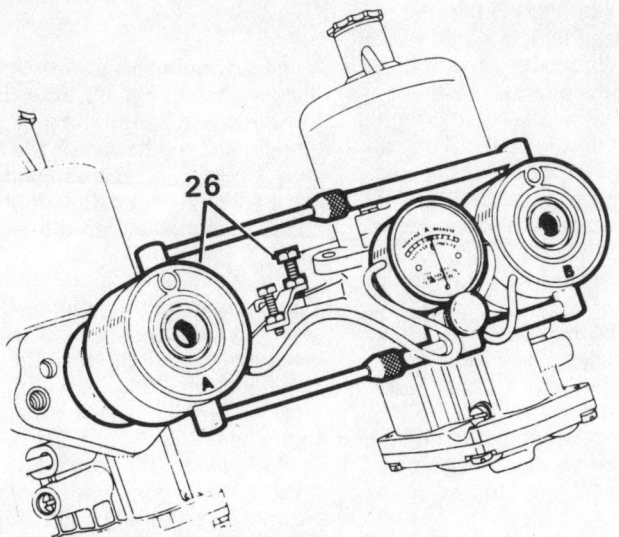

Fig 84

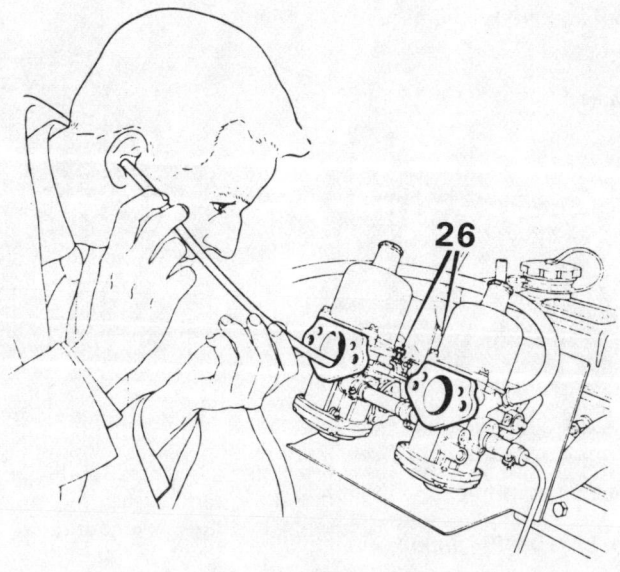

Fig 85

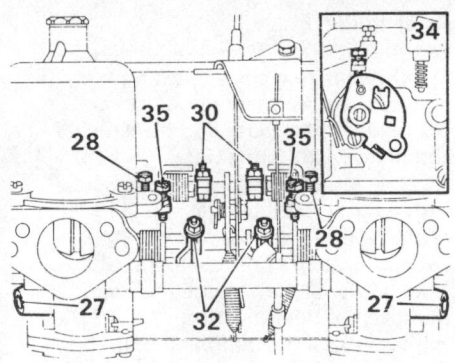

Fig 86

Servicing

When servicing carburetters it will be found advantageous to have a shallow metal bench tray available in which to strip the units and retain the parts. Immediately following carburetter removal the engine induction port faces should be covered to prevent inadvertent entry of foreign matter.

The following parts should be obtained for each carburetter in readiness for replacement as required:

> Throttle disc retaining screws (2)
> Jet needle retaining screw
> Seals, 'O' ring and gasket set

Thoroughly clean units externally before dismantling. Centre-pop, or otherwise mark the suction chamber rim and inlet flange adjacently for locating on reassembly.

Dismantling (Figs. 87, 88 and 89)

Standard Suction Chambers - refer to Fig. 87:

Remove the piston damper and washer (2).
Remove retaining screws and identity tag (3).
Lift the chamber assembly (4) vertically, without tilting.

Ball Bearing Suction Chambers - refer Fig. 87:

Hold the piston firmly in the choke.
Lift the chamber vertically, without tilting until the damper retainer is freed from the piston rod. Remove the damper (inset 5).
Remove the piston spring and lift out the piston assembly (6). Empty the oil from the piston rod.
Note the position of the needle guide etch mark in relation to the piston transfer holes for correct reassembly and unscrew the needle guide locking screw (7).
Withdraw the needle, guide and spring (8).

both jet adjusting screws by the minimum amount necessary to bring the readings just within the limits. If more than a half-turn of screw adjustment is required to achieve this the carburetters must be removed and serviced.

Set the throttle interconnection clamping levers (30, Fig.86), in accordance with vehicle maker's instructions, with clearance between the link pin and the lower edge of the fork. Tighten the clamp bolts, ensuring 0.05 in. interconnection rod end-float.

Run the engine 1500 rpm and check throttle linkage for correct connection by re-checking the carburetter balance.

With the fast idle cams against their stops, set the cold-start interconnections (32) so that all cams begin to move simultaneously.

With the fast idle cams against their stops see that there is 0.06 in free movement of the choke cable before the cable moves the cams. Pull out the choke until the arrow marked on the cam is positioned under the fast idling adjustment screw of each carburetter (inset 34).

Turn fast idle adjusting screws (35) to give correct fast idle rpm using vacuum balance meter or listening tube to ensure equal adjustment of carburetters.

83

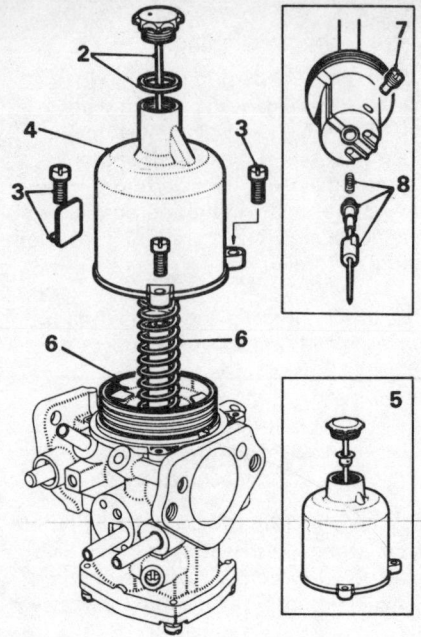

Fig 87

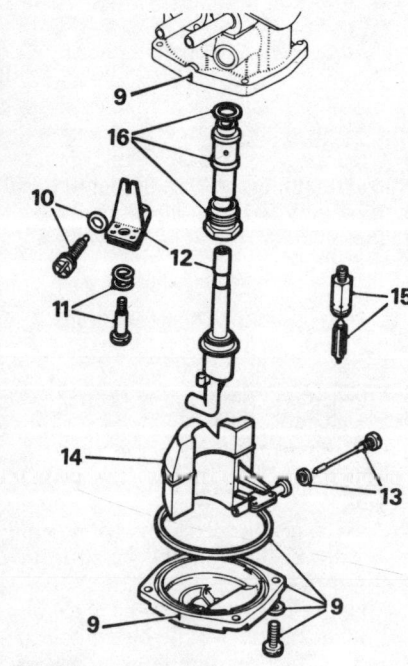

Fig 88

Refer to Fig. 88:

Mark the bottom coverplate and body (9) to ensure correct reassembly. Unscrew the retaining screws and remove the cover complete with sealing ring.
Remove jet adjusting screw complete with 'O' ring (10), and jet adjusting lever retaining screw with spring (11).
Withdraw the jet (12) complete with adjusting lever and disengage the lever.
Remove the float pivot spindle and fibre washer (13) and withdraw the float.
Remove the needle valve (15) and unscrew the valve seat.
Unscrew the jet bearing locking nut and withdraw the bearing complete with fibre washer (16).

Refer to Fig. 89:

Note the location of the ends of the fast idle cam lever return spring (17). Unlock and remove the cam lever retaining nut and locking washer (18).
With the return spring held towards the carburetter body, prise off the cam lever (19) and remove the return spring.
Unscrew the starter unit retaining screws and remove the coverplate (20).
Withdraw the starter unit assembly (21) and remove its gasket.

Withdraw the valve spindle and remove the 'O' rings, seals and dust cap (inset 22).
Note the location and loading of the ends of the throttle lever return spring (23) and remove the spring.
Unlock and remove the nut and tab washer (24) retaining the throttle levers.
Remove throttle lever and throttle actuating lever (25).
Remove the throttle disc retaining screws (26).

Close the throttle and mark the face of the throttle disc (27) relative to the adjacent flange. **Do not mark the disc in the vicinity of the overrun valve.** Open the throttle and carefully withdraw the disc from the throttle spindle taking care not to damage the overrun valve.

Note location of throttle spindle relative to carburetter body to ensure correct re-assembly; withdraw spindle (28) and remove seals.

Inspection

The inspection procedure consists of close examination of all unit parts as to their fitness for further service. In general, parts showing excessive wear or play, and fibre washers, 'O' rings, rubber seals and gaskets having worn or damaged surfaces, should be replaced. Particular points for checking are noted below.

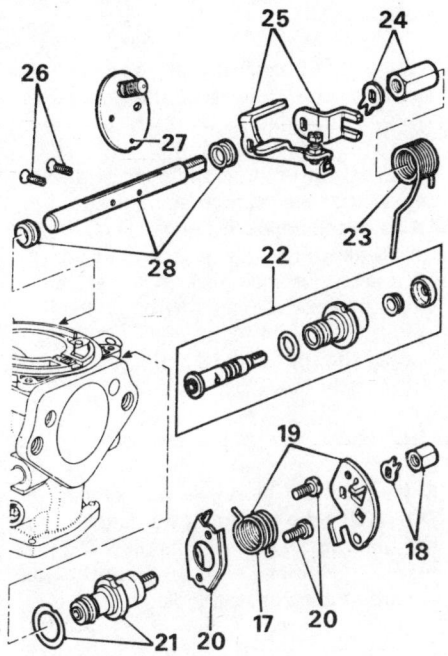

Fig 89

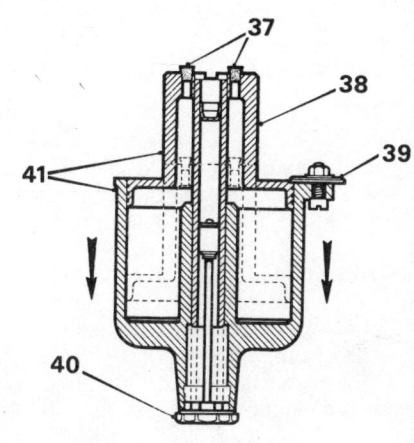

Fig 90

ITEM	EXAMINE FOR
Throttle spindle and bearings	Excessive play
Float needle and seating	Damage. Excessive wear
a) Rubber seals and 'O' rings	Damage. Deterioration
Fibre washers and gaskets	Condition
Carburetter body	Cracks. Damage. Security of brass connections and piston guide key
b) Suction chamber and piston	Damage. Foreign matter. Signs of scoring

a) The coverplate sealing ring **must** be replaced.
b) Clean the piston and the inside of the suction chamber with methylated spirits (denatured alcohol) and wipe dry. **Do not use abrasives.**

Ball Bearing Suction Chambers

Check that all the balls are in the piston ball race (2 rows, 6 per row). Fit the piston into the suction chamber, without the damper and spring, hold the assembly in a horizontal position and spin the

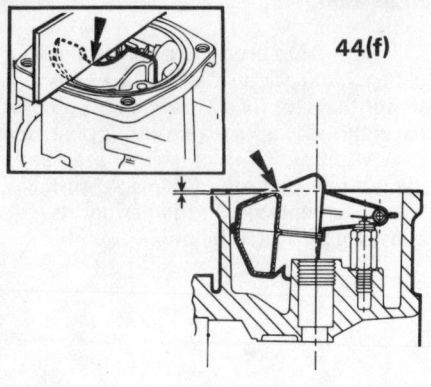

44(f)

Fig 91

piston. The piston should spin freely in the suction chamber without any tendency to stick.

Standard Suction Chambers

This check need only be carried out if the cause of the carburetter malfunction which necessitated the dismantling has not been located.

Temporarily plug the piston transfer holes (37, Fig.90) and fit the piston (38) into the chamber without its spring.

Fit a screw into one of the suction chamber fixing holes and retain with nut and washer (39) as shown to act as a piston stop. Fit the damper and washer (40).

Hold assembly (41) vertical with suction chamber uppermost; check that piston is fully entered into chamber.

Invert the assembly to allow chamber to descend until stopped by washer (39). Record the time taken for this travel.

For carburetters of 1.5 in to 1.875 in bore (38 to 47.6 mm) the time taken should be 5 to 7 seconds.

If the times are exceeded check the piston and chamber for presence of oil, foreign matter and damage. If after re-

checking the time is still not within these limits, renew the suction chamber assembly.

Reassembly

Reassembly is carried out in reverse order of dismantling, with special reference to the following:

Throttle. Ensure that the throttle disc is replaced in the correct facing position relative to the adjacent flange (as marked on dismantling). Use **new** throttle disc retaining screws and check that the disc closes properly before tightening them.

Spread the split ends of the screws sufficiently to secure.

Replace throttle spindle end seals.

Starter Valve. The starter unit valve is fitted with the cut-out towards the top retaining screw hole and its retaining plate is positioned with the slotted flange towards the throttle spindle.

Jet Assembly. When fitting the jet assembly to the adjusting lever ensure that the jet head moves freely in the bi-metal cut-out.

Check that the small diameter of the jet adjusting screw engages the slot in the adjusting lever and set the jet flush with the bridge of the body.

Float and Valve. After fitting the float and valve, invert the carburetter (Fig.91) so that the needle valve is held in the shut position by the weight of the float only. Check that the point indicated on the float (see illustration) is 0.04 ± 0.02 in (1.0 ± 0.5 mm) below the level of the float chamber face. Adjust the float position by carefully bending the brass pad. Check that the float pivots correctly about the spindle.

Jet Needle. When refitting the jet needle use a **new** retaining screw. Ensure that the needle guide etch mark aligns correctly with the piston transfer holes (alternative specifications illustrated). After fitting the needle assembly, check that the shoulder of the needle aligns the full face of the piston (Fig.92).

Ball Bearing Suction Chambers. Do not rotate the suction chamber when assembling; this will cause 'wind-up' of the piston spring. Hold the chamber above the piston with retaining screw holes and location mark to body in alignment. Engage suction chamber with piston rod and close vertically downwards.

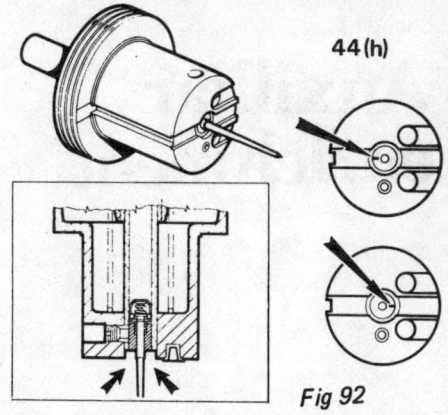

Fig 92

Chapter 8
Auxilliary enrichment

AUXILIARY ENRICHMENT (THERMO) CARBURETTER

Purpose

The auxiliary carburetter is shown in Fig. 93. It is used on certain installations to provide automatically differing degrees of mixture enrichment at:

(a) Starting.
(b) Idling and light cruising conditions.
(c) Full throttle conditions.

It may be used with single or multi-carburetter installations.

Control

The unit may be controlled by either:

(a) A thermostatically operated switch housed in the cylinder head coolant jacket and set to bring the apparatus into operation below $35°$ C. ($95°$ F.).

(b) A manually operated switch which is generally provided with a warning light.

Operation

The auxiliary carburetter is a separate unit attached to the main carburetter. When fitted to 'H'-type carburetters the construction of the main carburetter jet assembly differs from normal in the method of mixture adjustment.

The device consists of a solenoid operated valve and a fuel metering needle which draws its fuel from the base of the auxiliary jet supplied from the main carburetter.

When the device is operated, air is drawn from the atmosphere through the air intake into a chamber and is mixed with fuel as it passes the jet. The mixture then passes upwards past the shank of the needle, through a passage, and so past the

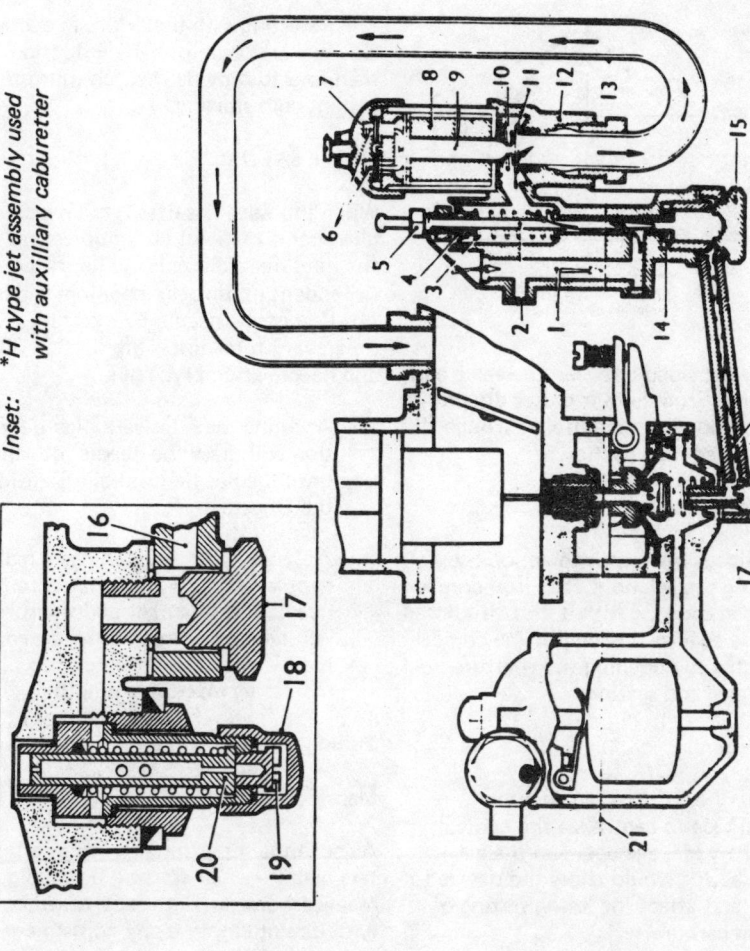

Inset: *H type jet assembly used with auxilliary caburetter

Fig. 93

1. Intake passage
2. Tapered needle
3. Spring (and needle disc chamber)
4. Suction disc — needle stop
5. Adjustable stop nut
6. Terminals
7. Securing strap screw
8. Solenoid
9. Plunger — iron core
10. Conical spring
11. Valve — ball jointed
12. Auxiliary-carburetter body
13. Feed pipe — external
14. Auxiliary jet
15. Bolt — pipe to body
16. Fuel passage
17. Bolt — pipe to carburetter
18. Cap nut.*
19. Adjusting screw*
20. Jet with flanged end*
21. Fuel level

The auxilliary enrichment (thermo) carburetter (shown as fitted to the 'HD' type carburetter)

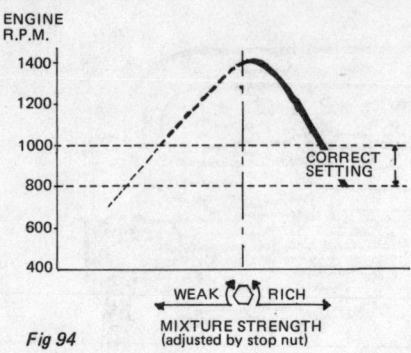

Fig 94

aperture provided between the valve and its seating. From here it passes directly to the main induction manifold through the external feed pipe as shown.

Solenoid and Valve

The device is brought into action by energizing the solenoid. The iron core is thus raised carrying with it the ball-jointed disc valve against the load of the conical spring, thereby opening the aperture between valve and seating.

Valve Seating

A cup washer is fitted against the solenoid face to centralize the conical spring. Any leakage between the valve and its seating would allow the device to operate and affect the idling setting of the main carburetter(s).

If the solenoid is energized while the engine is idling the valve will not normally lift owing to the high manifold depression; the act of opening the throttle will reduce manifold depression and allow the device to operate.

Fuel Level

The fuel level in the auxiliary carburetter is controlled by the main carburetter float-chamber. It can be seen from the illustration that this results in a reservoir of fuel remaining in the well of the auxiliary carburetter.

Fuel Well

When starting with the device in operation, this fuel is drawn into the induction manifold to provide the rich mixture for instant cold starting.

Needle and Disc

When the valve has lifted, the needle disc chamber is in direct communication with the inlet manifold and the depression, dependent on throttle opening, varies the position of the needle by exerting a downward force upon the suction disc and needle assembly. Thus:

(a) At idling the relatively high depression will draw the needle into the jet until the needle head abuts against the adjustable stop.

(b) At larger throttle openings a reduced depression is communicated to the needle disc chamber and the spring will tend to overcome the downward movement of the needle, thus increasing mixture strength.

Tuning and Adjustment

Main Carburetter(s)

As both the main and auxiliary carburetters operate when starting from cold, the main carburetter(s) must be tuned correctly before attempting any adjustment to the auxiliary carburetter. Reference should be made to the appropriate carburetter type and to the mixture adjustment instructions given below for 'H' type carburetters.

Mixture adjustment - 'H'-type carburetter

The procedure for mixture adjustment is the same as for normal 'H'-type carburetter except that a jet adjusting screw is used (see Inset Fig.93) in place of the normal jet adjusting nut as follows:

(1) Remove the cap nut.

(2) Adjust the jet as required, by turning the slotted screw up to weaken or down to enrich the mixture. The slight leakage of fuel through the jet during this operation can be ignored.

(3) Replace the cap nut with its sealing washer.

Auxiliary Carburetter

Tuning of the auxiliary carburetter is confined to adjustment of the stop nut which limits the downward movement of the needle, and is carried out with the engine running at normal temperature and the main carburetter(s) tuned.

Proceed as follows:

(1) Switch on the auxiliary carburetter:

  (a) Where the thermostat has automatically broken the circuit, energize the solenoid by short-circuiting the thermostatic switch to earth, or if this is inaccessible, earth the appropriate terminal of the auxiliary carburetter with a separate wire.

  (b) Where a manual switch is fitted, switch on.

(2) Open the throttle momentarily to allow the valve to lift.

(3) Adjust the stop nut:—

(a) Initially clockwise (to weaken) until the engine begins to run erratically.

(b) Then anti-clockwise (to enrich) through the phase where the engine speed has risen markedly (see Fig.94) to the point where over-richness results in the engine speed dropping to between 800-1,000 r.p.m. with the exhaust gases noticeably black in colour.

Chapter 9
Automatic enrichment device

Carburetter Automatic Enrichment
Device (A.E.D.)   AUH 300 Range

Description

The automatic Enrichment Device is a fully automatic auxiliary carburetter for providing an internal combustion petrol engine with the necessary fuel/air mixture in excess of that supplied by the standard carburetters, to achieve the degree of enrichment required whilst the engine is below its normal working temperatures.

It consists of a small carburetter complete with float-chamber and a throttle in the form of a valve opened or closed by the deflection of a temperature sensitive bi-metallic strip.

The main valve or throttle and the metering system of this self-contained unit are both temperature-sensitive; to a lesser extent the quantity of mixture is also affected by changes in manifold depression.

This sophisticated device provides efficient starting down to ambient temperatures of $-30°C$ and enables the vehicle to be driven away under these conditions with the minimum of delay. The AED automatically adjusts the quantity and strength of mixture it supplies until normal operating temperatures are reached: at this point the device will have smoothly gone out of action and will remain so until the temperature falls below a pre-determined level.

Referring to the diagram the main valve (10) and its seating (13) form the orifice controlling the volume of fuel/air mixture admitted to the engine.

The main valve is connected to the main bi-metal (22) by spindle (6) which slides freely in a low friction bush (8). By this means the valve orifice is determined by the temperature of the main bi-metal (22), the lower the temperature the larger the orifice.

The outlet pipe (32) is connected to the

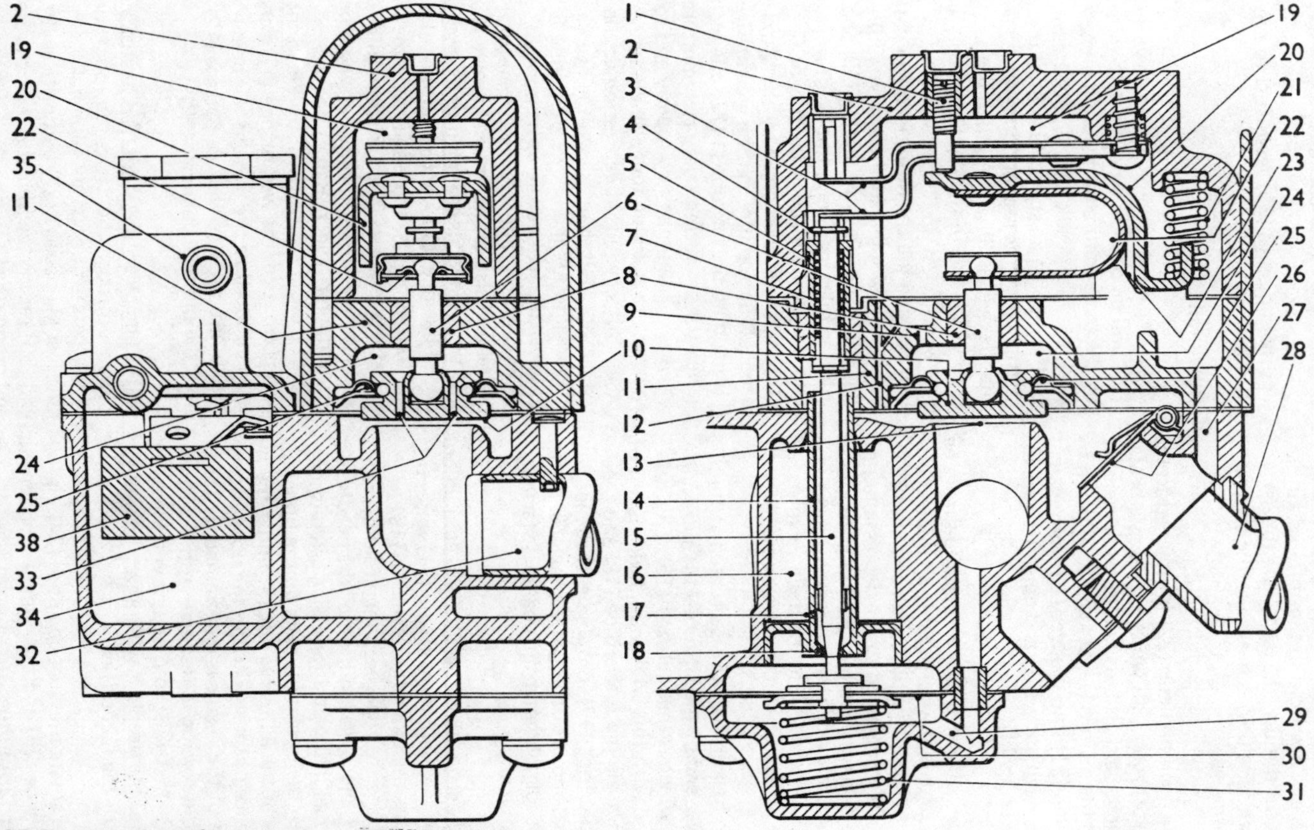

Fig 95 Cross section of automatic enrichment device

inlet manifold and the inlet pipe (28) is connected to a hot air pick-up on the exhaust manifold so that filtered air drawn through the device via the carburetter elbow is heated as the engine warms up.

The main bi-metal (22) is attached to the heat shroud (20) which serves as a heat storage and also as an adjustable member for the main valve, being loaded down by spring (21) into grooves (23) formed in the valve body (11) and abutting against the screw (1).

The main valve (10) is prevented from being drawn down by manifold depression on to its seating by the diaphragm (25) which is subjected to the depression in the balance chamber (24). This depression is provided by the matching of the two orifices (33) in the main valve and the orifice (9) in the valve body.

The fuel orifice (18) is situated at the lower end of the jet tube (14) surrounding which is the fuel well (16). This is filled with fuel whilst the device is out of action via the fuel orifice (18) and the well orifice (17) in the side of the jet tube, and is discharged via the well orifice immediately after the engine is started from cold.

The needle diaphragm (30) in conjuction with the diaphragm spring (31) raises or lowers the tapered fuel needle (15) in response to changes in manifold depression, the lower position of the needle, or normal idling position being established when the circlip (4) rests on the upper face of the adjusting nut (5) under the influence of spring (7) and the upper position of the needle is determined by the needle coming to rest against the secondary bi-metal (3) so that at low temperatures the needle is withdrawn further out of the fuel orifice.

Fuel enters the float-chamber (34) via fuel pipe (35) and the fine mesh nylon filter (36) to the viton-tipped and spring-loaded float needle (37) which in conjuction with the float (38) controls the level of fuel in the float chamber.

A drilled passage (39) feeds fuel to the fuel orifice.

Operation

Assuming a cold engine, the main valve (10) will be open to a degree determined by the temperature of the main bi-metal (22), the fuel needle (15) will be raised by the diaphragm spring (31) until it is restrained by the second bi-metal (3) and the fuel well (16) will be filled to the level of the fuel in the float-chamber.

On cranking the engine air is drawn past the lightly spring-loaded air valve (26) through the main valve seating (13) and into the inlet manifold. Fuel is drawn into the engine through the fuel orifice (18) temporarily enlarged by the lifted needle (15) also through the well orifice (17) and up the jet tube (14) to the main valve (10) producing a very rich mixture to wet the inlet manifold rapidly and so shorten the cranking time. When the engine runs, manifold depression acting via passage (29) draws down the needle diaphragm (30) and allows the spring (7) to lower the fuel needle to its normal idling position. The increased manifold depression also draws the main valve (10) slightly towards its seating due to small out-of-balance forces acting on the valve and its diaphragm. The engine will then run at the required speed as set by the adjusting screw (1) the mixture strength being temporarily increased by the discharge from the fuel well (16). When the well is emptied, the well orifice (17) acts as an air bleed to the jet tube, air being drawn into the fuel well via passage (12) from the bi-metal chamber (19).

As the engine temperature rises heated air is drawn through the device, a proportion of this passes through the bi-metal chamber via passage (27) and orifices (9) and (33) raising the bi-metal temperature and progressively closing the valve until the full working temperature is reached.

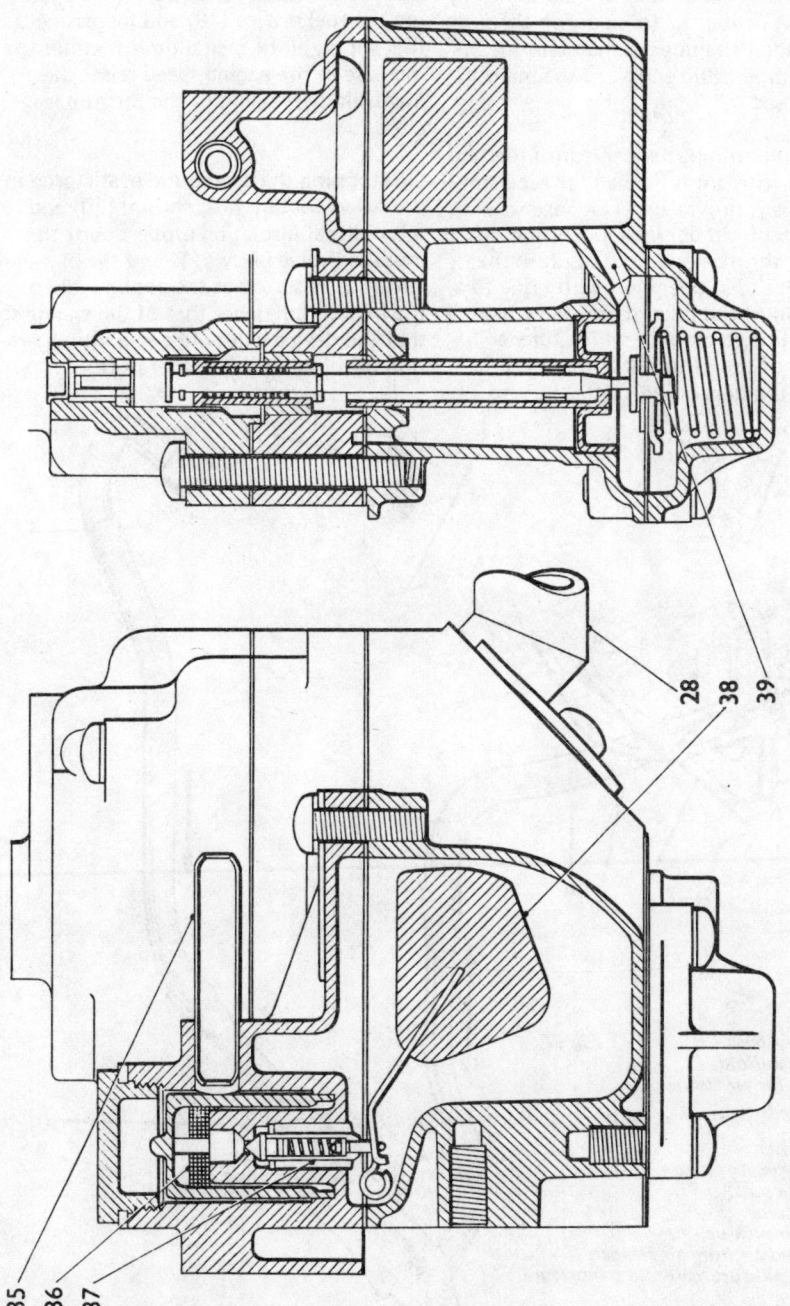

Fig 96 Cross section of automatic enrichment device

At this point the valve will be fully closed but subsequent running will induce sufficient heated air to be drawn through the bi-metal chamber to maintain the bi-metal temperature and keep the main valve closed.

Before full running temperature is reached extra enrichment is needed for acceleration. This is provided in response to falling manifold depression, small carburetter throttle openings result in the main valve (10) opening slightly due to a reduction of the pneumatic load which was tending to close it, whilst further opening of the carburetter throttles reduces the depression sufficiently to allow the needle diaphragm spring (31) to push the needle (15) upward thus opening the fuel orifice (18) and increasing the fuel supply until such a time as either the increase in the engine speed raises the manifold depression or the throttle is closed.

On stopping the engine the heat stored in the heavy section heat shroud (20) and the thermal insulating properties of the moulded valve body (11) and the bi-metal cover (2) ensure that the cooling rate of the bi-metal matches that of the engine so that the device will only come into operation at the required temperature.

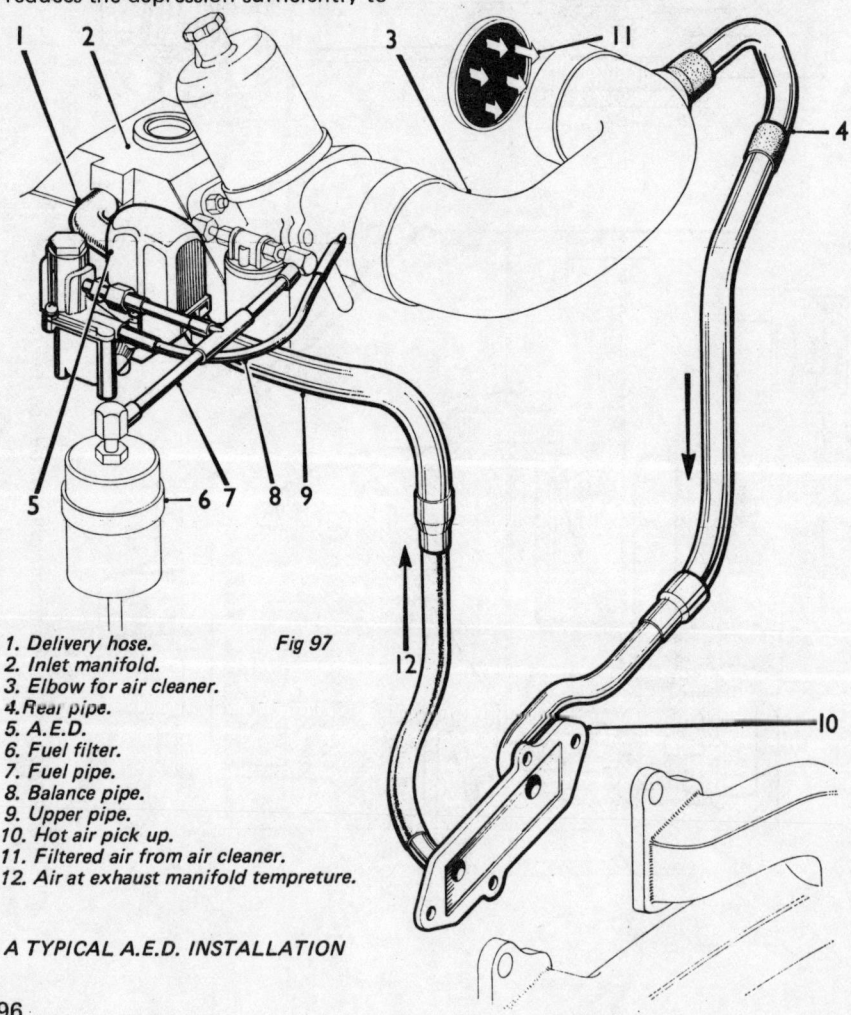

Fig 97

1. Delivery hose.
2. Inlet manifold.
3. Elbow for air cleaner.
4. Rear pipe.
5. A.E.D.
6. Fuel filter.
7. Fuel pipe.
8. Balance pipe.
9. Upper pipe.
10. Hot air pick up.
11. Filtered air from air cleaner.
12. Air at exhaust manifold tempreture.

A TYPICAL A.E.D. INSTALLATION

THE AUTOMATIC ENRICHMENT DEVICE COMPONENTS

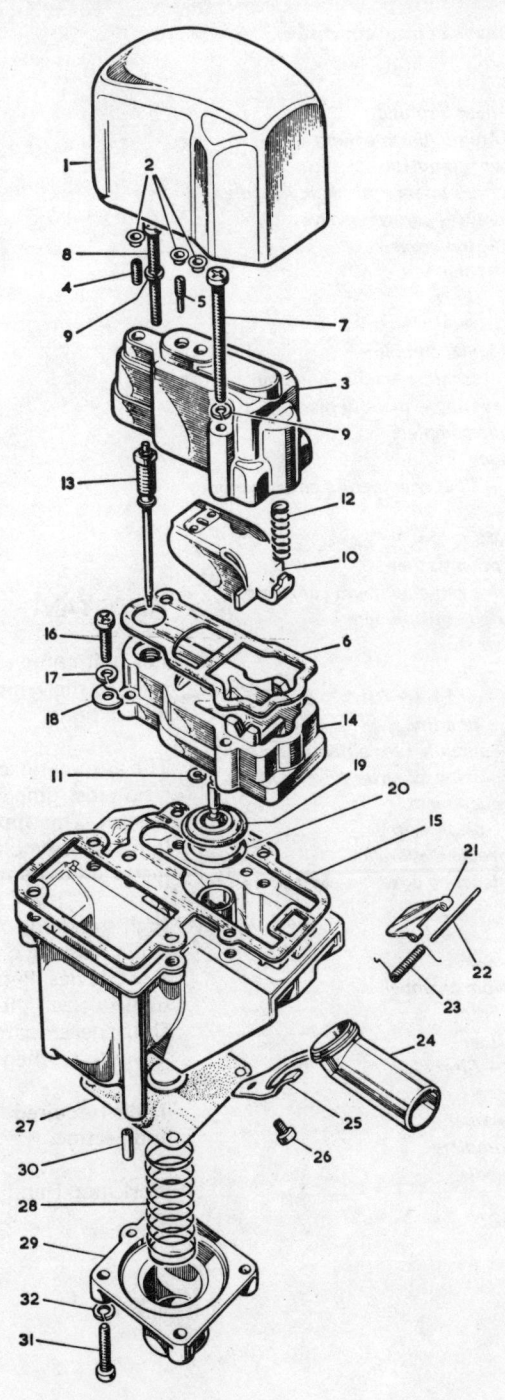

Fig 98

Key to automatic enrichment device components

1. Cover—heat insulation
2. Plugs—Aluminium blanking
3. Top cover complete
4. Hollow grub screw — adjusting needle
5. Grub screw — adjusting valve
6. Gasket — top cover
7. Screw — long
8. Screw — short
9. Spring washer
10. Main bi-metal complete
11. Washer — locating — main bi-metal
12. Loading spring — main bi-metal
13. Jet needle complete
14. Valve body
15. Gasket — float chamber lid and valve body
16. Screw
17. Spring washer
18. Special plain washer
19. Main valve and diaphragm complete
20. Clamp ring — diaphragm
21. Flap — air entry
22. Spindle — flap
23. Spring — return for flap
24. Elbow — air entry
25. Clamp — retaining for air entry below
26. Screw — fixing air entry pipe clamp
27. Needle diaphragm
28. Spring — diaphragm
29. Cap — needle diaphragm
30. Hollow locating dowel — cap and needle diaphragm
31. Screw
32. Spring washer
33. Lid — float chamber
34. Nylon filter
35. Plug — filter
36. Washer — filter plug
37. Screw
38. Spring washer
39. Float complete
40. Float needle

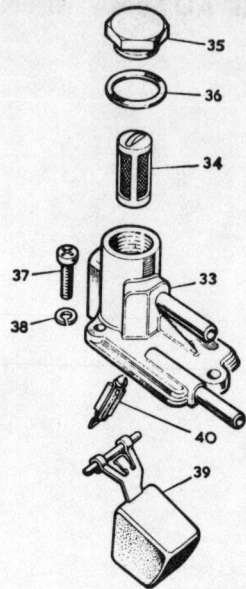

IMPORTANT

For unit removal and fitting information refer to the vehicle manufacturer's instructions.

The automatic enrichment device is a precision instrument and should be treated as such. This applies particularly to the bi-metal assemblies, which must not be distorted or bent in any way.

High standards of cleanliness are required when working on the automatic enrichment device. Petrol or paraffin may be used to clean the components. Use nylon cloth, never material that is fluffy or that leaves lint, when drying any components.

Tools Required for Dismantling, Servicing and Setting.

Workshop Hand Tools

Spanner   13/16 A/F open-ended

Screwdrivers   Small. Phillips medium
Rule   Flexible 6 inch.
Special Tools. (available from V.L. Churchill & Co. Ltd., P.O. Box 3, London Road, Daventry, Northants.)

Checking tool for float level, Part No. 9004.
Alignment tool for valve body/jet tube bore and setting screwdriver, Part No. 9005
Setting probe for main valve and needle lift, Part No. 9003.
Thermometer

DISMANTLING

1. Remove the polypropylene heat insulation cover from the unit, then use a penknife or thin-bladed screwdriver to prise out the three aluminium blanking plugs in the top cover.

2. Hold the unit upright, taking great care to avoid damage. Unscrew the two long screws retaining the moulded bakelite top cover and remove the cover carefully, separating it from the gasket if necessary. Remove the adjustment grub screws if replacement is necessary.

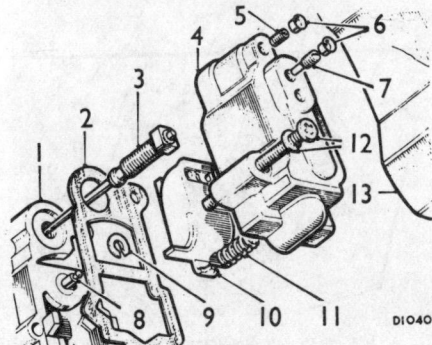

Top cover and main bi-metal

1. Valve body
2. Gasket for top cover
3. Jet needle complete
4. Top cover
5. Hollow grub screw, adjusting needle
6. Aluminium blanking plugs
7. Grub screw, adjusting valve
8. Valve stem
9. Locating washer for main bi-metal complete
10. Main bi-metal complete
11. Loading spring for main bi-metal complete
12. Screw and washer fixing top cover
13. Heat insulation cover

3. Carefully lift the main bi-metal complete out of the 'V' slots and disengage it from the top of the valve stem by sliding back over the 'V' slots. Remove the locating washer from the top of the valve stem. Unscrew the jet needle complete and withdraw it from the body. Remove the top cover gasket.

4. Unscrew the two screws retaining the moulded bakelite valve body and remove the body. If the body is stuck to the lower body gasket, separate by tapping the side of the valve body with the handle of a screwdriver.

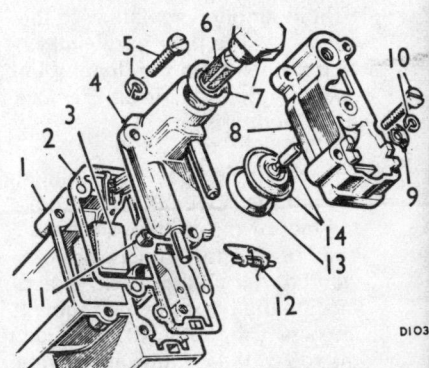

Valve body; aidphragm, float-chamber lid and float

1. Main body
2. Gasket for valve body and float chamber lid
3. Float
4. Float-chamber lid
5. Screw and washer fixing
6. Nylon filter
7. Plug and washer retaining nylon filter
8. Valve body
9. Special plain washer fixing valve body

10. Screw and spring washer fixing valve body
11. Jet tube
12. Air entry valve, spindle and spring
13. Clamp ring for diaphragm
14. Main valve and diaphragm

5. Depress the main valve then ease the pressed steel diaphragm clamp ring out of the valve body taking care not to damage the moulded rubber diaphragm surrounding the main valve head. Remove the main valve assembly, complete with the diaphragm, from the valve body. Lift the lower body gasket in order to remove the air entry flap valve, together with the spindle and spring.

6. Unscrew the large screw plug and remove the filter.

7. Unscrew the three screws retaining the float-chamber lid and remove the lid carefully. If it is stuck to the main body, separate by tapping the side of the lid with the handle of a screwdriver. Remove the float needle and float assembly complete with the hinge pin. The float needle may now be detached from the float by unhooking the wire stirrup. Remove the lower body gasket.

8. Take the main body and noting that the brass jet tube protrudes above the face of the casting, place the body upside down on a piece of wood having a hole drilled to accommodate the protruding jet tube. It is important that no load is applied to the top of the jet tube at any time, otherwise the jet location may be altered.

9. Unscrew the four screws retaining the needle diaphragm cap and hold the cap against the load of the spring inside it whilst withdrawing the screws. If the cap is stuck to the diaphragm, hold the unit firmly, then separate by tapping smartly at the side with the handle of a screwdriver. Remove the cap, spring, diaphragm,

and hollow locating dowel from the main body.

10. Unscrew the screw retaining the air entry pipe clamp and remove the air entry pipe and clamp.

INSPECTION

11. a. Wash all components, using clean petrol or paraffin only. Then examine all parts carefully for damage.

    b. Ensure that all drilled holes in the main body are free from obstructions.

    c. Examine the valve body and ensure that all holes are clear.

    d. Check that the valve stem articulates freely in the valve head and that the two air bleed holes in the head are clear.

    e. Check that the rubber diaphragm has not been damaged.

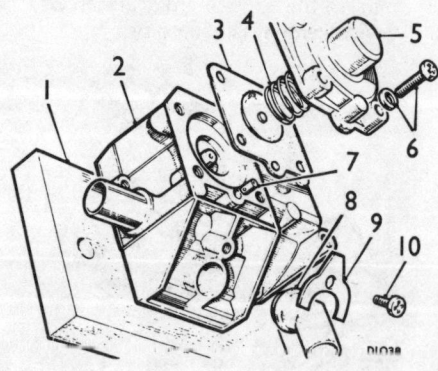

Diaphragm cap, diaphragm, and air entry pipe

1. Wooden block with a drilled hole to accommodate the brass jet tube.
2. Body casting.
3. Diaphragm.
4. Spring for diaphragm.
5. Diaphragm cap.
6. Screw and washer fixing diaphragm cap.
7. Hollow locating dowel.
8. Air entry pipe.
9. Clamp retaining air entry pipe.
10. Screw fixing clamp.

f. Examine the needle assembly and check for free movement in the adjuster screw and straightness of shaft.

g. Check that the bi-metal assembly in the top cover moves freely on its mounting screw. Do not remove bi-metal from cover.

h. Check that all pipes and drillings in the float-chamber lid are clear and that the filter is clean.

j. Examine the float needle tip for wear or damage, also the seating in the float-chamber lid.

k. Ensure that the float assembly pivots freely in the float-chamber with clearance all round and that there is side-play of the float spindle in the body recesses.

REASSEMBLING

1. Place the main body upside down on a piece of wood with a hole for the protruding jet tube.

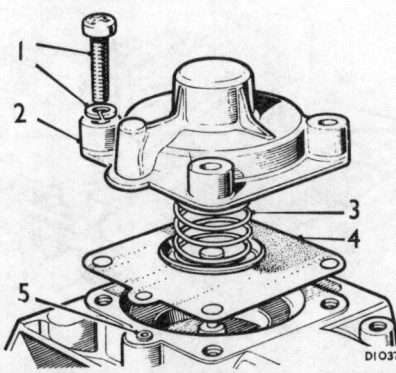

Diaphragm replacement

1. Screw and washer fixing diaphragm cap
2. Cap for diphragm
3. Sprimg for diaphragm
4. diphragm
5. Hollow dowel locating diphragm and cap

2. Ensure that the hollow dowel is free from obstruction, then fit it to the main body. Place the diaphragm over the dowel, with the flat rivet head downwards and align it with the screw holes. Position the spring in the locating plate of the diaphragm. Place the cap over the spring and press down taking care to engage with the hollow dowel and to keep the screw holes aligned. Whilst holding the cap down against the pressure of the springs check that the diaphragm has not puckered around the edges of screw holes.

Fit four screws with spring washers and tighten evenly.

3. Check the float level as follows:

a. Invert the float-chamber lid.

b. Locate the float needle and float to the lid, using checking tool for float lid, as illustrated.

c. Check the float level as illustrated; the float should rest lightly on the needle.

d. If the float is outside the limits, adjust by setting tongue on the float lever.

e. Remove the special tool together with the float and float needle.

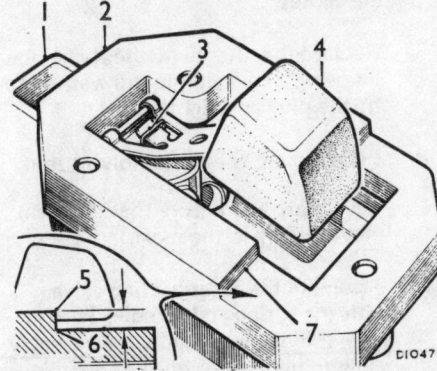

Checking the float level

1. Float-chamber lid

101

2. Checking tool, Part No. 9004
3. Stirrup for needle
4. Float
5. Upper setting limit
6. Lower setting limit
7. Setting limit indication

4. Hold unit correct way up.

5. Position the lower body gasket on the top face of the body and locate it with two screws opposite to the float-chamber

6. Drop the needle into the seating of the inverted float-chamber lid. Then ensure that the float needle is correctly located on the float lever by the wire stirrup. Holding the float assembly to the face of the lid with the tip of a steel rule or feeler gauge. Position the lid over the float-chamber close enough to allow the float assembly to be dropped, so that the hinge pin falls into the recesses in the body without disengaging the needle from the seating bore.

Lower the lid onto the main body, align the screw holes, fit three screws and spring washers, and tighten. Test that the float is moving freely in the chamber by rotating the whole unit around the float hinge pin axis and listen for the movement of the float. Remove the two screws used to locate the gasket.

7. Replace the filter in the float-chamber lid using a new aluminium washer; refit the plug and tighten.

8. Fit the main valve assembly to the valve body and ensure that the stem moves freely in the bush.

9. Assemble the air entry flap valve with the spring and spindle. Turn back the gasket to allow the air entry valve to be fitted with the spring in the loaded position. Replace the gasket and ensure that its edges do not foul the air entry valve.

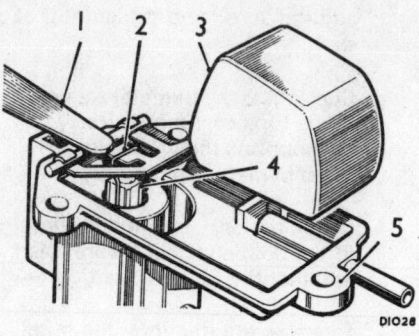

Float replacement in the lid

1. Float held against the face of the lid with a steel rule or feeler gauge
2. Stirrup on float needle
3. Float
4. Float needle
5. Float-chamber lid

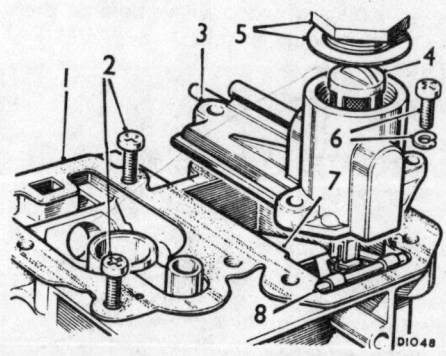

Float replacement in the body

1. Gasket
2. Locating screws for gasket
3. Float-chamber lid
4. Nylon filter
5. Plug and washer retaining nylon filter
6. Screw and washer fixing float-chamber lid
7. Float
8. Ensure hinge pin falls into recesses of body

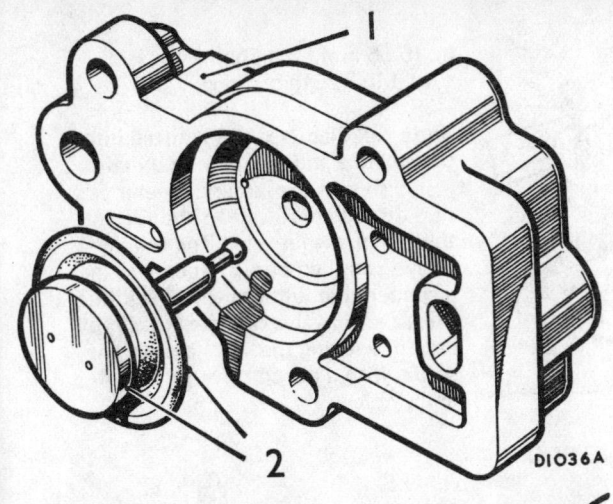

Main valve replacement

1. Valve body
2. Main valve and diaphragm

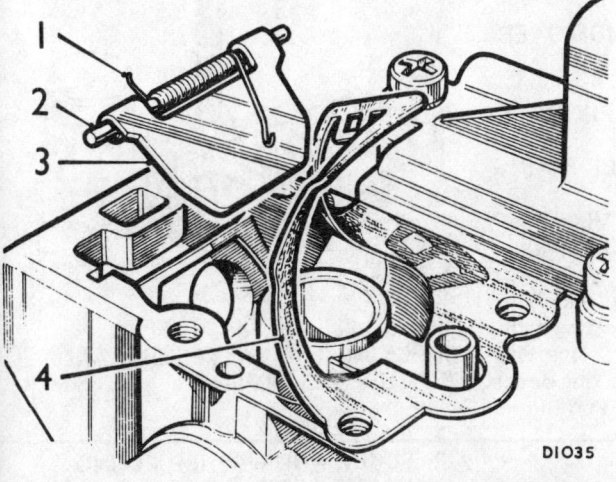

Air entry flap valve replacement

1. Spring in the loaded position
2. Spindle
3. Air entry flap valve
4. Gasket turned back to allow the valve to be fitted

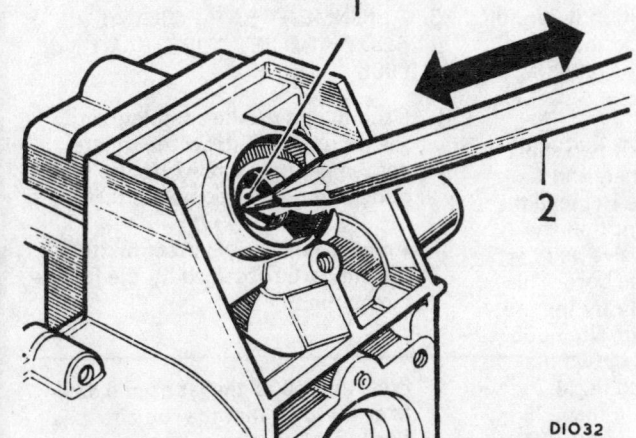

1. Air entry flap valve
2. Pencil

Checking the operation of the air entry flap valve

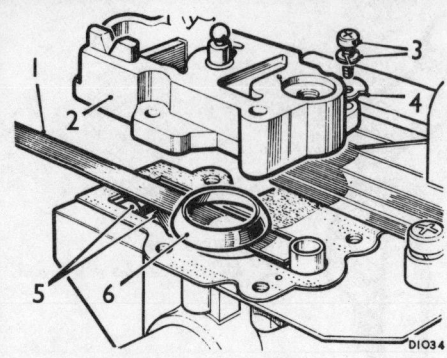

PREPARATION FOR VALVE BODY REPLACEMENT

1. STEEL RULE IN POSITION OVER MAIN BODY
2. VALVE BODY
3. SCREW AND WASHER FIXING VALVE BODY
4. SPECIAL PLAIN WASHER FIXING VALVE BODY
5. AIR ENTRY FLAP VALVE
6. DIAPHRAGM CLAMP RING

Place a steel rule along the main body to cover the valve seating and hold the air entry valve in place. Position the diaphragm clamp ring directly over the main valve seat on the steel rule.

Pick up the valve body by the top of the valve stem and position it carefully over the main body so that the clamp ring engages in the diaphragm recess.

Align the screw holes, fit two short screws with spring washers and fixing tags and lightly tighten. Remove the steel rule. It is important that the threaded insert in the valve body is aligned with the jet tube bore. This should be done carefully by the use of an alignment bar, Part No. 9005. This is a metal bar having two diameters; the smaller, .185 in. (4.7 mm.) dia. being not more than .75 in. (19 mm.) long, and the larger, .218 in. (5.55 mm.) dia., being not less than 1 in. (25 mm.) long.

The small diameter end is fitted into the jet tube and the valve body adjusted so that the larger diameter can pass through the insert to abut against the top of the jet tube. The retaining screws can then be tightened and the alignment bar withdrawn. Check that the air entry valve operates freely, by carefully lifting the valve against the spring with a pencil through the air entry hole.

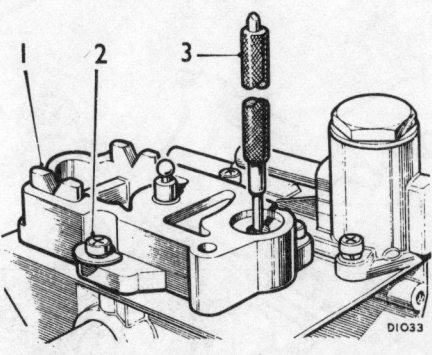

CHECKING THE VALVE BODY AND JET TUBE ALIGNMENT

1. VALVE BODY
2. SCREW AND WASHER FIXING VALVE BODY
3. ALIGNMENT BAR FOR VALVE BODY AND JET TUBE, PART No. 9005

10. Drop the jet needle complete into the jet tube and screw the square-headed adjuster screw into the valve body about three complete turns.

An approximately correct mixture setting can be obtained by the following method:

Press the top of the jet needle down as arrowed so that the top circlip is firmly against the top of the adjusting screw and proceed to screw the adjuster down. As soon as the jet needle can be felt to have seated in the jet (recognized when the adjuster leaves the circlip behind) screw the adjuster up until it can be seen to have abutted against the circlip. Release the pressure off the top of the jet needle. Now note the position of the needle adjuster and then turn it anti-clockwise three flats (¾ turn).

tions of the adjuster in one complete turn.
Before fitting the top cover therefore, the needle adjuster should be positioned to the nearest setting to line up with the serrations in the top cover cap.

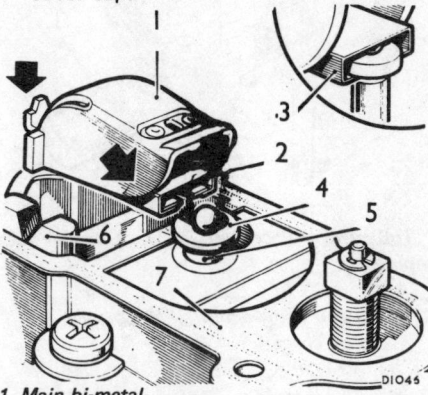

1. Main bi-metal
2. Spring clip
3. Valve stem and locating washer correctly assembled
4. Locating washer on valve stem
5. Valve stem
6. 'V' slots in valve body
7. Gasket on main body

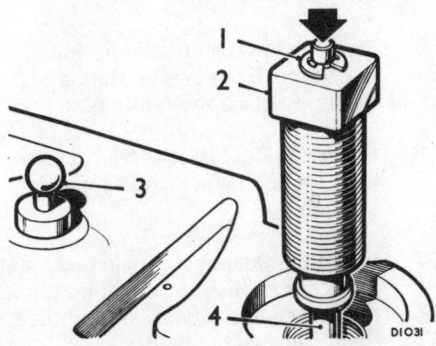

JET NEEDLE REPLACEMENT

1. CIRCLIP
2. ADJUSTER SCREW FOR JET NEEDLE
3. VALVE STEM
4. JET NEEDLE

11. Position the top cover gasket on the main body. Fit the locating washer to the ball top of the valve stem. Take the bi-metal complete and engage the spring clip with the locating washer on the valve stem. Position the ears of the bi-metal heat shroud in the 'V' slots of the valve body.

12. It should be noted before fitting the top cover that there are serrations moulded into the top cover to hold the needle adjusting screw in position. These serrations allow 12 posi-

13. Ensure that the main bi-metal loading spring is located in position in the top cover, then place the top cover squarely in position over the valve body taking care not to disturb the jet needle setting. Press the cover down firmly against the load of the main bi-metal loading spring and hold it in position.

Fit two long screws with spring washers, and tighten.

14. Fit the air inlet pipe as illustrated, then secure it with clamp and screws.

15. Adjust the main valve and jet needle lift (see later under setting)

16. Fit new blanking plugs to the top cover.

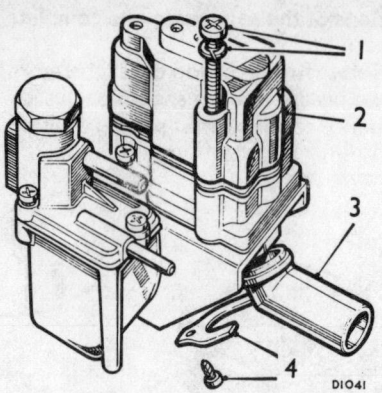

Top cover replacement 2nd stage, and air inlet pipe

1. Screw and washer fixing top cover
2. Top cover
3. Air inlet pipe correctly positioned
4. Clamp and fixing screw for the air inlet pipe

SERVICING

Filter cleaning and float level check

1. Remove the fuel inlet pipe and the float-chamber vent pipe.

2. Remove the heat insulation cover.

3. Unscrew the plug from the float-chamber lid and remove filter.

4. Remove the three retaining screws and washers. Tap the side of the float-chamber lid sharply with a screwdriver handle if necessary to separate it from the gasket.

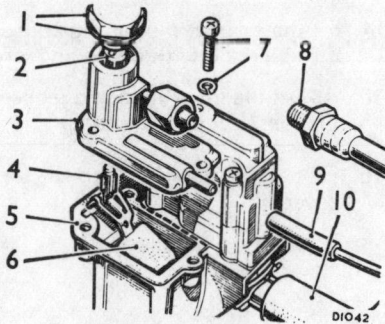

Float-chamber lid removal

1. Plug and washer for filter
2. Nylon filter
3. Float-chamber lid
4. Needle
5. Gasket for float-chamber, cut ad dotted line if replacement is required
6. Float
7. Screw and washer fixing float-chamber lid
8. Fuel inlet pipe
9. Float-chamber vent pipe
10. Air intake hose

5. Examine the float needle tip for wear or damage. Examine the seating in the lid. Replace any faulty parts.

6. Check the float level — refer reassembling section para. 3 and appropriate diagram.

7. Install the float in the main body and check for endfloat of the hinge pin in the body and clearance around the float. Remove the float.

8. If the gasket has been cut and part removed, obtain a new float-chamber and valve body gasket and cut it to fit adjacent to the existing valve body gasket. Place the cut gasket in position on the main body.

9. Float replacement — refer assembly section para. 6 and appropriate diagram.

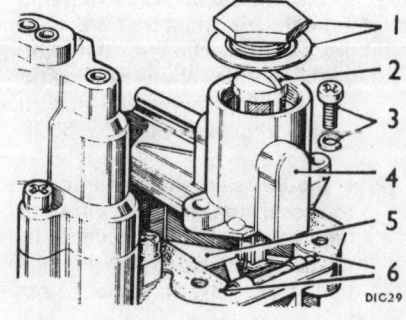

Float replacement in the body

1. Plug and washer retaining the nylon filter
2. Nylon filter
3. Screw and washer fixing the float-chamber lid
4. Float-chamber lid
5. Float
6. Ensure that the hinge pin falls into the recesses of the body

10. Clean and then replace the filter in the float-chamber lid, using a new aluminium washer; refit the plug and tighten.

SETTING

Main valve and jet needle

Note. If the setting operation is to be done with the unit installed, it is of paramount importance to ensure that the engine is at ambient room temperature before any adjustment is attempted. Failure to observe this rule will give incorrect setting.

1. If the unit is being set after overhaul, hold it securely in an upright position.

2. Remove the polypropylene heat insulation cover from the unit and prise out the three aluminium blanking plugs using a penknife or thin-bladed screwdriver.

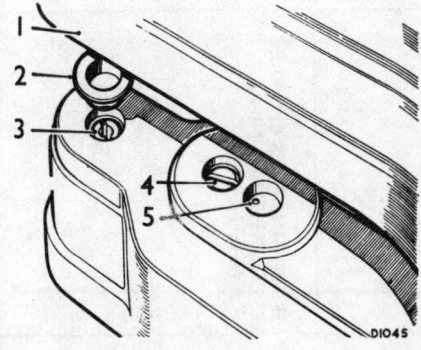

Heat insulation cover removal

1. Heat insulation cover
2. Aluminium blanking plugs
3. Hollow grub screw position, jet needle lift adjustment
4. Grub screw position adjacent to probe hole, main valve adjustment
5. Probe hole, centre of top cover

3. To measure the jet needle lift insert the probe through the hollow grub screw. With the knurled portion held firmly on the top cover and the sliding member of the probe abutting the knurled portion, press the probe down firmly to stop, and release. Continue to hold the knurled portion of the probe firmly against the top cover, then tighten the lock screw.

4. Remove the setting probe and measure the gap between the knurled portion of the probe and the sliding member.
Then refer to Chart 'A' and check that the gap is correct in relation to the ambient room temperature.

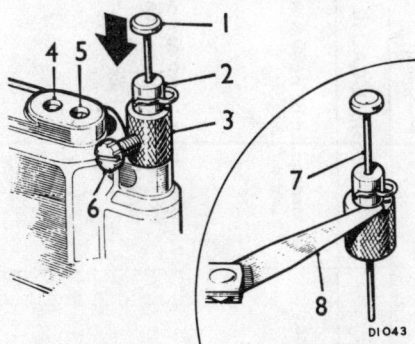

Setting probe in position

1. Probe inserted at hollow grub screw position for needle lift adjustment
2. Sliding member
3. Knurled portion of probe
4. Probe hole for the main valve
5. Main valve adjustment position
6. Lock screw
7. Probe removed
8. Feeler gauge

FAULT DIAGNOSIS

SYMPTOM	POSSIBLE CAUSE	REMEDY
A—ENGINE FAILS TO FIRE WHEN COLD	1. Inadequate or no fuel supply to the A.E.D.	1. Slacken the filter plug on the A.E.D. Crank the engine; fuel should leak from the plug. If no fuel, check the system leading to the A.E.D. If fuel is present, tighten the plug. Then carry out check 2 under symptom **A**.
	2. Inadequate or no fuel supply from the A.E.D. to the inlet manifold	2. Crank the engine for several seconds. Remove the pipe at the inlet manifold. If fuel is present, it indicates that the A.E.D. is satisfactory and the cause for failure to start must be traced to some other source. If no fuel is present this indicates a faulty A.E.D. Proceed as follows: **a.** Check that the main valve is open by inserting the probe down the centre hole—press down fully; the probe should return approximately ·030 in. (0·75 mm.) when released. NOTE:—This check is not applicable when temperature is above 35° C. (95° F.) **b.** Remove the float-chamber lid and check that the needle valve and float are free to move. If there is no fuel in the float chamber check that the fuel filter is clean and that ample fuel is being delivered to the unit. See **SERVICING (Float level)**.
B—ENGINE FIRES BUT FAILS TO KEEP RUNNING WHEN COLD	1. Sticking or faulty needle valve or float	1. Check the following: *a.* Remove the vent pipe from the float chamber and check that fuel is not discharged when cranking the engine. *b.* If fuel is discharged check the operation of the needle valve and float as detailed under **'A'** Item 2 **(b.)**.
	2. Faulty air flap valve	2. Remove the air inlet elbow on the A.E.D. and check that the flap valve is free to move and return under spring load. If jammed, dismantle the unit and rectify.
	3. Inadequate fuel supply	3. Check for lack of fuel as detailed under **'A'** 1 and **'A'** Item 2 **(b.)**.
	4. Faulty jet needle diaphragm	4. Remove the A.E.D. complete, remove the cap for the needle diaphragm, then withdraw the diaphragm and check for damage. Replace faulty parts. Reassemble as detailed in REASSEMBLING

C—ENGINE FAILS TO START WHEN HOT OR PART WARM OR FIRES AND FAILS TO KEEP RUNNING		If diaphragm is satisfactory, a complete overhaul of the unit is indicated.
	1. Incorrect starting procedure	1. Crank the engine and open the throttle slightly. If the unit is badly over-choked open the throttle fully do not over-rev. If the engine starts but fails to keep running, carry out check '4' below.
	2. Leaks from pipe layout	2. Ensure that all pipes are correctly fitted, particularly the pipe between the hot air pick-up and the A.E.D. Rectify as necessary, ensuring airtight joints. NOTE:—Air leaks at the hot air entry will result in excessive fuel consumption and the possibility of stalling at certain engine temperatures.
	3. Before carrying out further checks ensure that the A.E.D. is not the cause of failure to start	3. Remove the pipe from the A.E.D. to inlet manifold. Blank off the aperture in the manifold. If the engine starts this indicates that the A.E.D. is at fault, and further checks must be made. However, if the engine is flooded it may be necessary to crank for several seconds, with a slightly open throttle before the engine will fire.

	4. Sticking or faulty needle valve or float	4. Check the following:
		  a. Remove the vent pipe from the float-chamber and check that fuel is not discharged when cranking the engine.
		  b. If fuel is discharged, check the operation of the needle valve and float. Remove the float chamber lid; check that the needle valve and float are free to move.
		    If there is no fuel in the float-chamber check that the fuel filter is clean and that ample fuel is being delivered to the unit. See **SERVICING (Filter Cleaning)**.

	5. Main valve faulty. This fault and the checking procedure applies only when engine is really hot.	5. Check that the main valve is completely closed by inserting the probe down the centre hole, press down fully; probe should not return which indicates that the valve is fully seated. If probe returns under spring pressure dismantle the unit and rectify.
	6. Incorrect needle movement	6. Check the movement of the jet needle by inserting the probe down the hollow grub screw. Push down fully. If the engine is at its normal working temperature, probe should not return; if partly warm, probe should return approximately ·015 in. (0,40 mm.).
	7. Faulty needle diaphragm	7. Carry out checks as detailed under **'B'** Item 4.

Gap on setting probe for	Ambient room temperature of
·050 in. (1·25 mm.)	10° C. (50° F.)
·040 in. (1·00 mm.)	15·5° C. (60° F.)
·031 in. (0·80 mm.)	21° C. (70° F.)
·022 in. (0·60 mm.)	26·5° C. (80° F.)

Chart 'A'—Probe gap and room temperature for jet needle lift setting

5. If the gap is incorrect use the screwdriver end of the alignment bar, Part No. 9005, to adjust the hollow grub screw up or down to achieve the correct gap on the probe.

6. To measure the main valve opening insert the probe through the hole in the middle of the top cover and operate the probe as previously described. This time the gap indicates the distance the valve is off its seating.

7. Now refer to Chart 'B' and check that the gap is correct in relation to the ambient air temperature.

Gap on setting probe for	Ambient room temperature of
·045 in. (1·115 mm.)	10° C. (50° F.)
·038 in. (0·95 mm.)	15·5° C. (60° F.)
·030 in. (0·75 mm.)	21° C. (70° F.)
·023 in. (0·58 mm.)	26·5° C. (80° F.)

Chart 'B'—Probe gap and room temperature for main valve setting

If the gap is incorrect, adjust as previously, but this time use the grub screw adjacent to the centre probe hole.

8. When setting has been completed seal all three recesses in the top cover with new aluminium plugs. Replace the polypropylene heat insulation cover.

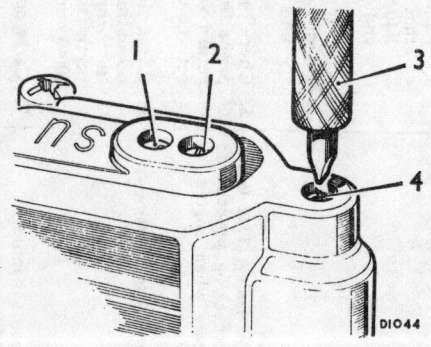

Setting the main valve and jet needle lift

1. Probe hole, for main valve
2. Main valve adjustment
3. Alignment bar and screw-driver, Part No. 9005
4. Hollow grub screw and probe hole for jet needle lift adjustment

Chapter 10
Electric fuel pumps

SU ELECTRIC FUEL PUMPS

Basic pump design

The present range of SU electric fuel pumps utilizes a well-developed and efficient diaphragm and electromagnet assembly as a pumping element. Of simple and modern design, a feature of these pumps is their insensitivity to dirt particles in the fuel. Electrical operation allows relative freedom of mounting position enabling good vapour handling to be achieved.

The method of operation is basic to all of the pumps and may be understood by reference to Fig. 99 and the following text. When the electromagnet is energised it attracts the diaphragm assembly, which constitutes a suction stroke, drawing fuel via an inlet valve into the pumping chamber; the circuit is then automatically interrupted by a contact-breaker, allowing a spring to return the diaphragm, so completing a delivery stroke and expelling fuel through an outlet valve.

The basic design and operation is common to the range of electric pumps described in the fuel pump type sections which follow.

Although enumerated for the L/HP single pump unit Figs. 100 and 101, for all practical purposes the descriptions covering common operational details apply to other pumps in the range when read in conjunction with the appropriate fuel pump type specific details and assembly diagrams.

The significant difference between types mainly concern earthing studs, valves, fuel flow smoothing devices and fuel pipe connections; these are indicated where appropriate.

FUEL PUMP COMMON OPERATIONAL FEATURES

Action of the pump

When the pump is at rest the outer rocker

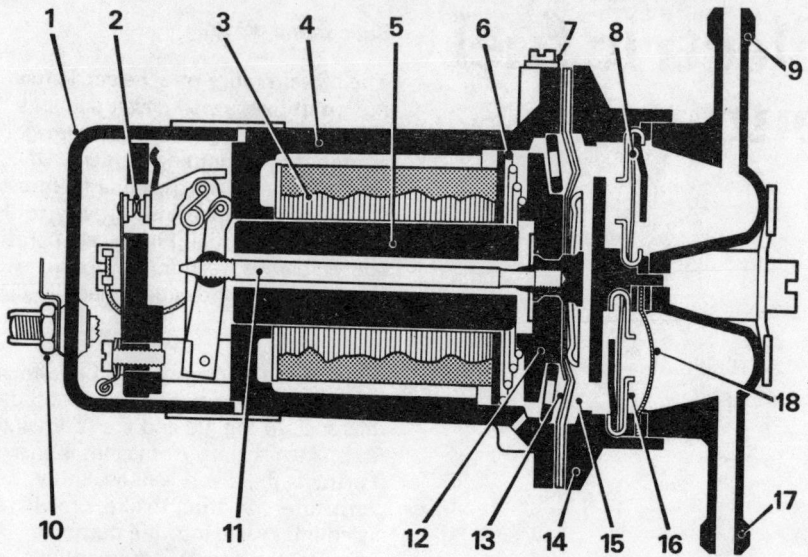

Fig 99 The main components of an SU electric fuel pump

1. Contact breaker cover
2. Contact breaker points
3. Magnet coil
4. Magnet housing
5. Magnet core
6. Return spring
7. Earth connection
8. Outlet valve
9. Outlet connection
10. Electrical supply connection
11. Push-rod
12. Magnet armature
13. Diaphragm assembly
14. Pump Body
15. Pumping chamber
16. Inlet valve
17. Inlet connection
18. Filter

30 lies in the position illustrated and the tungsten points 4 make contact. When switched on, current passes from the terminal stud 29 through the coil, back to the spring blade 32, through the points, and so to earth, thus energizing the coil and attracting the armature 24. The armature, together with the diaphragm assembly, moves towards the coil against pressure from the armature spring 9, drawing fuel through the inlet valve into the pumping chamber 21. When the armature has travelled well towards the end of its stroke the 'throw-over' mechanism operates and the outer rocker moves rapidly backwards, thus separating the contact points and breaking the circuit. The armature and diaphragm will now move away from the coil under the influence of the armature spring, thereby expelling the fuel through the outlet valve at a rate determined by the requirements of the engine. As the armature approaches the end of its stroke, away from the coil, the 'throw-over' mechanism again operates the tungsten points re-make contact, and the cycle of operations is repeated.

The diaphragm, armature, and magnet assembly.

The diaphragm (22) is clamped at its outer edge between the coil housing (2) and the body, and attatched at its centre to the iron armature (24). The armature spindle passes (7) freely through the magnet core (25) and is screwed into a trunnion (6) carried by the inner rocker (27). Eleven spherically-edged rollers (23) are fitted between the coil housing and the armature; these centralize the armature in the housing and allow freedom of movement in a longitudinal direction.

The contact breaker assembly

This consists of a bakerlite pedestal moulding (5) which carries two rockers, outer (30) and inner (27) both hinged to the moulding at one end by the rocker spindle (26), and interconnected at thier top ends by two small toggle springs (31) arranged to give a 'throw-over' action. The The inner rocker, as mentioned, carries a trunnion into which the inner rocker as mentioned carries a trunnion into which the armature spindle is screwed. The outer rocker (30) is fitted with one or two tungsten points (4) which contact other tungstan points carried by the spring blade (32). One end of the coil (8) is connected electrically to the spring blade and the other end is connected to the terminal stud (29). A short length of flexible wire (28) connects the outer rocker to one of the screws securing the pedestal moulding to the coil housing, thus providing an earth return. This must then be thoroughly earthed to the body or chassis of the vehicle via the earthing screw (10). A non-return valve may be fitted to the end cover moulding (33) to aid the circulation of air through the contact-breaker chamber. A condenser may be fitted in a wire clip to one of the pedestal retaining screws, the tag from it being secured under the contact blade attatchment screw.

Diaphragm and contact-breaker settings

Diaphragm

If the diaphragm has been disturbed, it is necessary to reset the position of the armature spindle in the rocker trunnion (6). This is done as follows:

(1) On modified rocker assemblies set the two stop fingers as described under the heading 'Contact breaker'.
(2) Slacken the screw securing the contact blade 32 and swing the blade to one side, so that the points no longer make contact.
(3) Holding the coil housing 2 in the left hand, screw the diaphragm in generously with the thumb of the right hand, alternately pressing gently and turning until the rocker 'throw-over' ceases.
(4) Unscrew the diaphragm one-sixth of a turn at a time in the same manner, slowly pressing and turning until the rocker 'throw-over' just operates.
(5) At this point, continue unscrewing until the nearest securing screw hole is just lined up, and then again four holes (two-thirds of a complete turn). The diaphragm is now correctly set.
(6) The contact blade, previously swung to one side, should now be replaced in its correct position. The slot for the attachment screw allows a degree of adjustment so that when correctly positioned, as the outer rocker operates to make or break the contacts, one pair of points wipes over the centre-line of the other in a symmetrical manner.

Contact breaker

Check that when the outer rocker is pressed on to the coil housing, the contact blade rests on the narrow rib which projects slightly above the main face of the pedestal. If it does not, slacken the contact blade attachment screw, swing the blade clear of the pedestal, and bend it downwards a sufficient amount so that when repositioned it rests against the rib lightly; over-tensioning of the blade will restrict the travel of the rocker mechanism.

Modified rocker assemblies

(Identified by stop fingers fitted to outer rockers.) Check the lift of the blade tip above the top of the pedestal with a feeler gauge, bending the stop finger beneath the pedestal, if necessary, to obtain a lift of $.035 \pm .005$ in. ($.9 \pm .13$ mm.).

Check the gap between the rocker finger and coil housing with a feeler gauge, bending the stop finger, if necessary, to obtain

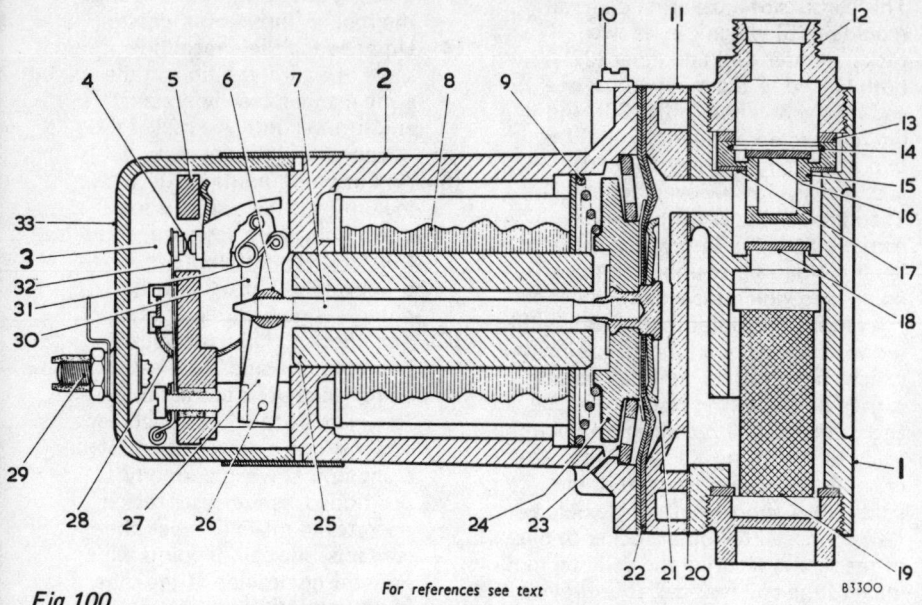

Fig 100
For references see text
Type L and HP fuel pump assembly

a gap of .070 ± .005 in. (1.8 ± .13 mm.).

Earlier-type rocker assemblies

Check the gap between the points indirectly by carefully holding the contact blade against the rib on the pedestal without pressing against the tip of the blade. Then check if a .030 in. (.8 mm.) feeler will pass between the fibre rollers and the face of the coil housing. If necessary, the tip of the blade can be set to correct the gap.

FAULT DIAGNOSIS

1. Suspected fuel feed failure

Disconnect the fuel line at the carburetter and check for flow.

(a) If normal, examine for obstructed float-chamber needle seating or gummed needle.

(b) If normal initially, but diminishing rapidly and accompanied by slow pump operation, check for correct tank venting by removing the filler cap. Inadequate venting causes a slow power stroke, with resultant excessive burning of contact points.

(c) If reduced flow is accompanied by slow operation of the pump, check for any restriction on the inlet side of the pump, such as a clogged filter, which should be removed and cleaned. In the case of reduced flow with rapid operation of the pump, check for an air leak on the suction side, dirt under the valves, or faulty valve cage sealing washers.

(d) If no flow, check for:

(i) *Electrical supply*
Disconnect the lead from the terminal and test for an electrical supply.

(ii) *Faulty contact points*
If electrical supply is satisfactory

the bakelite cover should be removed to check that the tungsten points are in contact. The lead should then be replaced on the terminal and a short piece of bared wire put across the contacts. If the pump then performs a stroke the fault is due to dirt, corrosion, or maladjustment of the tungsten points.

(iii) *Obstructed pipeline between fuel tank and pump*
The inlet pipe should be disconnected; if the pump then operates trouble is due to a restriction in the pipeline between the pump and the tank. This may be cleared by the use of compressed air after removing the fuel tank filler cap. It should be noted, however, that compressed air should not be passed through the pump, as this will cause serious damage to the valves.

(iv) *Faulty diaphragm action*
If the previous operations fail to locate the trouble, stiffening of the diaphragm fabric or abnormal friction in the rocker 'throwover' mechanism is to be suspected. To remedy these faults, the coil housing should be removed and the diaphragm flexed a few times, taking care not to lose any of the 11 rollers under it. Prior to reassembly, it is advisable to apply a little thin oil to the 'throw-over' spring spindles at a point where they pivot in the brass rockers. The diaphragm armature assembly should then be assembled and set in accordance with the instructions given under that heading.

2. Noisy pump

Air leaks. If the pump is noisy in operation, an air leak at one or other of the suction lines may be the cause. Such a leak may be checked by disconnecting the fuel pipe from the carburetter and allowing the pump to discharge into a suitable container with the end of the pipe submerged. The emission of continuous bubbles at this point will confirm the existence of an air leak.

The fault should be rectified by carrying out the following procedure:

(a) Check that all connections from the fuel tank to the pump are in good order.

(b) Check that the inlet union is tight.

(c) Check that the coil housing securing screws are well and evenly tightened. Air leaks on the suction side cause rapid operation of the pump and are the most frequent cause of premature failure.

3. *Pump operates without delivering fuel*

If the pump operates without delivering fuel the most likely causes are:

(a) A serious air leak on the suction side, or,

(b) Foreign matter lodged under one of the valves, particularly under the inlet valve.

To remedy (a) see para. 2 above.

To remove any foreign matter lodged under the valves these should be removed for cleaning.

FUEL PUMP COMMON DISMANTLING AND REASSEMBLING PROCEDURE (reference Fig. 101)

DISMANTLING

Contact breaker

1. Remove the insulated knob or sleeve (33), terminal nut (32), and connector (31), together with its shake-

proof washer. Remove the tape seal (if fitted) and take off the end-cover.

2. Unscrew the 5 B.A. screw (24) which secures the contact blade (22) to the pedestal (16) and remove the condenser (25) (if fitted) from its clip. This will allow the washer (23), the long-coil lead (11), and the contact blade to be removed.

Coil housing and diaphragm

3. Unscrew the coil housing securing screws (7), using a thick-bladed screw driver to avoid damaging the screw heads.

4. Remove the earthing screw (9). On earlier pumps a 2 B.A. earthing stud (Fig. 114) was fitted in the 9 o'clock position on 12-volt pumps, and in the 12 o'clock position on 6-volt pumps, looking at the front or pedestal end of the pump.

5. The coil housing (6) may now be removed from the body (1). Next remove the diaphragm and spindle assembly (2) by taking hold of the diaphragm and unscrewing it anticlockwise until the armature spring (5) pushes the diaphragm away from the coil housing. It is advisable to hold the housing over the bench so that the 11 brass rollers (3) will not fall onto the floor. The diaphragm and its spindle are serviced as a unit and should not be separated.

Pedestal and rocker

6. Remove the end-cover seal washer (21), unscrew the terminal nut (20), and remove the lead washer (19); this will have flattened on the terminal tag and thread and is best cut away with cutting pliers or a knife. Unscrew the two 2 B.A. screws (28), holding the pedestal to the coil housing, remove the earth terminal tag (13) together with the condenser clip (26) (if fitted). Tip the pedestal and withdraw the terminal stud (17) from the terminal tag (12). The pedestal (16) may now be removed with the rocker mechanism attached.

7. Push out the hardened steel pin (14) which holds the rocker mechanism to the pedestal and separate the two.

Body and valves

8. Remove the inlet union (44), the outlet union (37), the outlet valve cage (41), and the inlet valve disc (43). Remove the base plug (36) and filter (34).

Refer to specific pump type section for continuation of dismantling sequence

INSPECTION (except as noted)

If gum formation has occurred in the fuel used in the pump, the parts in contact with the fuel will have become coated with a substance similar to varnish. This has a strong stale smell and may attack the neoprene diaphragm. Brass and steel parts so affected can be cleaned by being boiled in a 20 per cent. solution of caustic soda, dipped in a strong nitric acid solution and finally washed in boiling water. Light alloy parts must be well soaked in methylated spirits and then cleaned.

    1. Clean the pump and inspect for cracks, damaged threads and joint faces.

a) 2. Remove the circlip in the outlet valve cage and examine the inlet and outlet valve discs for wear. Scrap if worn.

b) 3. Examine the plastic valve assemblies for kinks or damage to the valve plates. They can best be checked by blowing and sucking with the mouth.

b) 4. Check that the narrow tongue on the valve cage, which is bent over to retain the valve and to prevent it being forced out of position, has not been distorted but allows a

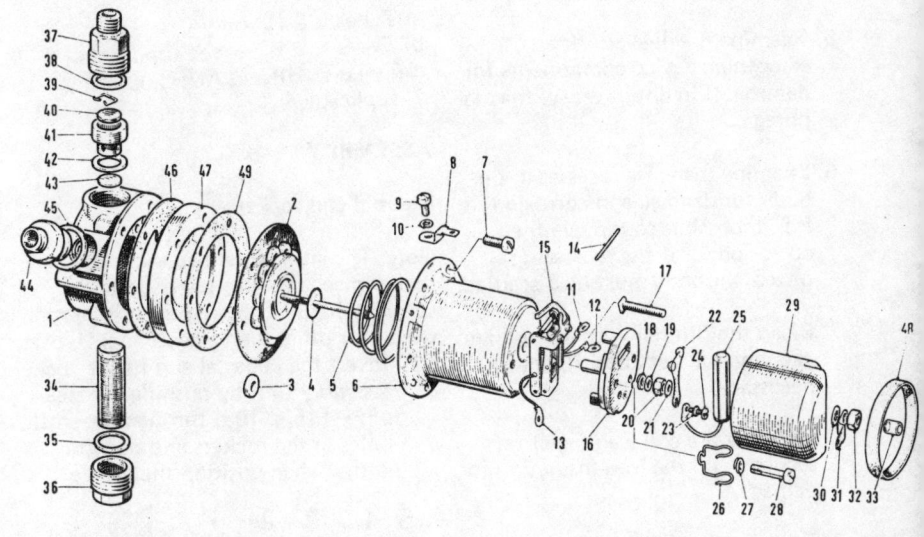

No.	Description	No.	Description	No.	Description
1.	Pump body.	17.	Stud—terminal.	33.	Sleeve—insulating.
2.	Diaphragm and spindle assembly.	18.	Washer—spring.	34.	Filter.
3.	Roller—armature centralizing.	19.	Washer—lead.	35.	Washer.
4.	Washer—impact.	20.	Nut—terminal.	36.	Plug—filter.
5.	Spring—armature.	21.	Washer—end cover seal.	37.	Connection—outlet.
6.	Housing—coil.	22.	Contact blade.	38.	Washer (Medium)—fibre.
7.	Screw—securing housing—2 B.A.	23.	Washer—5 B.A.	39.	Clip—spring.
8.	Connector—earth.	24.	Screw—contact blade—5 B.A.	40.	Valve—outlet.
9.	Screw—earth (4 B.A.—H, 2 B.A.—L).	25.	Condenser.	41.	Cage—outlet valve.
10.	Washer—spring.	26.	Clip—condenser.	42.	Washer (Thin)—fibre.
11.	Tag—terminal—5 B.A.	27.	Washer—spring, 2 B.A.	43.	Valve—inlet.
12.	Tag—terminal—2 B.A.	28.	Screw—pedestal to housing—2 B.A.	44.	Connection—inlet.
13.	Tag—earth—2 B.A.	29.	End cover.	45.	Washer—fibre.
14.	Pin—rocker pivot.	30.	Washer—shakeproof—2 B.A.	46.	Gasket—joint.
15.	Rocker mechanism.	31.	Connector—Lucar.	47.	Plate—sandwich.
16.	Pedestal.	32.	Nut—2 B.A.	48.	Band—sealing.
				49.	Gasket—diaphragm.

Fig 101 Type L and HP fuel pump details

valve lift of approximately 1/16 in. (1.6 mm) e.g. Fig. 117.

c) 5. Examine the delivery flow-smoothing device components for damage. If in doubt renew the diaphragm.

6. Examine the valve recesses in the body for damage and corrosion; if it is impossible to remove the corrosion, or if the recesses are pitted, the body must be discarded.

7. Clean the filter(s) with a brush and examine for fractures. Renew if necessary.

8. Examine the coil-lead tag(s) for security and the lead insulation for damage.

9. Examine the contact breaker points for signs of burning or pitting; if this is evident, the rocker assembly and spring blade must be removed.

10. Examine the pedestal for cracks or other damage, in particular to the narrow ridge on the edge of the rectangular hole, on which the contact blade rests.

11. If fitted: examine the non-return valve vent in the end cover for damage. Ensure that the small ball valve is free to move. Ensure that the coil housing vent tube is not blocked.

12. Examine the diaphragm for signs of deterioration. Replace if doubtful.

13. Renew the following parts: all fibre and cork washers, gaskets, 'O' section sealing rings, rollers showing signs of wear on their periphery, damaged bolts and unions.

NOTES.

a) Types L & HP only
b) Types L & HP — not applicable
c) Types L, HP and AUF 200 — not applicable

ASSEMBLY

Pedestal and rocker

Note. The steel pin which secures the rocker mechanism to the pedestal is specially hardened and must not be replaced by other than a genuine S.U. part.

1. Invert the pedestal and fit the rocker assembly to it by pushing the steel pin (1) (Fig. 103) through the small holes in the rockers and pedestal struts. Then position the centre

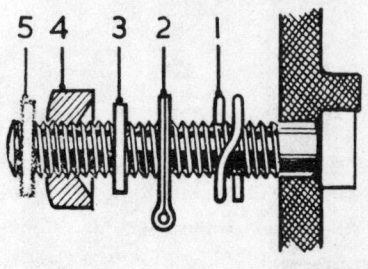

The correct assembly of components on the terminal stud

Fig 102

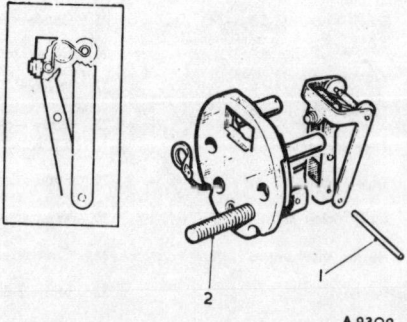

Fitting the rocker assembly to the pedestal. (Inset) the correct position of the centre toggle spring

Fig 103

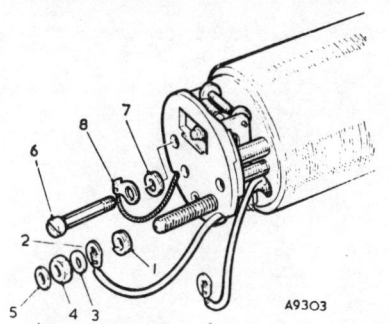

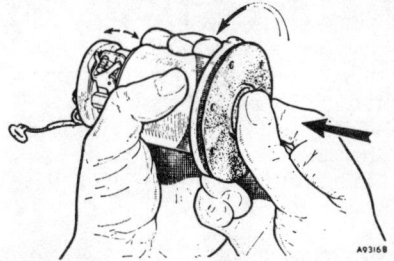

Fig 104
Attaching the pedestal to the coil housing

Fig 107
Setting the diaphragm. Unscrew until the rocker just 'throws over'

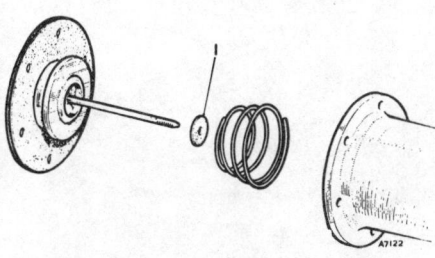

Fig 105
Fitting the diaphragm to the coil housing. Note the impact washer (1)

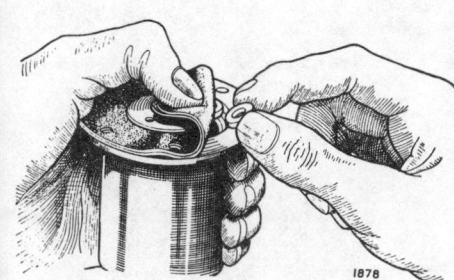

Fig 106
Inserting the diaphragm centralizing rollers

toggle so that, with the inner rocker spindle in tension against the rear of the contact point, the centre toggle spring is above the spindle on which the white rollers run. This positioning is important to obtain the correct 'throw over' action; it is also essential that the rockers are perfectly free to swing on the pivot pin and that the arms are not binding on the legs of the pedestal.
If necessary the rockers can be squared up with a pair of thin-nosed pliers.

2. Assemble the square-headed 2 B.A. terminal stud to the pedestal, the back of which is recessed to take the square head.

3. Assemble the 2 B.A. spring washer (1) (Fig. 104), and put the terminal stud through the 2 B.A. terminal tag (2), then fit the lead washer (3) and the coned nut with its coned face to the lead washer. (This makes better contact than an ordinary flat washer and nut.) Tighten the 2 B.A. nut and finally add the end-cover seal washer (5).

4. Assemble the pedestal to the coil housing (Fig. 104) by fitting the two 2 B.A. pedestal screws (6), ensuring that the spring washer (7) on the left-hand screw (9 o'clock position) is between the pedestal and the earthing tag (8). When a condenser is fitted, its wire clip base is placed under the earthing tag and the spring

119

washer is dispensed with.
5. Tighten the screws, taking care to prevent the earthing tag (8) from turning, as this will strain or break the earthing flex. Do not overtighten the screws or the pedestal will crack. **Do not fit the contact blade at this stage.**

Diaphragm assembly

6. Place the armature spring into the coil housing with its larger diameter towards the coil (Fig. 105).
7. Before fitting the diaphragm make sure that the impact washer is fitted to the armature. (This is a small neoprene washer that fits in the armature recess.) Do not use jointing compound or dope on the diaphragm.
8. Fit the diaphragm by inserting the spindle in the hole in the coil and screwing it into the threaded trunnion in the centre of the rocker assembly.
9. Screw in the diaphragm until the rocker will not 'throw over'; this must not be confused with jamming the armature on the coil housing internal steps.
10. Fit the 11 brass centralizing rollers (Fig. 106) by turning back the diaphragm edge and dropping the rollers into the coil recess. The pump should be held in the left hand, rocker end downwards, to prevent the rollers from falling out.
On later-type rocker mechanisms with adjustable fingers fit the contact blade and adjust the finger settings as described under those headings, then carefully remove the contact blade.
11. Holding the coil housing assembly in the left hand in an approximately horizontal position (see Fig. 107), push the diaphragm spindle in with the thumb of the right hand, pushing firmly but steadily. Unscrew the diaphragm, pressing and releasing with the thumb of the right hand until the rocker just 'throws over'. Now turn the diaphragm back (unscrew) to the nearest hole and again 4 holes (two-thirds of a complete turn). The diaphragm is now correctly set.
12. Press the centre of the armature and fit the retaining fork at the back of the rocker assembly (Fig. 108). This is done to prevent the rollers from falling out when the coil housing is placed on the bench prior to fitting the body, and is not intended to stretch the diaphragm before tightening the body screws.

Body components,
Refer to specific pump type section for continuation of assembly/sequence

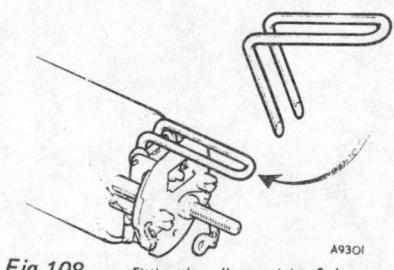

Fig 108 Fitting the roller retaining fork

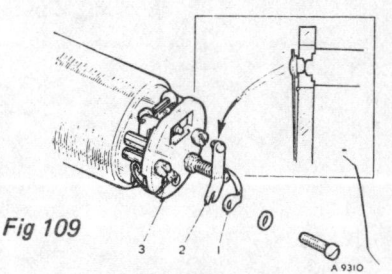

Fig 109

Setting the correct relative position of blade and rocker contact points

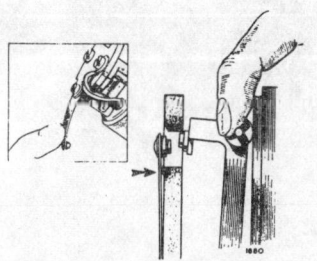

Setting the contact blade to ensure contact with the pedestal ridge

Fig 110

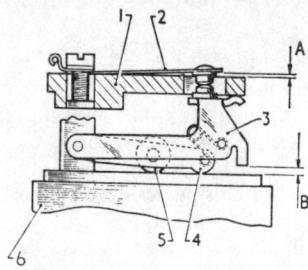

Fig 111

The rocker finger settings on modified rocker assemblies
1. Pedestal.
2. Contact blade.
3. Outer rocker.
4. Inner rocker.
5. Trunnion.
6. Coil housing.

A= ·035 in. (·9 mm.).   B= ·070 in. (1·8 mm.).

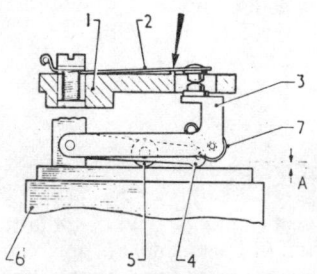

The contact gap setting on earlier-type rocker assemblies
1. Pedestal.
2. Contact blade.
3. Outer rocker.
4. Inner rocker.
5. Trunnion.
6. Coil housing.

A= ·030 in. (·8 mm.).

Fig 112

Contact blade

20. Fit the contact blade (2) (Fig. 109) and coil lead (1) to the pedestal (3) with the 5 B.A. washer and screw. When a condenser is fitted the tag on it is placed under the coil lead tag.
21. Adjust the contact blade so that the contact points on it are a little above the contact points on the rocker when the points are closed (see Fig. 109), also that when the contact points make or break, one pair of points wipes over the centre line of

the other in a symmetrical manner. As the contact blade is provided with a slot for the attachment screw, some degree of adjustment is possible.
22. Tighten the contact blade attachment screw when the correct setting is obtained.

Contact gap settings

23. Check that when the outer rocker is pressed onto the coil housing, the contact blade rests on the narrow rib or ridge which projects slightly above the main face of the pedestal (Fig. 110). If it does not, slacken the contact blade attachment screw, swing the blade clear of the pedestal, and bend it downwards a sufficient amount so that when repositioned it rests against the rib lightly, over-tensioning of the blade will restrict the travel of the rocker mechanism.

Modified rocker assemblies

24. Check the lift of the contact blade tip above the top of the pedestal (A) (Fig. 111) with a feeler gauge, bending the stop-finger beneath the pedestal, if necessary, to obtain a lift of .035 ± .005 in. (.9±.13 mm.).
25. Check the gap between rocker finger and coil housing (B) (Fig. 111) with a feeler gauge, bending the stop-finger, if necessary, to obtain a gap of .070±.005 in. (1.8±.13 mm.).

Earlier-type rocker assemblies

26. Check the gap between the points indirectly by carefully holding the contact blade against the rib on the pedestal without pressing against the tip (see Fig. 112). Then check if a .030 in. (.8 mm.) feeler will pass between the fibre rollers and the face of the coil housing. If necessary the tip of the blade can be set to correct the gap.

End-cover

27. Tuck all spare cable into position so

121

that it cannot foul the rocker mechanism. Ensure that the end-cover seal washer is in position on the terminal stud, fit the bakelite end-cover and lock washer, secure with the brass nut, fit the terminal tag or connector, and the insulated knob or sleeve.

28. The pump is now ready for test.

Pump testing

29. The performance testing of fuel pumps for flow rate, pressure and reduced voltage checks can only be safely and satisfactorily carried out on a special Pump Test Stand designed for the specific fuel pump type and having a controllable recirculating flow facility.

30. The following steps can be carried out with the pump in situ:-

Priming and Delivery Check

31. When switched on the pump should prime, from dry, within 10 - 15 seconds.

Valve Seat Check

32. After the pump has run for some time, it should hold without repeating for a minimum of 20 seconds. If it repeats it indicates a leak on the pressure side (e.g. float chamber needle valve), or that the inlet valve is not operating correctly. On earlier type pumps with metal disc valves this may be remedied by removing the discs and rubbing down the sealing face using fine lapping paste on a flat surface, and/or by re-bedding to the valve seat.

On pumps fitted with Melinex valves, malfunction of the inlet valve must be investigated.

Sparking Check

33. A moderate degree of sparking between the contact points is permissible, but there is a special 'leak' wire incorporated in the coil winding to keep this down to a minimum. If excessive sparking does occur it is probable that this comparatively delicate wire has fractured; on these rare occasions the complete coil unit must be replaced.

34. After test replace the rubber sealing band over the end cover gap and seal with adhesive tape. This may be removed to improve ventilation when the pump is mounted internally in a moisture-free region but MUST be retained otherwise.

TYPE L AND HP FUEL PUMP.
(Reference Fig. 100) (SPECIFIC DETAILS)

Installation

The 'L' type pump should be mounted in the region of the engine, at approximately carburetter level, in such a position that a minimum of exhaust manifold heat is radiated upon it, with the delivery pipe to the float chamber kept as short as possible.

The 'HP' type pump, because of its high delivery pressure, is suitable for mounting over the rear fuel tank, in which position it is free from vaporizing troubles arising from high underbonnet temperatures.

On both pumps, the filter plug should be positioned at the bottom and the delivery union at the top.

NOTE.— Earlier 'HP' pumps were fitted with a coil housing of about 9/16 in. greater length than 'L' type pumps; on current production the housing length is the same. On later 'HP' pumps the earthing screw has been reduced in size from 2 B.A. to 4 B.A., thus an 'L' type can be identified by the 2 B.A. earthing screw. Additionally, 'L' type pumps are normally fitted with a single-point contact blade. When a pump is being connected it must be primed by disconnecting the fuel pipe at the carburetter until a flow is obtained.

Description

The pump comprises three main assemblies: the body casting (1), the diaphragm, armature and magnet assembly (2), and the contact breaker assembly (3).

The body

This consists of the main body casting and a sandwich plate (11) which is assembled to it with a joint gasket (20). A filter (19) is screwed into the lower part of the body, and the inlet union, unseen in the diagram, is screwed in at an angle on one side. The outlet union (12) is screwed in to the top of the body, opposite to the filter, and tightens down on to the delivery valve cage (15), which is clamped between two fibre washers, (17) thin and (13) medium. In the top of the cage is the outlet valve, a thin brass disc (16) held in position by a spring clip (14). The inlet valve (18), a similar brass disc, rests on a seating machined in the body. A series of holes connect the space between the valves to the pumping chamber (21), which is a shallow depression on the forward face of the sandwich plate, bounded by the diaphragm (22).

Basic Details

The section 'Fuel Pump Common Operational Features' given earlier, sets out basic detail information.

Dismantling and Reassembly. *Fig 101*

Refer to 'Fuel Pump Common Dismantling and Reassembly Procedure' given earlier, and note the following specific details in sequential order.

Body and valves

8. Remove the inlet union (44), the outlet union (37), the outlet valve cage (41), and the inlet valve disc (43). Remove the base plug (36) and filter (34).

Body components

Note. — Outlet valve cages may be identified by the 4-hole drilling of the HP type and the 2-hole drilling of the L type.

13. Assemble the brass valve disc (4) (Fig. 113) to the outlet valve cage, (3) making sure that the smooth face of the disc faces the valve seat, retain it in position with the circlip (5) which must be located in the groove in the valve cage. The valve must rattle freely when the valve cage is shaken.

14. Drop the other valve disc (1) (Fig. 113) smooth face downwards onto the inlet valve seat in the body of the pump, insert the thin fibre washer (2), drop the valve cage (3) in position, insert the medium fibre washer (6), then screw in the outlet union (7), and tighten with a 3/8-in. Whitworth ring or box spanner. Fit the inlet union.

Body attachment

15. Place the sandwich plate gasket on the face of the body, lining up the holes in the body and gasket; fit the sandwich plate, concave face to diaphragm with the diaphragm gasket, again lining up the holes.

16. Offer up the coil housing to the body and sandwich plate and ensure correct seating between them. Outlet connection to the top and filter plug at bottom.

17. Line up the six securing screw holes, making sure that the two cast lugs on the coil housing are at the bottom, insert the six 2 B.A. screws finger-tight. Fit the earthing screw with its Lucar connector.

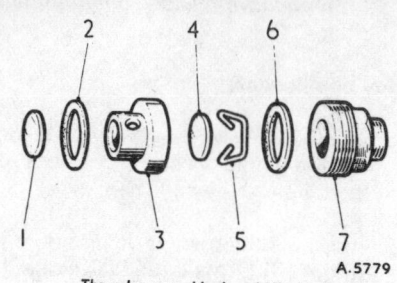

The valve assembly, L and HP **single** pumps

Fig 113

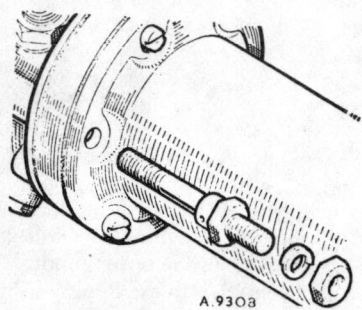

The earthing stud on earlier pumps

Fig 114

Note 1. On short HP pumps the earthing screw has been reduced in size from 2 B.A. to 4 B.A. thus an L-type pump can be identified externally by the 2 B.A. earthing screw.

Note 2. Earlier L and HP pumps have an earthing stud fitted in the 9 o'clock position (see Fig. 114).

18. **Remove the roller retaining fork before tightening the body securing screws,** making sure that the rollers retain their position, a displaced roller will cut the diaphragm. It is not necessary to stretch the diaphragm before tightening the securing screws.

19. **Tighten the securing screws in sequence as they appear diametrically opposite each other.**

Complete assembly sequence according to 'Fuel Pump Common Dismantling and Reassembly Procedure' given earlier, from 'Contact Blade' on.

FUEL PUMP TYPE AUF 200 RANGE SPECIFIC DETAILS *Fig 115*

INSTALLATION

The Type AUF 200 pump, in common with previous types of S.U. high-pressure electric fuel pump, is designed to be mounted in the vicinity of the fuel tank and at a level not appreciably above that of the top of the tank. This situation ensures freedom from vapour generation troubles, even under the most severe conditions of high ambient temperature and high-altitude operation. Mounted in this position and provided with fuel lines of approximately ¼ in. bore, the pump is capable of supplying approximately 75 pints of fuel per hour at a delivery point about 3 ft. above the level of the tank. It is thus capable of supplying fuel at this rate when ascending the most severe gradient liable to be encountered even by a vehicle of exceptionally long wheelbase.

The pump is normally provided with a Lucar connecting tag to the terminal screw (28), which can, however, be replaced by other types of connector tag if required. It is essential that a sound connection should be made to earth on the vehicle from the earthing screw (10). The most suitable method of mounting, particularly with regard to inaudibility of operation, is by a circular mounting clip surrounding the coil housing (2), from which it is separated by a soft rubber packing strip. The pump should be mounted in a horizontal position with the outlet nozzle (12) uppermost.

When a pump is being connected it must be primed by disconnecting the fuel pipe at the carburetter until a flow is obtained.

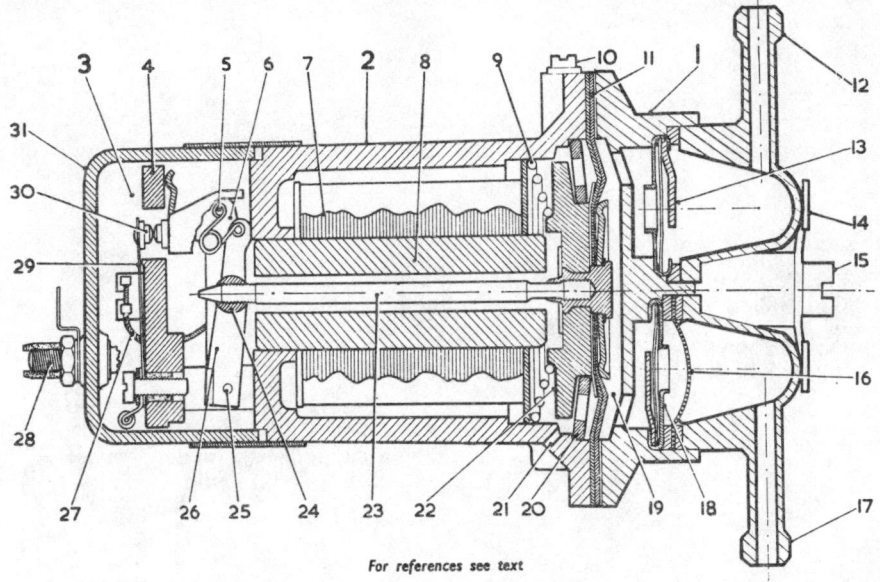

Fig 115 Type AUF 200 range fuel pump

DESCRIPTION

The pump comprises three main assemblies: the body casting (1), the diaphragm, armature, and magnet assembly (2), and the contact breaker assembly (3).

The body

The body (1) is a casting into which the clamp plate (14), retained by two screws (15), holds the inlet (17) and outlet (12), moulded nozzles, and both valve assemblies, all of which are arranged to be accessible from the outside of the pump. The inlet valve (18) consists of a thin plastic disc permanently assembled into a pressed-steel cage. The outlet valve (13) is an identical assembly, but reversed in direction. A dome-shaped filter (16) is provided on the entry side of the inlet valve (18). The valve allows passage to the pumping chamber (19), a shallow depression formed on the face of the body casting and bounded by the diaphragm (11).

Basic Detail

The section 'Fuel Pump Common Operational Features' given earlier provides basic detail information.

DISMANTLING AND REASSEMBLY. FIG. 116

Refer to 'Fuel Pump Common Dismantling and Reassembly Procedure' given earlier, and note the following specific details in sequential order.

Body and valves

8. Unscrew the two 2 B.A. screws (35) securing the spring clamp plate (34) holding the inlet and outlet nozzles (36). Remove the nozzles, filter (40), and valve assemblies (37) and (38).

Body components

13. In the AUF 200 range of pumps, inlet and outlet valves are identical

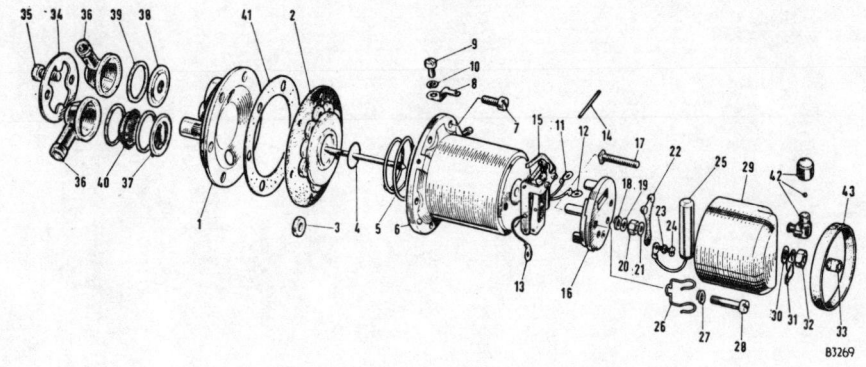

1. Pump body
2. Diaphragm and spindle assembly
3. Roller − armature centralizing
4. Washer − impact
5. Spring − armature
6. Housing − coil
7. Screw − securing housing − 2 B.A.
8. Connector − earth
9. Screw − 4 B.A.
10. Washer − Spring − 4 B.A.
11. Tag − Terminal − 5 B.A.
12. Tag − Terminal − 2 B.A.
13. Tag − earth − 2 B.A.
14. Pin − rocker pivot
15. Rocker Mechanism
16. Pedestal
17. Stud − terminal
18. Washer − spring
19. Washer − lead
20. Nut − Terminal
21. Washer − end cover seal
22. Contact blade
23. Washer − 5 B.A.
24. Screw − contact blade − 5 B.A.
25. Condenser
26. Clip − condenser
27. Washer − spring − 2 B.A.
28. Screw − pedestal to housing − 2 B.A.
29. End cover
30. Washer − shakeproof
31. Connector − lucar
32. Nut − 2 B.A.
33. Sleeve − insulating
34. Clamp − plate
35. Screw − securing − 2 B.A.
36. Nozzle − inlet and outlet
37. Valve − inlet
38. Valve − outlet
39. Washer − sealing
40. Filter
41. Gasket
42. Vent valve
43. Band − sealing

Fig. 116 − Type AUF 200 Range Fuel Pump Details

assemblies and are held in position in the one-piece body casting by a steel spring clamp plate secured by two 2 B.A. screws. This plate also secures the inlet and outlet nozzles, including the filter, all of which are arranged to be accessible from the outside of the pump (see Fig. 9). The inlet recess is deeper than the outlet to allow for the filter and extra washer.

14. Referring to Fig.118, place the outlet valve assembly, tongue side uppermost, in the recess marked 'outlet', place a joint washer on top of the valve assembly, and complete by adding the outlet nozzle.

15. Place the inlet valve assembly, tongue side downwards, in the recess marked 'inlet', follow this with a joint washer, then the filter, dome side upwards, then another joint washer, completing the assembly with the inlet nozzle.

16. Take care that both assemblies nest down evenly into their respective recesses. Position the nozzles as required, place the clamp plate on top, and tighten down firmly onto the body with the two 2 B.A. screws.

Body attatchment

17. Offer up the coil housing to the body, ensuring correct seating between them.

18. Line up the six securing screw holes, making sure that the cast lugs on the coil housing are at the bottom, insert the six 2 B.A. screws finger-tight. Fit the earthing screw with its Lucar connector.

19. Remove the roller retaining fork before tightening the body securing screws, making sure that the rollers retain their position; a displaced roller will cut the diaphragm. It is not necessary to stretch the diaphragm before tightening the securing screws.

20. Tighten the securing screws in sequence as they appear diametrically opposite each other.

Assembly Completion

Complete assembly sequence according to 'Fuel Pump Common Dismantling and Reassembly Procedure' given earlier, from 'Contact Blade' on.

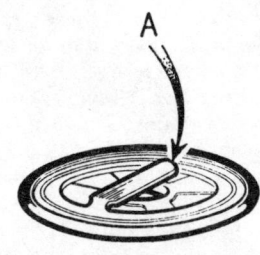

Fig. 117. The valve (inlet and outlet.)
A =   in. (1.6 mm.)

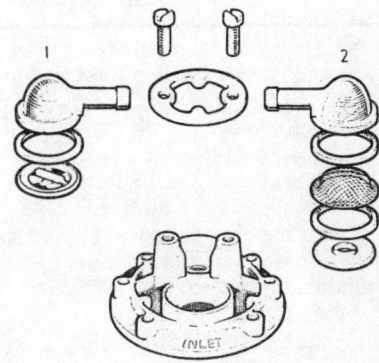

Fig. 118 - The valve assembly, AUF 200 range pump.

1. Outlet
2. Inlet

FUEL PUMP TYPE AUF 300 RANGE. SPECIFIC DETAILS *Fig 119*

Installation

The Type AUF 300 range of pumps, in common with previous types of S.U. high-pressure electric fuel pumps, is designed to be mounted in the vicinity of the fuel tank and at a level not appreciably above that of the top of the rank. This situation ensures freedom from vapour generation troubles, even under the most severe conditions of high ambient temperature and high-altitude operation. Mounted in this position, and provided with fuel lines of approximately 5/16 in. (7.9 mm.) diameter bore, the pump is capable of supplying approximately 140 pints (79.5 litres) of fuel per hour at a delivery point about 3 ft. (.9 m.) above the level of the tank. It is thus capable of supplying fuel at this rate when ascending the most severe gradients liable to be encountered, even with a vehicle of exceptionally long wheelbase.

The pump is normally provided with a Lucar connecting tag to the terminal screw (40), which can, however, be replaced by other types of connector tag if required. It is essential that a good electrical connection should be made to earth on the vehicle from the earthing screw (10). The most suitable method of mounting, particularly with regard to inaudibility of operation, is by a circular mounting clip surrounding the coil housing (2), from which it is separated by a soft rubber packing strip. Alternatively, the two tapped 5/16 in. B.S.F. holes provided on the main pump body casting (1) may be used. The pump should be mounted in a horizontal position with the outlet (17) uppermost. The coil housing (2) is provided with a vent (37), to which, on externally mounted pumps, a plastic tube must be fixed and led to a moisture-free region.

When a pump is being connected it must be primed by disconnecting the fuel pipe at the carburetter until a flow is obtained.

Description

The pump comprises three main assemblies: the body casting (1), the diaphragm, armature and magnet assembly (2), and the contact breaker assembly (3).

The body

The main fuel inlet (19) is in communication with an inlet air bottle (36—lower diagram), and connection to the main pumping chamber (24) is provided by the inlet valve assembly (21). This comprises a plastic valve disc permanently assembled within a pressed-steel cage, which is held in place by a valve cover (22). The outlet from the pumping chamber is provided with an identical valve assembly (11) reversed in direction.

A clamp plate (34), secured by self-tapping screws (see lower diagram), holds both inlet and outlet valve assemblies in position; the valves may be removed by releasing the clamp plate screws. A filter (20) is provided as shown on the entry side of the inlet valve assembly. A flexible plastic diaphragm and barrier (14) loaded by a spring (13) is contained between the vented cover (12) and the perforated diaphragm plate (16), and sealed by the rubber 'O' ring (15). The assembly, a flow smoothing device, is fitted across the extremity of the delivery chamber (18) which communicates with the outlet union (17).

The inlet valve (21) allows passage to the pumping chamber (24), which is formed by a shallow depression in the body casting and bounded by the diaphragm (23).

Basic Detail

The section 'Fuel Pump Common Operational Features' given earlier sets out basic detail information.

DISMANTLING AND REASSEMBLY
Fig 120

Refer to 'Fuel Pump Common Dismantling and Reassembly Procedure' given earlier, and note the following specific details in sequential order:

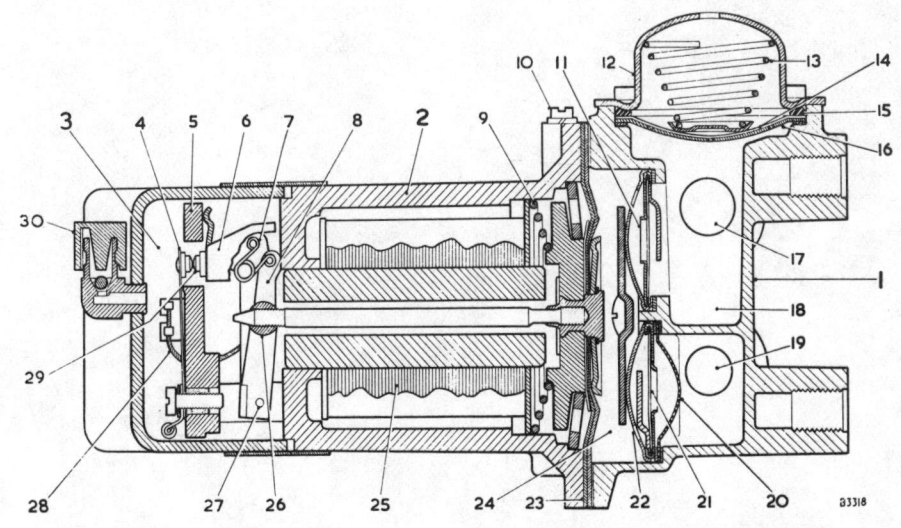

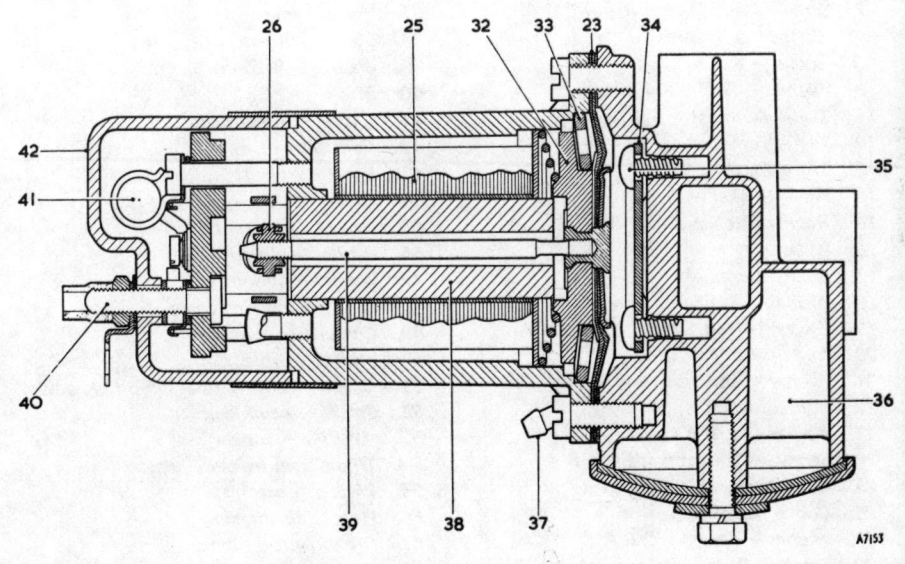

For references see text

Fig. 119. Type AUF 300 Range Fuel Pump Assembly

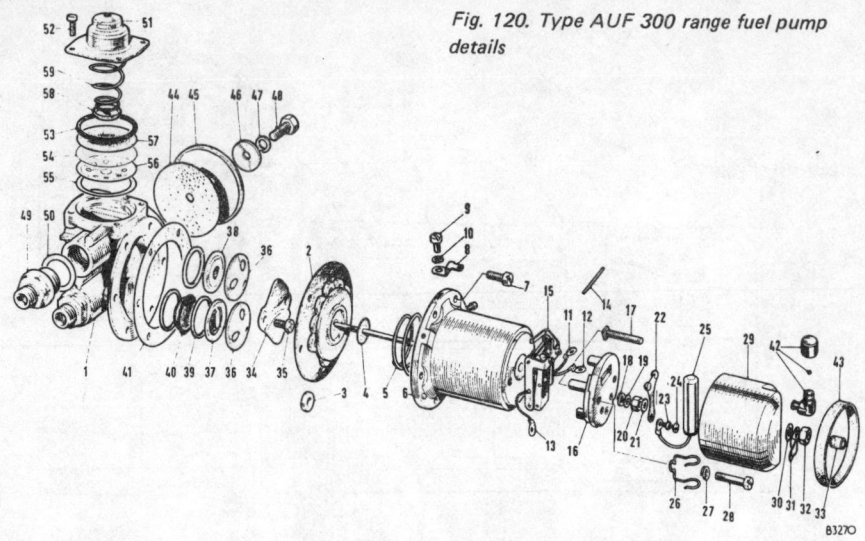

Fig. 120. Type AUF 300 range fuel pump details

1. Pump body
2. Diaphragm and spindle assembly
3. Roller – Armature centralizing
4. Washer – impact
5. Spring – armature
6. Housing – coil
7. Screw – securing housing – 2 B.A.
8. Connector – earth
9. Screw – 4 B.A.
10. Washer – Spring – 4 B.A.
11. Tag – Terminal – 5 B.A.
12. Tag – Terminal – 2 B.A.
13. Tag – Earth – 2 B.A.
14. Pin – Rocker – Pivot
15. Rocker Mechanism
16. Pedestal
17. Stud – terminal
18. Washer – Spring
19. Washer – lead
20. Nut – terminal
21. Washer – end cover seal
22. Contact blade
23. Washer – 5 B.A.
24. Screw – Contact blade – 5 B.A.
25. Condenser
26. Clip – condenser
27. Washer – Spring – 2 B.A.
28. Screw – Pedestal to housing – 2 B.A.
29. End cover
30. Washer – shakeproof

31. Connector – Lucar
32. Nut – 2 B.A.
33. Sleeve – Insulating
34. Plate – Clamp
35. Screw – Plate
36. Cap – Valve
37. Valve – Inlet
38. Valve – Outlet
39. Washer – Sealing
40. Filter
41. Gasket – Diaphragm
42. Vent valve
43. Band – sealing
44. Joint – Inlet air bottle cover
45. Cover – Inlet air bottle
46. Washer – dished
47. Washer – spring
48. Screw – securing cover
49. Connection – outlet
50. Washer – fibre
51. Cover – delivery flow smoothing device
52. Screw – securing cover
53. 'O' Ring – rubber
54. Diaphragm barrier – plastic
55. Washer – sealing
56. Plate – diaphragm
57. Diaphragm – rubber
58. Cap – spring end
59. Spring – diaphragm

Body and valves

8. Unscrew the two Phillips scres (35) securing the valve clamp plate (34), remove the valve caps (36), valves (37) and (38), sealing washers, and filter (40).
   Note. Dismantling of the delivery flow-smoothing device should only be undertaking if the operation of it is faulty, and if the necessary equipment for pressure-testing after assembly is available. On this understanding proceed as follows:

9. Remove the four 4 B.A. screws (52) securing the delivery flow-smoothing device vented cover (51), remove the cover, the diaphragm spring (59), rubber 'O' ring (53), spring cap (58), diaphragm (57), barrier (54), diaphragm plate (56) and sealing washer (55).

10. Remove the single 2 B.A. screw (48), securing the inlet air bottle cover (45). Remove the cover and gasket (44).

11. Unscrew the inlet and outlet connections.

Body components

13. In the AUF 300 range of pumps the valve assemblies are retained internally in the body by a clamp plate secured with self-tapping screws (see Fig. 121). The inlet valve recess in the body is deeper than the outlet recess to allow for the filter and extra washer. Another feature of these pumps is the incorporation of an air bottle on the inlet and a flow-smoothing device on the delivery side. The inlet air bottle is a chamber in the body casting blanked off by a simple cover and joint washer held by a single screw. The delivery flow-smoothing device is formed by a perforated metal plate which is in contact with a plastic barrier backed by a rubber diaphragm, all held in position by a spring and end-cap retained by a vented cover. This assembly seals the delivery chamber in the body.

14. Screw in the inlet and outlet connections with their sealing rings. Assemble the outlet valve components into the outlet recess in the following order, first a joint washer, then the valve, tongue side downwards, then the valve cap.

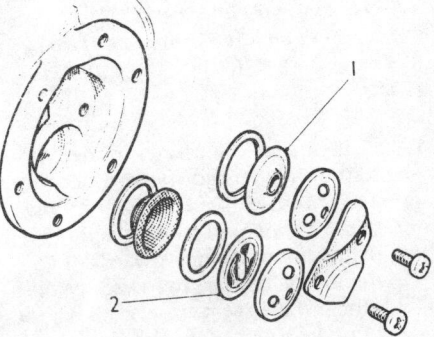

Fig. 121. The valve assembly, AUF 300 range pumps

1. Outlet valve
2. Inlet valve

15. Assemble the inlet valve into the inlet recess as follows: first a joint washer, then the filter, dome side downwards, then another join washer then the filter, dome side downwards, then another point washer, followed by the valve assembly, tongue side upwards, then the valve cap.

16. Take care that both valve assemblies nest down into their respective recesses, place the clamp plate on top and tighten down firmly to the body with the two screws.

17. Replace the inlet air bottle cover with its joint washer and tighten down the central screw.

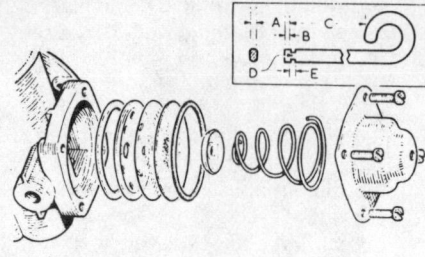

Fig. 122. The delivery flow smoothing device, AUF 300 range pumps. (Inset enlarged) and assembly tool made from 1/8 in. (3 mm.) dia. (10 S.W.G.) Iron wire. A, B, and E=1/16 in. (1.6 mm.) C = 2 in. (50 mm.). D = .090 in. (2 mm.)

18. Place the sealing washer in the bottom of the delivery flow-smoothing device recess, (see Fig. 122) follow this with the perforated diaphragm plate, dome side downwards, then the plastic barrier, followed by the rubber diaphragm. Insert the 'O' section sealing ring into the recess and ensure that it seats evenly. Place the diaphragm spring, large end towards the vented cover, into the cover, place the spring end-cap on the small end of the spring, pass the assembly tool (see inset) through the cover, spring, and end cap and turn it through 90° so that tension may be applied to the spring during assembly. Finally fit the spring and cap assembly onto the diaphragm, tighten the four retaining screws, and release the assembly tool. The pump should be pressure-tested after disturbance of the flow-smoothing device.

Body attachment

19. Fit the joint washer to the body, aligning the screw holes.
20. Offer up the coil housing to the body ensuring correct seating between them.
21. Line up the six securing screw holes, making sure that the cast lugs on the coil hosuing are at the bottom, insert the six 2 B.A. screws finger-tight. Fit the earthing screw with its Lucar connector.
22. **Remove the roller retaining fork before tightening the body securing screws,** making sure that the rollers retain their position; a displaced roller will cut the diaphragm. It is not necessary to stretch the diaphragm before tightening the securing screws.
23. Tighten the securing screws in sequence as they appear diametrically opposite each other.

Assembly Completion

Complete assembly sequence according to 'Fuel Pump Common Dismantling and Reassembly Procedure' given earlier, from 'Contact Blade' on.

FUEL PUMP TYPE AUF 400 RANGE. SPECIFIC DETAILS *Fig 123*

Description

The AUF 400 Type Dual pump is, constructionally, somewhat similar to the AUF 500 Type Double-entry pump as described in Service Sheet AUA 223 A. It differs, however, from the Double-entry pump in that the two pumping chambers with their associated pumping units operate simultaneously, being provided with a common inlet connection.

When a pump is being connected it must be primed by disconnecting the fuel pipe at the carburetter until a flow is obtained.

The pump comprises three main assemblies: the body casting (1), the diaphragm, armature and magnet assembly (3). For clarity, these will be described as single units.

The body

The body (1) consists of a die casting into which the inlet union (21), shown out of its true position on the diagram, is screwed. The inlet union is in communica-

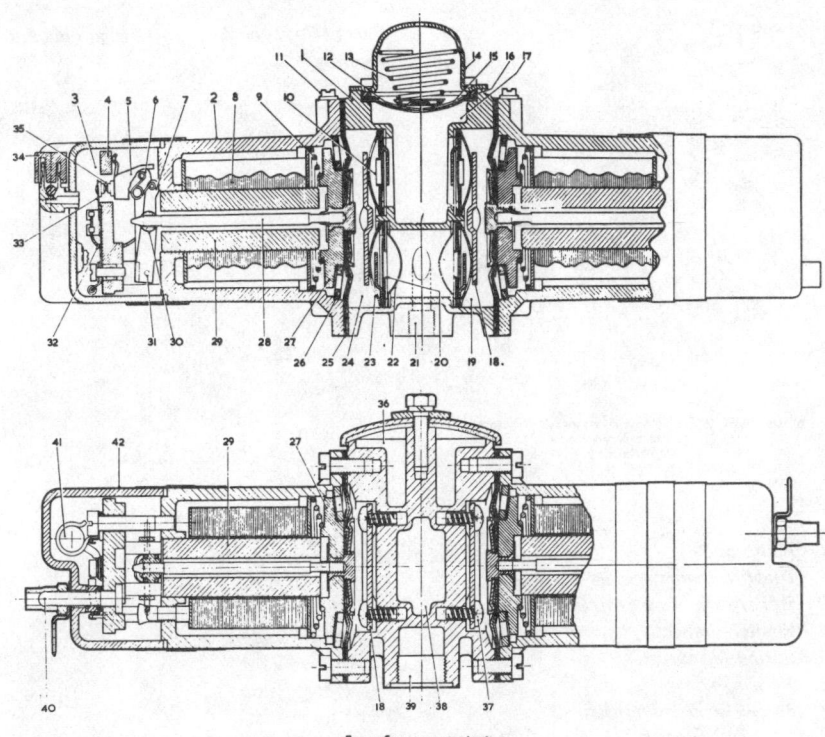

Fig 123 Type AUF 400 range fuel pump assembly

tion with an inlet air bottle (36). A flexible plastic diaphragm and barrier (15) loaded by a spring (13) is contained between the vented cover (14) and the perforated diaphragm plate (12), and sealed by the rubber 'O' ring (16). The assembly, a flow smoothing device, is fitted across the extremity of the delivery chamber (17) which communicates with the outlet union (39).

The inlet valve assembly (20) comprises a plastic disc permanently assembled into a pressed-steel cage which fits into a recess in the body casting. A domed filter (22) is provided on its entry side.

The outlet valve (10) is an identical assembly but reversed in direction. Both valves are held in position by valve covers (23) retained by a clamp plate (18) and two self-tapping screws (37).

The inlet valve (20) allows passage to the pumping chambers (19 and 24) formed by a shallow depression in the body casting and bounded by the diaphragm.

Basic Detail

The section 'Fuel Pump Common Operational Features' given earlier sets out basic detail information.

Dismantling and Reassembling *Fig 124*

The valves, delivery flow smoothing device and method of body attachment for the AUF 400 and AUF 300 pumps are identical. The 'Dismantling and Reassembly' text for the AUF 300 fuel pump may, therefore, be used.

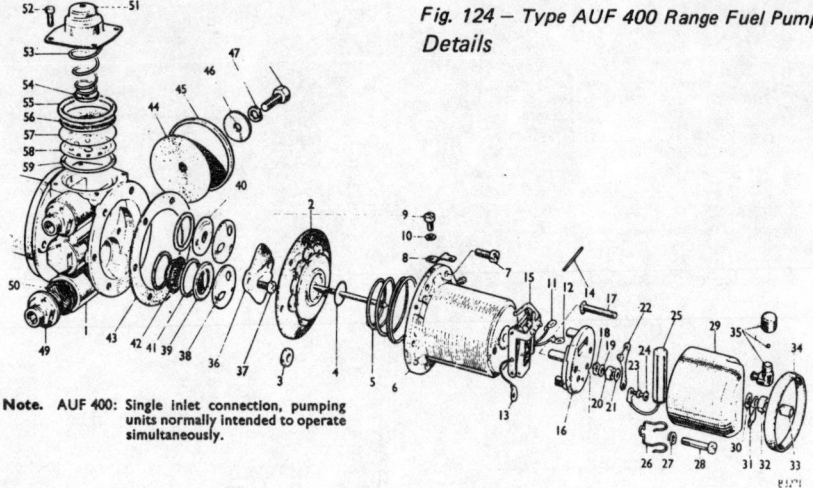

Fig. 124 – Type AUF 400 Range Fuel Pump
Details

Note. AUF 400: Single inlet connection, pumping units normally intended to operate simultaneously.

1. Pump body
2. Diaphragm and spindle assembly
3. Roller—armature centralizing
4. Washer—impact
5. Spring—armature
6. Housing—coil
7. Screw—securing housing—2 B.A.
8. Connector—earth
9. Screw—4 B.A.
10. Washer—Spring—4 b.A.
11. Tag—Terminal—5 B.A.
12. Tag—Terminal—2 B.A.
13. Tag—Earth—2 B.A.
14. Pin—Rocker pivot
15. Rocker mechanism
16. Pedestal
17. Stud—Terminal
18. Washer—Spring
19. Washer—Lead
20. Nut—Terminal
21. Washer—End cover seal
22. Contact blade
23. Washer—5 B.A.
24. Screw—Contact blade—5 B.A.
25. Condenser
26. Clip—Condenser
27. Washer—Spring—2 B.A.
28. Screw—Pedestal to housing—2 B.A.
29. End cover
30. Washer—Shakeproof
31. Connector—Lucar
32. Nut—2 B.A.
33. Sleeve—Insulating
34. Band—Sealing
35. Valve—Vent
36. Plate—Camp
37. Screw—Plate
38. Cap—Valve
39. Valve—Inlet
40. Valve—Outlet
41. Washer—Sealing
42. Filter
43. Gasket—Diaphragm
44. Joint—Inlet air bottle cover
45. Cover—Inlet air bottle
46. Washer—Dished
47. Washer—Spring
48. Screw—Securing cover
49. Connection—Sealing
50. Washer—Sealing
51. Cover—Delivery flow smoothing device
52. Screw—Securing cover
53. Spring—Diaphragm
54. Cap—Spring end
55. 'O' Ring—Rubber
56. Diaphragm—Rubber
57. Diaphragm Barrier—Plastic
58. Plate—Diaphragm
59. Washer—Sealing

FUEL PUMP TYPE AUF 500 RANGE. SPECIFIC DETAILS *Fig 125*

Description

The AUF 500 'double-entry' pump is, constructionally, somewhat similar to the AUF 400 'dual pump' as described in Service Sheet AUA 226. It differs, however, in that the two pumping chambers with their associated pumping units are not normally intended to operate simultaneously, the one being provided with an inlet connection supplied by a feed pipe which terminates short of the bottom of the fuel tank while the other feed pipe draws its fuel in the normal manner from the bottom of the tank. Thus, the pump is provided with two inlet passages marked, respectively, 'Main' and 'Reserve'. The two pumping units are alternatively energized by a two-way switch with corresponding 'Main' and 'Reserve' markings.

When a pump is being connected it must be primed by disconnecting the fuel pipe at the carburetter until a flow is obtained.

The pump comprises three main assemblies: the body casting (1), the diaphragm, armature, and magnet assembly (2), and the contact-breaker assembly (3).

The body

The body (1) is a die casting into which the main inlet union (19), shown out of its true position, is screwed; this is connected to one side of a divided compartment which is in communication with an inlet air bottle (34) separated from the corresponding inlet air bottle (35) which serves the 'Reserve' inlet connection (17). The delivery chamber (15), which is common to both main and reserve delivery, is bounded by a flexible plastic diaphragm (13), separating the delivery chamber from a seated volume of air contained in the air bottle cover (12), sealed by the 'O' ring (14). The inlet valve assembly (18) comprises a plastic disc permanently assembled in a pressed-steel cage; a domed filter (20) is provided on its entry side. The outlet valve (10) is an identical assembly, but reversed in direction. Both valves are held in position by valve covers (21), retained by a clamp plate (16) and two self-tapping screws (36). The inlet valve (18) allows passage to the pumping chamber (22), formed by a shallow depression in the body casting and bounded by the diaphragm (23).

Basic Detail

Basic detail information is set out in the section 'Fuel Pump Common Operational Features' given earlier in the chapter.

Dismantling and Reassembly *Fig 126*

Refer to 'Fuel Pump Common Dismantling and Reassembly Procedure' given earlier in the chapter and note the following specific details in sequential order:—

Body and valves

10. Unscrew the inlet and outlet unions.

11. Unscrew the self-tapping screws (35) securing the clamp plate (34) holding the valve assemblies on both sides of the body, remove the valve assemblies (37) and (38) with the perforated caps (36), filters (40) and joint washers (39).

12. Remove the inlet air bottle cover by unscrewing the single 2 B.A. securing screw (48).

Note. Dismantling of the delivery air bottle should only be undertaken if it is faulty in operation and if the necessary equipment for pressure-testing after assembly is available. On this understanding proceed as follows: Remove the delivery air bottle cover by unscrewing the four screws. Remove the 'O' ring (53), the plastic diaphragm (54), and joint washer (55).

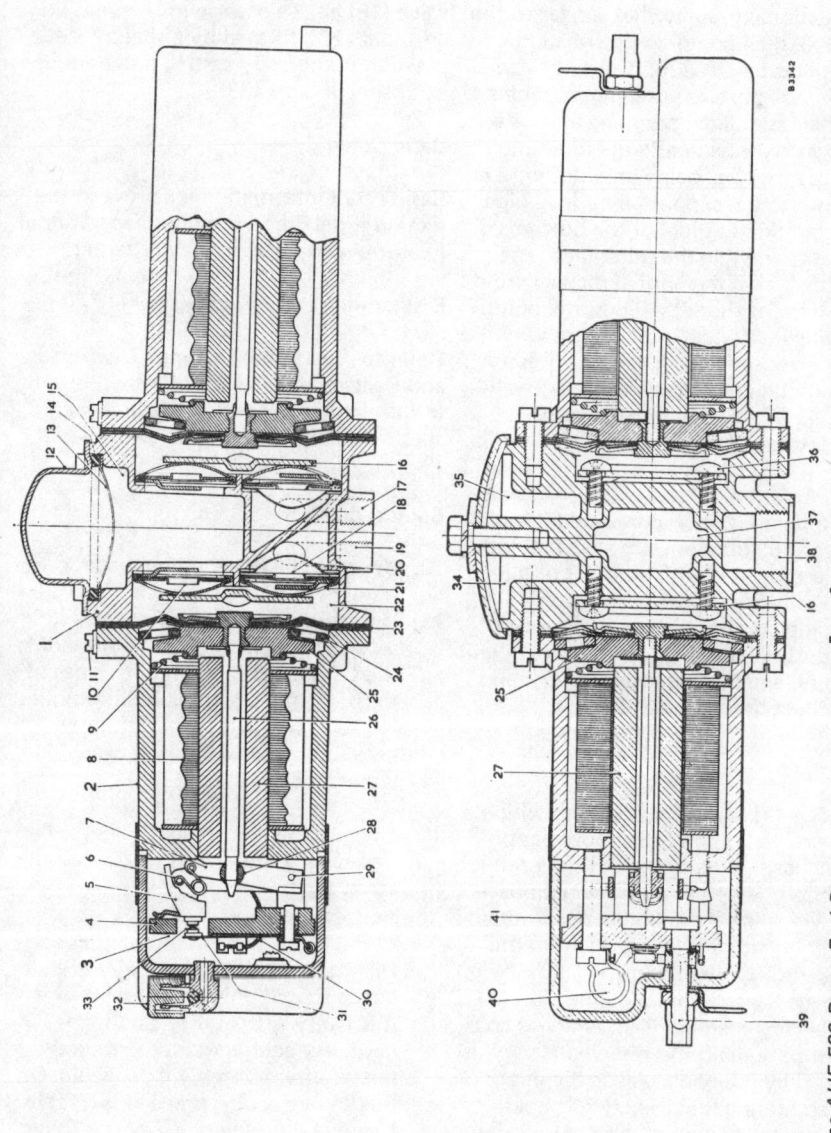

Fig. 125. Type AUF 500 Range Fuel Pump Assembly

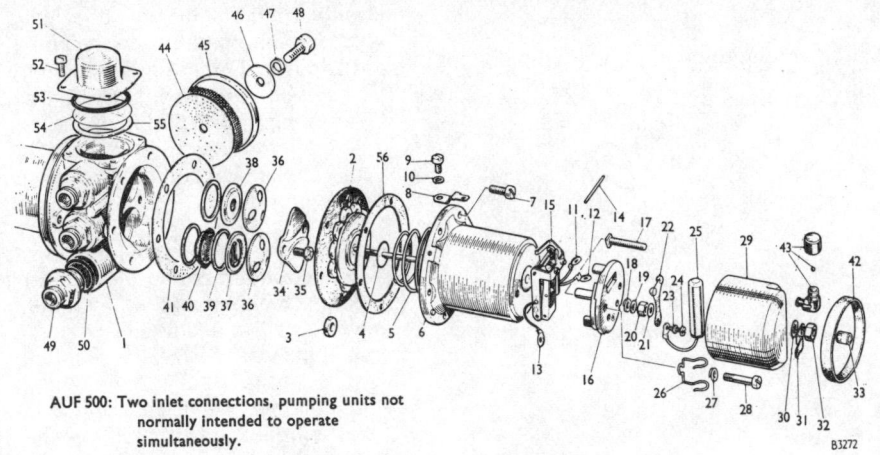

AUF 500: Two inlet connections, pumping units not normally intended to operate simultaneously.

1. Pump body
2. Diaphragm and spindle assembly
3. Roller—armature centralizing
4. Washer—impact
5. Spring—armature
6. Housing—coil
7. Screw—securing housing—2 B.A.
8. Connector—earth
9. Screw—4 B.A.
10. Washer—spring—4 B.A.
11. Tag—terminal—5 B.A.
12. Tag—terminal—2 B.A.
13. Tag—earth—2 B.A.
14. Pin—rocker pivot
15. Rocker mechanism
16. Pedestal
17. Stud terminal
18. Washer—spring
19. Washer—lead
20. Nut—terminal
21. Washer—end cover seal
22. Contact blade
23. Washer—5 B.A.
24. Screw—contact blade—5 B.A.
25. Condenser
26. Clip—condenser
27. Washer—spring—2 B.A.
28. Screw—pedestal to housing—2 B.A.
29. End cover
30. Washer—shakeproof
31. Connector—Lucar
32. Nut—2 B.A.
33. Sleeve—insulating
34. Plate—clamp
35. Screw—plate
36. Cap—valve
37. Valve—inlet
38. Valve—outlet
39. Washer—sealing
40. Filter
41. Gasket—diaphragm
42. Band—sealing
43. Valve—vent
44. Joint—inlet air bottle
45. Cover—inlet air bottle
46. Washer—dished
47. Washer—spring
48. Screw—cover
49. Connection—inlet
50. Washer—sealing
51. Cover—delivery air bottle
52. Screw—cover
53. 'O' Ring—rubber
54. Diaphragm—plastic
55. Washer—sealing
56. Gasket (single layer diaphragm only)

Fig. 126 Type AUF 500 Range Fuel Pump Details

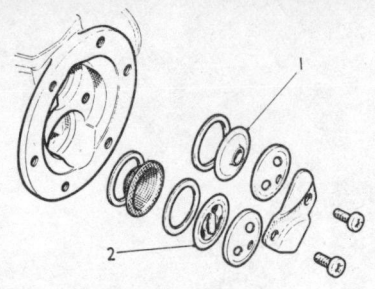

Fig. 127 — The valve assembly, AUF 500 range

1. Outlet
2. Inlet

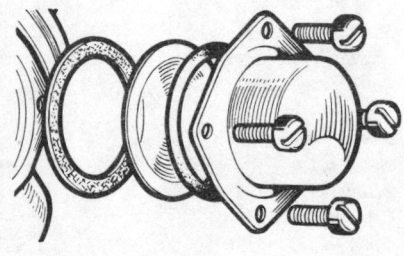

Fig 128 The delivery air bottle AUF 500 range pumps

Body components

13. In the AUF 500 range of pumps the valve assemblies are retained internally in the body by a clamp plate secured with self-tapping screws (see Fig. 127). The inlet valve recess in the body is deeper than the outlet valve recess to allow for the filter and extra washer.
    Another feature of the pumps is the incorporation of an air bottle on both the inlet and delivery sides. The inlet air bottle is a chamber in the body casting, blanked off by a simple cover and joint washer, held in position by a single screw.
    The delivery air bottle (Fig. 128) is formed by a flexible plastic diaphragm, separating the delivery chamber in the body from a sealed volume of air contained in the air bottle cover. This cover is secured by four screws and sealed by an 'O' section sealing ring and joint washer.

14. Screw in the inlet and outlet connections with their sealing rings.

15. Assemble the outlet valve components into the outlet recess in the following order: first a joint washer, then the valve assembly, tongue side downwards, then the perforated cap.

16. Assemble the inlet valve into the recess as follows: first a joint washer, then the filter, dome side downwards, then another joint washer, followed by the valve assembly, tongue side upwards, then the perforated cap.

17. Take care that both assemblies nest down evenly into their respective recesses. Place the clamping plate on the cap top and tighten down onto the body with the two screws.

18. Repeat these operations on the remaining valve assembly.

19. Replace the inlet air bottle cover with its joint washer and tighten down the central screw.

20. Place a sealing washer in the bottom of the delivery air bottle recess, place the plastic diaphragm, dome side downwards, then add the 'O' section sealing ring and tighten down the cap with its four screws. The pump should be pressure-tested after disturbance of the delivery air bottle.

Body attachment

21. Fit the joint washer to the body, aligning the screw holes. Offer up the coil housing to the body, ensuring a good seating between them.

22. Line up the six securing screw holes, making sure that the cast lugs in the

coil housing are at the bottom, insert the six 2 B.A. screws finger-tight.

23. Fit the earthing screw with its Lucar connector.

24. **Remove the roller-retaining fork before tightening the body securing screws,** making sure that the rollers retain their position; a displaced roller will cut the diaphragm. It is not necessary to stretch the diaphragm before tightening the securing screws.

25. Tighten the securing screws in sequence as they appear diametrically opposite each other.

Assembly Completion

Complete assembly sequence according to 'Fuel Pump Common Dismantling and Reassembly Procedure' given earlier, from 'Contact Blade' on.

Chapter 11
Mechanical fuel pumps

SU MECHANICAL FUEL PUMPS

TYPE AUF 700 SERIES *Fig 129,130*

Installation

The AUF 700 pump is mounted on the crankcase on two 5/16 in. U.N.F. studs with a heat insulating block and two gaskets, the total thickness of which should not be altered.

The pump rocker lever (1) abuts against the engine cam or push-rod in the space between the camshaft and the side of the crankcase. The rocker lever pivot pin (2) is retained by the walls of the insulating block.

Description

The cover

The outlet cover (3) and its sealing washer (4) are secured by three long No. 10 U.N.F. screws (5).

The body

The body (6) consists of an upper and lower diecasting, between which the diaphragm assembly (7) is clamped. Three short No. 10 U.N.F. screws secure the two halves of the body together, the upper casting containing the inlet and outlet valve moulding (8) and the lower casting containing the rocker lever (1), pivot pin (2), rocker lever tension spring (9), diaphragm spring (10), and the crankcase seal (11) beneath a pressed steel cup (12).

The valves

The larger diameter of the combined valve moulding (8) forms the inlet valve and the two lips at the peak of the moulding form the outlet valve. The valve is a press-fit into its housing on the under-side of the upper body.

Continues on page 146

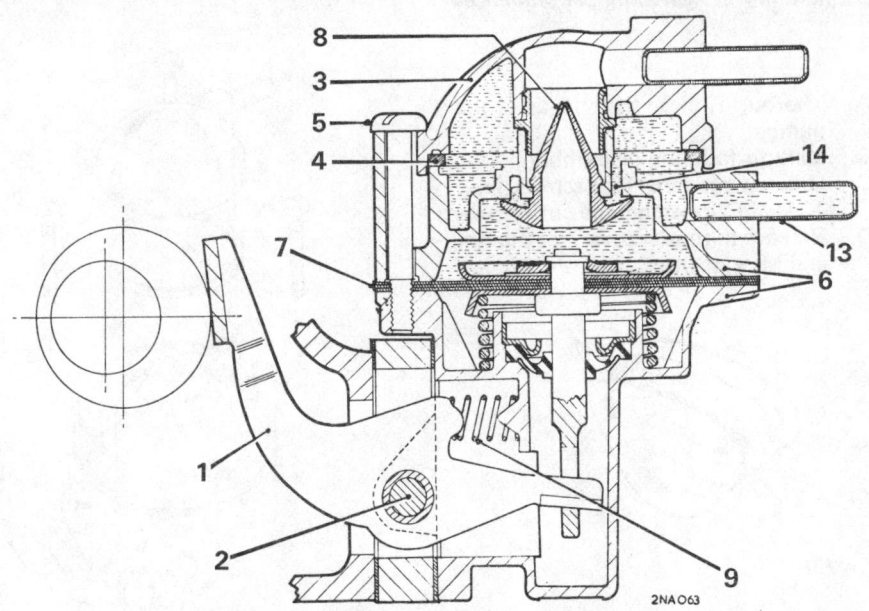

Fig. 129. Type AUF Series 700 Fuel Pump — Induction

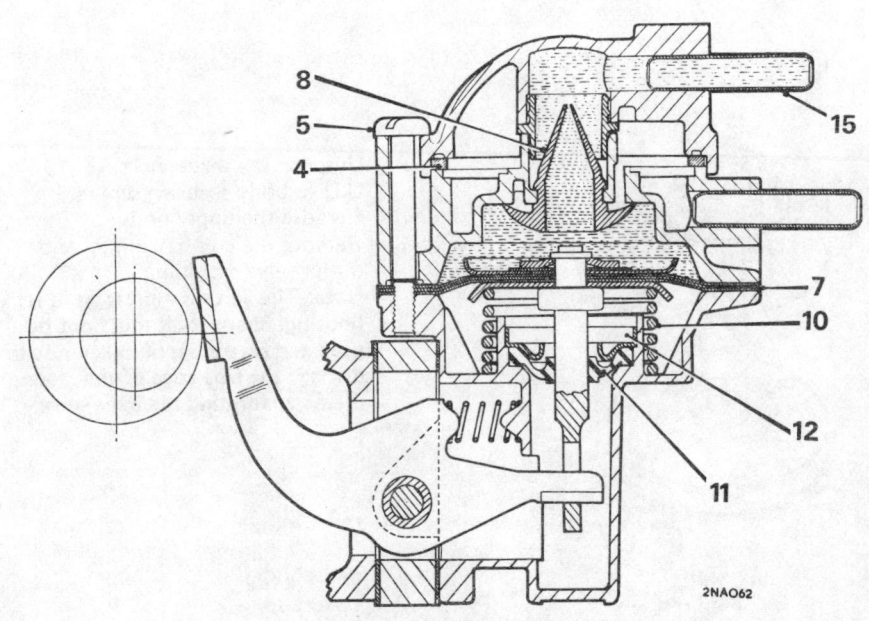

Fig. 130. Type AUF Series 700 Fuel Pump — Delivery

Dismantling *in figure number sequence*

A. Thoroughly clean the outside of the pump
B. Mark to facilitate reassembly
C. Unscrew the three long screws, No. 10 U.N.F., retaining the outlet cover.
D. Remove the outlet cover, sealing ring, and filter, if fitted.

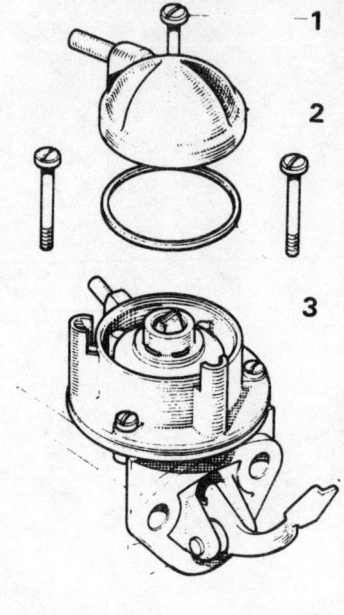

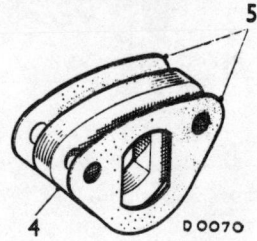

Fig. 131

1. Outlet cover retaining screws.
2. Outlet cover
3. Sealing ring
4. Insulating block
5. Gaskets

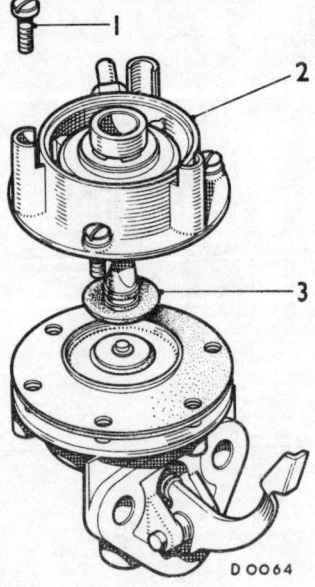

A. Unscrew the three short No. 10 U.N.F. body securing screws.
B. Remove the upper body
C. Remove the combined inlet and outlet valve moulding.
Note: The valve is a press-fit in its housing. Sharp tools must not be used and care must be taken not to damage the fine edge of the larger diameter forming the inlet valve.

Fig. 132

1. Securing screws
2. Upper body
3. Combined inlet/outlet valve

A. Release the diaphragm assembly by tapping out the rocker lever pivot pin from either direction using a soft metal punch, at the same time holding the diaphragm and rocker lever against spring pressure.

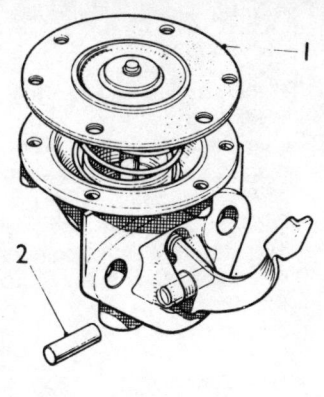

Fig. 133

1. Diaphragm assembly
2. Rocker lever pivot pin

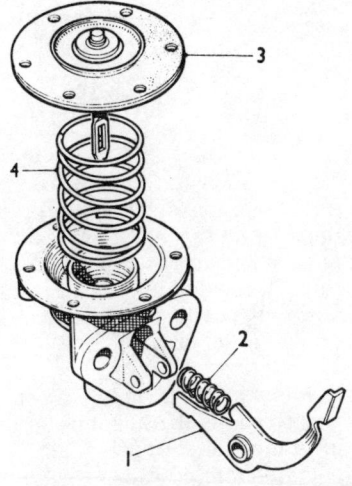

A. Withdraw the rocker lever and spring
B. Withdraw the diaphragm and spring

Fig. 134

1. Rocker lever
2. Rocker lever spring
3. Diaphragm assembly
4. Diaphragm spring

A. The crankcase seal is held in position by a pressed steel cup and should only be removed if a replacement cup is available.
B. When removing the steel cup, care must be taken not to damage the pump body.

Note: Before reassembly all components must be examined for damage and wear. Particular attention must be paid to the outlet valve lips, the fine edge of the large diameter inlet valve, and the plastic insert in the outlet cover. Unserviceable components must be renewed.

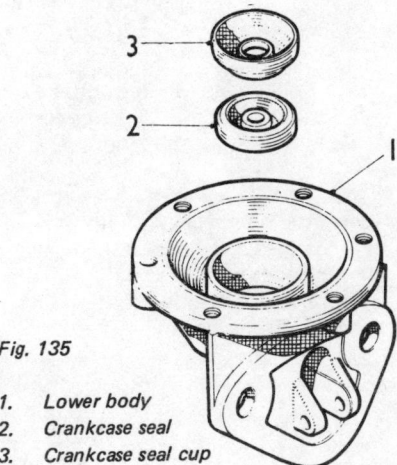

Fig. 135

1. Lower body
2. Crankcase seal
3. Crankcase seal cup

REASSEMBLING

A. Place the diaphragm spring in the lower body.
B. Remove any sharp edges from the diaphragm spindle and stirrup lightly smear with clean engine oil.
C. Position the diaphragm assembly over its spring, pushing the stirrup through the crankcase oil seal, so that the stirrup slot is lined up to receive the rocker lever.

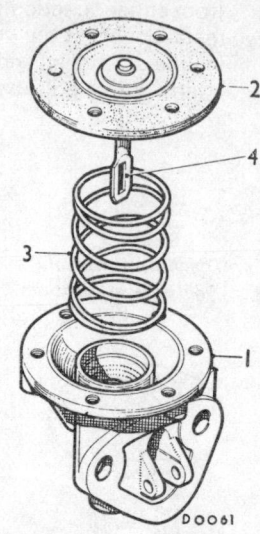

Fig. 136

1. Lower body
2. Diaphragm assembly
3. Diaphragm spring
4. Diaphragm stirrup slot

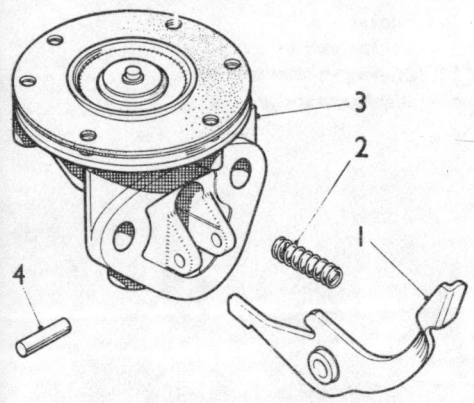

A. Fit the rocker lever and tension spring into the lower body with the rocker lever tip engaged in the diaphragm stirrup slot and the tension spring located both on the conical boss in the casting and the protrusion on the rocker lever.

B. Holding the rocker lever against its tension spring pressure, line up the pivot pin holes and gently tap the pivot pin into position.

Fig. 137

A. Insert the combined inlet/outlet valve into its housing in the upper body and press into position.

B. Ensure that the groove around the valve moulding registers with the ridge in the valve housing, and that the fine edge of the large diameter inlet valve lays evenly on its seating without puckering.

Fig. 138

1. Upper body
2. Combined inlet/outlet valve

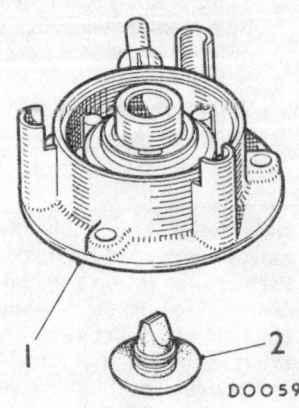

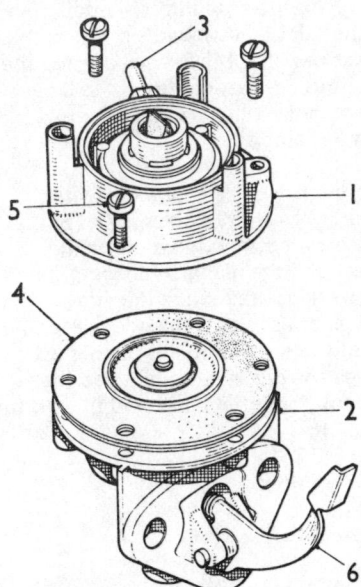

Fig. 139

1. Upper body
2. Lower body
3. Inlet pipe
4. Diaphragm
5. Body securing screws
6. Rocker lever

FIG. 139

A. Depress the rocker lever so that the diaphragm lies flat and position it so that the screw holes in diaphragm and lower body are lined up.

B. Attach the upper body to the lower body with the short screws, ensuring that the inlet pipe is in the correct position. Leave the screws slack at this stage.

REFER FIG 131

A. Replace the filter, if fitted, cover sealing ring, and outlet cover.

B. Insert the three long screws ensuring that they pass freely through the diaphragm holes.

C. Tighten the three short screws evenly.

D. Position the outlet nozzle and tighten the three long screws evenly.

Fuel Pump Dry Testing

The following sequence of tests are recommended when the pump performance is suspect or after dismantling and reassembly.

1. Suction Test — Fig. 140

A. Mount the pump in a soft-jawed vice and connect the lower (inlet) union with the tube to the gauge. (Inset) a pump actuating lever attached to a push-rod operated pump for testing purposes. (The gauge, tube and actuating lever are obtainable from V.L. Churchill and Co. Ltd., P.O. Box 3, London Road, Daventry, Northants under the same part number — 18G 1116)

B. Operate the pump lever through three full strokes. A minimum vacuum reading of 6 in. (152.4 mm.) Hg should be obtained which must not drop at a greater rate than 2 in. (50.8 mm.) in 15 seconds.

C. Disconnect the gauge before continuing.

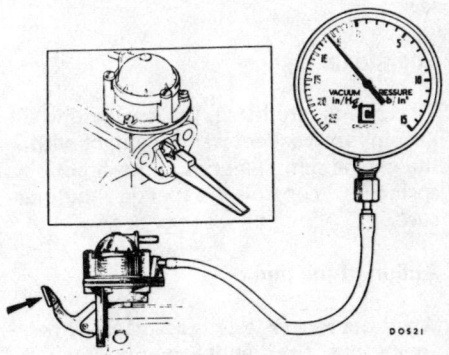

2. Delivery Test — Fig. 141

A. With the pump still mounted in the vice, connect the upper (outlet) union to the gauge using the same tube.

B. Operate the pump lever through two full strokes. A minimum reading of 3 lb./sq. in. (.21 kg./cm²) should be obtained which should not fall by more than ½ lb./sq. in. (.035 kg./cm²) in 15 seconds.

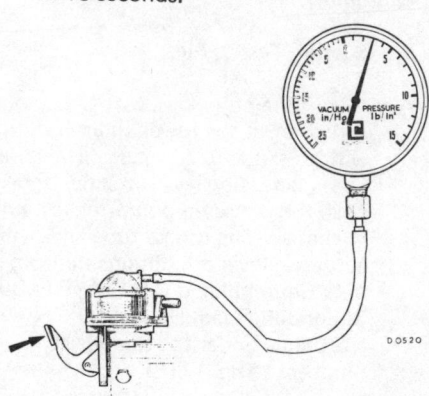

Continued from page 140

The diaphragm assembly

The assembly (7) is riveted and therefore cannot be separated in service. It comprises three separate layers attached to a stirrup which is operated by the rocker lever.

The springs

Two springs are fitted, the smaller one (9) keeping the rocker lever in contact with the engine cam at all times, the larger spring (10) controls the fuel delivery pressure.

Action of the pump

When the rocker lever is actuated by the engine cam, the diaphragm assembly moves downwards and fuel is drawn through the inlet nozzle (13) into the upper body. The fuel passes upwards through the filter (4) into the outer cover, and then flows downwards through an annular passage (14) formed outside the valve housing, past the lip of the large diameter inlet valve flap into the diaphragm chamber.

When the engine cam lobe passes the rocker lever pad, the diaphragm (7) is allowed to move upwards under the influence of the diaphragm spring. The pressure generated in the diaphragm chamber ensures that the inlet valve flap is firmly closed and fuel is discharged through the outlet valve lips into the centre of the outlet cover and thus to the nozzle (15).

Fault diagnosis

Suspected fuel starvation

To check the fuel flow, disconnect the carburetter end of the fuel line and place the line into a suitable container. With the **ignition switched off** rotate the engine:

(1) If the flow is normal, examine the carburetter for obstructed float-chamber needle seating or gummed needle valve.

(2) If the flow is normal initially, but falls off rapidly, check for adequate fuel tank venting by removing the filler cap.

(3) Other causes of a low fuel flow are a choked pump or tank filter.

(4) If quantities of air bubbles emerge from the fuel line whilst it is immersed in a container, check for an air leak in the inlet fuel line.

(5) If there is no flow, check as in (4) and if no air bubbles are present, dismantle the pump and examine the valves and diaphragm.

DO NOT PASS COMPRESSED AIR THROUGH THE PUMP

TYPE AUF 800 SERIES. FIGS. 143, 144

The type AUF 800 Series pump is of sealed unit construction developed to meet the need for a mechanical pump capable of handling fuel at the higher under bonnet temperatures now experienced.

The pumps are manufactured with push-on tube type, or screwed type inlet and outlet connections. An alternative body design provides for a detachable filter.

Installation

The AUF 800 pump is mounted vertically adjacent to an eccentric drive usually on the engine crankcase or camshaft housing. Holes are provided for mounting the pump on 2 X 5/16 in. (8 mm.) studs. Two gaskets with an insulating block between them provide for sealing, heat protection and determine the correct position relative to the pump drive. The pump is actuated by the rocker lever directly from the engine cam or by an intermediate push-rod.

Description

Construction

The AUF 800 pump comprises two main castings; the upper and lower bodies, and two nozzles; inlet and outlet.

Two versions of the pump are available, in one the castings and nozzles are formed into a sealed unit and in the other the nozzles are detachable.

The Body

The body (1) consists of an upper and lower die casting between which the diaphragm assembly (2) is clamped. A lip on the lower body is rolled over the upper casting to form an hermetic seal.

The upper casting houses the moulded inlet and outlet valves (3) & (4) and bosses are formed in it to accept the inlet and outlet nozzles (5) & (6). The lower casting contains the rocker lever (7), pivot pin (8), rocker lever tension spring (9), diaphragm spring (10) and the crankcase seal located beneath a pressed steel cup (11).

The Valves

The inlet and outlet valves (5) & (6) are identical mushroom-shaped elastomeric mouldings controlling ports formed in the upper body casting.

The Diaphragm Assembly

The riveted assembly consists of a single reinforced diaphragm with two large diameter backing plates and a stirrup.

The Springs

A small spring (9) acting on the rocker lever keeps it in contact with the engine cam or push-rod at all times, the diaphragm spring (10) controls the fuel delivery pressure.

Action of the Pump

Fuel Induction

When the diaphragm (2) is pulled down by the rocker lever (7) fuel is drawn into the inlet nozzle (5), passing downwards past the lip of the moulded inlet valve (3) into the diaphragm chamber (12).

Fuel Delivery

When pressure on the rocker lever is released the diaphragm (2) moved upwards under the influence of the diaphragm spring (10). The pressure in the diaphragm chamber ensures that the inlet valve is firmly closed and fuel is discharged past the lip of the moulded outlet valve (4) into the outlet nozzle (6).

Checking

Before removing a suspect pump, check that fault is not from a choked fuel filter

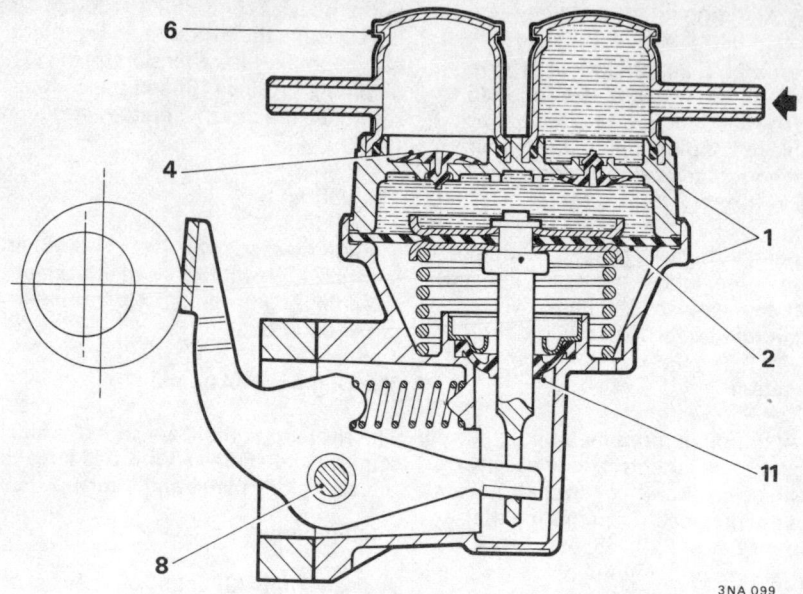

Fig. 142. Type AUF Series 800 Fuel Pump — Induction

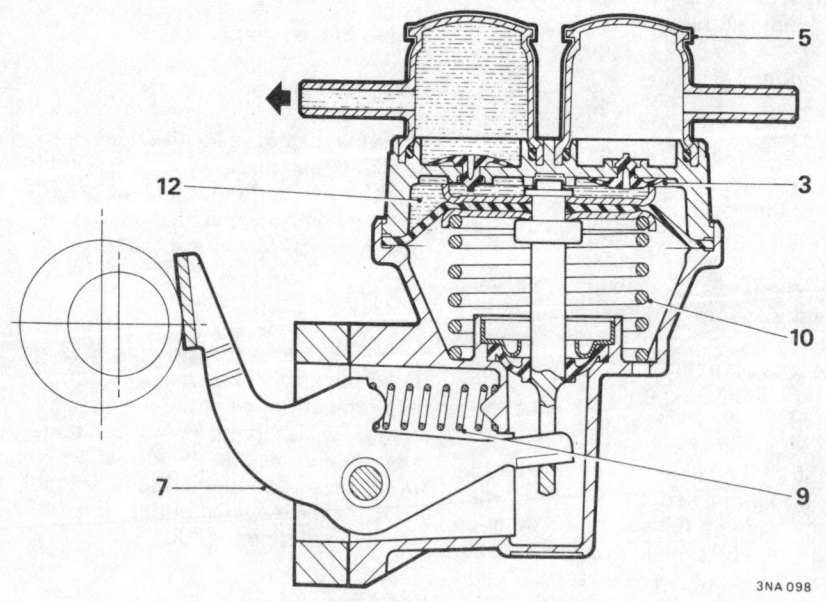

Fig. 143. Type AUF Series 800 Fuel Pump — Delivery

or an obstructed carburetter float valve, that the fuel tank vents are not blocked and that there are no leaks from the connections and pipes between the fuel tank and pump.

With the ignition switched off:

1. Disconnect the fuel pipe from the carburetter and place the end in a suitable container.

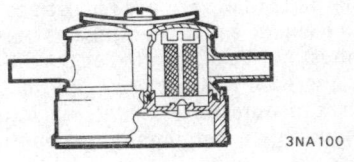

Fig. 144. Alternative body assembly with detachable filter.

2. Rotate the engine and check flow from the pump.

DO NOT PASS COMPRESSED AIR THROUGH THE PUMP

Fuel Pump Dry Testing

If a pump performance is suspect a dry test may be carried out in a similar manner to that described for the AUF 700 Series pumps, with hand operation as follows:—

1. **Suction Test**

With the inlet connected to the gauge, operate the pump lever through three full strokes. A minimum vacuum reading of 9 in (228.6 mm) Hg should be obtained which must not drop at a greater rate than 3 in (76.2 mm) in 5 seconds.

Disconnect the gauge before continuing.

2. **Delivery Test**

With the outlet connected to the gauge, operate the pump lever through two full strokes. A minimum pressure reading of 6 lbs/sq. in (0.42 kg./cm^2) should be obtained which should not fall by more than 2 lb/sq. in (0.14 kg./cm^2) in 5 seconds.

Appendix 1

APPENDIX I – SU FUEL SYSTEMS SPECIFICATION AND APPLICATION DATA

IMPORTANT – EMISSION CONTROLLED VEHICLES

Carburetter specifications appropriate to vehicle model details qualified by

USA   Canada   ECE   or   Sweden

satisfy particular statutory regulations regarding engine emissions. These carburetters must not be dismantled or the settings altered without reference to the relevant manufacturer's servicing instructions and legal constraints in the countries concerned.

Jet Needle Specifications

The jet needle recommendations given are correct at the time of printing and apply to the installation as designed by the relevant vehicle manufacturer. Any change of components related to the induction, engine, or exhaust system will affect the choice of jet needle necessary to maintain optimum performance and economy.

The weak needles given for carburetters fitted with fixed needles are not economy needles – they are to compensate for operation at high altitudes. There is no guarantee that greater economy will result from their use at normal altitudes.

The SU Carburetter Company will gladly give advice if any doubt arises as to the suitability of a needle type on a particular vehicle, or where it is felt that a change of needle is desirable because of modifications carried out to a given installation.

Carburetter Identification

For identification, the carburetter specification number appears on a metal tag attached by one of the float chamber or suction chamber (HIF) cover screws.

Piston Spring Identification

Paint Colour on End Coil	Load at	Length	Part No.	Remarks
Black and green	5¼ oz	2.500 in	AUC 5028	H1 Horizontal carburetters only (special)
Light blue	2½ oz	2.625 in	AUC 4587	
Red	4½ oz	2.635 in	AUC 4387	
Yellow	8 oz	2.750 in	AUC 1167	
Green	12 oz	3.000 in	AUC 1170	
Brown	14 oz	3.000 in	AUC 1168	
White	18 oz	3.562 in	AUC 1166	
Red	4½ oz	1.530 in	AUD 4355	
Yellow	8 oz	1.530 in	AUD 4398	Ball bearing suction chamber
Green	12 oz	1.530 in	JZX 1088	
Red and yellow	24 oz	4.812 in	AUC 4478	
Red and white	40½ oz	3.875 in	AUC 4869	
Red and green	11¼ oz	3.875 in	AUC 4826	2 in diameter throttle carburetters only
Light blue and black	4½ oz	3.875 in	AUC 2107*	
Light blue and red	18 oz	3.875 in	AUC 4818†	

* Used in place of AUC 5014 Red and Black † Used in place of AUC 2091 Blue and Green

SU4.6.

Starting Device (Thermo) Spring Identification

Colour on End Coil	Load at Length		Part No.
White	1¾ oz	1 in	AUC 1195
Blue	2¼ oz	1 in	AUC 1041
Yellow	2¾ oz	1 in	AUC 5021
Red	3¼ oz	1 in	AUC 3427
Green	3¾ oz	1 in	AUC 3127

Throttle Sizes

Throttle Diameter	Carburetter Type
1 1/8 in	H1
1¼ in	H2, HS2
1½ in	H4, HD4, HS4, HS4C, HIF4
1¾ in	H6, HD6, HS6, HIF6
1 7/8 in	HIF7
2 in	H8, HD8, HS8

Alternative Mechanical Pump Specifications

Important: When fitting an AUF 800 series alternative in place of the original AUF 700 series pump a replacement Insulator Assembly will be required as follows:

AUF 800 Insulator Part No. AUB 5029

Fuel systems application details

Model Details	Capacity	No. of Cyl.	Year	Spec.	Position[1]	Inter Connect	Type	Rich	Needle Std.	Weak
ALVIS										
TD 21	3 litre	6	1963/64	AUD 128F	F	—	HD6	—	AUD 1470	—
				AUD 128R	R	—	HD6TH[2]	—	AUD 1470	—
TF21 Series IV	3 litre	6	1965/66	AUD 226F	F	—	HD6	—	AUD 1319	—
				AUD 226C	C	—	HD6	—	AUD 1319	—
				AUD 226R	R	—	HD6TH[2]	—	AUD 1319	—
ASTON MARTIN										
DB5	3.7 litre	6	1962/64	AUD 88F	F	—	HD8	—	AUD 1498	—
				AUD 88C	C	—	HD8	—	AUD 1498	—
				AUD 88R	R	—	HD8	—	AUD 1498	—
DB6	4000cc	6	1965/67	AUD 88F	F	—	HD8	—	AUD 1498	—
				AUD 88C	C	—	HD8	—	AUD 1498	—
				AUD 88R	R	—	HD8	—	AUD 1498	—
AUSTIN										
A35 Van	848cc	4	1965/70	AUD 120	—	RHIC	HS2	AUD 1261	AUD 1149	AUD 1211
A40 Mk II	1098cc	4	1962/67	AUD 13	—	RHIC	HS2	AUD 1242	AUD 1478	AUD 1149
Westminster 110	2912cc	6	1967	AUD 240F	F	RHIC	H4	AUD 1002	AUD 1048	AUD 1230
				AUD 240R	R	LHIC	H4	AUD 1002	AUD 1048	AUD 1230
Austin Healey 3000 Mk III	2912cc	6	1964	AUD 124F	F	RHIC	HD8	AUD 1474	AUD 1370	AUD 1466
				AUD 124R	R	LHIC	HD8	AUD 1474	AUD 1370	AUD 1466
3 Litre	2912cc	6	1967/68	AUD 217F	F	RHIC	HS6	AUD 1361	AUD 1089	AUD 1117
				AUD 217R	R	LHIC	HS6	AUD 1361	AUD 1099	AUD 1117
A60	1622cc	4	1961/70	AUD 40	—	RHIC	HS2	AUD 1261	AUD 1227	AUD 1211
10cwt Van	1622cc	4	1971/72	AUD 523	—	RHIC	HS2	AUD 1261	AUD 1227	AUD 1211
Mini	848cc	4	1962/68	AUC 976	—	RHIC	HS2	AUD 1261	AUD 1149	AUD 1211
Mini Automatic	848cc	4	1965/67	AUD 170	—	LHIC	HS4	AUD 1242	AUD 1478	AUD 1149
Mini Automatic	848cc	4	1967/68	AUD 250	—	LHIC	HS4	AUD 1242	AUD 1478	AUD 1149
Mini Mk II	848cc	4	1968/70	AUD 239	—	RHIC	HS2	AUD 1261	AUD 1149	AUD 1211
Mini Mk II Automatic	848cc	4	1969/71	AUD 380	—	LHIC	HS4	AUD 1242	AUD 1478	AUD 1149
Mini Mk II	848cc	4	1969/74	AUD 359	—	RHIC	HS2	—	AUD 1149	—
Mini Mk II Automatic	848cc	4	1971/74	AUD 394	—	LHIC	HS4	—	AUD 1478	—
Mini (E.C.E.)	848cc	4	1971/74	AUD 449	—	RHIC	HS2	—	CUD 1019	—
Mini Van (G.P.O.)	848cc	4	1972/74	AUD 587	—	RHIC	HS2	—	CUD 1019	—
Mini Van (G.U.S.)	848cc	4	1974/75	AUD 713	—	LHIC	HS4	—	CUD 1040	—
Mini (E.C.E.)	848cc	4	1974/	AUD 611	—	LHIC	HS4	—	CUD 1040	—
Mini 850	848cc	4	1975	FZX 1043	—	LHIC	HS4	—	NZX 4008	—
Mini 850	848cc	4	1975/	FZX 1084	—	LHIC	HS4	—	NZX 4008	—
Mini 850	848cc	4	1976/	FZX 1142	—	LHIC	HS4	—	NZX 4008	—
Mini Mk II	998cc	4	1967/68	AUD 86	—	RHIC	HS2	AUD 1261	AUD 1227	AUD 1211
Mini Mk II Automatic	998cc	4	1967/68	AUD 184	—	LHIC	HS4	AUD 1267	AUD 1034	AUD 1230
Mini Mk II	998cc	4	1968/70	AUD 238	—	RHIC	HS2	AUD 1261	AUD 1227	AUD 1211
Mini Mk II Automatic	998cc	4	1969	AUD 366	—	LHIC	HS4	AUD 1267	AUD 1034	AUD 1230
Mini Mk II Automatic	998cc	4	1970	AUD 367	—	LHIC	HS4	AUD 1267	AUD 1034	AUD 1230
Mini Mk II	998cc	4	1970/71	AUD 363	—	RHIC	HS2	AUD 1261	AUD 1227	AUD 1211
Mini Mk II Automatic	998cc	4	1970/74	AUD 383	—	LHIC	HS4	AUD 1267	AUD 1034	AUD 1230
Mini Mk II (E.C.E.)	998cc	4	1971/75	AUD 509	—	RHIC	HS4	—	CUD 1019	—
Mini Mk II Man/Auto (E.C.E.)	998cc	4	1974/76	AUD 679	—	LHIC	HS4	—	CUD 1045	—
Mini Van (G.P.O.)	998cc	4	1974/	AUD 706	—	LHIC	HS4	—	CUD 1045	—
Mini (Canada)	998cc	4	1972/73	AUD 548	—	LHIC	HS4	—	CUD 1006	—
Mini (Canada)	998cc	4	1973	AUD 618	—	LHIC	HS4	—	CUD 1032	—
Mini (Canada)	998cc	4	1974/	AUD 654	—	LHIC	HS4	—	CUD 1032	—
Mini (Canada)	998cc	4	1975/	FZX 1016	—	LHIC	HS4	—	NZX 4004	—
Mini 1000	998cc	4	1975	FZX 1044	—	LHIC	HS4	—	NZX 4005	—
Mini 1000	998cc	4	1975/	FZX 1085	—	LHIC	HS4	—	NZX 4005	—
Mini 1000 (Sweden)	998cc	4	1975/	FZX 1094	—	LHIC	HS4	—	NZX 4006	—
Mini 1000	998cc	4	1976/	FZX 1146	—	LHIC	HS4	—	NZX 4005	—
Mini Mk II Man/Auto (E.C.E.)	1098cc	4	1973/75	AUD 608	—	LHIC	HS4	—	CUD 1037	—
Export only	1098cc	4	1975	FZX 1045	—	LHIC	HS4	—	CUD 1037	—
Mini 1100	1098cc	4	1975/	FZX 1086	—	LHIC	HS4	—	CUD 1037	—
Mini 1100	1098cc	4	1976/	FZX 1160	—	LHIC	HS4	—	CUD 1037	—
Mini Clubman	998cc	4	1969/71	AUD 363	—	RHIC	HS2	AUD 1261	AUD 1387	AUD 1211
Mini Clubman (E.C.E.)	998cc	4	1971/75	AUD 509	—	RHIC	HS2	—	CUD 1019	—
Mini Clubman Automatic	998cc	4	1970/74	AUD 383	—	LHIC	HS4	AUD 1267	AUD 1034	AUD 1230
Mini Clubman Automatic	998cc	4	1972/	AUD 460	—	LHIC	HS4	—	CUD 1006	—
Mini Clubman Man/Auto (E.C.E.)	998cc	4	1974/76	AUD 679	—	LHIC	HS4	—	CUD 1045	—
Mini Clubman 1275 GT	1275cc	4	1969/71	AUD 317	—	LHIC	HS4	AUD 1075	AUD 1528	AUD 1096
Mini Clubman 1275 GT	1275cc	4	1971/72	AUD 451	—	LHIC	HS4	—	CUD 1015	—
Mini Clubman 1275 GT (E.C.E.)	1275cc	4	1972/76	AUD 587	—	LHIC	HS4	—	CUD 1325	—
Mini Clubman 1275 GT	1275cc	4	1975/	FZX 1047	—	LHIC	HS4	—	CUD 1025	—
Mini 1275 GT	1275cc	4	1975	FZX 1046	—	LHIC	HS4	—	CUD 1025	—
Mini 1275 GT	1275cc	4	1976/	FZX 1164	—	LHIC	HS4	—	CUD 1025	—

[1] Front F, Centre C, Rear R, Right Hand RH, Left Hand LH. [2] Thermocarb gasket pack required in addition AUE 807.
[3] Air jet 0.116 in. diameter.

Spec. Repeated	Needle Guide	Needle Screw	Piston Spring	Damper	Jet	Needle and Seat	Float	Throttle Spindle	Throttle Disc	Gasket Pack	OE	Pump Alt.
AUD 128F	—	AUC 2057	AUC 4387	AUC 8102	AUC 8155	WZX 1102	WZX 1303	—	WZX 1321	AUE 805	—	—
AUD 128R	—	AUC 2057	AUC 4387	AUC 8102	AUC 8155	WZX 1102	WZX 1303	—	WZX 1321	AUE 805	—	—
AUD 226F	—	AUC 2057	AUC 4387	AUC 8102	AUC 8155	WZX 1101	WZX 1303	WZX 1214	WZX 1321	AUE 805	—	—
AUD 226C	—	AUC 2057	AUC 4387	AUC 8102	AUC 8155	WZX 1101	WZX 1303	WZX 1214	WZX 1321	AUE 805	—	—
AUD 226R	—	AUC 2057	AUC 4387	AUC 8102	AUC 8155	WZX 1101	WZX 1303	WZX 1197	WZX 1321	AUE 805	—	—
AUD 88F	—	AUC 2057	AUC 4826	AUC 8115	AUC 8156	WZX 1102	WZX 1303	WZX 1196	WZX 1373	AUE 806	AUB 161	AUF 406
AUD 88C	—	AUC 2057	AUC 4826	AUC 8115	AUC 8156	WZX 1102	WZX 1303	WZX 1196	WZX 1373	AUE 806	—	—
AUD 88R	—	AUC 2057	AUC 4826	AUC 8115	AUC 8156	WZX 1102	WZX 1303	WZX 1196	WZX 1373	AUE 806	—	—
AUD 88F	—	AUC 2057	AUC 4826	AUC 8115	AUC 8156	WZX 1102	WZX 1303	WZX 1196	WZX 1373	AUE 806	AUF 402	—
AUD 88C	—	AUC 2057	AUC 4826	AUC 8115	AUC 8156	WZX 1102	WZX 1303	WZX 1196	WZX 1373	AUE 806	—	—
AUD 88R	—	AUC 2057	AUC 4826	AUC 8115	AUC 8156	WZX 1102	WZX 1303	WZX 1196	WZX 1373	AUE 806	—	—
AUD 120	—	AUC 2057	AUC 4387	AUC 8103	AUD 9098	WZX 1100	WZX 1300	WZX 1310	WZX 1320	AUE 810	—	—
AUD 13	—	AUC 2057	AUC 4387	AUC 8103	AUD 9098	WZX 1100	WZX 1303	WZX 1310	WZX 1320	AUE 810	AUB 83	AUF 204
AUD 240F	—	AUC 2057	AUC 1167	AUC 8102	AUC 8182	WZX 1100	WZX 1303	WZX 1590	WZX 1592	AUE 801	AUF 208	AUF 204
AUD 240R	—	AUC 2057	AUC 1167	AUC 8102	AUC 8182	WZX 1100	WZX 1303	WZX 1591	WZX 1592	AUE 801	—	—
AUD 124F	—	AUC 2057	AUC 4826	AUC 8112	AUC 8156	WZX 1101	WZX 1303	WZX 1198	WZX 1373	AUE 806	AUA 173	AUF 303
AUD 124R	—	AUC 2057	AUC 4826	AUC 8112	AUC 8156	WZX 1101	WZX 1303	WZX 1199	WZX 1373	AUE 806	—	—
AUD 217F	—	AUC 2057	AUC 1167	AUC 8103	AUD 9105	WZX 1101	WZX 1300	WZX 1311	WZX 1321	AUE 812	AUF 708	AUF 811
AUD 217R	—	AUC 2057	AUC 1167	AUC 8103	AUD 9106	WZX 1101	WZX 1300	WZX 1311	WZX 1321	AUE 812	—	—
AUD 40	—	AUC 2057	AUC 1167	AUC 8103	AUD 9098	WZX 1100	WZX 1300	WZX 1310	WZX 1320	AUE 810	AUB 83	AUF 204
AUD 523	—	AUC 2057	AUC 1167	AUC 8103	AUD 9098	WZX 1100	WZX 1300	WZX 1310	WZX 1320	AUE 810	AUF 204	—
AUC 976	—	AUC 2057	AUC 4387	AUC 8103	AUD 9098	WZX 1100	WZX 1300	WZX 1310	WZX 1320	AUE 810	AUF 214	—
AUD 170	—	AUC 2057	AUC 4387	AUC 8103	AUD 9142	WZX 1100	WZX 1300	WZX 1312	WZX 1323	AUE 811	AUF 201	AUF 214
AUD 250	—	AUC 2057	AUC 4387	AUC 8103	AUD 9451	WZX 1100	WZX 1300	WZX 1312	WZX 1324	AUE 811	AUF 201	AUF 214
AUD 299	—	AUC 2057	AUC 4387	AUC 8103	AUD 9098	WZX 1100	WZX 1300	WZX 1310	WZX 1320	AUE 810	AUF 214	—
AUD 360	—	AUC 2057	AUC 4387	AUC 8103	AUD 9451	WZX 1100	WZX 1300	WZX 1312	WZX 1324	AUE 811	AUF 214	—
AUD 359	—	AUC 2057	AUC 4387	AUC 8103	AUD 9098	WZX 1100	WZX 1300	WZX 1310	WZX 1320	AUE 810	AUF 214/AUF 706	AUF 805
AUD 394	—	AUC 2057	AUC 4387	AUC 8103	AUD 9451	WZX 1100	WZX 1300	WZX 1312	WZX 1324	AUE 811	AUF 722	AUF 812
AUD 449	AUD 4288	AUD 4250	AUC 4387	AUC 8103	AUD 9098	WZX 1100	WZX 1300	WZX 1310	WZX 1320	AUE 810	AUF 706	AUF 805
AUD 587	AUD 4288	AUD 4250	AUC 4387	AUC 8103	AUD 9098	WZX 1100	WZX 1300	WZX 1310	WZX 1320	AUE 810	AUF 706	AUF 805
AUD 713	AUD 4288	AUD 4251	AUC 4387	CUD 4103	AUD 9451	WZX 1100	WZX 1300	WZX 1312	WZX 1324	AUE 811	AUF 706	AUF 805
AUD 611	AUD 4288	AUD 4251	AUC 4387	CUD 4103	LZX 1111	WZX 1100	WZX 1300	WZX 1312	WZX 1324	AUE 811	AUF 812	—
FZX 1043	AUD 4288	AUD 4251	AUC 4387	CUD 4103	LZX 1111	WZX 1100	WZX 1300	WZX 1312	WZX 1324	AUE 811	AUF 812	—
FZX 1064	AUD 4288	AUD 4251	AUC 4387	CUD 4103	AUD 9451	WZX 1100	WZX 1300	WZX 1312	WZX 1324	AUE 811	AUF 812	—
FZX 1142	AUD 4288	AUD 4251	AUC 4387	CUD 4103	LZX 1111	WZX 1100	WZX 1300	WZX 1312	WZX 1324	AUE 811	AUF 812	—
AUD 86	—	AUC 2057	AUC 4387	AUC 8103	AUD 9098	WZX 1100	WZX 1300	WZX 1310	WZX 1320	AUE 810	AUF 201	AUF 214
AUD 184	—	AUC 2057	AUC 4387	AUC 8103	AUD 9451	WZX 1100	WZX 1300	WZX 1312	WZX 1324	AUE 811	AUF 201	AUF 214
AUD 298	—	AUC 2057	AUC 4387	AUC 8103	AUD 9098	WZX 1100	WZX 1300	WZX 1310	WZX 1320	AUE 810	AUF 214	—
AUD 366	—	AUC 2057	AUC 4387	AUC 8103	AUD 9451	WZX 1100	WZX 1300	WZX 1312	WZX 1324	AUE 811	AUF 201	AUF 214
AUD 367	—	AUC 2057	AUC 4387	AUC 8103	AUD 9451	WZX 1100	WZX 1300	WZX 1312	WZX 1324	AUE 811	AUF 214	—
AUD 363	—	AUC 2057	AUC 4387	AUC 8103	AUD 9098	WZX 1100	WZX 1300	WZX 1310	WZX 1320	AUE 810	AUF 214	—
AUD 393	—	AUC 2057	AUC 4387	AUC 8193	AUD 9451	WZX 1100	WZX 1300	WZX 1312	WZX 1323	AUE 811	AUF 214/AUF 722	AUF 812
AUD 509	AUD 4288	AUD 4250	AUC 4387	AUC 8103	AUD 9098	WZX 1100	WZX 1300	WZX 1310	WZX 1320	AUE 810	AUF 706	AUF 805
AUD 679	AUD 4288	AUD 4251	AUC 4387	AUC 8103	AUD 9451	WZX 1100	WZX 1300	WZX 1312	WZX 1324	AUE 811	AUF 706	AUF 805
AUD 706	AUD 4288	AUD 4251	AUC 4387	AUC 8103	AUD 9451	WZX 1100	WZX 1300	WZX 1312	WZX 1324	AUE 811	AUF 722	AUF 812
AUD 548	AUD 4288	AUD 4251	AUC 4387	AUC 8103	AUD 9451	WZX 1100	WZX 1300	WZX 1312	WZX 1325	AUE 811	AUF 722	AUF 812
AUD 618	AUD 4288	AUD 4251	AUC 4387	AUC 8103	AUD 9451	WZX 1100	WZX 1300	WZX 1312	WZX 1325	AUE 811	AUF 722	AUF 812
AUD 654	AUD 4288	AUD 4251	AUC 4387	AUC 8103	AUD 9451	WZX 1100	WZX 1300	WZX 1312	WZX 1325	AUE 811	AUF 812	—
FZX 1016	AUD 4288	AUD 4251	AUC 4387	AUC 8103	AUD 9451	WZX 1100	WZX 1300	WZX 1312	WZX 1325	AUE 811	AUF 812	—
FZX 1044	AUD 4288	AUD 4251	AUC 4387	AUC 8103	LZX 1111	WZX 1100	WZX 1300	WZX 1312	WZX 1324	AUE 811	AUF 812	—
FZX 1065	AUD 4288	AUD 4251	AUC 4387	AUC 8103	AUD 9451	WZX 1100	WZX 1300	WZX 1312	WZX 1324	AUE 811	AUF 812	—
FZX 1094	AUD 4288	AUD 4251	AUC 4387	AUC 8103	AUD 9451	WZX 1100	WZX 1300	WZX 1312	WZX 1325	AUE 811	AUF 812	—
FZX 1146	AUD 4288	AUD 4251	AUC 4387	AUC 8103	LZX 1111	WZX 1100	WZX 1300	WZX 1312	WZX 1324	AUE 811	AUF 812	—
AUD 608	AUD 4288	AUD 4251	AUC 4387	AUC 8103	AUD 9451	WZX 1100	WZX 1300	WZX 1312	WZX 1325	AUE 811	AUF 706	AUF 805
FZX 1045	AUD 4288	AUD 4251	AUC 4387	AUC 8103	LZX 1111	WZX 1100	WZX 1300	WZX 1312	WZX 1325	AUE 811	AUF 812	—
FZX 1066	AUD 4288	AUD 4251	AUC 4387	AUC 8103	AUD 9451	WZX 1100	WZX 1300	WZX 1312	WZX 1325	AUE 811	AUF 812	—
FZX 1160	AUD 4288	AUD 4251	AUC 4387	AUC 8103	LZX 1111	WZX 1100	WZX 1300	WZX 1312	WZX 1325	AUE 811	AUF 812	—
AUD 363	—	AUC 2057	AUC 4387	AUC 8103	AUD 9098	WZX 1100	WZX 1300	WZX 1310	WZX 1320	AUE 810	AUF 705	AUF 812
AUD 509	AUD 4288	AUC 4250	AUC 4387	AUC 8103	AUD 9098	WZX 1100	WZX 1300	WZX 1310	WZX 1320	AUE 810	AUF 706	AUF 805
AUD 393	—	AUC 2057	AUC 4387	AUC 8103	AUD 9451	WZX 1100	WZX 1300	WZX 1312	WZX 1323	AUE 811	AUF 722	AUF 812
AUD 450	AUD 4288	AUD 4251	AUC 4387	AUC 8103	AUD 9451	WZX 1101	WZX 1300	WZX 1312	WZX 1324	AUE 811	AUF 706	AUF 805
AUD 679	AUD 4288	AUD 4251	AUC 4387	AUC 8103	AUD 9451	WZX 1100	WZX 1300	WZX 1312	WZX 1324	AUE 811	AUF 722	—
AUD 317	—	AUC 2057	AUC 4387	AUC 8103	AUD 9451	WZX 1100	WZX 1300	WZX 1312	WZX 1323	AUE 811	AUF 722	AUF 812
AUD 451	AUD 4288	AUC 4251	AUC 4387	AUC 8103	AUD 9451	WZX 1100	WZX 1300	WZX 1312	WZX 1324	AUE 811	AUF 722	AUF 812
AUD 567	AUD 4288	AUD 4251	AUC 4387	AUC 8103	AUD 9451	WZX 1100	WZX 1300	WZX 1312	WZX 1390	AUE 811	AUF 812	—
FZX 1147	AUD 4288	AUD 4251	AUC 4387	AUC 8103	AUD 9451	WZX 1100	WZX 1300	WZX 1312	WZX 1390	AUE 811	AUF 812	—
FZX 1046	AUD 4288	AUD 4251	AUC 4387	AUC 8103	LZX 1111	WZX 1100	WZX 1300	WZX 1312	WZX 1390	AUE 811	AUF 812	—
FZX 1164	AUD 4288	AUD 4251	AUC 4387	AUC 8103	LZX 1111	WZX 1100	WZX 1300	WZX 1312	WZX 1390	AUE 811	AUF 812	—

[3] AED Unit TZX 1002 supersedes AUH 308, 309, 310 and 317/(1 per installation). [4] Service AED Unit AUH 300 (1 per installation).
[6] Air jet 0.102 in. diameter.   [7] Service AED Unit AUH 305 1 per installation Rover (U.S.A.) spec. only.

Model Details	Capacity	No. of Cyl.	Year	Spec.	¹ Position	Inter Connect	Type	Rich	Needle Std.	Weak
Mini Cooper Mk I & Mk II	998cc	4	1964/69	AUD 104L	LH	RHIC	HS2	AUD 1261	AUD 1468	AUD 1211
				AUD 104R	RH	LHIC	HS2	AUD 1261	AUD 1468	AUD 1211
Mini Cooper 'S'	970cc	4	1964	AUD 151L	LH	RHIC	HS2	AUD 1242	AUD 1478	AUD 1149
				AUD 151R	RH	LHIC	HS2	AUD 1242	AUD 1478	AUD 1149
Mini Cooper 'S'	1070cc	4	1963/64	AUD 99L	LH	RHIC	HS2	AUD 1002	AUD 1242	AUD 1149
				AUD 99R	RH	LHIC	HS2	AUD 1002	AUD 1242	AUD 1149
Mini Cooper 'S'	1275cc	4	1964/70	AUD 146L	LH	RHIC	HS2	AUD 1059	AUD 1261	AUD 1149
				AUD 146R	RH	LHIC	HS2	AUD 1059	AUD 1261	AUD 1149
Mini Cooper 'S'	1275cc	4	1970/71	AUD 440L	LH	RHIC	HS2	AUD 1059	AUD 1261	AUD 1149
				AUD 440R	RH	LHIC	HS2	AUD 1059	AUD 1261	AUD 1149
1100	1098cc	4	1962/67	AUD 13	—	RHIC	HS2	AUD 1242	AUD 1478	AUD 1149
1100 Automatic	1098cc	4	1965/67	AUD 185	—	LHIC	HS4	AUD 1076	AUD 1522	AUD 1151
1100 Mk II	1098cc	4	1967/71	AUD 13	—	RHIC	HS2	AUD 1242	AUD 1478	AUD 1149
1100 Mk II Automatic	1098cc	4	1967/68	AUD 251	—	LHIC	HS4	AUD 1076	AUD 1522	AUD 1151
1100 Mk II Automatic	1098cc	4	1969/71	AUD 370	—	LHIC	HS4	AUD 1076	AUD 1522	AUD 1151
1100 Mk II	1098cc	4	1971/72	AUD 368	—	RHIC	HS2	AUD 1242	AUD 1478	AUD 1149
1100 Mk III	1098cc	4	1971/74	AUD 368	—	RHIC	HS2	AUD 1242	AUD 1478	AUD 1149
1100 Mk III Automatic	1098cc	4	1971/74	AUD 371	—	LHIC	HS4	AUD 1076	AUD 1522	AUD 1151
1100 Mk III (E.C.E.)	1098cc	4	1971/74	AUD 508	—	LHIC	HS4	—	CUD 1022	—
1300	1275cc	4	1967/68	AUD 186	—	LHIC	HS4	AUD 1076	AUD 1528	AUD 1096
1300 Automatic	1275cc	4	1967/68	AUD 271	—	LHIC	HS4	AUD 1076	AUD 1528	AUD 1096
1300	1275cc	4	1969/70	AUD 374	—	LHIC	HS4	AUD 1076	AUD 1528	AUD 1096
1300 Automatic	1275cc	4	1969/70	AUD 376	—	LHIC	HS4	AUD 1076	AUD 1528	AUD 1096
1300 GT	1275cc	4	1969/71	AUD 344L	L	RHIC	HS2	AUD 1261	AUD 1468	AUD 1211
				AUD 344R	R	LHIC	HS2	AUD 1261	AUD 1468	AUD 1211
1300	1275cc	4	1971	AUD 472	—	LHIC	HS4	AUD 1076	AUD 1528	AUD 1096
1300 GT	1275cc	4	1971	AUD 431L	L	RHIC	HS2	AUD 1261	AUD 1468	AUD 1211
				AUD 431R	R	LHIC	HS2	AUD 1261	AUD 1468	AUD 1211
1300	1275cc	4	1971/72	AUD 480	—	LHIC	HS4	AUD 1076	AUD 1528	AUD 1096
1300 GT	1275cc	4	1971/72	AUD 454L	LH	RHIC	HS2	—	CUD 1013	—
				AUD 454R	RH	LHIC	HS2	—	CUD 1013	—
1300 Mk III (E.C.E.)	1275cc	4	1971/72	AUD 453	—	LHIC	HS4	—	CUD 1015	—
1300 GT (E.C.E.)	1275cc	4	1971/72	AUD 496L	LH	RHIC	HS2	—	CUD 1013	—
				AUD 496R	RH	LHIC	HS2	—	CUD 1013	—
1300 Mk I & III (E.C.E.)	1275cc	4	1972/73	AUD 559	—	LHIC	HS4	—	CUD 1025	—
1300 Mk III (E.C.E.)	1275cc	4	1972/73	AUD 585	—	LHIC	HS4	—	CUD 1015	—
1300 Mk III (E.C.E.)	1275cc	4	1973/4	AUD 594	—	LHIC	HS4	—	CUD 1025	—
1300 Mk III (E.C.E.)	1275cc	4	1973/	AUD 595	—	LHIC	HS4	—	CUD 1015	—
1300 Mk III Automatic (E.C.E.)	1275cc	4	1971/74	AUD 486	—	LHIC	HS4	—	CUD 1015	—
1300 Mk III Automatic (E.C.E.)	1275cc	4	1972/76	AUD 567	—	LHIC	HS4	—	CUD 1025	—
Austin-Healey Sprite Mk III	1098cc	4	1964/66	AUD 136F	F	RHIC	HS2	AUD 1242	AUD 1478	AUD 1211
				AUD 136R	R	LHIC	HS2	AUD 1242	AUD 1478	AUD 1211
Austin-Healey Sprite Mk IV	1275cc	4	1967/68	AUD 136F	F	RHIC	HS2	AUD 1242	AUD 1478	AUD 1211
				AUD 136R	R	LHIC	HS2	AUD 1242	AUD 1478	AUD 1211
Austin-Healey Sprite Mk IV	1275cc	4	1968/71	AUD 327F	F	RHIC	HS2	AUD 1242	AUD 1478	AUD 1211
				AUD 327R	R	LHIC	HS2	AUD 1242	AUD 1478	AUD 1211
Austin Sprite Mk IV	1275cc	4	1971	AUD 327F	F	RHIC	HS2	AUD 1242	AUD 1478	AUD 1211
				AUD 327R	R	LHIC	HS2	AUD 1242	AUD 1478	AUD 1211
Austin-Healey Sprite Mk IV (U.S.A.)	1275cc	4	1968	AUD 266F	F	RHIC	HS2	—	AUD 1478	—
				AUD 266R	R	LHIC	HS2	—	AUD 1478	—
Austin-Healey Sprite Mk IV (U.S.A.)	1275cc	4	1968/69	AUD 328F	F	RHIC	HS2	—	CUD 1002	—
				AUD 328R	R	LHIC	HS2	—	CUD 1002	—
Austin-Healey Sprite Mk IV (U.S.A.)	1275cc	4	1969/71	AUD 404F	F	RHIC	HS2	—	CUD 1002	—
				AUD 404R	R	LHIC	HS2	—	CUD 1002	—
Austin Sprite (U.S.A.)	1275cc	4	1972/74	AUD 549F	F	RHIC	HS2	—	CUD 1026	—
				AUD 549R	R	LHIC	HS2	—	CUD 1026	—
Austin America Automatic	1275cc	4	1968	AUD 296	--	LHIC	HS4	—	AUD 1528	—
Austin America	1275cc	4	1968	AUD 281	—	LHIC	HS4	—	AUD 1528	—
Austin America Automatic	1275cc	4	1969	AUD 380	—	LHIC	HS4	—	CUD 1006	—
Austin America	1275cc	4	1969	AUD 379	—	LHIC	HS4	—	CUD 1006	—
Austin America	1275cc	4	1969/71	AUD 345	—	LHIC	HS4	—	CUD 1006	—
Austin America Automatic	1275cc	4	1969/71	AUD 346	—	LHIC	HS4	—	CUD 1006	—
Austin Marina (U.S.A.)	1798cc	4	1972	AUD 494	—	RHIC	HIF6	—	CUD 1128	—
Austin Marina Automatic (U.S.A.)	1798cc	4	1972	AUD 495	—	RHIC	HIF6	—	CUD 1128	—
Austin Marina (U.S.A.)	1798cc	4	1972/74	AUD 583	—	RHIC	HIF6	—	CUD 1138	—
Austin Marina Automatic (U.S.A.)	1798cc	4	1972/74	AUD 584	—	RHIC	HIF6	—	CUD 1138	—
Austin Marina (Canada)	1798cc	4	1973/	AUD 575	—	RHIC	HIF6	—	CUD 1108	▪
Austin Marina Auto (Canada)	1798cc	4	1973/	AUD 576	—	RHIC	HIF6	—	CUD 1106	—
Austin 7 cwt Van	1098cc	4	1972/73	AUD 368	—	RHIC	HS2	AUD 1242	AUD 1478	AUD 1149
Austin 7 cwt Van (E.C.E.)	1098cc	4	1973/	AUD 627	—	RHIC	HS4	—	CUD 1036	—
Austin 10 cwt Van (E.C.E.)	1275cc	4	1972/	AUD 541	—	RHIC	HS4	—	CUD 1023	—
Austin 10 cwt G.P.O. Van	1275cc	4	1972/73	AUD 589	—	RHIC	HS4	—	CUD 1023	—
Allegro 1100 (E.C.E.)	1098cc	4	1973/75	AUD 608	—	LHIC	HS4	—	CUD 1037	—
Allegro 1100	1098cc	4	1976/	FZX 1170	—	LHIC	HS4	—	CUD 1037	—
Allegro 1100	1098cc	4	1975/	FZX 1022	—	LHIC	HS4	—	CUD 1037	—
Allegro 1100	1098cc	4	1975/	FZX 1067	—	LHIC	HS4	—	CUD 1037	—
Allegro 1300 (E.C.E.)	1275cc	4	1973/75	AUD 594	—	LHIC	HS4	—	CUD 1025	—

¹ Front F, Centre C, Rear R, Right Hand RH, Left Hand LH.   ² Thermocarb gasket pack required in addition AUE 807.
⁵ Air jet 0.116 in. diameter.

Spec. Repeated	Needle Guide	Needle Screw	Piston Spring	Damper	Jet	Needle and Seat	Float	Throttle Spindle	Throttle Disc	Gasket Pack	Pump OE	Pump Alt.
AUD 104L	—	AUC 2057	AUC 4387	AUC 8103	AUD 9141	WZX 1100	WZX 1300	WZX 1310	WZX 1320	AUE 810	—	—
AUD 104R	—	AUC 2057	AUC 4387	AUC 8103	AUD 9142	WZX 1100	WZX 1300	WZX 1310	WZX 1320	AUE 810	AUF 201	AUF 214
AUD 151L	—	AUC 2057	AUC 4387	AUC 8103	AUD 9141	WZX 1100	WZX 1300	WZX 1310	WZX 1320	AUE 810	—	—
AUD 151R	—	AUC 2057	AUC 4387	AUC 8103	AUD 9142	WZX 1100	WZX 1300	WZX 1310	WZX 1320	AUE 810	—	—
AUD 99L	—	AUC 2057	AUC 4387	AUC 8103	AUD 9141	WZX 1100	WZX 1300	WZX 1310	WZX 1320	AUE 810	AUF 201	AUF 214
AUD 99R	—	AUC 2057	AUC 4387	AUC 8103	AUD 9142	WZX 1100	WZX 1300	WZX 1310	WZX 1320	AUE 810	—	—
AUD 146L	—	AUC 2057	AUC 4387	AUC 8103	AUD 9141	WZX 1100	WZX 1300	WZX 1310	WZX 1320	AUE 810	AUF 201	AUF 214
AUD 146R	—	AUC 2057	AUC 4387	AUC 8103	AUD 9142	WZX 1100	WZX 1300	WZX 1310	WZX 1320	AUE 810	—	—
AUD 440L	—	AUC 2057	AUC 4387	AUC 8103	AUD 9141	WZX 1100	WZX 1300	WZX 1310	WZX 1320	AUE 810	AUF 214	—
AUD 440R	—	AUC 2057	AUC 4387	AUC 8103	AUD 9142	WZX 1100	WZX 1300	WZX 1310	WZX 1320	AUE 810	—	—
AUD 13	—	AUC 2057	AUC 4387	AUC 8103	AUD 9098	WZX 1100	WZX 1300	WZX 1310	WZX 1320	AUE 810	AUB 83	AUF 204
AUD 185	—	AUC 2057	AUC 4387	AUC 8103	AUD 9142	WZX 1100	WZX 1300	WZX 1310	WZX 1323	AUE 811	AUF 204	AUF 207
AUD 13	—	AUC 2057	AUC 4387	AUC 8103	AUD 9098	WZX 1100	WZX 1300	WZX 1310	WZX 1320	AUE 810	AUF 207	AUF 204
AUD 251	—	AUC 2057	AUC 4387	AUC 8103	AUD 9451	WZX 1100	WZX 1300	WZX 1312	WZX 1324	AUE 811	AUF 207	AUF 204
AUD 370	—	AUC 2057	AUC 4387	AUC 8103	AUD 9451	WZX 1100	WZX 1300	WZX 1312	WZX 1324	AUE 811	AUF 207	AUF 204
AUD 368	—	AUC 2057	AUC 4387	AUC 8103	AUD 9098	WZX 1100	WZX 1300	WZX 1310	WZX 1320	AUE 810	AUF 207	AUF 204
AUD 368	—	AUC 2057	AUC 4387	AUC 8103	AUD 9098	WZX 1100	WZX 1300	WZX 1310	WZX 1320	AUE 810	AUF 706	AUF 805
AUD 371	—	AUC 2057	AUC 4387	AUC 8103	AUD 9451	WZX 1100	WZX 1300	WZX 1312	WZX 1324	AUE 811	AUF 705	AUF 812
AUD 508	AUD 4288	AUC 4251	AUC 4387	AUC 8103	AUD 9451	WZX 1100	WZX 1300	WZX 1312	WZX 1324	AUE 811	AUF 705	AUF 812
AUD 186	—	AUC 2057	AUC 4387	AUC 8103	AUD 9451	WZX 1100	WZX 1300	WZX 1312	WZX 1324	AUE 811	AUF 207	AUF 204
AUD 271	—	AUC 2057	AUC 4387	AUC 8103	AUD 9451	WZX 1100	WZX 1300	WZX 1312	WZX 1324	AUE 811	AUF 207	AUF 204
AUD 374	—	AUC 2057	AUC 4387	AUC 8103	AUD 9451	WZX 1100	WZX 1300	WZX 1312	WZX 1324	AUE 811	AUF 207	AUF 204
AUD 376	—	AUC 2057	AUC 4387	AUC 8103	AUD 9451	WZX 1100	WZX 1300	WZX 1312	WZX 1324	AUE 811	AUF 207	AUF 204
AUD 344L	—	AUC 2057	AUC 4587	AUC 8103	AUD 9141	WZX 1100	WZX 1300	WZX 1310	WZX 1320	AUE 810	—	—
AUD 344R	—	AUC 2057	AUC 4587	AUC 8103	AUD 9142	WZX 1100	WZX 1300	WZX 1310	WZX 1320	AUE 810	—	—
AUD 472	—	AUC 2057	AUC 4387	AUC 8103	AUD 9451	WZX 1100	WZX 1300	WZX 1312	WZX 1324	AUE 811	AUF 207	AUF 204
AUD 431L	—	AUC 2057	AUC 4587	AUC 8103	AUD 9141	WZX 1100	WZX 1300	WZX 1310	WZX 1320	AUE 810	AUF 207	AUF 204
AUD 431R	—	AUC 2057	AUC 4587	AUC 8103	AUD 9142	WZX 1100	WZX 1300	WZX 1310	WZX 1320	AUE 810	—	—
AUD 480	—	AUC 2057	AUC 4387	AUC 8103	AUD 9451	WZX 1100	WZX 1300	WZX 1312	WZX 1324	AUE 811	AUF 705	AUF 812
AUD 454L	AUD 4288	AUD 4250	AUC 4387	AUC 8103	AUD 9141	WZX 1100	WZX 1300	WZX 1310	WZX 1380	AUE 810	AUF 207	AUF 204
AUD 454R	AUD 4288	AUD 4250	AUC 4387	AUC 8103	AUD 9142	WZX 1100	WZX 1300	WZX 1310	WZX 1380	AUE 810	—	—
AUD 453	AUD 4288	AUD 4251	AUC 4387	AUC 8103	AUD 9451	WZX 1100	WZX 1300	WZX 1312	WZX 1329	AUE 811	AUF 207	AUF 204
AUD 496L	AUD 4288	AUD 4250	AUC 4587	AUC 8103	AUD 9141	WZX 1100	WZX 1300	WZX 1310	WZX 1380	AUE 810	AUF 207	AUF 204
AUD 496R	AUD 4288	AUD 4250	AUC 4587	AUC 8103	AUD 9142	WZX 1100	WZX 1300	WZX 1310	WZX 1380	AUE 810	—	—
AUD 559	AUD 4288	AUD 4251	AUC 4387	AUC 8103	AUD 9451	WZX 1100	WZX 1300	WZX 1312	WZX 1324	AUE 811	AUF 705	AUF 812
AUD 585	AUD 4288	AUD 4251	AUC 4387	AUC 8103	AUD 9451	WZX 1100	WZX 1300	WZX 1312	WZX 1324	AUE 811	AUF 705	AUF 812
AUD 594	AUD 4288	AUD 4251	AUC 4387	AUC 8103	AUD 9451	WZX 1100	WZX 1300	WZX 1312	WZX 1324	AUE 811	AUF 709	AUF 806
AUD 595	AUD 4288	AUD 4251	AUC 4387	AUC 8103	AUD 9451	WZX 1100	WZX 1300	WZX 1312	WZX 1324	AUE 811	AUF 709	AUF 806
AUD 486	AUD 4288	AUD 4251	AUC 4387	AUC 8103	AUD 9451	WZX 1100	WZX 1300	WZX 1312	WZX 1329	AUE 811	AUF 705	AUF 812
AUD 567	AUD 4288	AUD 4251	AUC 4387	AUC 8103	AUD 9451	WZX 1100	WZX 1300	WZX 1312	WZX 1324	AUE 811	AUF 705	AUF 812
AUD 136F	—	AUC 2057	AUC 4587	AUC 8114	AUD 9141	WZX 1100	WZX 1300	WZX 1310	WZX 1320	AUE 810	AUF 206	AUF 201
AUD 136R	—	AUC 2057	AUC 4587	AUC 8114	AUD 9142	WZX 1100	WZX 1300	WZX 1310	WZX 1320	AUE 810	—	—
AUD 136F	—	AUC 2057	AUC 4587	AUC 8114	AUD 9141	WZX 1100	WZX 1300	WZX 1310	WZX 1320	AUE 810	AUF 206	AUF 201
AUD 136R	—	AUC 2057	AUC 4587	AUC 8114	AUD 9142	WZX 1100	WZX 1300	WZX 1310	WZX 1320	AUE 810	—	—
AUD 327F	—	AUC 2057	AUC 4587	AUC 8114	AUD 9141	WZX 1100	WZX 1300	WZX 1310	WZX 1320	AUE 810	AUF 216	AUF 214
AUD 327R	—	AUC 2057	AUC 4587	AUC 8114	AUD 9142	WZX 1100	WZX 1300	WZX 1310	WZX 1320	AUE 810	—	—
AUD 327F	—	AUC 2057	AUC 4587	AUC 8114	AUD 9141	WZX 1100	WZX 1300	WZX 1310	WZX 1320	AUE 810	AUF 216	AUF 214
AUD 327R	—	AUC 2057	AUC 4587	AUC 8114	AUD 9142	WZX 1100	WZX 1300	WZX 1310	WZX 1320	AUE 810	—	—
AUD 266F	—	AUC 2057	AUC 4587	AUC 8114	AUD 9141	WZX 1100	WZX 1300	WZX 1310	WZX 1383	AUE 810	AUF 206	AUF 201
AUD 266R	—	AUC 2057	AUC 4587	AUC 8114	AUD 9142	WZX 1100	WZX 1300	WZX 1310	WZX 1383	AUE 810	—	—
AUD 328F	AUD 4288	AUD 4250	AUC 4587	AUC 8114	AUD 9141	WZX 1100	WZX 1300	WZX 1310	WZX 1383	AUE 810	AUF 216	AUF 214
AUD 328R	AUD 4288	AUD 4250	AUC 4587	AUC 8114	AUD 9142	WZX 1100	WZX 1300	WZX 1310	WZX 1383	AUE 810	—	—
AUD 404F	AUD 4288	AUD 4250	AUC 4587	AUC 8114	AUD 9141	WZX 1100	WZX 1300	WZX 1310	WZX 1383	AUE 810	AUF 305	AZX 1304
AUD 404R	AUD 4288	AUD 4250	AUC 4587	AUC 8114	AUD 9142	WZX 1100	WZX 1300	WZX 1310	WZX 1383	AUE 810	—	—
AUD 549F	AUD 4288	AUD 4250	AUC 4587	AUC 8114	AUD 9141	WZX 1100	WZX 1300	WZX 1310	WZX 1322	AUE 810	AUF 305	AZX 1304
AUD 549R	AUD 4288	AUD 4250	AUC 4587	AUC 8114	AUD 9142	WZX 1100	WZX 1300	WZX 1310	WZX 1322	AUE 810	—	—
AUD 296	—	AUC 2057	AUC 4387	AUC 8103	AUD 9451	WZX 1100	WZX 1300	WZX 1312	WZX 1325	AUE 811	AUF 207	AUF 204
AUD 281	—	AUC 2057	AUC 4387	AUC 8103	AUD 9451	WZX 1100	WZX 1300	WZX 1312	WZX 1325	AUE 811	AUF 207	AUF 204
AUD 380	AUD 4288	AUD 4251	AUC 4387	AUC 8103	AUD 9451	WZX 1100	WZX 1300	WZX 1312	WZX 1325	AUE 811	AUF 207	AUF 204
AUD 379	AUD 4288	AUD 4251	AUC 4387	AUC 8103	AUD 9451	WZX 1100	WZX 1300	WZX 1312	WZX 1325	AUE 811	AUF 207	AUF 204
AUD 345	AUD 4288	AUD 4251	AUC 4387	AUC 8103	AUD 9451	WZX 1100	WZX 1300	WZX 1312	WZX 1325	AUE 811	AUF 207	AUF 204
AUD 346	AUD 4288	AUD 4251	AUC 4387	AUC 8103	AUD 9451	WZX 1100	WZX 1300	WZX 1312	WZX 1325	AUE 811	AUF 207	AUF 204
AUD 494	AUD 4287	AUD 4252	AUC 1167	AUC 8103	WZX 1452	WZX 1100	WZX 1401	WZX 1170	WZX 1326	WZX 1505	—	—
AUD 495	AUD 4287	AUD 4252	AUC 1167	AUC 8103	WZX 1452	WZX 1100	WZX 1401	WZX 1170	WZX 1326	WZX 1505	—	—
AUD 583	AUD 4287	AUD 4252	AUC 1167	AUC 8103	WZX 1452	WZX 1100	WZX 1401	WZX 1170	WZX 1326	WZX 1505	—	—
AUD 584	AUD 4287	AUD 4252	AUC 1167	AUC 8103	WZX 1452	WZX 1100	WZX 1401	WZX 1170	WZX 1326	WZX 1505	—	—
AUD 575	AUD 4287	AUD 4252	AUC 1167	AUC 8103	WZX 1452	WZX 1100	WZX 1401	WZX 1170	WZX 1326	WZX 1505	—	—
AUD 576	AUD 4287	AUD 4252	AUC 1167	AUC 8103	WZX 1452	WZX 1100	WZX 1401	WZX 1170	WZX 1326	WZX 1505	—	—
AUD 368	—	AUC 2057	AUC 4387	AUC 8103	AUD 9098	WZX 1100	WZX 1300	WZX 1310	WZX 1320	AUE 810	AUF 718	AUF 804
AUD 627	AUD 4288	AUD 4251	AUC 4387	AUC 8103	AUD 9450	WZX 1100	WZX 1300	WZX 1312	WZX 1384	AUE 811	AUF 715	AUF 804
AUD 541	AUD 4288	AUD 4251	AUC 4387	AUC 8103	AUD 9450	WZX 1100	WZX 1300	WZX 1312	WZX 1384	AUE 811	AUF 715	AUF 804
AUD 589	AUD 4288	AUD 4251	AUC 4387	AUC 8103	AUD 9450	WZX 1100	WZX 1300	WZX 1312	WZX 1323	AUE 811	AUF 705	AUF 812
AUD 608	AUD 4288	AUD 4251	AUC 4387	AUC 8103	AUD 9451	WZX 1100	WZX 1300	WZX 1312	WZX 1324	AUE 811	AUF 804	—
FZX 1170	AUD 4288	AUD 4251	AUC 4387	AUC 8103	LZX 1111	WZX 1100	WZX 1300	WZX 1312	WZX 1324	AUE 811	AUF 804	—
FZX 1022	AUD 4288	AUD 4251	AUC 4387	AUC 8103	AUD 9451	WZX 1100	WZX 1300	WZX 1312	WZX 1324	AUE 811	AUF 804	—
FZX 1067	AUD 4288	AUD 4251	AUC 4387	AUC 8103	LZX 1111	WZX 1100	WZX 1300	WZX 1312	WZX 1324	AUE 811	AUF 804	—
AUD 594	AUD 4288	AUD 4251	AUC 4387	AUC 8103	AUD 9451	WZX 1100	WZX 1300	WZX 1312	WZX 1324	AUE 811	AUF 804	—

[3] AED Unit TZX 1002 supersedes AUH 308, 309, 310 and 317 (1 per installation).
[6] Air jet 0.102 in. diameter.   [7] Service AED Unit AUH 305 1 per installation Rover (U.S.A.) spec. only.
[4] Service AED Unit AUH 300 (1 per installation).

Model Details	Capacity	No. of Cyl.	Year	Spec.	1 Position	Inter Connect	Type	Rich	Needle Std.	Weak
Allegro 1300 Automatic (E.C.E.)	1275cc	4	1973/76	AUD 567	—	LHIC	HS4	—	CUD 1025	—
Allegro 1300	1275cc	4	1975/	FZX 1023	—	LHIC	HS4	—	CUD 1025	—
Allegro 1300 (Sweden)	1275cc	4	1975/	FZX 1106	—	LHIC	HS4	—	CUD 1025	—
Allegro 1300 Automatic	1275cc	4	1975/	FZX 1086	—	LHIC	HS4	—	CUD 1017	—
Allegro 1300	1275cc	4	1975/	FZX 1068	—	LHIC	HS4	—	CUD 1017	—
Allegro 1300	1275cc	4	1976/	FZX 1172	—	LHIC	HS4	—	CUD 1017	—
Allegro 1300 Automatic	1275cc	4	1976/	FZX 1174	—	LHIC	HS4	—	CUD 1017	—
Allegro 1500 Automatic (E.C.E.)	1485cc	4	1973/75	AUD 628	—	RHIC	HS6	—	CUD 1116	—
Allegro 1500 (E.C.E.)	1485cc	4	1973/76	AUD 556	—	RHIC	HS6	—	CUD 1116	—
Allegro 1500	1485cc	4	1974	AUD 711	—	RHIC	HS6	—	CUD 1116	—
Allegro 1500 Automatic	1485cc	4	1975/76	FZX 1074	—	RHIC	HS6	—	CUD 1116	—
Allegro 1500	1485cc	4	1976/	FZX 1178	—	RHIC	HS6	—	CUD 1116	—
Allegro 1500	1485cc	4	1975/	FZX 1076	—	RHIC	HS6	—	CUD 1116	—
Allegro 1500 Automatic	1485cc	4	1976/	FZX 1180	—	RHIC	HS6	—	CUD 1116	—
Allegro 1750 (E.C.E.)	1748cc	4	1973/76	AUD 557	—	RHIC	HS6	—	CUD 1131	—
Allegro 1750 Automatic (E.C.E.)	1748cc	4	1973/76	AUD 619	—	RHIC	HS6	—	CUD 1131	—
Allegro HL/Sport (E.C.E.)	1748cc	4	1974/76	AUD 539L	LH	RHIC	HS6	—	CUD 1139	—
				AUD 539R	RH	LHIC	HS6	—	CUD 1139	—
Allegro Hiline	1748cc	4	1975/	FZX 1093L	LH	RHIC	HS6	—	CUD 1139	—
				FZX 1093R	RH	LHIC	HS6	—	CUD 1139	—
Allegro 1750 HL/Sport	1748cc	4	1976/	FZX 1183L	LH	RHIC	HS6	—	CUD 1139	—
				FZX 1183R	RH	LHIC	HS6	—	CUD 1139	—
Maxi 1500	1485cc	4	1969/71	AUD 258	—	RHIC	HS6	—	AUD 1541	—
Maxi 1500	1485cc	4	1971	AUD 468	—	RHIC	HS6	—	CUD 1116	—
Maxi 1500 (E.C.E.)	1485cc	4	1971/72	AUD 498	—	RHIC	HS6	—	CUD 1116	—
Maxi 1500	1485cc	4	1972/73	AUD 555	—	RHIC	HS6	—	CUD 1116	—
Maxi 1500 (E.C.E.)	1485cc	4	1972/76	AUD 556	—	RHIC	HS6	—	CUD 1116	—
Maxi 1500	1485cc	4	1975/	FZX 1076	—	RHIC	HS6	—	CUD 1116	—
Maxi 1500	1485cc	4	1976/	FZX 1178	—	RHIC	HS6	—	CUD 1116	—
Maxi 1500 Automatic	1485cc	4	1976/	FZX 1180	—	RHIC	HS6	—	CUD 1116	—
Maxi 1750	1748cc	4	1970/71	AUD 462	—	RHIC	HS6	—	CUD 1115	—
Maxi 1750 Automatic	1748cc	4	1972	AUD 463	—	RHIC	HS6	—	CUD 1115	—
Maxi 1750 (E.C.E.)	1748cc	4	1971/72	AUD 528	—	RHIC	HS6	—	CUD 1131	—
Maxi 1750 HL (E.C.E.)	1748cc	4	1972/76	AUD 539L	LH	RHIC	HS6	—	CUD 1139	—
				AUD 539R	RH	LHIC	HS6	—	CUD 1139	—
Maxi 1750	1748cc	4	1972/73	AUD 558	—	RHIC	HS6	—	CUD 1115	—
Maxi 1750 (E.C.E.)	1748cc	4	1972/76	AUD 557	—	RHIC	HS6	—	CUD 1131	—
Maxi 1750 Automatic (E.C.E.)	1748cc	4	1973/76	AUD 619	—	RHIC	HS6	—	CUD 1131	—
Maxi Hiline	1748cc	4	1975/	FZX 1093L	LH	RHIC	HS6	—	CUD 1139	—
				FZX 1093R	RH	LHIC	HS6	—	CUD 1139	—
Maxi 1750	1748cc	4	1975/	FZX 1077	—	RHIC	HS6	—	NZX 8005	—
Maxi 1750 Automatic (E.C.E.)	1748cc	4	1975/	FZX 1087	—	RHIC	HS6	—	NZX 8005	—
Maxi 1750	1748cc	4	1976/	FZX 1207	—	RHIC	HS6	—	NZX 8005	—
Maxi 1750 Automatic	1748cc	4	1976/	FZX 1209	—	RHIC	HS6	—¹	NZX 8005	—
Maxi 1750 Hiline	1748cc	4	1976/	FZX 1211L	LH	RHIC	HS6	—	CUD 1139	—
				FZX 1211R	RH	LHIC	HS6	—	CUD 1139	—
1800	1798cc	4	1964/66	AUD 147	—	RHIC	HS6	AUD 1337	AUD 1362	AUD 1117
1800	1798cc	4	1966/67	AUD 223	—	RHIC	HS6	AUD 1337	AUD 1362	AUD 1117
1800 Mk II	1798cc	4	1968/70	AUD 280	—	RHIC	HS6	AUD 1317	AUD 1490	AUD 1117
1800 Mk II Automatic	1798cc	4	1968/70	AUD 291	—	RHIC	HS6	AUD 1317	AUD 1490	AUD 1117
1800 Automatic (Canada)	1798cc	4	1968/72	AUD 315	—	RHIC	HS6	—	CUD 1108	—
1800 (Canada)	1798cc	4	1969/72	AUD 314	—	RHIC	HS6	—	CUD 1108	—
1800 'S'	1798cc	4	1969/71	AUD 171L	LH	RHIC	HS6	AUD 1099	AUD 1469	AUD 1117
				AUD 171R	RH	LHIC	HS6	AUD 1099	AUD 1469	AUD 1117
1800 Mk II	1798cc	4	1971/72	AUD 524	—	RHIC	HS6	AUD 1317	AUD 1490	AUD 1117
1800 Mk II Automatic	1798cc	4	1971/74	AUD 525	—	RHIC	HS6	AUD 1317	AUD 1490	AUD 1117
1800 Mk II (E.C.E.)	1798cc	4	1971/72	AUD 355	—	RHIC	HS6	—	CUD 1129	—
1800 Mk II Automatic (E.C.E.)	1798cc	4	1973/	AUD 356	—	RHIC	HS6	—	CUD 1129	—
1800 Mk II (E.C.E.)	1798cc	4	1973/	AUD 564	—	RHIC	HS6	—	CUD 1129	—
1800 Mk II	1798cc	4	1972/73	AUD 565	—	RHIC	HS6	—	AUD 1490	—
1800 Mk II Automatic	1798cc	4	1972/73	AUD 568	—	RHIC	HS6	—	AUD 1490	—
Princess 1800	1798cc	4	1974	AUD 684	—	RHIC	HS6	—	CUD 1129	—
Princess 1800 Automatic	1798cc	4	1975/76	AUD 635	—	RHIC	HS6	—	CUD 1129	—
Princess 1800	1798cc	4	1976/	FZX 1215	—	RHIC	HS6	—	CUD 1129	—
Princess 1800 Automatic	1798cc	4	1976	FZX 1217	—	RHIC	HS6	—	CUD 1129	—
Princess 1800 (Sweden)	1798cc	4	1976/	FZX 1030	—	RHIC	HS6	—	NZX 8028	—
2200	2227cc	6	1972/74	AUD 409F	LH	LHIC	HS6	—	CUD 1127	—
				AUD 409R	RH	LHIC	HS6	—	CUD 1127	—
2200 (E.C.E.)	2227cc	6	1972/73	AUD 546F	LH	RHIC	HIF6	—	CUD 1136	—
2200 Automatic (E.C.E.)	2227cc	6	1972/75	AUD 546R	RH	LHIC	HIF6	—	CUD 1136	—
				AUD 581F	LH	RHIC	HIF6	—	CUD 1136	—
				AUD 581R	RH	LHIC	HIF6	—	CUD 1136	—
Princess 2200	2227cc	6	1974/76	AUD 697F	LH	RHIC	HIF6	—	CUD 1161	—
				AUD 697R	RH	LHIC	HIF6	—	CUD 1161	—
Princess 2200	2227cc	6	1974/76	AUD 698F	LH	RHIC	HIF6	—	CUD 1161	—
				AUD 698R	RH	LHIC	HIF6	—	CUD 1161	—
Princess 2200	2227cc	6	1975/	FZX 1095F	LH	RHIC	HIF6	—	CUD 1161	—
				FZX 1095R	RH	LHIC	HIF6	—	CUD 1161	—
Princess 2200 Automatic	2227cc	6	1975/	FZX 1096F	LH	RHIC	HIF6	—	CUD 1161	—
				FZX 1096R	RH	LHIC	HIF6	—	CUD 1161	—

¹ Front F, Centre C, Rear R, Right Hand RH, Left Hand LH.   ² Thermocarb gasket pack required in addition AUE 807.
³ Air jet 0.116 in. diameter.

Spec. Repeated	Needle Guide	Needle Screw	Piston Spring	Damper	Jet	Needle and Seat	Float	Throttle Spindle	Throttle Disc	Gasket Pack	Pump OE	Alt.
AUD 567	AUD 4288	AUD 4251	AUC 4387	AUC 8103	AUD 9451	WZX 1100	WZX 1300	WZX 1312	WZX 1324	AUE 811	AUF 804	—
FZX 1023	AUD 4288	AUD 4251	AUC 4387	AUC 8103	AUD 9451	WZX 1100	WZX 1300	WZX 1312	WZX 1324	AUE 811	AUF 804	—
FZX 1106	AUD 4288	AUD 4251	AUC 4387	AUC 8103	AUD 9451	WZX 1100	WZX 1300	WZX 1312	WZX 1325	AUE 811	AUF 804	—
FZX 1086	AUD 4288	AUD 4251	AUC 4387	AUC 8103	LZX 1111	WZX 1100	WZX 1300	WZX 1312	WZX 1324	AUE 811	AUF 804	—
FZX 1068	AUD 4288	AUD 4251	AUC 4387	AUC 8103	LZX 1111	WZX 1100	WZX 1300	WZX 1312	WZX 1324	AUE 811	AUF 804	—
FZX 1172	AUD 4288	AUD 4251	AUC 4387	AUC 8103	LZX 1111	WZX 1100	WZX 1300	WZX 1312	WZX 1324	AUE 811	AUF 804	—
FZX 1174	AUD 4288	AUD 4251	AUC 4387	AUC 8103	LZX 1111	WZX 1100	WZX 1300	WZX 1312	WZX 1324	AUE 811	AUF 804	—
AUD 628	AUD 4288	AUD 4252	AUC 4387	AUC 8103	AUD 9105	WZX 1100	WZX 1300	WZX 1311	WZX 1321	AUE 812	AUF 809	—
AUD 556	AUD 4288	AUD 4252	AUC 4387	AUC 8103	AUD 9105	WZX 1100	WZX 1300	WZX 1311	WZX 1321	AUE 812	AUE 809	—
AUD 711	AUD 4288	AUD 4252	AUC 4387	AUC 8103	AUD 9105	WZX 1100	WZX 1300	WZX 1311	WZX 1321	AUE 812	AUF 809	—
FZX 1074	AUD 4288	AUD 4252	AUC 4387	AUC 8103	LZX 1118	WZX 1100	WZX 1300	WZX 1311	WZX 1321	AUE 812	AUF 800	—
FZX 1178	AUD 4288	AUD 4252	AUC 4387	AUC 8103	LZX 1118	WZX 1100	WZX 1300	WZX 1311	WZX 1321	AUE 812	AUF 800	—
FZX 1076	AUD 4288	AUD 4252	AUC 4387	AUC 8103	LZX 1118	WZX 1100	WZX 1300	WZX 1311	WZX 1321	AUE 812	AUF 800	—
FZX 1180	AUD 4288	AUD 4252	AUC 4387	AUC 8103	LZX 1118	WZX 1100	WZX 1300	WZX 1311	WZX 1321	AUE 812	AUF 809	—
AUD 557	AUD 4288	AUD 4252	AUC 4387	AUC 8103	AUD 9105	WZX 1100	WZX 1300	WZX 1311	WZX 1321	AUE 812	AUF 809	—
AUD 619	AUD 4288	AUD 4252	AUC 4387	AUC 8103	AUD 9105	WZX 1100	WZX 1300	WZX 1311	WZX 1321	AUE 812	AUF 809	—
AUD 539L	AUD 4288	AUD 4252	AUC 4387	AUC 8114	AUD 9148	WZX 1100	WZX 1300	WZX 1311	WZX 1321	AUE 812	AUF 702	AUF 800
AUD 539R	AUD 4288	AUD 4252	AUC 4387	AUC 8114	AUD 9149	WZX 1100	WZX 1300	WZX 1311	WZX 1321	AUE 812	—	—
FZX 1093L	AUD 4288	AUD 4252	AUC 4387	AUC 8114	LZX 1126	WZX 1100	WZX 1300	WZX 1311	WZX 1321	AUE 812	AUF 800	—
FZX 1093R	AUD 4288	AUD 4252	AUC 4387	AUC 8114	LZX 1127	WZX 1100	WZX 1300	WZX 1311	WZX 1321	AUE 812	—	—
FZX 1183L	AUD 4288	AUD 4252	AUC 4387	AUC 8114	LZX 1126	WZX 1100	WZX 1300	WZX 1311	WZX 1321	AUE 812	AUF 800	—
FZX 1183R	AUD 4288	AUD 4252	AUC 4387	AUC 8114	LZX 1127	WZX 1100	WZX 1300	WZX 1311	WZX 1321	AUE 812	—	—
AUD 258	—	AUC 2057	AUC 4387	AUC 8103	AUD 9105	WZX 1100	WZX 1300	WZX 1311	WZX 1321	AUE 812	AUF 702	AUF 800
AUD 468	AUD 4288	AUD 4252	AUC 4387	AUC 8103	AUD 9105	WZX 1100	WZX 1300	WZX 1311	WZX 1321	AUE 812	AUF 702	AUF 800
AUD 498	AUD 4288	AUD 4252	AUC 4387	AUC 8103	AUD 9105	WZX 1100	WZX 1300	WZX 1311	WZX 1321	AUE 812	AUF 702	AUF 800
AUD 555	AUD 4288	AUD 4252	AUC 4387	AUC 8103	AUD 9105	WZX 1100	WZX 1300	WZX 1311	WZX 1321	AUE 812	AUF 702	AUF 800
AUD 556	AUD 4288	AUD 4252	AUC 4387	AUC 8103	AUD 9105	WZX 1100	WZX 1300	WZX 1311	WZX 1321	AUE 812	AUF 702	AUF 800
FZX 1076	AUD 4288	AUD 4252	AUC 4387	AUC 8103	LZX 1118	WZX 1100	WZX 1300	WZX 1311	WZX 1321	AUE 812	AUF 800	—
FZX 1178	AUD 4288	AUD 4252	AUC 4387	AUC 8103	LZX 1118	WZX 1100	WZX 1300	WZX 1311	WZX 1321	AUE 812	AUF 800	—
FZX 1180	AUD 4288	AUD 4252	AUC 4387	AUC 8103	LZX 1118	WZX 1100	WZX 1300	WZX 1311	WZX 3121	AUE 812	AUF 800	—
AUD 462	AUD 4288	AUD 4252	AUC 4387	AUC 8103	AUD 9105	WZX 1100	WZX 1300	WZX 1311	WZX 1321	AUE 812	AUF 702	AUF 800
AUD 463	AUD 4288	AUD 4252	AUC 4387	AUC 8103	AUD 9105	WZX 1100	WZX 1300	WZX 1311	WZX 1321	AUE 812	AUF 702	AUF 800
AUD 528	AUD 4288	AUD 4252	AUC 4387	AUC 8103	AUD 9105	WZX 1100	WZX 1300	WZX 1311	WZX 1321	AUE 812	AUF 702	AUF 800
AUD 539L	AUD 4288	AUD 4252	AUC 4387	AUC 8114	AUD 9148	WZX 1100	WZX 1300	WZX 1311	WZX 1321	AUE 812	AUF 702	AUF 800
AUD 539R	AUD 4288	AUD 4252	AUC 4387	AUC 8114	AUD 9149	WZX 1100	WZX 1300	WZX 1311	WZX 1321	AUE 812	—	—
AUD 558	AUD 4288	AUD 4252	AUC 4387	AUC 8103	AUD 9105	WZX 1100	WZX 1300	WZX 1311	WZX 1321	AUE 812	AUF 702	AUF 800
AUD 557	AUD 4288	AUD 4252	AUC 4387	AUC 8103	AUD 9105	WZX 1100	WZX 1300	WZX 1311	WZX 1321	AUE 812	AUF 702	AUF 800
AUD 619	AUD 4288	AUD 4252	AUC 4387	AUC 8103	AUD 9105	WZX 1100	WZX 1300	WZX 1311	WZX 1321	AUE 812	AUF 702/809	AUF 800
FZX 1093L	AUD 4288	AUD 4252	AUC 4387	AUC 8114	LZX 1126	WZX 1100	WZX 1300	WZX 1311	WZX 1321	AUE 812	AUF 800	—
FZX 1093R	AUD 4288	AUD 4252	AUC 4387	AUC 8114	LZX 1127	WZX 1100	WZX 1300	WZX 1311	WZX 1321	AUE 812	—	—
FZX 1077	AUD 4288	AJD 4252	AUC 4387	AUC 8103	LZX 1118	WZX 1100	WZX 1300	WZX 1311	WZX 1321	AUE 812	AUF 800	—
FZX 1087	AUD 4288	AUD 4252	AUC 4387	AUC 8103	LZX 1118	WZX 1100	WZX 1300	WZX 1311	WZX 1321	AUE 812	AUF 800	—
FZX 1207	AUD 4288	AUD 4252	AUC 4387	AUC 8103	LZX 1118	WZX 1100	WZX 1300	WZX 1311	WZX 1321	AUE 812	AUF 800	—
FZX 1209	AUD 4288	AUD 4252	AUC 4387	AUC 8103	LZX 1118	WZX 1100	WZX 1300	WZX 1311	WZX 1321	AUE 812	AUF 800	—
FZX 1211	AUD 4288	AUD 4252	AUC 4387	AUC 8114	LZX 1116	WZX 1100	WZX 1300	WZX 1311	WZX 1321	AUE 812	AUF 800	—
FZX 1211	AUD 4288	AUD 4252	AUC 4387	AUC 8114	LZX 1117	WZX 1100	WZX 1300	WZX 1311	WZX 1321	AUE 812	—	—
AUD 147	—	AUC 2057	AUC 1167	AUC 8103	AUD 9148	WZX 1100	WZX 1300	WZX 1311	WZX 1321	AUE 812	AUF 209	AUF 201
AUD 223	—	AUC 2057	AUC 1167	AUC 8103	AUD 9451	WZX 1100	WZX 1300	WZX 1311	WZX 1321	AUE 812	AUF 209	AUF 201
AUD 280	—	AUC 2057	AUC 1167	AUC 8103	AUD 9148	WZX 1100	WZX 1300	WZX 1311	WZX 1321	AUE 812	AUF 704	AUF 803
AUD 291	—	AUC 2057	AUC 1167	AUC 8103	AUD 9148	WZX 1100	WZX 1300	WZX 1311	WZX 1321	AUE 812	AUF 704	AUF 803
AUD 315	AUD 4288	AUD 4252	AUC 1167	AUC 8103	AUD 9148	WZX 1100	WZX 1300	WZX 1311	WZX 1326	AUE 812	AUF 704	AUF 803
AUD 314	AUD 4288	AUD 4252	AUC 1167	AUC 8103	AUD 9148	WZX 1100	WZX 1300	WZX 1311	WZX 1326	AUE 812	AUF 704	AUF 803
AUD 171L	—	AUC 2057	AUC 4387	AUC 8103	AUD 9149	WZX 1100	WZX 1300	WZX 1311	WZX 1321	AUE 812	AUF 704	AUF 803
AUD 171R	—	AUC 2057	AUC 4387	AUC 8103	AUD 9148	WZX 1100	WZX 1300	WZX 1311	WZX 1321	AUE 812	—	—
AUD 524	—	AUC 2057	AUC 1167	AUC 8103	AUD 9148	WZX 1100	WZX 1300	WZX 1311	WZX 1321	AUE 812	AUF 704	AUF 803
AUD 525	—	AUC 2057	AUC 1167	AUC 8103	AUD 9148	WZX 1100	WZX 1300	WZX 1311	WZX 1321	AUE 812	AUF 704	AUF 803
AUD 355	AUD 4288	AUD 4252	AUC 1167	AUC 8103	AUD 9148	WZX 1100	WZX 1300	WZX 1311	WZX 1321	AUE 812	AUF 704	AUF 803
AUD 356	AUD 4288	AUD 4252	AUC 1167	AUC 8103	AUD 9148	WZX 1100	WZX 1300	WZX 1311	WZX 1321	AUE 812	AUF 704	AUF 803
AUD 564	AUD 4288	AUD 4252	AUC 1167	AUC 8103	AUD 9148	WZX 1100	WZX 1300	WZX 1311	WZX 1321	AUE 812	AUF 704	AUF 803
AUD 565	—	AUC 2057	AUC 1167	AUC 8103	AUD 9148	WZX 1100	WZX 1300	WZX 1311	WZX 1321	AUE 812	AUF 704	AUF 803
AUD 568	—	AUC 2057	AUC 1167	AUC 8103	AUD 9148	WZX 1100	WZX 1300	WZX 1311	WZX 1321	AUE 812	AUF 704	AUF 803
AUD 684	AUD 4288	AUD 4252	AUC 1167	AUC 8103	AUD 9148	WZX 1100	WZX 1300	WZX 1311	WZX 1321	AUE 812	AUF 817	—
AUD 635	AUD 4288	AUD 4252	AUC 1167	AUC 8103	AUD 9148	WZX 1100	WZX 1300	WZX 1311	WZX 1321	AUE 812	AUF 803	—
FZX 1215	AUD 4288	AUD 4252	AUC 1167	AUC 8103	LZX 1114	WZX 1100	WZX 1300	WZX 1311	WZX 1321	AUE 812	AUF 803	—
FZX 1217	AUD 4288	AUD 4252	AUC 1167	AUC 8103	LZX 1114	WZX 1100	WZX 1300	WZX 1311	WZX 1321	AUE 812	AUF 803	—
FZX 1030	JZX 1039	AUD 4252	AUC 1167	CUD 4105	LZX 1052	WZX 1100	WZX 1300	WZX 1311	WZX 1378	AUE 812	AUF 803	—
AUD 409F	AUD 4288	AUD 4252	AUC 4387	AUC 8103	AUD 9106	WZX 1101	WZX 1300	WZX 1314	WZX 1321	AUE 812	AUF 222	—
AUD 409R	AUD 4288	AUD 4252	AUC 4387	AUC 8103	AUD 9106	WZX 1101	WZX 1300	WZX 1314	WZX 1321	AUE 812	or AUF 305	—
AUD 546F	AUD 4288	AUD 4252	AUC 4387	CUD 2901	WZX 1452	WZX 1102	WZX 1401	WZX 1170	WZX 1326	WZX 1505	AUF 305	AZX 1304
AUD 546R	AUD 4288	AUD 4252	AUC 4387	CUD 2901	WZX 1453	WZX 1102	WZX 1400	WZX 1170	WZX 1326	WZX 1505	—	—
AUD 581F	AUD 4288	AUD 4252	AUC 4387	CUD 2901	WZX 1452	WZX 1102	WZX 1401	WZX 1170	WZX 1326	WZX 1505	AUF 305	AZX 1304
AUD 581R	AUD 4288	AUD 4252	AUC 4387	CUD 2901	WZX 1453	WZX 1102	WZX 1400	WZX 1171	WZX 1326	WZX 1505	—	—
AUD 697F	AUD 4288	AUD 4252	AUD 4355	CUD 2907	WZX 1452	WZX 1102	WZX 1401	WZX 1170	WZX 1379	WZX 1505	AUF 818	—
AUD 697R	AUD 4288	AUD 4252	AUD 4355	CUD 2907	WZX 1452	WZX 1102	WZX 1400	WZX 1170	WZX 1379	WZX 1505	—	—
AUD 698F	AUD 4288	AUD 4252	AUD 4355	CUD 2907	WZX 1452	WZX 1102	WZX 1401	WZX 1170	WZX 1379	WZX 1505	AUF 818	—
AUD 698R	AUD 4288	AUD 4252	AUD 4355	CUD 2907	WZX 1453	WZX 1102	WZX 1400	WZX 1171	WZX 1379	WZX 1505	—	—
FZX 1095F	AUD 4288	AUD 4252	AUD 4355	LZX 1150	WZX 1452	WZX 1102	WZX 1401	WZX 1170	WZX 1379	WZX 1505	AUF 818	—
FZX 1095R	AUD 4288	AUD 4252	AUD 4355	LZX 1150	WZX 1453	WZX 1102	WZX 1400	WZX 1170	WZX 1379	WZX 1505	—	—
FZX 1096F	AUD 4288	AUD 4252	AUD 4355	LZX 1150	WZX 1452	WZX 1102	WZX 1401	WZX 1170	WZX 1379	WZX 1505	AUF 818	—
FZX 1096R	AUD 4288	AUD 4252	AUD 4355	LZX 1150	WZX 1453	WZX 1102	WZX 1400	WZX 1170	WZX 1379	WZX 1505	—	—

[3] AED Unit TZX 1002 supersedes AUH 308, 309, 310 and 317 (1 per installation)   [4] Service AED Unit AUH 300 (1 per installation).
[6] Air jet 0.102 in. diameter.   [7] Service AED Unit AUH 305 1 per installation Rover (U.S.A.) spec. only.

Model Details	Capacity	No. of Cyl.	Year	Spec.	Position	Inter Connect	Type	Rich	Needle Std.	Weak
Princess 2200	2227cc	6	1976/	FZX 1219F	F	RHIC	HIF6	—	CUD 1161	—
				FZX 1219R	R	LHIC	HIF6	—	CUD 1161	—
Princess 2200	2227cc	6	1976/	FZX 1221F	F	RHIC	HiF6	—	CUD 1161	—
				FZX 1221R	R	LHIC	HIF6	—	CUD 1161	—
BENTLEY										
S3 V8	6230cc	8	1963/64	AUD 54 'A'	RH	—	HD8	—	AUD 1485	—
				AUD 54 'B'	LH	—	HD8	—	AUD 1485	—
T Series (SY)	6230cc	8	1965/68	AUD 177 'A'	RH	—	HD8	—	AUD 1517	—
				AUD 177 'B'	LH	—	HD8	—	AUD 1517	—
T Series (SY) (U.S.A.)	6230cc	8	1968	AUD 269 'A'	RH	—	HD8	—	AUD 1532	—
				AUD 269 'B'	LH	—	HD8	—	AUD 1532	—
T Series (SY) (U.S.A.)	6750cc	8	1969	AUD 389 'A'	RH	—	HD8	—	CUD 1104	—
				AUD 389 'B'	LH	—	HD8	—	CUD 1104	—
T Series (SY) (U.S.A.)	6750cc	8	1969/71	AUD 387 'A'	RH	—	HD8	—	CUD 1104	—
				AUD 387 'B'	LH	—	HD8	—	CUD 1104	—
CHRYSLER										
Hillman Hunter	1496cc	4	1972/73	AUD 554	—	LHIC	HS4	—	CUD 1009	—
Hillman Hunter	1724cc	4	1972/73	AUD 554	—	LHIC	HS4	—	CUD 1009	—
Hillman Hunter 1500	1496cc	4	1975	AUD 660	—	LHIC	HS4C	—	CUD 1044	—
Hillman Hunter 1724	1724cc	4	1975	AUD 660	—	LHIC	HS4C	—	CUD 1044	—
Hillman Avenger 1300 ..	1295cc	4	1973/74	AUD 572	—	RHIC	HS4C	—	CUD 1039	—
Avenger 1300	1295cc	4	1974/76	AUD 690	—	RHIC	HS4C	—	CUD 1048	—
Hillman Avenger 1600 ..	1600cc	4	1973/74	AUD 572	—	RHIC	HS4C	—	CUD 1039	—
Chrysler Avenger 1800 (Brazil) ..	1800cc	4	1975	AUD 689	—	RHIC	HS6	—	CUD 1107	—
Chrysler Avenger 1800 Hiline (Brazil)	1800cc	4	1976/	FZX 1250	—	RHIC	HS6	—	CUD 1107	—
Dodge 1800	1800cc	4	1973/	AUD 672	—	RHIC	HS4C	—	CUD 1018	—
CONVERSION SETTINGS										
Ford Escort 1100 & 1300			4	1968/	AUD 674	—	LHIC	HS2	—	CUD 1002	—
Maxi BLMC (Special Tuning) ..	1485cc	4	1969/71	AUD 438L	LH	RHIC	HS4	—	CUD 1001	—
				AUD 438R	RH	LHIC	HS4	—	CUD 1001	—
Princess 1800 (Special Tuning) ..	1798cc	4	1975/	FZX 1098F	F	RHIC	HS6	—	NZX 8016	—
				FZX 1098R	R	LIHC	HS6	—	NZX 8016	—
Triumph 2000 & Vitesse	1998cc	6	1966/73	AUD 704F	F	LHIC	HS4C	—	CUD 1034	—
				AUD 704R	R	RHIC	HS4C	—	CUD 1034	—
Triumph 2.5 PI Conversion	2498cc	6	1974/	AUD 607F	F	LHIC	HS4	—	CUD 1042	—
				AUD 607R	R	RHIC	HS4	—	CUD 1042	—
Jaguar 'E' Type V12	5343cc	12	1972/	AUD 547 NSF	NS F	RHIC	HIF6	—	CUD 1130	—
				AUD 547 NSR	NS R	LHIC	HIF6	—	CUD 1130	—
				AUD 547 OSF	OS F	LHIC	HIF6	—	CUD 1130	—
				AUD 547 OSR	OS R	RHIC	HIF6	—	CUD 1130	—
DAIMLER										
V8 Saloon Automatic	2548cc	8	1964/68	AUD 180L	LH	—	HD6	AUD 1353	AUD 1469	—
				AUD 180R	RH	—	HD6	AUD 1353	AUD 1469	—
V8 Saloon Manual	2548cc	8	1967/68	AUD 180L	LH	—	HD6	AUD 1353	AUD 1469	—
				AUD 180R	RH	—	HD6	AUD 1353	AUD 1469	—
V8 Majestic Major	4561cc	8	1964	AUD 139L	LH	—	HD8	—	AUD 1466	—
				AUD 139R	RH	—	HD8	—	AUD 1466	—
V8 Majestic	4561cc	8	1964	AUD 139L	LH	—	HD8	—	AUD 1466	—
				AUD 139R	RH	—	HD8	—	AUD 1466	—
V8 Majestic Major	4561cc	8	1964/68	AUD 181L	LH	—	HD8	—	AUD 1466	—
				AUD 181R	RH	—	HD8	—	AUD 1466	—
Limousine	4235cc	6	1970/72	AUD 357F	F	—	HD8Th[2]	—	AUD 1467	—
				AUD 357R	R	—	HD8	—	AUD 1467	—
Limousine	4235cc	6	1973/74	AUD 647F	F	LHIC	HS8AED[3]	—	CUD 1120	
				AUD 647R	R	RHIC	HS8	—	CUD 1120	—
Limousine	4235cc	6	1974/76	AUD 667F	F	LHIC	HS8AED[3]	—	CUD 1150	—
				AUD 667R	R	RHIC	HS8	—	CUD 1150	—
Sovereign	2792cc	6	1968/71	AUD 321F	F	LHIC	HD8Th[2]	—	AUD 1586	—
				AUD 321R	R	RHIC	HD8	—	AUD 1586	—
Sovereign (LHD)	2792cc	6	1971/72	AUD 537F	F	LHIC	HS8AED[3]	—	CUD 1134	—
				AUD 537R	R	RHIC	HS8	—	CUD 1134	—
Sovereign	2792cc	6	1971/73	AUD 415F	F	LHIC	HS8AED[3]	—	CUD 1118	—
				AUD 415R	R	RHIC	HS8	—	CUD 1118	—
Sovereign	4235cc	6	1967/68	AUD 245F	F	LHIC	HD8Th[2]	—	AUD 1467	—
				AUD 245R	R	RHIC	HD8	—	AUD 1467	—
Sovereign	4235cc	6	1968/71	AUD 357F	F	LHIC	HD8Th[2]	—	AUD 1467	—
				AUD 357R	R	RHIC	HD8	—	AUD 1467	—

[1] Front F, Centre C, Rear R, Right Hand RH, Left Hand LH. [2] Thermocarb gasket pack required in addition AUE 807.
[5] Air jet 0.116 in. diameter.

Spec. Repeated	Needle Guide	Needle Screw	Piston Spring	Damper	Jet	Needle and Seat	Float	Throttle Spindle	Throttle Disc	Gasket Pack	Pump OE	Pump Alt.
FZX 1219F	AUD 4288	AUD 4252	AUD 4355	LZX 1150	WZX 1452	WZX 1102	WZX 1401	WZX 1170	WZX 1379	WZX 1505	AUF 817	—
FZX 1219R	AUD 4288	AUD 4252	AUD 4355	LZX 1150	WZX 1453	WZX 1102	WZX 1400	WZX 1170	WZX 1379	WZX 1505	—	—
FZX 1221F	AUD 4288	AUD 4252	AUD 4355	LZX 1150	WZX 1452	WZX 1102	WZX 1401	WZX 1170	WZX 1379	WZX 1505	AUF 817	—
FZX 1221R	AUD 4288	AUD 4252	AUD 4355	LZX 1150	WZX 1453	WZX 1102	WZX 1400	WZX 1170	WZX 1379	WZX 1505	—	—
AUD 54'A'	—	AUC 2057	AUC 4818	AUC 8111	AUD 9030	WZX 1102	WZX 1303	WZX 1218	WZX 1373	AUE 806	AUA 146	AUF 406
AUD 54'B'	—	AUC 2057	AUC 4818	AUC 8111	AUD 9030	WZX 1102	WZX 1303	WZX 1219	WZX 1373	AUE 806	—	—
AUD 177'A'	—	AUC 2057	AUC 4818	AUC 8111	AUD 9030	WZX 1102	WZX 1303	WZX 1202	WZX 1373	AUE 806	AUF 400	—
AUD 177'B'	—	AUC 2057	AUC 4818	AUC 8111	AUD 9030	WZX 1102	WZX 1303	WZX 1203	WZX 1373	AUE 806	—	—
AUD 269'A'	—	AUC 2057	AUC 4818	AUC 8111	AUD 9825	WZX 1102	WZX 1303	WZX 1202	WZX 1373	AUE 806	AUF 400	—
AUD 269'B'	—	AUC 2057	AUC 4818	AUC 8111	AUD 9825	WZX 1102	WZX 1303	WZX 1203	WZX 1373	AUE 806	—	—
AUD 389'A'	AUD 4288	AUD 4253	AUC 4818	AUC 8111	CUD 2637	WZX 1102	WZX 1303	WZX 1202	WZX 1373	AUE 806	AUF 402	—
AUD 389'B'	AUD 4288	AUD 4253	AUC 4818	AUC 8111	CUD 2637	WZX 1102	WZX 1303	WZX 1203	WZX 1373	AUE 806	—	—
AUD 387'A'	AUD 4288	AUD 4253	AUC 4818	AUC 8111	CUD 2637	WZX 1102	WZX 1303	WZX 1200	WZX 1373	AUE 806	AUF 402	—
AUD 387'B'	AUD 4288	AUD 4253	AUC 4818	AUC 8111	CUD 2637	WZX 1102	WZX 1303	WZX 1201	WZX 1373	AUE 806	—	—
AUD 554	AUD 4288	AUD 4251	AUC 1170	AUC 8103	AUD 9451	WZX 1100	WZX 1300	WZX 1312	WZX 1323	AUE 811	—	—
AUD 554	AUD 4288	AUD 4251	AUC 1170	AUC 8103	AUD 9451	WZX 1100	WZX 1300	WZX 1312	WZX 1323	AUE 811	—	—
AUD 660	AUD 4288	AUD 4251	AUC 1167	CUD 4103	AUD 9814	WZX 1100	WZX 1300	WZX 1316	WZX 1387	—	—	—
AUD 660	AUD 4288	AUD 4251	AUC 1167	CUD 4103	AUD 9814	WZX 1100	WZX 1300	WZX 1316	WZX 1387	—	—	—
AUD 572	AUD 4288	AUD 4251	AUC 1167	CUD 4103	AUD 9815	WZX 1100	WZX 1300	WZX 1316	WZX 1388	—	—	—
AUD 690	AUD 4288	AUD 4251	AUC 4387	AUC 8103	AUD 9815	WZX 1100	WZX 1300	WZX 1316	WZX 1387	—	—	—
AUD 572	AUD 4288	AUD 4251	AUC 1167	CUD 4103	AUD 9815	WZX 1100	WZX 1300	WZX 1316	WZX 1388	—	—	—
AUD 689	AUD 4288	AUD 4252	AUC 4387	AUC 8103	AUD 9105	WZX 1101	WZX 1300	WZX 1311	WZX 1321	AUE 812	—	—
FZX 1250	AUD 4288	AUD 4252	AUC 4387	AUC 8103	AUD 9105	WZX 1101	WZX 1300	WZX 1311	WZX 1321	AUE 812	—	—
AUD 672	AUD 4288	AUD 4251	AUC 1170	AUC 8103	AUD 9815	WZX 1100	WZX 1300	WZX 1316	WZX 1387	—	—	—
AUD 674	AUD 4288	AUD 4250	AUC 4387	AUC 8103	AUD 9142	WZX 1100	WZX 1300	WZX 1310	WZX 1320	AUE 810	—	—
AUD 438L	AUD 4288	AUD 4251	AUC 4387	AUC 8114	AUD 9141	WZX 1100	WZX 1300	WZX 1312	WZX 1323	AUE 811	AUF 702	AUF 800
AUD 438R	AUD 4288	AUD 4251	AUC 4387	AUC 8114	AUD 9142	WZX 1100	WZX 1300	WZX 1312	WZX 1323	AUE 811	—	—
FZX 1098F	AUD 4288	AUD 4252	AUC 4387	AUC 8114	AUD 9148	WZX 1101	WZX 1300	WZX 1311	WZX 1321	AUE 812	AUF 817	—
FZX 1098R	AUD 4288	AUD 4252	AUC 4387	AUC 8114	AUD 9149	WZX 1101	WZX 1300	WZX 1311	WZX 1321	AUE 812	—	—
AUD 704F	AUD 4288	AUD 4251	AUC 1167	AUC 8103	AUD 9814	WZX 1100	WZX 1300	WZX 1316	WZX 1387	—	—	—
AUD 704R	AUD 4288	AUD 4251	AUC 1167	AUC 8103	AUD 9815	WZX 1100	WZX 1300	WZX 1316	WZX 1387	—	—	—
AUD 607F	AUD 4288	AUD 4251	AUC 1167	AUC 8103	AUD 9451	WZX 1100	WZX 1300	WZX 1312	WZX 1323	AUE 811	AUF 301	AZX 1301
AUD 607R	AUD 4288	AUD 4251	AUC 1167	AUC 8103	AUD 9450	WZX 1100	WZX 1300	WZX 1312	WZX 1323	AUE 811	—	—
AUD 547 NSF	AUD 4287	AUD 4252	AUC 1167	AUC 8103	WZX 1452	WZX 1100	WZX 1401	WZX 1170	WZX 1321	WZX 1505	AUF 406	—
AUD 547 NSR	AUD 4287	AUD 4252	AUC 1167	AUC 8103	WZX 1453	WZX 1100	WZX 1400	WZX 1172	WZX 1321	WZX 1505	—	—
AUD 547 OSF	AUD 4287	AUD 4252	AUC 1167	AUC 8103	WZX 1453	WZX 1100	WZX 1400	WZX 1170	WZX 1321	WZX 1505	—	—
AUD 547 OSR	AUD 4287	AUD 4252	AUC 1167	AUC 8103	WZX 1452	WZX 1100	WZX 1401	WZX 1172	WZX 1321	WZX 1505	—	—
AUD 180L	—	AUC 2057	AUC 4387	AUC 8102	AUC 8155	WZX 1102	WZX 1303	WZX 1214	WZX 1321	AUE 805	AUF 303	AUF 306
AUD 180R	—	AUC 2057	AUC 4387	AUC 8102	AUC 8155	WZX 1102	WZX 1303	WZX 1214	WZX 1321	AUE 805	—	—
AUD 180L	—	AUC 2057	AUC 4387	AUC 8102	AUC 8155	WZX 1102	WZX 1303	WZX 1214	WZX 1321	AUE 805	AUF 303	AUF 306
AUD 180R	—	AUC 2057	AUC 4387	AUC 8102	AUC 8155	WZX 1102	WZX 1303	WZX 1214	WZX 1321	AUE 805	—	—
AUD 139L	—	AUC 2057	AUC 4826	AUC 8113	AUC 8156	WZX 1102	WZX 1303	WZX 1213	WZX 1373	AUE 806	AUA 161	AUF 406
AUD 139R	—	AUC 2057	AUC 4826	AUC 8113	AUC 8156	WZX 1102	WZX 1303	WZX 1213	WZX 1373	AUE 806	—	—
AUD 139L	—	AUC 2057	AUC 4826	AUC 8113	AUC 8156	WZX 1102	WZX 1303	WZX 1213	WZX 1373	AUE 806	AUA 161	AUF 406
AUD 139R	—	AUC 2057	AUC 4826	AUC 8113	AUC 8156	WZX 1102	WZX 1303	WZX 1213	WZX 1373	AUE 806	—	—
AUD 181L	—	AUC 2057	AUC 4826	AUC 8113	AUC 8156	WZX 1102	WZX 1303	WZX 1213	WZX 1373	AUE 806	AUA 161	AUF 406
AUD 181R	—	AUC 2057	AUC 4826	AUC 8113	AUC 8156	WZX 1102	WZX 1303	WZX 1213	WZX 1373	AUE 806	—	—
AUD 357F	—	AUC 2057	AUC 4826	AUC 8115	AUC 8156	WZX 1102	WZX 1303	WZX 1209	WZX 1373	AUE 806[2]	AUF 301 (2)	AZX 1301 (2)
AUD 357R	—	AUC 2057	AUC 4826	AUC 8115	AUC 8156	WZX 1102	WZX 1303	WZX 1212	WZX 1373	AUE 806	—	—
AUD 647F	AUD 4288	AUD 4253	AUC 4826	AUC 8102	CUD 2753	WZX 1102	WZX 1300	WZX 1317	WZX 1328	AUE 813	AUF 301 (2)	AZX 1301 (2)
AUD 647R	AUD 4288	AUD 4253	AUC 4826	AUC 8102	CUD 2753	WZX 1102	WZX 1300	WZX 1313	WZX 1328	AUE 813	—	—
AUD 667F	AUD 4288	AUD 4253	AUC 4826	AUC 8102	CUD 2752	WZX 1102	WZX 1300	WZX 1317	WZX 1328	AUE 813	AUF 301 (2)	AZX 1301 (2)
AUD 667R	AUD 4288	AUD 4253	AUC 4826	AUC 8102	CUD 2752	WZX 1102	WZX 1300	WZX 1313	WZX 1328	AUE 813	—	—
AUD 321F	—	AUC 2057	AUC 4826	AUC 8115	AUC 8156	WZX 1102	WZX 1303	WZX 1209	WZX 1373	AUE 806[2]	AUF 301 (2)	AZX 1301 (2)
AUD 321R	—	AUC 2057	AUC 4826	AUC 8115	AUC 8156	WZX 1102	WZX 1303	WZX 1212	WZX 1373	AUE 806	—	—
AUD 537F	AUD 4288	AUD 4253	AUC 4826	AUC 8102	CUD 2753	WZX 1102	WZX 1300	WZX 1317	WZX 1389	AUE 813	AUF 301 (2)	AZX 1301 (2)
AUD 537R	AUD 4288	AUD 4253	AUC 4826	AUC 8102	CUD 2752	WZX 1102	WZX 1300	WZX 1313	WZX 1389	AUE 813	—	—
AUD 415F	AUD 4288	AUD 4253	AUC 2107	AUC 8102	CUD 2753	WZX 1102	WZX 1300	WZX 1317	WZX 1389	AUE 813	AUF 301 (2)	AZX 1301 (2)
AUD 415R	AUD 4288	AUD 4253	AUC 2107	AUC 8102	CUD 2752	WZX 1102	WZX 1300	WZX 1313	WZX 1389	AUE 813	—	—
AUD 245F	—	AUC 2057	AUC 4826	AUC 8110	AUC 8156	WZX 1102	WZX 1303	WZX 1207	WZX 1373	AUE 806[2]	AUF 301 (2)	AZX 1301 (2)
AUD 245R	—	AUC 2057	AUC 4826	AUC 8110	AUC 8156	WZX 1102	WZX 1303	WZX 1208	WZX 1373	AUE 806	—	—
AUD 357F	—	AUC 2057	AUC 4826	AUC 8115	AUC 8156	WZX 1102	WZX 1303	WZX 1209	WZX 1373	AUE 806[2]	AUF 301 (2)	AZX 1301 (2)
AUD 357R	—	AUC 2057	AUC 4826	AUC 8115	AUC 8156	WZX 1102	WZX 1303	WZX 1212	WZX 1373	AUE 806	—	—

[3] AED Unit TZX 1002 supersedes AUH 308, 309, 310 and 317 (1 per installation) [4] Service AED Unit AUH 300 (1 per installation)
[6] Air jet 0.102 in. diameter. [7] Service AED Unit AUH 305 1 per installation Rover (U.S.A.) spec. only.

Model Details	Capacity	No. of Cyl.	Year	Spec.[1]	Position	Inter Connect	Type	Rich	Needle Std.	Weak
Sovereign (LHD)	4235cc	6	1971/72	AUD 538F	F	LHIC	HS8AED[3]	—	CUD 1133	—
				AUD 538R	R	RHIC	HS8	—	CUD 1133	—
Sovereign	4235cc	6	1971/73	AUD 397F	F	LHIC	HS8AED[3]	—	CUD 1120	—
				AUD 397R	R	RHIC	HS8	—	CUD 1120	—
Sovereign	4235cc	6	1973	AUD 647F	F	LHIC	HS8AED[3]	—	CUD 1120	—
				AUD 647R	R	RHIC	HS8	—	CUD 1120	—
Sovereign	4235cc	6	1973/76	AUD 653F	F	LHIC	HS8AED[3]	—	CUD 1150	—
				AUD 653R	R	RHIC	HS8	—	CUD 1150	—
Sovereign	4235cc	6	1974/75	AUD 667F	F	LHIC	HS8AED	—	CUD 1150	—
				AUD 667R	R	RHIC	HS8	—	CUD 1150	—
Sovereign	4235cc	6	1975/76	FZX 1049F	F	LHIC	HIF7AED[3]	—	NZX 8013	—
				FZX 1049R	R	LHIC	HIF7	—	NZX 8013	—
Sovereign	4235cc	6	1976/	FZX 1252F	F	LHIC	HIF7AED[3]	—	NZX 8023	—
				FZX 1252R	R	LHIC	HIF7	—	NZX 8023	—
INNOCENTI										
Mini	848cc	4	1965/66	AUD 210	—	RHIC	HS2	AUD 1261	AUD 1149	AUD 1211
Mini Automatic	848cc	4	1967/68	AUD 262	—	LHIC	HS4	AUD 1242	AUD 1478	AUD 1149
Mini	848cc	4	1975	FZX 1060	—	LHIC	HS4	—	CUD 1023	—
Mini	998cc	4	1968/69	AUD 324L	LH	RHIC	HS2	AUD 1261	AUD 1468	AUD 1211
				AUD 324R	RH	LHIC	HS2	AUD 1261	AUD 1468	AUD 1211
Mini Clubman	998cc	4	1970/71	AUD 365L	LH	RHIC	HS2	AUD 1261	AUD 1468	AUD 1211
				AUD 365R	RH	LHIC	HS2	AUD 1261	AUD 1468	AUD 1211
Minimatic	998cc	4	1970/71	AUD 460	—	LHIC	HS4	AUD 1522	AUD 1116	AUD 1468
Mini 1001 Automatic	998cc	4	1971/74	AUD 513	—	LHIC	HS4	—	CUD 1015	—
Mini 90	998cc	4	1974/75	AUD 693	—	LHIC	HS4	—	CUD 1025	—
1100 IM3	1098cc	4	1963/64	AUD 132L	LH	RHIC	HS2	AUD 1144	AUD 1142	AUD 1225
				AUD 132R	RH	LHIC	HS2	AUD 1144	AUD 1142	AUD 1225
1100 IM3	1098cc	4	1964	AUD 160L	LH	RHIC	HS2	AUD 1144	AUD 1142	AUD 1225
				AUD 160R	RH	LHIC	HS2	AUD 1144	AUD 1142	AUD 1225
1100 IM3	1098cc	4	1967/68	AUD 168	—	LHIC	HS2	AUD 1242	AUD 1478	AUD 1149
1100 IM3 Automatic	1098cc	4		AUD 263	—	LHIC	HS4	AUD 1076	AUD 1522	AUD 1151
1100 IM3	1098cc	4	1970/71	AUD 490L	LH	RHIC	HS2	AUD 1261	AUD 1149	AUD 1211
				AUD 490R	RH	LHIC	HS2	AUD 1261	AUD 1149	AUD 1211
1100 IM3	1098cc	4	1971/72	AUD 532L	LH	RHIC	HS2	AUD 1261	AUD 1149	AUD 1211
				AUD 532R	RH	LHIC	HS2	AUD 1261	AUD 1149	AUD 1211
Mini 1300 (E.C.E.)	1275cc	4	1972	AUD 534L	LH	RHIC	HS2	—	CUD 1013	—
				AUD 534R	RH	LHIC	HS2	—	CUD 1013	—
Mini 120	1275cc	4	1974/75	AUD 692	—	LHIC	HS6	—	CUD 1118	—
Regent 1300	1275cc	4	1974/	AUD 534L	LH	RHIC	HS2	—	CUD 1013	—
				AUD 534R	RH	LHIC	HS2	—	CUD 1013	—
Regent 1500	1498cc	4	1974/	AUD 633L	LH	RHIC	HS4	—	CUD 1025	—
				AUD 633R	RH	LHIC	HS4	—	CUD 1025	—
JAGUAR										
Mk X	3781cc	6	1963/64	AUD 111F	F	—	HD8Th[2]	—	AUD 1467	—
				AUD 111C	C	—	HD8	—	AUD 1467	—
				AUD 111R	R	—	HD8	—	AUD 1467	—
Mk X 8:1 & 9:1 CR	3781cc	6	1964	AUD 144F	F	—	HD8Th[2]	—	AUD 1467	—
				AUD 144C	C	—	HD8	—	AUD 1467	—
				AUD 144R	R	—	HD8	—	AUD 1467	—
Mk X Automatic and Overdrive	3781cc	6	1964	AUD 156F	F	—	HD8Th[2]	—	AUD 1467	—
				AUD 156C	C	—	HD8	—	AUD 1467	—
				AUD 156R	R	—	HD8	—	AUD 1467	—
Mk X	3781cc	6	1964	AUD 157F	F	—	HD8Th[2]	—	AUD 1467	—
				AUD 157C	C	—	HD8	—	AUD 1467	—
				AUD 157R	R	—	HD8	—	AUD 1467	—
Mk X 8:1 & 9:1 CR	4235 cc	6	1964	AUD 144F	F	—	HD8Th[2]	—	AUD 1467	—
				AUD 144C	C	—	HD8	—	AUD 1467	—
				AUD 144R	R	—	HD8	—	AUD 1467	—
Mk X Automatic and Overdrive	4235cc	6	1964	AUD 156F	F	—	HD8Th[2]	—	AUD 1467	—
				AUD 156C	C	—	HD8	—	AUD 1467	—
				AUD 156R	R	—	HD8	—	AUD 1467	—
Mk X	4235cc	6	1964	AUD 157F	F	—	HSD8Th[2]	—	AUD 1467	—
				AUD 157C	C	—	HD0	—	AUD 1467	—
				AUD 157R	R	—	HD8	—	AUD 1467	—
240	2483cc	6	1967/68	AUD 256F	F	LHIC	HS6	—	AUD 1353	—
				AUD 256R	R	RHIC	HS6	—	AUD 1353	—
240 Automatic	2483cc	6	1967/68	AUD 297F	F	LHIC	HS6	—	AUD 1353	—
				AUD 297R	R	RHIC	HS6	—	AUD 1353	—
240	2483cc	6	1968/69	AUD 309F	F	LHIC	HS6	—	AUD 1353	—
				AUD 309R	R	RHIC	HS6	—	AUD 1353	—
240 Automatic	2483cc	6	1968/69	AUD 310F	F	LHIC	HS6	—	AUD 1353	—
				AUD 310R	R	RHIC	HS6	—	AUD 1353	—
3.4 Mk III	3442cc	6	1963/64	AUD 109F	F	—	HD6Th[2]	—	AUD 1353	—
				AUD 109R	R	—	HD6	—	AUD 1353	—
3.4 'S' Type 8:1 & 9:1 CR Automatic/Manual (AC Paper Cleaner)	3442cc	6	1967/68	AUD 243F	F	—	HD6Th[2]	—	AUD 1353	—
				AUD 243R	R	—	HD6	—	AUD 1353	—

[1] Front F, Centre C, Rear R, Right Hand RH, Left Hand LH.   [2] Thermocarb gasket pack required in addition AUE 807.
[3] Air jet 0.116 in. diameter.

Spec. Repeated	Needle Guide	Needle Screw	Piston Spring	Damper	Jet	Needle and Seat	Float	Throttle Spindle	Throttle Disc	Gasket Pack	Pump OE	Pump Alt.
AUD 538F	AUD 4288	AUD 4253	AUC 4826	AUC 8102	CUD 2753	WZX 1102	WZX 1300	WZX 1317	WZX 1328	AUE 813	AUF 301 (2)	AZX 1301 (2)
AUD 538R	AUD 4288	AUD 4253	AUC 4826	AUC 8102	CUD 2752	WZX 1102	WZX 1300	WZX 1313	WZX 1328	AUE 813	—	—
AUD 397F	AUD 4288	AUD 4253	AUC 4826	AUC 8102	CUD 2753	WZX 1102	WZX 1300	WZX 1317	WZX 1328	AUE 813	AUF 301 (2)	AZX 1301 (2)
AUD 397R	AUD 4288	AUD 4253	AUC 4826	AUC 8102	CUD 2752	WZX 1102	WZX 1300	WZX 1313	WZX 1328	AUE 813	—	—
AUD 647F	AUD 4288	AUD 4253	AUC 4826	AUC 8102	CUD 2753	WZX 1102	WZX 1300	WZX 1317	WZX 1328	AUE 813	AUF 301 (2)	AZX 1301 (2)
AUD 647R	AUD 4288	AUD 4253	AUC 4826	AUC 8102	CUD 2752	WZX 1102	WZX 1300	WZX 1313	WZX 1328	AUE 813	—	—
AUD 653F	AUD 4288	AUD 4253	AUC 4826	AUC 8102	CUD 2753	WZX 1102	WZX 1300	WZX 1317	WZX 1328	AUE 813	AUF 301 (2)	AZX 1301 (2)
AUD 653R	AUD 4288	AUD 4253	AUC 4826	AUC 8102	CUD 2752	WZX 1102	WZX 1300	WZX 1313	WZX 1328	AUE 813	—	—
AUD 667F	AUD 4288	AUD 4253	AUC 4826	AUC 8102	CUD 2753	WZX 1102	WZX 1300	WZX 1317	WZX 1328	AUE 813	AUF 301 (2)	AZX 1301 (2)
AUD 667R	AUD 4288	AUD 4253	AUC 4826	AUC 8102	CUD 2752	WZX 1102	WZX 1300	WZX 1313	WZX 1328	AUE 813	—	—
FZX 1049F	JZX 1039	AUD 4252	AUD 4355	CUD 2952	WZX 1456	WZX 1100	WZX 1401	WZX 1173	WZX 1188	WZX 1505	—	—
FZX 1049R	JZX 1039	AUD 4252	AUD 4355	CUD 2952	WZX 1456	WZX 1100	WZX 1401	WZX 1174	WZX 1188	WZX 1505	—	—
FZX 1252F	JZX 1039	AUD 4252	AUD 4355	CUD 2952	WZX 1456	WZX 1100	WZX 1401	WZX 1174	WZX 1188	WZX 1505	—	—
FZX 1252R	JZX 1039	AUD 4252	AUD 4355	CUD 2952	WZX 1456	WZX 1100	WZX 1401	WZX 1173	WZX 1188	WZX 1505	—	—
AUD 210	—	AUC 2057	AUC 4387	AUC 8103	AUD 9098	WZX 1100	WZX 1300	WZX 1310	WZX 1320	AUE 810	AUF 201	AUF 214
AUD 262	—	AUC 2057	AUC 4387	AUC 8103	AUD 9451	WZX 1100	WZX 1300	WZX 1312	WZX 1324	AUE 811	AUF 201	AUF 214
FZX 1060	AUD 4288	AUD 4251	AUC 1167	AUC 8103	AUD 9451	WZX 1100	WZX 1300	WZX 1312	WZX 1324	AUE 811	AUF 816	—
AUD 324L	—	AUC 2057	AUC 4587	AUC 8103	AUD 9141	WZX 1100	WZX 1300	WZX 1310	WZX 1320	AUE 810	AUF 214	—
AUD 324R	—	AUC 2057	AUC 4587	AUC 8103	AUD 9142	WZX 1100	WZX 1300	WZX 1310	WZX 1320	AUE 810	—	—
AUD 365L	—	AUC 2057	AUC 4587	AUC 8103	AUD 9141	WZX 1100	WZX 1300	WZX 1310	WZX 1320	AUE 810	AUF 214	—
AUD 365R	—	AUC 2057	AUC 4587	AUC 8103	AUD 9142	WZX 1100	WZX 1300	WZX 1310	WZX 1320	AUE 810	—	—
AUD 460	—	AUC 2057	AUC 4387	AUC 8103	AUD 9451	WZX 1100	WZX 1300	WZX 1312	WZX 1324	AUE 811	AUF 214	—
AUD 513	AUD 4288	AUD 4251	AUC 4387	AUC 8103	AUD 9451	WZX 1100	WZX 1300	WZX 1312	WZX 1324	AUE 811	AUF 705	AUF 812
AUD 693	AUD 4288	AUD 4251	AUC 1167	AUC 8103	AUD 9451	WZX 1100	WZX 1300	WZX 1312	WZX 1324	AUE 811	AUF 816	—
AUD 132L	—	AUC 2057	AUC 4587	AUC 8103	AUD 9141	WZX 1100	WZX 1300	WZX 1310	WZX 1320	AUE 810	AUF 201	AUF 214
AUD 132R	—	AUC 2057	AUC 4587	AUC 8103	AUD 9142	WZX 1100	WZX 1300	WZX 1310	WZX 1320	AUE 810	—	—
AUD 160L	—	AUC 2057	AUC 4587	AUC 8103	AUD 9141	WZX 1100	WZX 1300	WZX 1310	WZX 1320	AUE 810	AUF 207	AUF 204
AUD 160R	—	AUC 2057	AUC 4587	AUC 8103	AUD 9142	WZX 1100	WZX 1300	WZX 1310	WZX 1320	AUE 810	—	—
AUD 168	—	AUC 2057	AUC 4387	AUC 8103	AUD 9098	WZX 1100	WZX 1300	WZX 1310	WZX 1320	AUE 810	AUF 207	AUF 204
AUD 263	—	AUC 2057	AUC 4387	AUC 8103	AUD 9451	WZX 1100	WZX 1300	WZX 1312	WZX 1324	AUE 811	AUF 211	AUF 204
AUD 490L	—	AUC 2057	AUC 4587	AUC 8103	AUD 9141	WZX 1100	WZX 1300	WZX 1310	WZX 1320	AUE 810	AUF 207	AUF 204
AUD 490R	—	AUC 2057	AUC 4587	AUC 8103	AUD 9142	WZX 1100	WZX 1300	WZX 1310	WZX 1320	AUE 810	—	—
AUD 532L	—	AUC 2057	AUC 4587	AUC 8103	AUD 9141	WZX 1100	WZX 1300	WZX 1310	WZX 1320	AUE 810	AUF 207	AUF 204
AUD 532R	—	AUC 2057	AUC 4587	AUC 8103	AUD 9142	WZX 1100	WZX 1300	WZX 1310	WZX 1320	AUE 810	—	—
AUD 534L	AUD 4288	AUD 4250	AUC 4587	AUC 8103	AUD 9141	WZX 1100	WZX 1300	WZX 1310	WZX 1320	AUE 810	AUF 214	—
AUD 534R	AUD 4288	AUD 4250	AUC 4587	AUC 8103	AUD 9142	WZX 1100	WZX 1300	WZX 1310	WZX 1320	AUE 810	—	—
AUD 692	AUD 4290	AUD 4252	AUC 1167	AUC 8103	AUD 9106	WZX 1100	WZX 1300	WZX 1311	WZX 1321	AUE 812	—	—
AUD 534L	AUD 4288	AUD 4250	AUC 4587	AUC 8103	AUD 9141	WZX 1100	WZX 1300	WZX 1310	WZX 1320	AUE 810	AUF 214	—
AUD 534R	AUD 4288	AUD 4250	AUC 4587	AUC 8103	AUD 9142	WZX 1100	WZX 1300	WZX 1310	WZX 1320	AUE 810	—	—
AUD 633L	AUD 4288	AUD 4251	AUC 4387	AUC 8114	AUD 9141	WZX 1100	WZX 1300	WZX 1312	WZX 1323	AUE 811	AUF 809	—
AUD 633R	AUD 4288	AUD 4251	AUC 4387	AUC 8114	AUD 9142	WZX 1100	WZX 1300	WZX 1312	WZX 1323	AUE 811	—	—
AUD 111F	—	AUC 2057	AUC 2107	AUC 8110	AUC 8156	WZX 1101	WZX 1303	WZX 1206	WZX 1373	AUE 806[2]	AUF 301 (2)	AZX 1301 (2)
AUD 111C	—	AUC 2057	AUC 2107	AUC 8110	AUC 8156	WZX 1101	WZX 1303	WZX 1206	WZX 1373	AUE 806	—	—
AUD 111R	—	AUC 2057	AUC 2107	AUC 8110	AUC 8156	WZX 1101	WZX 1303	WZX 1206	WZX 1373	AUE 806	—	—
AUD 144F	—	AUC 2057	AUC 2107	AUC 8110	AUC 8156	WZX 1101	WZX 1303	WZX 1206	WZX 1373	AUE 806[2]	AUF 301 (2)	AZX 1301 (2)
AUD 144C	—	AUC 2057	AUC 2107	AUC 8110	AUC 8156	WZX 1101	WZX 1303	WZX 1206	WZX 1373	AUE 806	—	—
AUD 144R	—	AUC 2057	AUC 2107	AUC 8110	AUC 8156	WZX 1101	WZX 1303	WZX 1206	WZX 1373	AUE 806	—	—
AUD 156F	—	AUC 2057	AUC 2107	AUC 8110	AUC 8156	WZX 1102	WZX 1303	WZX 1206	WZX 1373	AUE 806[2]	AUF 301 (2)	AZX 1301 (2)
AUD 156C	—	AUC 2057	AUC 2107	AUC 8110	AUC 8156	WZX 1102	WZX 1303	WZX 1206	WZX 1373	AUE 806	—	—
AUD 156R	—	AUC 2057	AUC 2107	AUC 8110	AUC 8156	WZX 1102	WZX 1303	WZX 1206	WZX 1373	AUE 806	—	—
AUD 157F	—	AUC 2057	AUC 2107	AUC 8110	AUC 8156	WZX 1102	WZX 1303	WZX 1206	WZX 1373	AUE 806[2]	AUF 301 (2)	AZX 1301 (2)
AUD 157C	—	AUC 2057	AUC 2107	AUC 8110	AUC 8156	WZX 1102	WZX 1303	WZX 1206	WZX 1373	AUE 806	—	—
AUD 157R	—	AUC 2057	AUC 2107	AUC 8110	AUC 8156	WZX 1102	WZX 1303	WZX 1206	WZX 1373	AUE 806	—	—
AUD 144F	—	AUC 2057	AUC 2107	AUC 8110	AUC 8156	WZX 1101	WZX 1303	WZX 1206	WZX 1373	AUE 806[2]	—	—
AUD 144C	—	AUC 2057	AUC 2107	AUC 8110	AUC 8156	WZX 1101	WZX 1303	WZX 1206	WZX 1373	AUE 806	—	—
AUD 144R	—	AUC 2057	AUC 2107	AUC 8110	AUC 8156	WZX 1101	WZX 1303	WZX 1206	WZX 1373	AUE 806	—	—
AUD 156F	—	AUC 2057	AUC 2107	AUC 8110	AUC 8156	WZX 1102	WZX 1303	WZX 1206	WZX 1373	AUE 806[2]	AUF 301 (2)	AZX 1301 (2)
AUD 156C	—	AUC 2057	AUC 2107	AUC 8110	AUC 8156	WZX 1102	WZX 1303	WZX 1206	WZX 1373	AUE 806	—	—
AUD 156R	—	AUC 2057	AUC 2107	AUC 8110	AUC 8156	WZX 1102	WZX 1303	WZX 1206	WZX 1373	AUE 806	—	—
AUD 157F	—	AUC 2057	AUC 2107	AUC 8110	AUC 8156	WZX 1102	WZX 1303	WZX 1206	WZX 1373	AUE 806[2]	AUF 301 (2)	AZX 1301 (2)
AUD 157C	—	AUC 2057	AUC 2107	AUC 8110	AUC 8156	WZX 1102	WZX 1303	WZX 1206	WZX 1373	AUE 806	—	—
AUD 157R	—	AUC 2057	AUC 2107	AUC 8110	AUC 8156	WZX 1102	WZX 1303	WZX 1206	WZX 1373	AUE 806	—	—
AUD 256F	—	AUC 2057	AUC 4387	AUC 8102	AUD 9106	WZX 1102	WZX 1300	WZX 1311	WZX 1321	AUE 812	AUF 301	AZX 1301
AUD 256R	—	AUC 2057	AUC 4387	AUC 8102	AUD 9105	WZX 1102	WZX 1300	WZX 1311	WZX 1321	AUE 812	—	—
AUD 297F	—	AUC 2057	AUC 4387	AUC 8102	AUD 9106	WZX 1102	WZX 1300	WZX 1311	WZX 1321	AUE 812	AUF 301	AZX 1301
AUD 297R	—	AUC 2057	AUC 4387	AUC 8102	AUD 9105	WZX 1102	WZX 1300	WZX 1311	WZX 1321	AUE 812	—	—
AUD 309F	—	AUC 2057	AUC 4387	AUC 8102	AUD 9106	WZX 1102	WZX 1300	WZX 1311	WZX 1321	AUE 812	AUF 301	AZX 1301
AUD 309R	—	AUC 2057	AUC 4387	AUC 8102	AUD 9105	WZX 1102	WZX 1300	WZX 1311	WZX 1321	AUE 812	—	—
AUD 310F	—	AUC 2057	AUC 4387	AUC 8102	AUD 9106	WZX 1102	WZX 1300	WZX 1311	WZX 1321	AUE 812	AUF 301	AZX 1301
AUD 310R	—	AUC 2057	AUC 4387	AUC 8102	AUD 9105	WZX 1102	WZX 1300	WZX 1311	WZX 1321	AUE 812	—	—
AUD 109F	—	AUC 2057	AUC 4387	AUC 8102	AUC 8155	WZX 1101	WZX 1303	WZX 1204	WZX 1205	AUE 805[2]	AUF 301	AZX 1301
AUD 109R	—	AUC 2057	AUC 4387	AUC 8102	AUC 8155	WZX 1101	WZX 1303	WZX 1205	WZX 1321	AUE 805	—	—
AUD 243F	—	AUC 2057	AUC 4387	AUC 8102	AUC 8155	WZX 1102	WZX 1303	WZX 1204	WZX 1205	AUE 805[2]	AUF 301 (2)	AZX 1301 (2)
AUD 243R	—	AUC 2057	AUC 4387	AUC 8102	AUC 8155	WZX 1102	WZX 1303	WZX 1205	WZX 1321	AUE 805	—	—

[3] AED Unit TZX 1002 supersedes AUH 308, 309, 310 and 317 (1 per installation).
[4] Service AED Unit AUH 300 (1 per installation).
[6] Air jet 0.102 in. diameter.
[7] Service AED Unit AUH 305 1 per installation Rover (U.S.A.) spec. only.

Model Details	Capacity	No. of Cyl.	Year	Spec.	Position	Inter Connect	Type	Rich	Needle Std.	Weak
3.8 Mk II	3781cc	6	1963/64	AUD 109F	F	—	HD6Th[2]	—	AUD 1353	—
				AUD 109R	R	—	HD6	—	AUD 1353	—
3.8 7:1 CR (Cooper Cleaner) ..	3781cc	6	1964	AUD 155F	F	—	HD6Th[2]	—	AUD 1354	—
				AUD 155R	R	—	HD6	—	AUD 1354	—
3.8 'S' Type Mk III 8:1 & 9:1 CR (Paper Cleaner)	3781cc	6	1964	AUD 153F	F	—	HD6Th[2]	—	AUD 1353	—
				AUD 153R	R	—	HD6	—	AUD 1353	—
3.8 'S' Type Mk III 8:1 & 9:1 CR (Oil Bath Cleaner)	3781cc	6	1964	AUD 154F	F	—	HD6Th[2]	—	AUD 1099	—
				AUD 154R	R	—	HD6	—	AUD 1099	—
3.8 'S' Type 8:1 and 9:1 CR Manual/ Automatic (AC Paper Cleaner)	3781cc	6	1967/68	AUD 243F	F	—	HD6Th[2]	—	AUD 1353	—
				AUD 243R	R	—	HD6	—	AUD 1353	—
340 7:1 CR Manual/Automatic (AC Paper Cleaner)	3442cc	6	1967/68	AUD 241F	F	—	HD6Th[2]	—	AUD 1354	—
				AUD 241R	R	—	HD6	—	AUD 1354	—
340 8:1 & 9:1 CR Manual/Automatic (AC Paper Cleaner) ..	3442cc	6	1967/68	AUD 242F	F	—	HD6Th[2]	—	AUD 1099	—
				AUD 242R	R	—	HD6	—	AUD 1099	—
420 Manual 8:1 & 9:1 CR (AC Paper Cleaner)	4235cc	6	1967/68	AUD 239F	F	—	HD8Th[2]	—	AUD 1467	—
				AUD 239R	R	—	HD8	—	AUD 1467	—
420 Automatic 8:1 & 9:1 CR (AC Paper Cleaner)	4235cc	6	1967/68	AUD 245F	F	—	HD8Th[2]	—	AUD 1467	—
				AUD 245R	R	—	HD8	—	AUD 1467	—
420G Manual 8:1 & 9:1 CR (AC Paper Cleaner)	4235cc	6	1967/68	AUD 157F	F	—	HD8Th[2]	—	AUD 1524	—
				AUD 157C	C	—	HD8	—	AUD 1524	—
				AUD 157R	R	—	HD8	—	AUD 1524	—
420G Automatic 8:1 and 9:1 CR (AC Paper Cleaner	4235cc	6	1967/68	AUD 156F	F	—	HD8Th[2]	—	AUD 1467	—
				AUD 156C	C	—	HD8	—	AUD 1467	—
				AUD 156R	R	—	HD8	—	AUD 1467	—
'E' Type	3781cc	6	1963/64	AUD 112F	F	—	HD8	—	AUD 1467	—
				AUD 112C	C	—	HD8	—	AUD 1467	—
				AUD 112R	R	—	HD8	—	AUD 1467	—
'E' Type 8:1 and 9:1 CR	4235cc	6	1967/68	AUD 227F	F	—	HD8	—	AUD 1467	—
				AUD 227C	C	—	HD8	—	AUD 1467	—
				AUD 227R	R	—	HD8	—	AUD 1467	—
'E' Type 5.3 litre	5343cc	12	1971/73	—	—	—	—	—	—	—
XJ12 5.3 litre ..	5343cc	12	1972/73	—	—	—	—	—	—	—
2.8 XJ6	2792cc	6	1968/71	AUD 321F	F	—	HD8Th[2]	—	AUD 1548	—
				AUD 321R	R	—	HD8	—	AUD 1548	—
2.8 XJ6	2792cc	6	1971/72	AUD 415F	F	LHIC	HS8AED[3]	—	CUD 1118	—
				AUD 415R	R	RHIC	HS8	—	CUD 1118	—
2.8 XJ6 (LHD)	2792cc	6	1972/73	AUD 537F	F	LHIC	HS8AED[3]	—	CUD 1134	—
				AUD 537R	R	RHIC	HS8	—	CUD 1134	—
3.4 XJ6	3442cc	6	1975/76	AUD 710F	F	LHIC	HS8AED[3]	—	CUD 1169	—
				AUD 710R	R	RHIC	HS8	—	CUD 1169	—
3.4 XJ6	3442cc	6	1975/76	FZX 1049F	F	LHIC	HIF7AED[3]	—	NZX 8013	—
				FZX 1049R	R	LHIC	HIF7	—	NZX 8013	—
3.4 XJ6	3442cc	6	1976/	FZX 1053F	F	LHIC	HIF7AED[3]	—	NZX 8021	—
				FZX 1053R	R	LHIC	HIF7	—	NZX 8021	—
4.2 XJ6	4235cc	6	1968/71	AUD 357F	F	—	HD8Th[2]	—	AUD 1467	—
				AUD 357R	R	—	HD8	—	AUD 1467	—
4.2 XJ6 (LHD)	4235cc	6	1972/73	AUD 538F	F	LHIC	HS8AED[3]	—	CUD 1133	—
				AUD 538R	R	RHIC	HS8	—	CUD 1133	—
4.2 XJ6	4235cc	6	1971/73	AUD 397F	F	LHIC	HS8AED[3]	—	CUD 1120	—
				AUD 397R	R	RHIC	HS8	—	CUD 1120	—
4.2 XJ6	4235cc	6	1973	AUD 647F	F	LHIC	HS8AED[3]	—	CUD 1120	—
				AUD 647R	R	RHIC	HS8	—	CUD 1120	—
4.2 XJ6	4235cc	6	1973/74	AUD 653F	F	LHIC	HS8AED[3]	—	CUD 1150	—
				AUD 653R	R	RHIC	HS8	—	CUD 1150	—
4.2 XJ6	4235cc	6	1974/75	AUD 667F	F	LHIC	HS8AED[3]	—	CUD 1150	—
				AUD 667R	R	RHIC	HS8	—	CUD 1150	—
4.2XJ6	4235cc	6	1975/76	FZX 1049F	F	LHIC	HIF7AED[3]	—	NZX 8013	—
				FZX 1049R	R	LHIC	HIF7	—	NZX 8013	—
4.2 XJ6	4235cc	6	1976/	FZX 1252F	F	LHIC	HIF7AED[3]	—	NZX 8023	—
				FZX 1252R	R	LHIC	HIF7	—	NZX 8023	—

JENSEN
Jensen-Healey Mk I & Mk II .. | — | — | — | — | — | — | — | — | — | —

LEYLAND INTERNATIONAL

Model Details	Capacity	No. of Cyl.	Year	Spec.	Position	Inter Connect	Type	Rich	Needle Std.	Weak
185, 215, 220, Van etc.	1622cc	4	1974/75	AUD 620	—	RHIC	HS6	—	CUD 1183	—
215, 220, 240, 250, LC Van etc. ..	1798cc	4	1974/75	AUD 631	—	RHIC	HS6	—	CUD 1166	—
215, 220, 240, 250, LC Auto Van etc.	1798cc	4	1974/76	AUD 658	—	RHIC	HS6	—	CUD 1166	—
Sherpa (Cyclopack Air Cleaner)	1622cc	4	1975	FZX 1035	—	RHIC	HS6	—	NZX 8017	—
Sherpa 185/215/220	1622cc	4	1975/	FZX 1041	—	RHIC	HS6	—	CUD 1165	—
Sherpa CV306 215-240	1622cc	4	1975/76	FZX 1042	—	RHIC	HS6	—	CUD 1166	—
Sherpa CV306 185/215/220	1622cc	4	1976/	FZX 1223	—	RHIC	HS6	—	CUD 1165	—
Sherpa 1800 (Cyclopack Air Cleaner)	1798cc	4	1975	FZX 1033	—	RHIC	HS6	—	NZX 8018	—
Sherpa 1800 CV306	1798cc	4	1976/	FZX 1225	—	RHIC	HS6	—	CUD 1166	—
Sherpa 1800 CV306 (Automatic) ..	1798cc	4	1976/	FZX 1227	—	RHIC	HS6	—	CUD 1166	—
Mini (S.A.)	1097cc	4	1971	AUD 481	—	LHIC	HS4	AUD 1522	AUD 1116	AUD 1468
Apache 1300 (S.A.)	1275cc	4	1970/71	AUD 469	—	LHIC	HS4	AUD 1076	AUD 1528	AUD 1096
Apache 1300TC (S.A.)	1275cc	4	1971	AUD 431L	LH	RHIC	HS2	—	AUD 1468	—
				AUD 431R	RH	LHIC	HS2	—	AUD 1468	—

[1] Front F, Centre C, Rear R, Right Hand RH, Left Hand LH.   [2] Thermocarb gasket pack required in addtiion AUE 807.
[3] Air jet 0.116 in. diameter.

Spec. Repeated	Needle Guide	Needle Screw	Piston Spring	Damper	Jet	Needle and Seat	Float	Throttle Spindle	Throttle Disc	Gasket Pack	Pump OE	Pump Alt.
AUD 109F	—	AUC 2057	AUC 4387	AUC 8102	AUC 8155	WZX 1101	WZX 1303	WZX 1204	WZX 1321	AUE 805[2]	AUF 301	AZX 1301
AUD 109R	—	AUC 2057	AUC 4387	AUC 8102	AUC 8155	WZX 1101	WZX 1303	WZX 1204	WZX 1321	AUE 805	—	—
AUD 155F	—	AUC 2057	AUC 4387	AUC 8102	AUC 8155	WZX 1102	WZX 1303	WZX 1205	WZX 1321	AUE 805[2]	AUF 301	AZX 1301
AUD 155R	—	AUC 2057	AUC 4387	AUC 8122	AUC 8155	WZX 1102	WZX 1303	WZX 1205	WZX 1321	AUE 805	—	—
AUD 153F	—	AUC 2057	AUC 4387	AUC 8102	AUC 8155	WZX 1102	WZX 1303	WZX 1205	WZX 1321	AUE 805[2]	AUF 301 (2)	AZX 1301 (2)
AUD 153R	—	AUC 2057	AUC 4387	AUC 8102	AUC 8155	WZX 1102	WZX 1303	WZX 1205	WZX 1321	AUE 805	—	—
AUD 154F	—	AUC 2057	AUC 4387	AUC 8102	AUC 8155	WZX 1102	WZX 1303	WZX 1204	WZX 1321	AUE 805[2]	AUF 031 (2)	AZX 1301 (2)
AUD 154R	—	AUC 2057	AUC 4387	AUC 8102	AUC 8155	WZX 1102	WZX 1303	WZX 1205	WZX 1321	AUE 805	—	—
AUD 243F	—	AUC 2057	AUC 4387	AUC 8102	AUC 8155	WZX 1102	WZX 1303	WZX 1204	WZX 1321	AUE 805[2]	AUF 301 (2)	AZX 1301 (2)
AUD 243R	—	AUC 2057	AUC 4387	AUC 8102	AUC 8155	WZX 1102	WZX 1303	WZX 1205	WZX 1321	AUE 805	—	—
AUD 241F	—	AUC 2057	AUC 4387	AUC 8102	AUC 8155	WZX 1102	WZX 1303	WZX 1204	WZX 1321	AUE 805[2]	AUF 301	AZX 1301
AUD 241R	—	AUC 2057	AUC 4387	AUC 8102	AUC 8155	WZX 1102	WZX 1303	WZX 1205	WZX 1321	AUE 805	—	—
AUD 242F	—	AUC 2057	AUC 4387	AUC 8102	AUC 8155	WZX 1102	WZX 1303	WZX 1204	WZX 1321	AUE 805[2]	AUF 301	AZX 1301
AUD 242R	—	AUC 2057	AUC 4387	AUC 8102	AUC 8155	WZX 1102	WZX 1303	WZX 1205	WZX 1321	AUE 805	—	—
AUD 239F	—	AUC 2057	AUC 2107	AUC 8110	AUC 8156	WZX 1102	WZX 1303	WZX 1206	WZX 1373	AUE 806[2]	AUF 301 (2)	AZX 1301 (2)
AUD 239R	—	AUC 2057	AUC 2107	AUC 8110	AUC 8156	WZX 1102	WZX 1303	WZX 1207	WZX 1373	AUE 806	—	—
AUD 245F	—	AUC 2057	AUC 4826	AUC 8110	AUC 8156	WZX 1102	WZX 1303	WZX 1206	WZX 1373	AUE 806[2]	AUF 301 (2)	AZX 1301 (2)
AUD 245R	—	AUC 2057	AUC 4826	AUC 8110	AUC 8156	WZX 1102	WZX 1303	WZX 1207	WZX 1373	AUE 806	—	—
AUD 157F	—	AUC 2057	AUC 2107	AUC 8110	AUC 8156	WZX 1102	WZX 1303	WZX 1206	WZX 1373	AUE 806[2]	AUF 301 (2)	AZX 1301 (2)
AUD 157C	—	AUC 2057	AUC 2107	AUC 8110	AUC 8156	WZX 1102	WZX 1303	WZX 1206	WZX 1373	AUE 806	—	—
AUD 157R	—	AUC 2057	AUC 2107	AUC 8110	AUC 8156	WZX 1102	WZX 1303	WZX 1206	WZX 1373	AUE 806	—	—
AUD 156F	—	AUC 2057	AUC 2107	AUC 8110	AUC 8156	WZX 1102	WZX 1303	WZX 1206	WZX 1309	AUE 806[2]	AUF 301 (2)	AZX 1301 (2)
AUD 156C	—	AUC 2057	AUC 2107	AUC 8110	AUC 8156	WZX 1102	WZX 1303	WZX 1206	WZX 1309	AUE 806	—	—
AUD 156R	—	AUC 2057	AUC 2107	AUC 8110	AUC 8156	WZX 1102	WZX 1303	WZX 1206	WZX 1309	AUE 806	—	—
AUD 112F	—	AUC 2057	AUC 2107	AUC 8115	AUC 8156	WZX 1102	WZX 1303	WZX 1206	WZX 1309	AUE 806	AUF 301	AZX 1301
AUD 112C	—	AUC 2057	AUC 2107	AUC 8115	AUC 8156	WZX 1102	WZX 1303	WZX 1206	WZX 1309	AUE 806	—	—
AUD 112F	—	AUC 2057	AUC 2107	AUC 8115	AUC 8156	WZX 1102	WZX 1303	WZX 1206	WZX 1309	AUE 806	—	—
AUD 112R	—	AUC 2057	AUC 2107	AUC 8115	AUC 8156	WZX 1102	WZX 1303	WZX 1206	WZX 1309	AUE 806	AUF 301 (2)	AZX 1301 (2)
AUD 227F	—	AUC 2057	AUC 2107	AUC 8115	AUC 8156	WZX 1102	WZX 1303	WZX 1206	WZX 1309	AUE 806	—	—
AUD 227C	—	AUC 2057	AUC 2107	AUC 8115	AUC 8156	WZX 1102	WZX 1303	WZX 1206	WZX 1309	AUE 806	—	—
AUD 227R	—	AUC 2057	AUC 2107	AUC 8115	AUC 8156	WZX 1102	WZX 1303	WZX 1206	WZX 1309	AUE 806	AUF 406 (2)	AUF 411 (2)
—	—	—	—	—	—	—	—	—	—	—	AUF 406 (2)	AUF 411 (2)
AUD 321F	—	AUC 2057	AUC 2107	AUC 8115	AUC 8156	WZX 1102	WZX 1303	WZX 1209	WZX 1309	AUE 806	AUF 301 (2)	AZX 1301 (2)
AUD 321R	—	AUC 2057	AUC 2107	AUC 8115	AUC 8156	WZX 1102	WZX 1303	WZX 1212	WZX 1309	AUE 806	—	—
AUD 415F	AUD 4288	AUD 4253	AUC 2107	AUC 8102	CUD 2752	WZX 1102	WZX 1300	WZX 1317	WZX 1389	AUE 813	AUF 301 (2)	AZX 1301 (2)
AUD 415R	AUD 4288	AUD 4253	AUC 2107	AUC 8102	CUD 2752	WZX 1102	WZX 1300	WZX 1313	WZX 1389	AUE 813	—	—
AUD 537F	AUD 4288	AUD 4253	AUC 4826	AUC 8102	CUD 2753	WZX 1102	WZX 1300	WZX 1317	WZX 1389	AUE 813	AUF 301 (2)	AZX 1301 (2)
AUD 537R	AUD 4288	AUD 4253	AUC 4826	AUC 8102	CUD 2752	WZX 1102	WZX 1300	WZX 1313	WZX 1389	AUE 813	—	—
AUD 710F	AUD 4288	AUD 4253	AUC 4826	AUC 8102	CUD 2753	WZX 1102	WZX 1300	WZX 1317	WZX 1328	AUE 813	AUF 301 (2)	AZX 1301 (2)
AUD 710R	AUD 4288	AUD 4253	AUC 4826	AUC 8102	CUD 2752	WZX 1102	WZX 1300	WZX 1313	WZX 1328	AUE 813	—	—
FZX 1049F	JZX 1039	AUD 4253	AUD 4355	CUD 2952	WZX 1456	WZX 1100	WZX 1401	WZX 1174	WZX 1188	WZX 1505	—	—
FZX 1049R	JZX 1039	AUD 4253	AUD 4355	CUD 2952	WZX 1456	WZX 1100	WZX 1401	WZX 1173	WZX 1188	WZX 1505	—	—
FZX 1053F	JZX 1039	AUD 4253	AUD 4355	CUD 2952	WZX 1456	WZX 1100	WZX 1401	WZX 1174	WZX 1188	WZX 1505	—	—
FZX 1053R	JZX 1039	AUD 4253	AUD 4355	CUD 2952	WZX 1456	WZX 1100	WZX 1401	WZX 1173	WZX 1188	WZX 1505	—	—
AUD 357F	—	AUC 2057	AUC 4826	AUC 8115	AUC 8156	WZX 1102	WZX 1303	WZX 1209	WZX 1473	AUE 806[2]	AUF 301 (2)	AZX 1301 (2)
AUD 357R	—	AUC 2057	AUC 4826	AUC 8115	AUC 8156	WZX 1102	WZX 1303	WZX 1212	WZX 1473	AUE 806	—	—
AUD 538F	AUD 4288	AUD 4253	AUC 4826	AUC 8102	CUD 2753	WZX 1102	WZX 1300	WZX 1317	WZX 1328	AUE 813	AUF 301 (2)	AZX 1301 (2)
AUD 538R	AUD 4288	AUD 4253	AUC 4826	AUC 8102	CUD 2752	WZX 1102	WZX 1300	WZX 1313	WZX 1328	AUE 813	—	—
AUD 397F	AUD 4288	AUD 4253	AUC 4826	AUC 8102	CUD 2753	WZX 1102	WZX 1300	WZX 1317	WZX 1328	AUE 813	AUF 301 (2)	AZX 1301 (2)
AUD 397R	AUD 4288	AUD 4253	AUC 4826	AUC 8102	CUD 2752	WZX 1102	WZX 1300	WZX 1313	WZX 1328	AUE 813	—	—
AUD 647F	AUD 4288	AUD 4253	AUC 4826	AUC 8102	CUD 2753	WZX 1102	WZX 1300	WZX 1317	WZX 1328	AUE 813	AUF 301 (2)	AZX 1301 (2)
AUD 647R	AUD 4288	AUD 4253	AUC 4826	AUC 8102	CUD 2752	WZX 1102	WZX 1300	WZX 1313	WZX 1328	AUE 813	—	—
AUD 653F	AUD 4288	AUD 4253	AUC 4826	AUC 8102	CUD 2753	WZX 1102	WZX 1300	WZX 1317	WZX 1328	AUE 813	AUF 301 (2)	AZX 1301 (2)
AUD 653R	AUD 4288	AUD 4253	AUC 4826	AUC 8102	CUD 2752	WZX 1102	WZX 1300	WZX 1313	WZX 1328	AUE 813	—	—
AUD 667F	AUD 4288	AUD 4253	AUC 4826	AUC 8102	CUD 2753	WZX 1102	WZX 1300	WZX 1317	WZX 1328	AUE 813	AUF 301 (2)	AZX 1301 (2)
AUD 667R	AUD 4288	AUD 4253	AUC 4826	AUC 8102	CUD 2752	WZX 1102	WZX 1300	WZX 1313	WZX 1328	AUE 813	—	—
FZX 1049F	JZX 1039	AUD 4252	AUD 4355	CUD 2952	WZX 1456	WZX 1100	WZX 1401	WZX 1174	WZX 1188	WZX 1505	—	—
FZX 1049R	JZX 1039	AUD 4252	AUD 4355	CUD 2952	WZX 1456	WZX 1100	WZX 1401	WZX 1173	WZX 1188	WZX 1505	—	—
FZX 1252F	JZX 1039	AUD 4252	AUD 4355	CUD 2952	WZX 1456	WZX 1100	WZX 1401	WZX 1174	WZX 1188	WZX 1505	—	—
FZX 1252R	JZX 1039	AUD 4252	AUD 4355	CUD 2952	WZX 1456	WZX 1100	WZX 1401	WZX 1173	WZX 1188	WZX 1505	—	—
—	—	—	—	—	—	—	—	—	—	—	AUF 301	AZX 1302
AUD 620	AUD 4288	AUD 4252	AUC 1167	AUC 8103	AUD 9148	WZX 1100	WZX 1300	WZX 1311	WZX 1382	AUE 812	AUF 802	—
AUD 621	AUD 4288	AUD 4252	AUC 1167	AUC 8103	AUD 9148	WZX 1100	WZX 1300	WZX 1311	WZX 1382	AUE 812	AUF 802	—
AUD 658	AUD 4288	AUD 4252	AUC 1167	AUC 8103	AUD 9148	WZX 1100	WZX 1300	WZX 1311	WZX 1321	AUE 812	AUF 802	—
FZX 1035	AUD 4288	AUD 4252	AUC 1167	AUC 8103	AUD 9148	WZX 1100	WZX 1300	WZX 1311	WZX 1382	AUE 812	AUF 802	—
FZX 1041	AUD 4288	AUD 4252	AUC 1167	AUC 8103	AUD 9148	WZX 1100	WZX 1300	WZX 1311	WZX 1382	AUE 812	AUF 802	—
FZX 1042	AUD 4288	AUD 4252	AUC 1167	AUC 8103	AUD 9148	WZX 1100	WZX 1300	WZX 1311	WZX 1382	AUE 812	AUF 802	—
FZX 1223	AUD 4288	AUD 4252	AUC 1167	AUC 8103	LZX 1114	WZX 1100	WZX 1300	WZX 1311	WZX 1382	AUE 812	AUF 802	—
FZX 1033	AUD 4288	AUD 4252	AUC 4387	AUC 8103	AUD 9148	WZX 1100	WZX 1300	WZX 1311	WZX 1382	AUE 812	AUF 802	—
FZX 1225	AUD 4288	AUD 4252	AUC 1167	AUC 8103	LZX 1114	WZX 1100	WZX 1300	WZX 1311	WZX 1382	AUE 812	AUF 802	—
FZX 1227	AUD 4288	AUD 4252	AUC 1167	AUC 8103	LZX 1114	WZX 1100	WZX 1300	WZX 1311	WZX 1321	AUE 812	AUF 802	—
AUD 481	—	AUC 4387	AUC 4387	AUC 8103	AUD 9451	WZX 1100	WZX 1300	WZX 1312	WZX 1324	AUE 811	AUF 705	AUF 812
AUD 469	—	AUC 2057	AUC 4387	AUC 8103	AUD 9451	WZX 1100	WZX 1300	WZX 1312	WZX 1324	AUE 811	AUF 207	AUF 204
AUD 431L	—	AUC 2057	AUC 4587	AUC 8103	AUD 9142	WZX 1100	WZX 1300	WZX 1310	WZX 1320	AUE 810	AUF 207	AUF 204
AUD 431R	—	AUC 2057	AUC 4587	AUC 8103	AUD 9141	WZX 1100	WZX 1300	WZX 1310	WZX 1320	AUE 810	—	—

[3] AED Unit TZX 1002 supersedes AUH 308, 309, 310 and 317 (1 per installation) [4] Service AED Unit AUH 300 (1 per installation).
[6] Air jet 0.102 in. diameter. [7] Service AED Unit AUH 305 1 per installation Rover (U.S.A.) spec. only.

Model Details	Capacity	No. of Cyl.	Year	Spec.	Position[1]	Inter Connect	Type	Rich	Needle Std.	Weak
Apache 1300 (S.A.)	1275cc	4	1973/74	AUD 595	—	LHIC	HS4	—	CUD 1015	—
Apache 1300 Automatic (S.A.)	1275cc	4	1970/74	AUD 317	—	LHIC	HS4	AUD 1076	AUD 1528	AUD 1096
Mini GTS (S.A.)	1275cc	4	1971/	AUD 431L	LH	RHIC	HS2	—	AUD 1468	—
				AUD 431R	RH	LHIC	HS2	—	AUD 1468	—
Marina 1.7 Manual/Automatic (S.A.)	1748cc	4	1972	AUD 503	—	RHIC	HS6	—	CUD 1112	—
Marina 2.6 Manual/Automatic (S.A.)	2620cc	6	1973/75	AUD 588	—	RHIC	HS6	—	CUD 1148	—
Marina 1.7 Manual/Automatic (S.A.)	1748cc	4	1975/76	FZX 1099	—	RHIC	HS6	—	CUD 1131	—
Marina 1750 Automatic (S.A.)	1748cc	4	1975/76	FZX 1100	—	RHIC	HS6	—	CUD 1131	—
Marina 2.6 Automatic (S.A.)	2620cc	6	1975/76	FZX 1102	—	RHIC	HS6	—	CUD 1148	—
Mini Sal./Van/Moke (Australia)	1098cc	4	1974	AUD 668	—	RHIC	HS2	—	CUD 1043	—
1500 TC (Australia)	1485cc	4	1968	AUD 385L	LH	RHIC	HS6	—	AUD 1553	—
				AUD 385R	RH	LHIC	HS6	—	AUD 1553	—
1500 (Australia)	1485cc	4	1969	AUD 288	—	RHIC	HS6	—	AUD 1346	—
Marina 1500 (Australia)	1485cc	4	1972	AUD 487	—	RHIC	HS4	—	CUD 1004	—
Marina 1750 (Australia)	1748cc	4	1972/75	AUD 503	—	RHIC	HS6	—	CUD 1112	—
Marina 1750 TC (Australia)	1748cc	4	1972	AUD 504F	F	RHIC	HS6	—	CUD 1103	—
				AUD 504R	R	LHIC	HS6	—	CUD 1103	—
Marina 1.7 (Australia)	1748cc	4	1974	AUD 700	—	RHIC	HS6	—	CUD 1157	—
1800 Mk II (Australia)	1798cc	4	1968	AUD 381	—	RHIC	HS6	—	AUD 1327	—
1800 Mk II Automatic (Australia)	1798cc	4	1968	AUD 382	—	RHIC	HS6	—	AUD 1327	—
1800 Mk II TC (Australia)	1798cc	4	1968	AUD 385F	LH	RHIC	HS6	—	AUD 1553	—
				AUD 385R	RH	LHIC	HS6	—	AUD 1553	—
2200 (Australia)	2227cc	6	1971/72	AUD 419	—	RHIC	HS6	—	AUD 1583	—
Marina P76 (Australia)	2620cc	6	1973/75	AUD 588	—	RHIC	HS6	—	CUD 1148	—
Triumph 2.5 (Australia)	2498cc	6	1976	FZX 1105F	F	LHIC	HS6	—	NZX 8019	—
				FZX 1105R	R	RHIC	HS6	—	NZX 8019	—
Triumph 2500 (Australia)	2498cc	6	1976/	FZX 1117F	F	LHIC	HS6	—	NZX 8019	—
				FZX 1117R	R	RHIC	HS6	—	NZX 8019	—
Mini 850 (Spain)	848cc	4	1971/74	AUD 449	—	RHIC	HS2	—	CUD 1019	—
Mini 1000 (Spain)	998cc	4	1971/75	AUD 509	—	RHIC	HS2	—	CUD 1019	—
Mini GT (Spain)	1275cc	4	1972/74	AUD 559	—	LHIC	HS4	—	CUD 1025	—
1100 (Spain)	1098cc	4	1971/	AUD 368	—	RHIC	HS2	—	AUD 1478	—
Victoria 1300 (Spain)	1275cc	4	1972/74	AUD 559	—	LHIC	HS4	—	CUD 1025	—
Victoria 1300 TC (Spain)	1275cc	4	—	AUD 496L	LH	RHIC	HS2	—	CUD 1013	—
				AUD 496R	RH	LHIC	HS2	—	CUD 1013	—
Victoria 1300 (Spain)	1275cc	4	1973/	AUD 593	—	LHIC	HS6	—	CUD 1155	—

M.G.

Model Details	Capacity	No. of Cyl.	Year	Spec.	Position[1]	Inter Connect	Type	Rich	Needle Std.	Weak
MG Magnette Mk IV	1622cc	4	1961/68	AUD 41F	F	—	HD4	AUD 1200	AUD 1231	AUD 1190
				AUD 41R	R	—	HD4	AUD 1200	AUD 1231	AUD 1190
MG 1100	1098cc	4	1962/68	AUD 69L	L	RHIC	HS2	AUD 1144	AUD 1142	AUD 1468
				AUD 69R	R	LHIC	HS2	AUD 1144	AUD 1142	AUD 1468
Sedan (U.S.A.)	1275cc	4	1967/68	AUD 281	—	LHIC	HS4	—	AUD 1528	—
Sedan Automatic (U.S.A.)	1275cc	4	1968	AUD 296	—	LHIC	HS4	—	AUD 1528	—
MGC	2912cc	6	1967/68	AUD 150F	F	RHIC	HS6	AUD 1332	AUD 1335	AUD 1117
				AUD 150R	R	LHIC	HS6	AUD 1332	AUD 1335	AUD 1117
MGC	2912cc	6	1969	AUD 341F	F	RHIC	HS6	—	AUD 1335	—
				AUD 341R	R	LHIC	HS6	—	AUD 1335	—
MGC (U.S.A.)	2912cc	6	1968	AUD 287F	F	RHIC	HS6	—	AUD 1537	—
				AUD 287R	R	LHIC	HS6	—	AUD 1537	—
MGC (U.S.A.)	2912cc	6	1969	AUD 342F	F	RHIC	HS6	—	CUD 1103	—
				AUD 342R	R	LHIC	HS6	—	CUD 1103	—
Midget Mk II	1098cc	4	1964	AUD 136F	F	RHIC	HS2	AUD 1242	AUD 1478	AUD 1211
				AUD 136R	R	LHIC	HS2	AUD 1242	AUD 1478	AUD 1211
Midget Mk III	1275cc	4	1967/68	AUD 136F	F	RHIC	HS2	AUD 1242	AUD 1478	AUD 1211
				AUD 136R	R	LHIC	HS2	AUD 1242	AUD 1478	AUD 1211
Midget Mk III	1275cc	4	1968/71	AUD 327F	F	RHIC	HS2	AUD 1242	AUD 1478	AUD 1211
				AUD 327R	R	LHIC	HS2	AUD 1242	AUD 1478	AUD 1211
Midget Mk III	1275cc	4	1971/72	AUD 502F	F	RHIC	HS2	—	CUD 1017	—
				AUD 502R	R	LHIC	HS2	—	CUD 1017	—
Midget Mk III (E.C.E.)	1275cc	4	1973/74	AUD 662F	F	RHIC	HS2	—	CUD 1002	—
				AUD 662R	R	LHIC	HS2	—	CUD 1002	—
Midget Mk III (U.S.A.)	1275cc	4	1968	AUD 266F	F	RHIC	HS2	—	AUD 1478	—
				AUD 266R	R	LHIC	HS2	—	AUD 1478	—
Midget Mk III (U.S.A.)	1275cc	4	1968/69	AUD 328F	F	RHIC	HS2	—	CUD 1002	—
				AUD 328R	R	LHIC	HS2	—	BUB 180L	—
Midget Mk III (U.S.A.)	1275cc	4	1969/70	AUD 404F	F	RHIC	HS2	—	CUD 1002	—
				AUD 404R	R	LHIC	HS2	—	CUD 1002	—
Midget Mk III (U.S.A.)	1275cc	4	1972/74	AUD 549F	F	RHIC	HS2	—	CUD 1026	—
				AUD 549R	R	LHIC	HS2	—	CUD 1026	—
Midget 1500 (E.C.E.)	1493cc	4	1974/76	AUD 665F	F	LHIC	HS4	—	CUD 1041	—
				AUD 665R	R	RHIC	HS4	—	CUD 1041	—
MG 1300	1275cc	4	1967	AUD 186	—	LHIC	HS4	AUD 1076	AUD 1528	AUD 1096
MG 1300 Automatic	1275cc	4	1967/68	AUD 271	—	LHIC	HS4	AUD 1076	AUD 1528	AUD 1096
MG 1300	1275cc	4	1969	AUD 318L	LH	RHIC	HS2	AUD 1261	AUD 1149	AUD 1211
				AUD 318R	RH	LHIC	HS2	AUD 1261	AUD 1149	AUD 1211
MG 1300	1275cc	4	1969	AUD 374	—	LHIC	HS4	AUD 1076	AUD 1528	AUD 1096
MG 1300 Mk II	1275cc	4	1969/71	AUD 344L	LH	RHIC	HS2	AUD 1261	AUD 1468	AUD 1211
				AUD 344R	RH	LHIC	HS2	AUD 1261	AUD 1468	AUD 1211

[1] Front F, Centre C, Rear R, Right Hand RH, Left Hand LH. [2] Thermocarb gasket pack required in addition AUE 807.
[3] Air jet 0.116 in. diameter.

Spec. Repeated	Needle Guide	Needle Screw	Piston Spring	Damper	Jet	Needle and Seat	Float	Throttle Spindle	Throttle Disc	Gasket Pack	OE	Pump Alt.
AUD 595	AUD 4288	AUD 4251	AUC 4387	AUC 8103	AUD 9451	WZX 1100	WZX 1300	WZX 1312	WZX 1324	AUE 811	AUF 806	—
AUD 317	—	AUC 2057	AUC 4387	AUC 8103	AUD 9451	WZX 1100	WZX 1300	WZX 1312	WZX 1324	AUE 811	AUF 709	AUF 806
AUD 431L	—	AUC 2057	AUC 4587	AUC 8103	AUD 9142	WZX 1100	WZX 1300	WZX 1310	WZX 1320	AUE 810	AUF 214	—
AUD 431R	—	AUC 2057	AUC 4587	AUC 8103	AUD 9141	WZX 1100	WZX 1300	WZX 1310	WZX 1320	AUE 810	—	—
AUD 503	AUD 4288	AUD 4252	AUC 4387	AUC 8103	AUD 9148	WZX 1101	WZX 1300	WZX 1311	WZX 1321	AUE 812	AZX 1306	—
AUD 588	AUD 4288	AUD 4252	AUC 1170	AUC 8103	AUD 9148	WZX 1101	WZX 1300	WZX 1311	WZX 1321	AUE 812	AZX 1306	—
FZX 1099	AUD 4288	AUD 4252	AUC 4387	AUC 8103	AUD 9148	WZX 1100	WZX 1300	WZX 1311	WZX 1321	AUE 812	AUF 1305	—
FZX 1100	AUD 4288	AUD 4252	AUC 4387	AUC 8103	AUD 9148	WZX 1100	WZX 1300	WZX 1311	WZX 1321	AUE 812	AZX 1306	—
FZX 1102	AUD 4288	AUD 4252	AUC 1170	AUC 8103	AUD 9148	WZX 1101	WZX 1300	WZX 1311	WZX 1321	AUE 812	AZX 1306	—
AUD 668	AUD 4288	AUD 4250	AUC 4387	AUC 8103	AUD 9098	WZX 1100	WZX 1300	WZX 1310	WZX 1320	AUE 810	—	—
AUD 385L	—	AUC 2057	AUC 4587	AUC 8103	AUD 9105	WZX 1100	WZX 1300	WZX 1311	WZX 1321	AUE 812	—	—
AUD 385R	—	AUC 2057	AUC 4587	AUC 8103	AUD 9106	WZX 1100	WZX 1300	WZX 1311	WZX 1321	AUE 812	—	—
AUD 288	—	AUC 2057	AUC 4387	AUC 8103	AUD 9105	WZX 1101	WZX 1300	WZX 1311	WZX 1321	AUE 812	—	—
AUD 487	AUD 4288	AUD 4251	AUC 1167	AUC 8103	AUD 9141	WZX 1100	WZX 1300	WZX 1312	WZX 1324	AUE 811	—	—
AUD 530	AUD 4288	AUD 4252	AUC 1167	AUC 8103	AUD 9148	WZX 1101	WZX 1300	WZX 1311	WZX 1321	AUE 812	—	—
AUD 504F	AUD 4288	AUD 4252	AUC 4387	AUC 8103	AUD 9148	WZX 1100	WZX 1300	WZX 1311	WZX 1321	AUE 812	—	—
AUD 504R	AUD 4288	AUD 4252	AUC 4387	AUC 8103	AUD 9149	WZX 1100	WZX 1300	WZX 1311	WZX 1321	AUE 812	—	—
AUD 700	AUD 4288	AUD 4252	AUC 4387	AUC 8103	AUD 9148	WZX 1101	WZX 1300	WZX 1311	WZX 1321	AUE 812	—	—
AUD 381	—	AUC 2057	AUC 1167	AUC 8103	AUD 9148	WZX 1100	WZX 1300	WZX 1311	WZX 1321	AUE 812	—	—
AUD 382	—	AUC 2057	AUC 1167	AUC 8103	AUD 9148	WZX 1100	WZX 1300	WZX 1311	WZX 1321	AUE 812	—	—
AUD 385F	—	AUC 2057	AUC 4587	AUC 8103	AUD 9105	WZX 1101	WZX 1300	WZX 1311	WZX 1321	AUE 812	—	—
AUD 385R	—	AUC 2057	AUC 4587	AUC 8103	AUD 9106	WZX 1101	WZX 1300	WZX 1311	WZX 1321	AUE 812	—	—
AUD 419	—	AUC 2057	AUC 4387	AUC 8103	AUD 9148	WZX 1101	WZX 1300	WZX 1311	WZX 1321	AUE 812	—	—
AUD 588	AUD 4288	AUD 4252	AUC 1170	AUC 8103	AUD 9148	WZX 1101	WZX 1300	WZX 1311	WZX 1321	AUE 812	—	—
FZX 1105F	JZX 1039	AUD 4252	AUD 4398	CUD 2904	LZX 1059	WZX 1100	WZX 1300	WZX 1311	WZX 1379	AUE 812	—	—
FZX 1105R	JZX 1039	AUD 4252	AUD 4398	CUD 2904	LZX 1058	WZX 1100	WZX 1300	WZX 1311	WZX 1379	AUE 812	—	—
FZX 1117F	JZX 1039	AUD 4252	AUD 4398	CUD 2904	LZX 1059	WZX 1100	WZX 1300	WZX 1311	WZX 1379	AUE 812	—	—
FZX 1117R	JZX 1039	AUD 4252	AUD 4398	CUD 2904	LZX 1058	WZX 1100	WZX 1300	WZX 1311	WZX 1379	AUE 812	—	—
AUD 449	AUD 4288	AUD 4250	AUC 4387	AUC 8103	AUD 9098	WZX 1100	WZX 1300	WZX 1310	WZX 1320	AUE 810	AUF 706	AUF 805
AUD 509	AUD 4288	AUD 4250	AUC 4387	AUC 8103	AUD 9098	WZX 1100	WZX 1300	WZX 1310	WZX 1320	AUE 810	AUF 706	AUF 805
AUD 559	AUD 4288	AUC 4587	AUC 4387	AUC 8103	AUD 9451	WZX 1100	WZX 1300	WZX 1312	WZX 1324	AUE 811	—	—
AUD 368	—	AUC 2057	AUC 4387	AUC 8103	AUD 9098	WZX 1100	WZX 1300	WZX 1310	WZX 1320	AUE 810	—	—
AUD 559	AUD 4288	AUD 4251	AUC 4387	AUC 8103	AUD 9451	WZX 1100	WZX 1300	WZX 1312	WZX 1324	AUE 811	—	—
AUD 496L	AUD 4288	AUD 4250	AUC 4587	AUC 8103	AUD 9141	WZX 1100	WZX 1300	WZX 1310	WZX 1380	AUE 810	—	—
AUD 496R	AUD 4288	AUD 4250	AUC 4587	AUC 8103	AUD 9142	WZX 1100	WZX 1300	WZX 1310	WZX 1380	AUE 810	—	—
AUD 593	AUD 4288	AUD 4252	AUC 4387	AUC 8103	AUD 9106	WZX 1100	WZX 1300	WZX 1311	WZX 1321	AUE 812	—	—
AUD 41F	—	AUC 2057	AUC 4387	AUC 8114	AUC 8154	WZX 1100	WZX 1303	WZX 1215	WZX 1323	—	AUB 83	AUF 204
AUD 41R	—	AUC 2057	AUC 4387	AUC 8114	AUC 8154	WZX 1100	WZX 1303	WZX 1215	WZX 1323	—	—	—
AUD 69L	—	AUC 2057	AUC 4587	AUC 8103	AUD 9141	WZX 1100	WZX 1300	WZX 1310	WZX 1320	AUE 810	AUB 83	AUF 201
AUD 69R	—	AUC 2057	AUC 4587	AUC 8103	AUD 9142	WZX 1100	WZX 1300	WZX 1310	WZX 1320	AUE 810	—	—
AUD 281	—	AUC 2057	AUC 4387	AUC 8103	AUD 9894	WZX 1100	WZX 1300	WZX 1312	WZX 1325	AUE 811	AUF 207	AUF 204
AUD 296	—	AUC 2057	AUC 4387	AUC 8103	AUD 9894	WZX 1100	WZX 1300	WZX 1312	WZX 1325	AUE 811	AUF 207	AUF 204
AUD 150F	—	AUC 2057	AUC 1167	AUC 8103	AUD 9105	WZX 1100	WZX 1300	WZX 1311	WZX 1321	AUE 812	AUF 305	AZX 1304
AUD 150R	—	AUC 2057	AUC 1167	AUC 8103	AUD 9106	WZX 1100	WZX 1300	WZX 1311	WZX 1321	AUE 812	—	—
AUD 341F	—	AUC 2057	AUC 1167	AUC 8103	AUD 9105	WZX 1100	WZX 1300	WZX 1311	WZX 1321	AUE 812	AUF 305	AZX 1304
AUD 341R	—	AUC 2057	AUC 1167	AUC 8103	AUD 9106	WZX 1100	WZX 1300	WZX 1311	WZX 1321	AUE 812	—	—
AUD 287F	—	AUC 2057	AUC 1167	AUC 8103	AUD 9105	WZX 1100	WZX 1300	WZX 1311	WZX 1326	AUE 812	AUF 305	AZX 1304
AUD 287R	—	AUC 2057	AUC 1167	AUC 8103	AUD 9106	WZX 1100	WZX 1300	WZX 1311	WZX 1326	AUE 812	—	—
AUD 342F	AUD 4288	AUD 4252	AUC 1167	AUC 8103	AUD 9105	WZX 1100	WZX 1300	WZX 1311	WZX 1326	AUE 812	AUF 305	AZX 1304
AUD 342R	AUD 4288	AUD 4252	AUC 1167	AUC 8103	AUD 9106	WZX 1100	WZX 1300	WZX 1311	WZX 1326	AUE 812	—	—
AUD 136F	—	AUC 2057	AUC 4587	AUC 8114	AUD 9141	WZX 1100	WZX 1300	WZX 1310	WZX 1320	AUE 810	AUF 206	AUF 201
AUD 136R	—	AUC 2057	AUC 4587	AUC 8114	AUD 9142	WZX 1100	WZX 1300	WZX 1310	WZX 1320	AUE 810	—	—
AUD 136F	—	AUC 2057	AUC 4587	AUC 8114	AUD 9141	WZX 1100	WZX 1300	WZX 1310	WZX 1320	AUE 810	AUF 206	AUF 201
AUD 136R	—	AUC 2057	AUC 4587	AUC 8114	AUD 9142	WZX 1100	WZX 1300	WZX 1310	WZX 1320	AUE 810	—	—
AUD 327F	—	AUC 2057	AUC 4587	AUC 8114	AUD 9141	WZX 1100	WZX 1300	WZX 1310	WZX 1380	AUE 810	AUF 216	AUF 214
AUD 327R	—	AUC 2057	AUC 4587	AUC 8114	AUD 9142	WZX 1100	WZX 1300	WZX 1310	WZX 1380	AUE 810	—	—
AUD 502F	AUD 4288	AUD 4250	AUC 4587	AUC 8114	AUD 9141	WZX 1100	WZX 1300	WZX 1310	WZX 1380	AUE 810	AUF 216	AUF 214
AUD 502R	AUD 4288	AUD 4250	AUC 4587	AUC 8114	AUD 9142	WZX 1100	WZX 1300	WZX 1310	WZX 1380	AUE 810	—	—
AUD 662F	AUD 4288	AUD 4250	AUC 4587	AUC 8103	AUD 9141	WZX 1100	WZX 1300	WZX 1310	WZX 1320	AUE 810	AUF 206	AUF 201
AUD 662R	AUD 4288	AUD 4250	AUC 4587	AUC 8103	AUD 9142	WZX 1100	WZX 1300	WZX 1310	WZX 1320	AUE 810	—	—
AUD 266F	—	AUC 2057	AUC 4587	AUC 8114	AUD 9141	WZX 1100	WZX 1300	WZX 1310	WZX 1383	AUE 810	AUF 206	AUF 201
AUD 266R	—	AUC 2057	AUC 4587	AUC 8114	AUD 9142	WZX 1100	WZX 1300	WZX 1310	WZX 1383	AUE 810	AUF 216	AUF 214
AUD 328F	AUD 4288	AUD 4250	AUC 4587	AUC 8114	AUD 9141	WZX 1100	WZX 1300	WZX 1310	WZX 1383	AUE 810	—	—
AUD 328R	AUD 4288	AUD 4250	AUC 4587	AUC 8114	AUD 9142	WZX 1100	WZX 1300	WZX 1310	WZX 1383	AUE 810	AUF 216	AUF 214
AUD 404F	AUD 4290	AUD 4250	AUC 4587	AUC 8114	AUD 9141	WZX 1100	WZX 1300	WZX 1310	WZX 1383	AUE 810	—	—
AUD 404R	AUD 4290	AUD 4250	AUC 4587	AUC 8114	AUD 9142	WZX 1100	WZX 1300	WZX 1310	WZX 1383	AUE 810	AUF 305	AZX 1304
AUD 549F	AUD 4288	AUD 4250	AUC 4587	AUC 8114	AUD 9141	WZX 1100	WZX 1300	WZX 1310	WZX 1322	AUE 810	—	—
AUD 549R	AUD 4288	AUD 4250	AUC 4587	AUC 8114	AUD 9142	WZX 1100	WZX 1300	WZX 1310	WZX 1322	AUE 810	—	—
AUD 665F	AUD 4288	AUD 4251	AUC 4387	AUC 8114	AUD 9451	WZX 1100	WZX 1300	WZX 1312	WZX 1385	AUE 811	—	—
AUD 665R	AUD 4288	AUD 4251	AUC 4387	AUC 8103	AUD 9450	WZX 1100	WZX 1300	WZX 1312	WZX 1385	AUE 811	—	—
AUD 186	—	AUC 2057	AUC 4587	AUC 8103	AUD 9451	WZX 1100	WZX 1300	WZX 1312	WZX 1324	AUE 811	AUF 207	AUF 204
AUD 271	—	AUC 2057	AUC 4387	AUC 8103	AUD 9451	WZX 1100	WZX 1300	WZX 1312	WZX 1324	AUE 811	AUF 207	AUF 204
AUD 318L	—	AUC 2057	AUC 4587	AUC 8103	AUD 9141	WZX 1100	WZX 1300	WZX 1310	WZX 1320	AUE 810	—	—
AUD 318R	—	AUC 2057	AUC 4587	AUC 8103	AUD 9142	WZX 1100	WZX 1300	yZX 1310	WZX 1320	AUE 810	—	—
AUD 374	—	AUC 2057	AUC 4387	AUC 8103	AUD 9451	WZX 1100	WZX 1300	WZX 1312	WZX 1324	AUE 811	AUF 207	AUF 204
AUD 344L	—	AUC 2057	AUC 4587	AUC 8103	AUD 9141	WZX 1100	WZX 1300	WZX 1310	WZX 1320	AUE 810	AUF 207	AUF 204
AUD 344R	—	AUC 2057	AUC 4587	AUC 8103	AUD 9142	WZX 1100	WZX 1300	WZX 1310	WZX 1320	AUE 810	—	—

[3] AED Unit TZX 1002 supersedes AUH 308, 309, 310 and 317 (1 per installation).
[6] Air jet 0.102 in. diameter.   [7] Service AED Unit AUH 305 1 per installation Rover (U.S.A.) spec. only.
[4] Service AED Unit AUH 300 (1 per installation).

Model Details	Capacity	No. of Cyl.	Year	Spec.	Position¹	Inter Connect	Type	Rich	Needle Std.	Weak
MG 1300 Mk II	1275cc	4	1971	AUD 431L	LH	RHIC	HS2	AUD 1261	AUD 1468	AUD 1211
				AUD 431R	RH	LHIC	HS2	AUD 1261	AUD 1468	AUD 1211
MG 1300 Mk II	1275cc	4	1971/72	AUD 454L	LH	RHIC	HS2	—	CUD 1013	—
				AUD 454R	RH	LHIC	HS2	—	CUD 1013	—
MG 1300 Mk II (E.C.E.)	1275cc	4	1971/72	AUD 496L	LH	RHIC	HS2	—	CUD 1013	—
				AUD 496R	RH	LHIC	HS2	—	CUD 1013	—
MGB (U.S.A.)	1798cc	4	1968	AUD 265F	F	RHIC	HS4	—	AUD 1530	—
				AUD 265R	R	LHIC	HS4	—	AUD 1530	—
MGB Mk II (U.S.A.)	1798cc	4	1968/69	AUD 326F	F	RHIC	HS4	—	CUD 1004	—
				AUD 326R	R	LHIC	HS4	—	CUD 1004	—
MGB Mk II (U.S.A.)	1798cc	4	1970/71	AUD 405F	F	RHIC	HS4	—	CUD 1004	—
				AUD 405R	R	LHIC	HS4	—	CUD 1004	—
MGB Mk II (U.S.A.)	1798cc	4	1971	AUD 465F	F	RHIC	HS4	—	CUD 1010	—
				AUD 465R	R	LHIC	HS4	—	CUD 1010	—
MGB	1798cc	4	1972	AUD 492F	F	RHIC	HS4	—	CUD 1018	—
				AUD 492R	R	LHIC	HS4	—	CUD 1018	—
MGB Mk II (U.S.A.)	1798cc	4	1972	AUD 493F	F	RHIC	HIF4	—	CUD 1018	—
				AUD 493R	R	LHIC	HIF4	—	CUD 1018	—
MGB (U.S.A.)	1798cc	4	1972/74	AUD 550F	F	RHIC	HIF4	—	CUD 1027	—
				AUD 550R	R	LHIC	HIF4	—	CUD 1027	—
MGB (U.S.A.)	1798cc	4	1974/	AUD 630F	F	RHIC	HIF4	—	CUD 1027	—
				AUD 630R	R	LHIC	HIF4	—	CUD 1027	—
MGB Competition	1798cc	4	1963/64	AUD 129F	F	—	HD8	—.	AUD 1376	—
				AUD 129R	R	—	HD8	—	AUD 1376	—
MGB & GT	1798cc	4	1965/66	AUD 135F	F	RHIC	HS4	AUD 1005	AUD 1004	AUD 1008
				AUD 135R	R	LHIC	HS4	AUD 1005	AUD 1004	AUD 1008
MGB & GT	1798cc	4	1967/68	AUD 278F	F	RHIC	HS4	AUD 1004	AUD 1530	AUD 1473
				AUD 278R	R	LHIC	HS4	AUD 1004	AUD 1530	AUD 1473
MGB	1798cc	4	1969/71	AUD 325F	F	RHIC	HS4	AUD 1004	AUD 1530	AUD 1473
				AUD 325R	R	LHIC	HS4	AUD 1004	AUD 1530	AUD 1473
MGB	1798cc	4	1972	AUD 434F	F	RHIC	HIF4	—	CUD 1018	—
				AUD 434R	R	LHIC	HIF4	—	CUD 1018	—
MGB (E.C.E.)	1798cc	4	1973/74	AUD 616F	F	RHIC	HIF4	—	CUD 1018	—
				AUD 616R	R	LHIC	HIF4	—	CUD 1018	—
MGB (E.C.E.)	1798cc	4	1974/76	FZX 1001F	F	RHIC	HIF4	—	CUD 1051	—
				FZX 1001R	R	LHIC	HIF4	—	CUD 1051	—
MGB	1798cc	4	1976/	FZX 1229F	F	RHIC	HIF4	—	CUD 1051	—
				FZX 1229R	R	LHIC	HIF4	—	CUD 1051	—
MGB GT V8 (E.C.E.)	3528cc	8	1973/76	AUD 613L	LH	RHIC	HIF6	—	CUD 1142	—
				AUD 613R	RH	LHIC	HIF6	—	CUD 1142	—

MORRIS

Model Details	Capacity	No. of Cyl.	Year	Spec.	Position¹	Inter Connect	Type	Rich	Needle Std.	Weak
Minor	1098cc	4	1962/70	AUD 13	—	RHIC	HS2	AUD 1242	AUD 1478	AUD 1149
Oxford	1622cc	4	1961/71	AUD 40	—	RHIC	HS2	AUD 1261	AUD 1478	AUD 1211
Mini	848cc	4	1962/68	AUC 976	—	RHIC	HS2	AUD 1261	AUD 1149	AUD 1211
Mini Automatic	848cc	4	1965/66	AUD 170	—	LHIC	HS4	AUD 1242	AUD 1478	AUD 1149
Mini Automatic	848cc	4	1967	AUD 250	—	LHIC	HS4	AUD 1242	AUD 1478	AUD 1149
Mini	848cc	4	1968/71	AUD 299	—	RHIC	HS2	AUD 1242	AUD 1478	AUD 1149
Mini Automatic	848cc	4	1969	AUD 360	—	LHIC	HS4	AUD 1261	AUD 1478	AUD 1211
Mini Mk II	848cc	4	1969/75	AUD 359	—	RHIC	HS2	—	AUD 1149	—
Mini (E.C.E.)	848cc	4	1971/74	AUD 449	—	RHIC	HS2	—	CUD 1019	—
Mini Van (G.P.O.)	848cc	4	1972/73	AUD 587	—	RHIC	HS2	—	CUD 1019	—
Mini Mk II	998cc	4	1967/68	AUD 86	—	RHIC	HS2	AUD 1261	AUD 1227	AUD 1211
Mini Mk II Automatic	998cc	4	1967/68	AUD 184	—	LHIC	HS4	AUD 1267	AUD 1034	AUD 1230
Mini Mk II	998cc	4	1968/71	AUD 298	—	RHIC	HS2	AUD 1261	AUD 1227	AUD 1211
Mini Mk II Automatic	998cc	4	1969	AUD 366	—	LHIC	HS4	AUD 1267	AUD 1034	AUD 1230
Mini Mk II	998cc	4	1969	AUD 363	—	RHIC	HS2	AUD 1261	AUD 1227	AUD 1211
Mini Mk II Automatic	998cc	4	1970	AUD 367	—	LHIC	HS4	AUD 1267	AUD 1034	AUD 1230
Mini Mk II Automatic	998cc	4	1970/74	AUD 393	—	LHIC	HS4	AUD 1267	AUD 1034	AUD 1230
Mini (E.C.E.)	998cc	4	1971/74	AUD 509	—	RHIC	HS2	—	CUD 1019	—
Mini Mk II Automatic (E.C.E.)	988cc	4	1974/	AUD 679	—	LHIC	HS4	—	CUD 1045	—
Mini Clubman	998cc	4	1969	AUD 363	—	RHIC	HS2	AUD 1261	AUD 1227	AUD 1211
Mini Clubman Automatic	998cc	4	1970/74	AUD 393	—	LHIC	HS4	AUD 1267	AUD 1034	AUD 1230
Mini Clubman (E.C.E.)	998cc	4	1971/75	AUD 509	—	RHIC	HS2	—	CUD 1019	—
Mini Clubman Automatic	998cc	4	1972/	AUD 450	—	LHIC	HS4	—	CUD 1006	—
Mini Clubman Man/Auto (E.C.E.)	998cc	4	1974/76	AUD 679	—	LHIC	HS4	—	CUD 1045	—
Mini Van (G.P.O.)	998cc	4	1974/75	AUD 706	—	LHIC	HS4	—	CUD 1045	—
Mini Mk II Man/Auto (E.C.E.) Exp. only	1098cc	4	1973/75	AUD 608	—	LHIC	HS4	—	CUD 1037	—
Mini Clubman 1275 GT	1275cc	4	1969	AUD 317	—	LHIC	HS4	AUD 1076	AUD 1528	AUD 1096
Mini Clubman 1275 GT (E.C.E.)	1275cc	4	1971/72	AUD 451	—	LHIC	HS4	—	CUD 1015	—
Mini Clubman 1275 GT (E.C.E.)	1275cc	4	1972/76	AUD 567	—	LHIC	HS4	—	CUD 1025	—
Mini Cooper	998cc	4	1964/69	AUD 104L	L	RHIC	HS2	AUD 1261	AUD 1468	AUD 1211
				AUD 104R	R	LHIC	HS2	AUD 1261	AUD 1468	AUD 1211
Mini Cooper 'S'	970cc	4	1964	AUD 151L	L	RHIC	HS2	AUD 1242	AUD 1478	AUD 1149
				AUD 151R	R	LHIC	HS2	AUD 1242	AUD 1478	AUD 1149
Mini Cooper 'S'	1070cc	4	1963/64	AUD 99L	L	RHIC	HS2	AUD 1002	AUD 1242	AUD 1149
				AUD 99R	R	LHIC	HS2	AUD 1002	AUD 1242	AUD 1149
Mini Cooper 'S'	1275cc	4	1964/70	AUD 146L	L	RHIC	HS2	AUD 1059	AUD 1261	AUD 1149
				AUD 146R	R	LHIC	HS2	AUD 1059	AUD 1261	AUD 1149

¹ Front F, Centre C, Rear R, Right Hand RH, Left Hand LH. ² Thermocarb gasket pack required in addition AUE 807.
³ Air jet 0.116 in. diameter.

Spec. Repeated	Needle Guide	Needle Screw	Piston Spring	Damper	Jet	Needle and Seat	Float	Throttle Spindle	Throttle Disc	Gasket Pack	Pump OE	Pump Alt.
AUD 431 L	—	AUC 2057	AUC 4587	AUC 8103	AUD 9141	WZX 1100	WZX 1300	WZX 1310	WZX 1320	AUE 810	AUF 207	AUF 204
AUD 431 R	—	AUC 2057	AUC 4587	AUC 8103	AUD 9142	WZX 1100	WZX 1300	WZX 1310	WZX 1320	AUE 810	—	—
AUD 454 L	AUD 4288	AUC 4250	AUC 4587	AUC 8103	AUD 9141	WZX 1100	WZX 1300	WZX 1310	WZX 1380	AUE 810	AUF 207	AUF 204
AUD 454 R	AUD 4288	AUC 4250	AUC 4587	AUC 8103	AUD 9142	WZX 1100	WZX 1300	WZX 1310	WZX 1380	AUE 810	—	—
AUD 496 L	AUD 4288	AUC 4250	AUC 4587	AUC 8103	AUD 9141	WZX 1100	WZX 1300	WZX 1310	WZX 1380	AUE 810	AUF 207	AUF 204
AUD 496 R	AUD 4288	AUC 4250	AUC 4587	AUC 8103	AUD 9142	WZX 1100	WZX 1300	WZX 1310	WZX 1380	AUE 810	—	—
AUD 265 F	—	AUC 2057	AUC 4387	AUC 8114	AUD 9141	WZX 1100	WZX 1300	WZX 1312	WZX 1329	AUE 811	AUF 305	AZX 1304
AUD 265 R	—	AUC 2057	AUC 4387	AUC 8114	AUD 9142	WZX 1100	WZX 1300	WZX 1312	WZX 1329	AUE 811	—	—
AUD 326 F	AUD 4288	AUC 4251	AUC 4387	AUC 8114	AUD 9141	WZX 1100	WZX 1300	WZX 1312	WZX 1329	AUE 811	AUF 305	AZX 1304
AUD 326 R	AUD 4288	AUC 4251	AUC 4387	AUC 8114	AUD 9142	WZX 1100	WZX 1300	WZX 1312	WZX 1329	AUE 811	—	—
AUD 405 F	AUD 4288	AUC 4251	AUC 4387	AUC 8114	AUD 9141	WZX 1100	WZX 1300	WZX 1312	WZX 1329	AUE 811	AUF 305	AZX 1304
AUD 405 R	AUD 4288	AUC 4251	AUC 4387	AUC 8114	AUD 9142	WZX 1100	WZX 1300	WZX 1312	WZX 1329	AUE 811	—	—
AUD 465 F	AUD 4288	AUC 4251	AUC 4387	AUC 8114	AUD 9141	WZX 1100	WZX 1300	WZX 1312	WZX 1329	AUE 811	AUF 305	AZX 1304
AUD 465 R	AUD 4288	AUC 4251	AUC 4387	AUC 8114	AUD 9142	WZX 1100	WZX 1300	WZX 1312	WZX 1329	AUE 811	—	—
AUD 492 F	AUD 4288	AUC 4251	AUC 4387	AUC 8114	AUD 9141	WZX 1100	WZX 1300	WZX 1312	WZX 1323	AUE 811	AUF 305	AZX 1304
AUD 492 R	AUD 4288	AUC 4251	AUC 4387	AUC 8114	AUD 9142	WZX 1100	WZX 1300	WZX 1312	WZX 1323	AUE 811	—	—
AUD 493 F	AUD 4287	AUC 4251	AUC 4387	AUC 8114	WZX 1454	WZX 1100	WZX 1401	WZX 1170	WZX 1329	WZX 1505	AUF 305	AZX 1304
AUD 493 R	AUD 4287	AUC 4251	AUC 4387	AUC 8114	WZX 1455	WZX 1100	WZX 1400	WZX 1170	WZX 1329	WZX 1505	—	—
AUD 550 F	AUD 4287	AUC 4251	AUC 4387	AUC 8114	WZX 1454	WZX 1100	WZX 1401	WZX 1170	WZX 1329	WZX 1505	AUF 305	AZX 1304
AUD 550 R	AUD 4287	AUC 4251	AUC 4387	AUC 8114	WZX 1455	WZX 1100	WZX 1400	WZX 1170	WZX 1329	WZX 1505	—	—
AUD 630 F	JZX 1039	AUC 4251	AUC 4387	CUD 2904	WZX 1454	WZX 1100	WZX 1401	WZX 1170	WZX 1329	WZX 1505	AUF 305	AZX 1304
AUD 630 R	JZX 1039	AUC 4251	AUC 4387	CUD 2904	WZX 1455	WZX 1100	WZX 1400	WZX 1170	WZX 1329	WZX 1505	—	—
AUD 129 F	—	AUC 2057	AUC 2107	AUC 8102	AUC 8156	WZX 1101	WZX 1303	AUC 4837	WZX 1373	AUE 806	AUA 150	AUF 305
AUD 129 R	—	AUC 2057	AUC 2107	AUC 8102	AUC 8156	WZX 1101	WZX 1303	AUC 4837	WZX 1373	AUE 806	—	—
AUD 135 F	—	AUC 2057	AUC 4387	AUC 8114	AUD 9141	WZX 1100	WZX 1300	WZX 1312	WZX 1323	AUE 811	AUF 301	AUF 305
AUD 135 R	—	AUC 2057	AUC 4387	AUC 8114	AUD 9142	WZX 1100	WZX 1300	WZX 1312	WZX 1323	AUE 811	—	—
AUD 278 F	—	AUC 2057	AUC 4387	AUC 8114	AUD 9141	WZX 1100	WZX 1300	WZX 1312	WZX 1323	AUE 811	AUF 305	AZX 1304
AUD 278 R	—	AUC 2057	AUC 4387	AUC 8114	AUD 9142	WZX 1100	WZX 1300	WZX 1312	WZX 1323	AUE 811	—	—
AUD 325 F	—	AUC 2057	AUC 4387	AUC 8114	AUD 9141	WZX 1100	WZX 1300	WZX 1312	WZX 1323	AUE 811	AUF 305	AZX 1304
AUD 325 R	—	AUC 2057	AUC 4387	AUC 8114	AUD 9142	WZX 1100	WZX 1300	WZX 1312	WZX 1323	AUE 811	—	—
AUD 434 F	AUD 4287	AUC 4251	AUC 4387	AUC 8114	WZX 1454	WZX 1100	WZX 1401	WZX 1170	WZX 1323	WZX 1505	AUF 305	AZX 1304
AUD 434 R	AUD 4287	AUC 4251	AUC 4387	AUC 8114	WZX 1455	WZX 1100	WZX 1400	WZX 1170	WZX 1323	WZX 1505	—	—
AUD 616 F	AUD 4287	AUC 4251	AUC 4387	AUC 8114	WZX 1454	WZX 1100	WZX 1401	WZX 1170	WZX 1329	WZX 1505	AUF 305	AZX 1304
AUD 616 R	AUD 4287	AUC 4251	AUC 4387	AUC 8114	WZX 1455	WZX 1100	WZX 1400	WZX 1170	WZX 1329	WZX 1505	—	—
FZX 1001 F	AUD 4287	AUC 4251	AUC 4387	AUC 8114	WZX 1454	WZX 1100	WZX 1401	WZX 1170	WZX 1329	WZX 1505	AUF 305	AZX 1304
FZX 1001 R	AUD 4287	AUC 4251	AUC 4387	AUC 8114	WZX 1455	WZX 1100	WZX 1400	WZX 1170	WZX 1329	WZX 1505	—	—
FZX 1229 F	AUD 4287	AUC 4251	AUC 4387	AUC 8114	WZX 1454	WZX 1102	WZX 1401	WZX 1170	WZX 1329	WZX 1505	AUF 305	AZX 1304
FZX 1229 R	AUD 4287	AUC 4251	AUC 4387	AUC 8114	WZX 1455	WZX 1102	WZX 1400	WZX 1170	WZX 1329	WZX 1505	—	—
AUD 613 L	AUD 4288	AUC 4252	AUD 4398	CUD 2902	WZX 1452	WZX 1100	WZX 1401	WZX 1171	WZX 1326	WZX 1505	AUF 305	AZX 1304
AUD 613 R	AUD 4288	AUC 4252	AUD 4398	CUD 2902	WZX 1453	WZX 1100	WZX 1400	WZX 1171	WZX 1326	WZX 1505	—	—
AUD 13	—	AUC 2057	AUC 4387	AUC 8103	AUD 9098	WZX 1100	WZX 1300	WZX 1310	WZX 1320	AUE 810	AUA 66	—
AUD 40	—	AUC 2057	AUC 1167	AUC 8103	AUD 9098	WZX 1100	WZX 1300	WZX 1310	WZX 1320	AUE 810	AUA 83	AUF 204
AUC 976	—	AUC 2057	AUC 4387	AUC 8103	AUD 9142	WZX 1100	WZX 1300	WZX 1310	WZX 1323	AUE 811	AUF 214	—
AUD 170	—	AUC 2057	AUC 4387	AUC 8103	AUD 9451	WZX 1100	WZX 1300	WZX 1312	WZX 1324	AUE 811	AUF 201	AUF 214
AUD 250	—	AUC 2057	AUC 4387	AUC 8103	AUD 9098	WZX 1100	WZX 1300	WZX 1310	WZX 1320	AUE 810	AUF 214	—
AUD 299	—	AUC 2057	AUC 4387	AUC 8103	AUD 9451	WZX 1100	WZX 1300	WZX 1312	WZX 1324	AUE 811	AUF 214	—
AUD 360	—	AUC 2057	AUC 4387	AUC 8103	AUD 9098	WZX 1100	WZX 1300	WZX 1310	WZX 1320	AUE 810	AUF 706	AUF 805
AUD 359	—	AUC 2057	AUC 4387	AUC 8103	AUD 9098	WZX 1100	WZX 1300	WZX 1310	WZX 1320	AUE 810	—	—
AUD 449	AUD 4288	AUC 4250	AUC 4387	AUC 8103	AUD 9098	WZX 1100	WZX 1300	WZX 1310	WZX 1320	AUE 810	AUF 706	AUF 805
AUD 587	AUD 4288	AUC 4250	AUC 4387	AUC 8103	AUD 9098	WZX 1100	WZX 1300	WZX 1310	WZX 1320	AUE 810	AUF 706	AUF 805
AUD 86	—	AUC 2057	AUC 4387	AUC 8103	AUD 9098	WZX 1100	WZX 1300	WZX 1310	WZX 1320	AUE 810	AUF 201	AUF 214
AUD 184	—	AUC 2057	AUC 4387	AUC 8103	AUD 9451	WZX 1100	WZX 1300	WZX 1312	WZX 1324	AUE 811	AUF 201	AUF 214
AUD 298	—	AUC 2057	AUC 4387	AUC 8103	AUD 9098	WZX 1100	WZX 1300	WZX 1310	WZX 1320	AUE 810	AUF 214	—
AUD 366	—	AUC 2057	AUC 4387	AUC 8103	AUD 9451	WZX 1100	WZX 1300	WZX 1312	WZX 1324	AUE 811	AUF 214	—
AUD 363	—	AUC 2057	AUC 4387	AUC 8103	AUD 9098	WZX 1100	WZX 1300	WZX 1310	WZX 1320	AUE 810	AUF 214	—
AUD 367	—	AUC 2057	AUC 4387	AUC 8103	AUD 9451	WZX 1100	WZX 1300	WZX 1312	WZX 1324	AUE 811	AUF 214	—
AUD 393	—	AUC 2057	AUC 4387	AUC 8103	AUD 9451	WZX 1100	WZX 1300	WZX 1312	WZX 1323	AUE 811	AUF 214	—
AUD 509	AUD 4288	AUC 4250	AUC 4387	AUC 8103	AUD 9098	WZX 1100	WZX 1300	WZX 1312	WZX 1324	AUE 811	AUF 706	AUF 805
AUD 679	AUD 4288	AUC 4251	AUC 4387	AUC 8103	AUD 9451	WZX 1100	WZX 1300	WZX 1310	WZX 1320	AUE 810	AUF 705	AUF 812
AUD 363	—	AUC 2057	AUC 4387	AUC 8103	AUD 9098	WZX 1100	WZX 1300	WZX 1310	WZX 1323	AUE 811	AUF 722	AUF 812
AUD 393	—	AUC 2057	AUC 4387	AUC 8103	AUD 9451	WZX 1100	WZX 1300	WZX 1310	WZX 1320	AUE 810	AUF 706	AUF 805
AUD 509	AUD 4288	AUC 4250	AUC 4387	AUC 8103	AUD 9098	WZX 1100	WZX 1300	WZX 1312	WZX 1324	AUE 811	AUF 722	AUF 812
AUD 450	AUD 4288	AUC 4251	AUC 4387	AUC 8103	AUD 9451	WZX 1100	WZX 1300	WZX 1312	WZX 1324	AUE 811	AUF 706	AUF 805
AUD 679	AUD 4288	AUC 4251	AUC 4387	AUC 8103	AUD 9451	WZX 1100	WZX 1300	WZX 1312	WZX 1324	AUE 811	AUF 722	AUF 812
AUD 706	AUD 4288	AUC 4251	AUC 4387	AUC 8103	AUD 9451	WZX 1100	WZX 1300	WZX 1312	WZX 1324	AUE 811	AUF 722	AUF 812
AUD 608	AUD 4288	AUC 4251	AUC 4387	AUC 8103	AUD 9451	WZX 1100	WZX 1300	WZX 1312	WZX 1324	AUE 811	AUF 706	AUF 805
AUD 317	—	AUC 2057	AUC 4387	AUC 8103	AUD 9451	WZX 1100	WZX 1300	WZX 1312	WZX 1323	AUE 811	AUF 722	AUF 812
AUD 451	AUD 4288	AUC 4251	AUC 4387	AUC 8103	AUD 9451	WZX 1100	WZX 1300	WZX 1312	WZX 1324	AUE 811	AUF 722	AUF 812
AUD 567	AUD 4288	AUC 4251	AUC 4387	AUC 8103	AUD 9451	WZX 1100	WZX 1300	WZX 1310	WZX 1320	AUE 810	AUF 201	AUF 214
AUD 104 L	—	AUC 2057	AUC 4587	AUC 8103	AUD 9141	WZX 1100	WZX 1300	WZX 1310	WZX 1320	AUE 810	—	—
AUD 104 R	—	AUC 2057	AUC 4587	AUC 8103	AUD 9142	WZX 1100	WZX 1300	WZX 1310	WZX 1320	AUE 810	—	—
AUD 151 L	—	AUC 2057	AUC 4387	AUC 8103	AUD 9141	WZX 1100	WZX 1300	WZX 1310	WZX 1320	AUE 810	AUF 201	AUF 214
AUD 151 R	—	AUC 2057	AUC 4387	AUC 8103	AUD 9142	WZX 1100	WZX 1300	WZX 1310	WZX 1320	AUE 810	—	—
AUD 99 L	—	AUC 2057	AUC 4387	AUC 8103	AUD 9141	WZX 1100	WZX 1300	WZX 1310	WZX 1320	AUE 810	AUB 83	AUF 201
AUD 99 R	—	AUC 2057	AUC 4387	AUC 8103	AUD 9142	WZX 1100	WZX 1300	WZX 1310	WZX 1320	AUE 810	—	—
AUD 146 L	—	AUC 2057	AUC 4387	AUC 8103	AUD 9141	WZX 1100	WZX 1300	WZX 1310	WZX 1320	AUE 810	AUF 201	AUF 214
AUD 146 R	—	AUC 2057	AUC 4387	AUC 8103	AUD 9142	WZX 1100	WZX 1300	WZX 1310	WZX 1320	AUE 810	—	—

[3] AED Unit TZX 1002 supersedes AUH 308, 309, 310 and 317 (1 per installation).
[6] Air jet 0.102 in. diameter.   [7] Service AED Unit AUH 305 1 per installation Rover (U.S.A.) spec. only.

[4] Service AED Unit AUH 300 (1 per installation).
IMPORTANT
Mechanical Fuel Pumps, see note on inside of back cover

Model Details	Capacity	No. of Cyl.	Year	Spec.	Position	Inter Connect	Type	Rich	Needle Std.	Weak
Mini Cooper 'S'	1275cc	4	1970/71	AUD 440L	L	RHIC	HS2	AUD 1059	AUD 1261	AUD 1149
				AUD 440R	R	LHIC	HS2	AUD 1059	AUD 1261	AUD 1149
1100 Automatic	1098cc	4	1965/66	AUD 185	—	LHIC	HS4	AUD 1076	AUD 1522	AUD 1151
1100 Automatic	1098cc	4	1967	AUD 251	—	LHIC	HS4	AUD 1076	AUD 1522	AUD 1151
1100 Mk II	1098cc	4	1967/68	AUD 13	—	RHIC	HS2	AUD 1242	AUD 1478	AUD 1149
1100 Mk II Automatic	1098cc	4	1969/71	AUD 370	—	LHIC	HS4	AUD 1076	AUD 1522	AUD 1151
1300	1275cc	4	1967/68	AUD 186	—	LHIC	HS4	AUD 1076	AUD 1528	AUD 1096
1300 Automatic	1275cc	4	1967/68	AUD 271	—	LHIC	HS4	AUD 1076	AUD 1528	AUD 1096
1300	1275cc	4	1969/70	AUD 374	—	LHIC	HS4	AUD 1076	AUD 1528	AUD 1096
1300 Automatic	1275cc	4	1969/70	AUD 376	—	LHIC	HS4	AUD 1076	AUD 1528	AUD 1096
1300 GT	1275cc	4	1969/71	AUD 344L	L	RHIC	HS2	AUD 1261	AUD 1468	AUD 1211
				AUD 344R	R	LHIC	HS2	AUD 1261	AUD 1468	AUD 1211
1300	1275cc	4	1971	AUD 472	—	LHIC	HS4	AUD 1076	AUD 1528	AUD 1096
1300 GT	1275cc	4	1971/75	AUD 431L	L	RHIC	HS2	AUD 1261	AUD 1468	AUD 1211
				AUD 431R	R	LHIC	HS2	AUD 1261	AUD 1468	AUD 1211
1300	1275cc	4	1971	AUD 480	—	LHIC	HS4	AUD 1076	AUD 1528	AUD 1096
1300 Traveller (E.C.E.)	1275cc	4	1971/72	AUD 453	—	LHIC	HS4	—	CUD 1015	—
1300 Traveller	1275cc	4	1972/73	AUD 559	—	LHIC	HS4	—	CUD 1025	—
1300 Mk III Traveller	1275cc	4	1972/73	AUD 585	—	LHIC	HS4	—	CUD 1015	—
1300 Mk III Traveller (E.C.E.)	1275cc	4	1973/75	AUD 594	—	LHIC	HS4	—	CUD 1025	—
1300 Mk III Traveller	1275cc	4	1973	AUD 595	—	LHIC	HS4	—	CUD 1015	—
1300 Traveller Automatic (E.C.E.)	1275cc	4	1971/72	AUD 486	—	LHIC	HS4	—	CUD 1015	—
1300 Mk III Traveller Automatic (E.C.E.)	1275cc	4	1972/76	AUD 567	—	LHIC	HS4	—	CUD 1025	—
Marina 1100 Van	1098cc	4	1976/	FZX 1187	—	RHIC	HS4	—	CUD 1036	—
Marina 1.3	1275cc	4	1971/72	AUD 354	—	RHIC	HS4	—	CUD 1014	—
Marina 1.3 Automatic	1275cc	4	1971/76	AUD 436	—	RHIC	HS4	—	CUD 1014	—
Marina 1.3 (E.C.E.)	1275cc	4	1972/76	AUD 541	—	RHIC	HS4	—	CUD 1023	—
Marina 1.3 Automatic (E.C.E.)	1275cc	4	1972/	AUD 542	—	RHIC	HS4	—	CUD 1023	—
Marina 1.3 (E.C.E.)	1275cc	4	1976/6	AUD 670	—	RHIC	HS4	—	NZX 4007	—
Marina 1.3	1275cc	4	1976/	FZX 1189	—	RHIC	HS4	—	NZX 4007	—
Marina 1.3 Automatic	1275cc	4	1975/	FZX 1071	—	RHIC	HS4	—	NZX 4007	—
Marina 1.3 Automatic	1275cc	4	1976/	FZX 1191	—	RHIC	HS4	—	NZX 4007	—
Marina 1.8	1798cc	4	1971/72	AUD 428	—	RHIC	HS6	—	CUD 1114	—
Marina 1.8 Automatic	1798cc	4	1971/72	AUD 479	—	RHIC	HS6	—	CUD 1114	—
Marina 1.8 TC	1798cc	4	1971/72	AUD 445F	F	RHIC	HS4	—	CUD 1016	—
				AUD 445R	R	LHIC	HS4	—	CUD 1016	—
Marina 1.8 TC Automatic	1798cc	4	1971/72	AUD 464F	F	RHIC	HS4	—	CUD 1016	—
				AUD 464R	R	LHIC	HS4	—	CUD 1016	—
Marina 1.8 (E.C.E.)	1798cc	4	1972/75	AUD 535	—	RHIC	HS6	—	CUD 1116	—
Marina 1.8 Automatic (E.C.E.)	1798cc	4	1972/75	AUD 536	—	RHIC	HS6	—	CUD 1116	—
Marina 1.8 TC (E.C.E.)	1798cc	4	1972/74	AUD 543F	F	RHIC	HS4	—	CUD 1024	—
				AUD 543R	R	LHIC	HS4	—	CUD 1024	—
Marina 1.8 (E.C.E.)	1798cc	4	1972/76	AUD 566	—	RHIC	HS6	—	CUD 1116	—
Marina 1.8 TC (E.C.E.) Automatic	1798cc	4	1973/4	AUD 673F	F	RHIC	HS4	—	CUD 1016	—
				AUD 673R	R	LHIC	HS4	—	CUD 1016	—
Marina 1.8 (E.C.E.)	1798cc	4	1974/	FZX 1011	—	RHIC	HS6	—	CUD 1168	—
Marina 1.8 Automatic (E.C.E.)	1798cc	4	1974/76	FZX 1012	—	RHIC	HS6	—	CUD 1168	—
Marina 1.8 TC (E.C.E.)	1798cc	4	1974/76	FZX 1013F	F	RHIC	HS4	—	CUD 1052	—
				FZX 1013R	R	LHIC	HS4	—	CUD 1052	—
Marina 1.8 TC Automatic (E.C.E.)	1798cc	4	1974/76	FZX 1014F	F	RHIC	HS4	—	CUD 1052	—
				FZX 1014R	R	LHIC	HS4	—	CUD 1052	—
Marina 1.8 SC (E.C.E.)	1798cc	4	1976/	FZX 1199	—	RHIC	HS6	—	CUD 1168	—
Marina 1.8 SC Automatic	1798cc	4	1976/	FZX 1201	—	RHIC	HS6	—	CUD 1168	—
Marina 1.8 TC	1798cc	4	1976/	FZX 1203F	F	RHIC	HS4	—	CUD 1052	—
				FZX 1203R	R	LHIC	HS4	—	CUD 1052	—
7 cwt Van	1098cc	4	1972/73	AUD 368	—	RHIC	HS2	—	AUD 1478	—
7 cwt Van (E.C.E.)	1098cc	4	1973/76	AUD 627	—	RHIC	HS4	—	CUD 1036	—
10 cwt Van (E.C.E.)	1275cc	4	1972/76	AUD 541	—	RHIC	HS4	—	CUD 1023	—
10 cwt G.P.O. Van	1275cc	4	1972/74	AUD 589	—	RHIC	HS4	—	CUD 1023	—
1800	1798cc	4	1964	AUD 147	—	RHIC	HS6	AUD 1337	AUD 1362	AUD 1117
1800	1798cc	4	1966	AUD 223	—	RHIC	HS6	AUD 1337	AUD 1362	AUD 1117
1800 Mk II	1798cc	4	1968	AUD 280	—	RHIC	HS6	AUD 1317	AUD 1490	AUD 1117
1800 Mk II Automatic	1798cc	4	1968	AUD 291	—	RHIC	HS6	AUD 1317	AUD 1490	AUD 1117
1800 'S'	1798cc	4	1969/71	AUD 171L	LH	LHIC	HS6	AUD 1099	AUD 1469	AUD 1117
				AUD 171R	RH	LHIC	HS6	AUD 1099	AUD 1469	AUD 1117
1800 Mk II	1798cc	4	1971/72	AUD 524	—	RHIC	HS6	AUD 1317	AUD 1490	AUD 1117
1800 Mk II Automatic	1798cc	4	1971/72	AUD 525	±	RHIC	HS6	AUD 1317	AUD 1490	AUD 1117
1800 Mk II (E.C.E.)	1798cc	4	1971/72	AUD 388	—	RHIC	HS6	—	CUD 1129	—
1800 Mk II (E.C.E.)	1798cc	4	1973/74	AUD 564	—	RHIC	HS6	—	CUD 1129	—
1800 Mk II	1798cc	4	1972/73	AUD 565	—	RHIC	HS6	—	AUD 1490	—
1800 Mk II Automatic	1798cc	4	1972/73	AUD 568	—	RHIC	HS6	—	AUD 1490	—
1800 Mk II Automatic (E.C.E.)	1798cc	4	1971/74	AUD 356	—	RHIC	HS6	—	CUD 1129	—
2200	2227cc	6	1972/74	AUD 409F	LH	LHIC	HS6	—	CUD 1127	—
				AUD 409R	RH	LHIC	HS6	—	CUD 1127	—
2200 (E.C.E.)	2227cc	6	1972/75	AUD 546F	LH	RHIC	HIF6	—	CUD 1136	—
				AUD 546R	RH	LHIC	HIF6	—	CUD 1136	—
2200 Automatic (E.C.E.)	2227cc	6	1972/75	AUD 581F	LH	RHIC	HIF6	—	CUD 1136	—
				AUD 581R	RH	LHIC	HIF6	—	CUD 1136	—

[1] Front F, Centre C, Rear R, Right Hand RH, Left Hand LH.   [2] Thermocarb gasket pack required in addition AUE 807.
[3] Air jet 0.116 in. diameter.

Spec. Repeated	Needle Guide	Needle Screw	Piston Spring	Damper	Jet	Needle and Seat	Float	Throttle Spindle	Throttle Disc	Gasket Pack	Pump OE	Pump Alt.
AUD 440L	—	AUC 2057	AUC 4387	AUC 8103	AUD 9141	WZX 1100	WZX 1300	WZX 1310	WZX 1320	AUE 810	AUF 214	—
AUD 440R	—	AUC 2057	AUC 4387	AUC 8103	AUD 9142	WZX 1100	WZX 1300	WZX 1310	WZX 1320	AUE 810	—	—
AUD 185	—	AUC 2057	AUC 4387	AUC 8103	AUD 9142	WZX 1100	WZX 1300	WZX 1312	WZX 1323	AUE 811	AUF 204	AUF 207
AUD 251	—	AUC 2057	AUC 4387	AUC 8103	AUD 9451	WZX 1100	WZX 1300	WZX 1312	WZX 1324	AUE 811	AUF 207	AUF 204
AUD 13	—	AUC 2057	AUC 4387	AUC 8103	AUD 9098	WZX 1100	WZX 1300	WZX 1312	WZX 1320	AUE 810	AUF 207	AUF 204
AUD 370	—	AUC 2057	AUC 4387	AUC 8103	AUD 9451	WZX 1100	WZX 1300	WZX 1312	WZX 1324	AUE 811	AUF 207	AUF 204
AUD 186	—	AUC 2057	AUC 4387	AUC 8103	AUD 9451	WZX 1100	WZX 1300	WZX 1312	WZX 1324	AUE 811	AUF 207	AUF 204
AUD 271	—	AUC 2057	AUC 4387	AUC 8103	AUD 9451	WZX 1100	WZX 1300	WZX 1312	WZX 1324	AUE 811	AUF 207	AUF 204
AUD 374	—	AUC 2057	AUC 4387	AUC 8103	AUD 9451	WZX 1100	WZX 1300	WZX 1312	WZX 1324	AUE 811	AUF 207	AUF 204
AUD 376	—	AUC 2057	AUC 4387	AUC 8103	AUD 9451	WZX 1100	WZX 1300	WZX 1312	WZX 1324	AUE 811	AUF 207	AUF 204
AUD 344L	—	AUC 2057	AUC 4587	AUC 8103	AUD 9141	WZX 1100	WZX 1300	WZX 1310	WZX 1320	AUE 810		
AUD 344R	—	AUC 2057	AUC 4587	AUC 8103	AUD 9142	WZX 1100	WZX 1300	WZX 1310	WZX 1320	AUE 810		
AUD 472	—	AUC 2057	AUC 4387	AUC 8103	AUD 9451	WZX 1100	WZX 1300	WZX 1312	WZX 1324	AUE 811	AUF 207	AUF 204
AUD 431L	—	AUC 2057	AUC 4587	AUC 8103	AUD 9141	WZX 1100	WZX 1300	WZX 1310	WZX 1320	AUE 810	AUF 207	—
AUD 431R	—	AUC 2057	AUC 4587	AUC 8103	AUD 9142	WZX 1100	WZX 1300	WZX 1310	WZX 1320	AUE 810		
AUD 480	—	AUC 2057	AUC 4387	AUC 8103	AUD 9451	WZX 1100	WZX 1300	WZX 1312	WZX 1324	AUE 811	AUF 705	AUF 812
AUD 453	AUD 4288	AUD 4251	AUC 4387	AUC 8103	AUD 9451	WZX 1100	WZX 1300	WZX 1312	WZX 1329	AUE 811	AUF 207	AUF 204
AUD 559	AUD 4288	AUD 4251	AUC 4387	AUC 8103	AUD 9451	WZX 1100	WZX 1300	WZX 1312	WZX 1324	AUE 811	AUF 207	AUF 204
AUD 585	AUD 4288	AUD 4251	AUC 4387	AUC 8103	AUD 9451	WZX 1100	WZX 1300	WZX 1312	WZX 1324	AUE 811	AUF 207	AUF 204
AUD 594	AUD 4288	AUD 4251	AUC 4387	AUC 8103	AUD 9451	WZX 1100	WZX 1300	WZX 1312	WZX 1324	AUE 811	AUF 207	AUF 204
AUD 595	AUD 4288	AUD 4251	AUC 4387	AUC 8103	AUD 9451	WZX 1100	WZX 1300	WZX 1312	WZX 1324	AUE 811	AUF 207	AUF 204
AUD 486	AUD 4288	AUD 4251	AUC 4387	AUC 8103	AUD 9451	WZX 1100	WZX 1300	WZX 1312	WZX 1329	AUE 811	AUF 207	AUF 204
AUD 567	AUD 4288	AUD 4251	AUC 4387	AUC 8103	AUD 9451	WZX 1100	WZX 1300	WZX 1312	WZX 1324	AUE 811	AUF 207	AUF 204
FZX 1187	AUD 4288	AUD 4251	AUC 4387	AUC 8103	LZX 1110	WZX 1100	WZX 1300	WZX 1312	WZX 1325	AUE 811	AUF 804	—
AUD 354	AUD 4288	AUD 4251	AUC 4387	AUC 8103	AUD 9450	WZX 1100	WZX 1300	WZX 1312	WZX 1325	AUE 811	AUF 707	AUF 804
AUD 436	AUD 4288	AUD 4251	AUC 4387	AUC 8103	AUD 9450	WZX 1100	WZX 1300	WZX 1312	WZX 1384	AUE 811	AUF 707	AUF 804
AUD 541	AUD 4288	AUD 4251	AUC 4387	AUC 8103	AUD 9451	WZX 1100	WZX 1300	WZX 1312	WZX 1384	AUE 811	AUF 715	AUF 804
AUD 542	AUD 4288	AUD 4251	AUC 4387	AUC 8103	AUD 9450	WZX 1100	WZX 1300	WZX 1312	WZX 1384	AUE 811	AUF 715	AUF 804
AUD 670	AUD 4288	AUD 4251	AUC 4387	AUC 8103	LZX 1110	WZX 1100	WZX 1300	WZX 1312	WZX 1324	AUE 811	AUF 804	—
FZX 1189	AUD 4288	AUD 4251	AUC 4387	AUC 8103	LZX 1110	WZX 1100	WZX 1300	WZX 1312	WZX 1324	AUE 811	AUF 802	—
FZX 1071	AUD 4288	AUD 4251	AUC 4387	AUC 8103	LZX 1110	WZX 1100	WZX 1300	WZX 1312	WZX 1324	AUE 811	AUF 804	—
FZX 1191	AUD 4288	AUD 4251	AUC 4387	AUC 8103	LZX 1110	WZX 1100	WZX 1300	WZX 1312	WZX 1324	AUE 811	AUF 804	—
AUD 428	AUD 4288	AUD 4252	AUC 1167	AUC 8103	AUD 9148	WZX 1100	WZX 1300	WZX 1311	WZX 1326	AUE 812	AUF 711	AUF 802
AUD 479	AUD 4288	AUD 4252	AUC 1167	AUC 8103	AUD 9148	WZX 1100	WZX 1300	WZX 1311	WZX 1326	AUE 812	AUF 711	AUF 802
AUD 445F	AUD 4288	AUD 4251	AUC 4387	AUC 8103	AUD 9141	WZX 1100	WZX 1300	WZX 1312	WZX 1329	AUE 811	AUF 711	AUF 802
AUD 445R	AUD 4288	AUD 4251	AUC 4387	AUC 8103	AUD 9142	WZX 1100	WZX 1300	WZX 1312	WZX 1329	AUE 811		
AUD 464F	AUD 4288	AUD 4251	AUC 4387	AUC 8103	AUD 9141	WZX 1100	WZX 1300	WZX 1312	WZX 1329	AUE 811	AUF 711	AUF 802
AUD 464R	AUD 4288	AUD 4251	AUC 4387	AUC 8114	AUD 9142	WZX 1100	WZX 1300	WZX 1306	WZX 1329	AUE 811		
AUD 535	AUD 4288	AUD 4252	AUC 1167	AUC 8103	AUD 9148	WZX 1100	WZX 1300	WZX 1311	WZX 1386	AUE 812	AUF 711	AUF 802
AUD 536	AUD 4288	AUD 4252	AUC 1167	AUC 8103	AUD 9148	WZX 1100	WZX 1300	WZX 1311	WZX 1386	AUE 812	AUF 711	AUF 802
AUD 543F	AUD 4288	AUD 4251	AUC 4387	AUC 8114	AUD 9141	WZX 1100	WZX 1300	WZX 1312	WZX 1329	AUE 811	AUF 711	AUF 802
AUD 543R	AUD 4288	AUD 4251	AUC 4387	AUC 8114	AUD 9142	WZX 1100	WZX 1300	WZX 1312	WZX 1329	AUE 811	—	—
AUD 566	AUD 4288	AUD 4252	AUC 1167	AUC 8103	AUD 9148	WZX 1100	WZX 1300	WZX 1311	WZX 1329	AUE 812	AUF 711	AUF 802
AUD 673F	AUD 4288	AUD 4251	AUC 4387	AUC 8114	AUD 9141	WZX 1100	WZX 1300	WZX 1312	WZX 1323	AUE 811	AUF 711	AUF 802
AUD 673R	AUD 4288	AUD 4251	AUC 4387	AUC 8114	AUD 9142	WZX 1100	WZX 1300	WZX 1306	WZX 1323	AUE 811		
FZX 1011	AUD 4288	AUD 4252	AUC 1167	AUC 8103	AUD 9148	WZX 1100	WZX 1300	WZX 1311	WZX 1321	AUE 812	AUF 711	AUF 802
FZX 1012	AUD 4288	AUD 4252	AUC 1167	AUC 8103	AUD 9148	WZX 1100	WZX 1300	WZX 1311	WZX 1321	AUE 812	AUF 711	AUF 802
FZX 1013F	AUD 4288	AUD 4251	AUC 4387	AUC 8103	AUD 9141	WZX 1100	WZX 1300	WZX 1312	WZX 1329	AUE 811		
FZX 1013R	AUD 4288	AUD 4251	AUC 4387	AUC 8103	AUD 9142	WZX 1100	WZX 1300	WZX 1312	WZX 1323	AUE 811	AUF 711	AUF 802
FZX 1014F	AUD 4288	AUD 4251	AUC 4387	AUC 8103	AUD 9141	WZX 1100	WZX 1300	WZX 1312	WZX 1323	AUE 811		
FZX 1014R	AUD 4288	AUD 4251	AUC 4387	AUC 8103	AUD 9142	WZX 1100	WZX 1300	WZX 1306	WZX 1323	AUE 811		
FZX 1199	AUD 4288	AUD 4252	AUC 1167	AUC 8103	AUD 9148	WZX 1100	WZX 1300	WZX 1311	WZX 1321	AUE 812	AUF 802	—
FZX 1201	AUD 4288	AUD 4252	AUC 1167	AUC 8103	AUD 9148	WZX 1100	WZX 1300	WZX 1311	WZX 1321	AUE 812	AUF 802	—
FZX 1203F	AUD 4288	AUD 4251	AUC 4387	AUC 8103	AUD 9141	WZX 1100	WZX 1300	WZX 1312	WZX 1329	AUE 811	AUF 802	—
FZX 1203R	AUD 4288	AUD 4251	AUC 4387	AUC 8103	AUD 9142	WZX 1100	WZX 1300	WZX 1312	WZX 1329	AUE 811		
AUD 368	—	AUC 2057	AUC 4387	AUC 8103	AUD 9098	WZX 1100	WZX 1300	WZX 1310	WZX 1320	AUE 810	AUF 718	AUF 804
AUD 627	AUD 4288	AUD 4251	AUC 4387	AUC 8103	AUD 9450	WZX 1100	WZX 1300	WZX 1312	WZX 1324	AUE 811	AUF 715	AUF 804
AUD 541	AUD 4288	AUD 4251	AUC 4387	AUC 8103	AUD 9450	WZX 1100	WZX 1300	WZX 1312	WZX 1384	AUE 811	AUF 715	AUF 804
AUD 589	AUD 4288	AUD 4251	AUC 4387	AUC 8103	AUD 9450	WZX 1100	WZX 1300	WZX 1312	WZX 1323	AUE 811	AUF 705	AUF 812
AUD 147	—	AUC 2057	AUC 4387	AUC 8103	AUD 9148	WZX 1100	WZX 1300	WZX 1311	WZX 1321	AUE 812	AUF 209	AUF 201
AUD 223	—	AUC 2057	AUC 1167	AUC 8103	AUD 9148	WZX 1100	WZX 1300	WZX 1311	WZX 1321	AUE 812	AUF 209	AUF 201
AUD 280	—	AUC 2057	AUC 1167	AUC 8103	AUD 9148	WZX 1100	WZX 1300	WZX 1311	WZX 1321	AUE 812	AUF 704	AUF 803
AUD 291	—	AUC 2057	AUC 1167	AUC 8103	AUD 9148	WZX 1100	WZX 1300	WZX 1311	WZX 1321	AUE 812	AUF 704	AUF 803
AUD 171L	—	AUC 2057	AUC 4387	AUC 8103	AUD 9149	WZX 1100	WZX 1300	WZX 1311	WZX 1321	AUE 812	—	—
AUD 171R	—	AUC 2057	AUC 4387	AUC 8103	AUD 9148	WZX 1100	WZX 1300	WZX 1311	WZX 1321	AUE 812	—	—
AUD 524	—	AUC 2057	AUC 1167	AUC 8103	AUD 9148	WZX 1100	WZX 1300	WZX 1311	WZX 1321	AUE 812	AUF 704	AUF 803
AUD 525	—	AUC 2057	AUC 1167	AUC 8103	AUD 9148	WZX 1100	WZX 1300	WZX 1311	WZX 1321	AUE 812	AUF 704	AUF 803
AUD 355	AUD 4288	AUD 4252	AUC 1167	AUC 8103	AUD 9148	WZX 1100	WZX 1300	WZX 1311	WZX 1321	AUE 812	AUF 704	AUF 803
AUD 564	AUD 4288	AUD 4252	AUC 1167	AUC 8103	AUD 9148	WZX 1100	WZX 1300	WZX 1311	WZX 1321	AUE 812	AUF 704	AUF 803
AUD 565	—	AUC 2057	AUC 1167	AUC 8103	AUD 9148	WZX 1100	WZX 1300	WZX 1311	WZX 1321	AUE 812	AUF 704	AUF 803
AUD 568	—	AUC 2057	AUC 1167	AUC 8103	AUD 9148	WZX 1100	WZX 1300	WZX 1311	WZX 1321	AUE 812	AUF 704	AUF 803
AUD 356	AUD 4288	AUD 4252	AUC 1167	AUC 8103	AUD 9148	WZX 1100	WZX 1300	WZX 1311	WZX 1321	AUE 812	AUF 222 or	—
AUD 409F	AUD 4288	AUD 4252	AUC 4387	AUC 8103	AUD 9106	WZX 1101	WZX 1300	WZX 1314	WZX 1321	AUE 812	AUF 305	—
AUD 409R	AUD 4288	AUD 4252	AUC 4387	AUC 8103	AUD 9106	WZX 1101	WZX 1300	WZX 1314	WZX 1321	AUE 812		
AUD 546F	AUD 4288	AUD 4252	AUC 4387	CUD 2901	WZX 1452	WZX 1102	WZX 1401	WZX 1170	WZX 1326	WZX 1505	AUF 305	AZX 1304
AUD 546R	AUD 4288	AUD 4252	AUC 4387	CUD 2901	WZX 1453	WZX 1102	WZX 1400	WZX 1170	WZX 1326	WZX 1505		
AUD 581F	AUD 4288	AUD 4252	AUC 4387	CUD 2901	WZX 1452	WZX 1102	WZX 1401	WZX 1170	WZX 1326	WZX 1505	AUF 305	AZX 1304
AUD 581R	AUD 4288	AUD 4252	AUC 4387	CUD 2901	WZX 1453	WZX 1102	WZX 1400	WZX 1171	WZX 1326	WZX 1505	—	—

[3] AED Unit TZX 1002 supersedes AUH 308, 309, 310 and 317 (1 per installation).
[4] Service AED Unit AUH 300 (1 per installation).
[6] Air jet 0.102 in. diameter.
[7] Service AED Unit AUH 305 1 per installation Rover (U.S.A.) spec. only.

Model Details	Capacity	No. of Cyl.	Year	Spec.	Position[1]	Inter Connect	Type	Rich	Needle Std.	Weak
LAND-ROVER										
2.6 109 FWD (Forward Control)		6	1963/67	AUD 81	—	—	HD6	—	AUD 1334	—
2.6 Station Wagon 109 WB (LC)		6	1967	AUD 247	—	—	HD6	—	AUD 1334	—
2.6 109 WB (LHD)		6	1967/68	AUD 201	—	—	HD8	—	AUD 1481	—
RELIANT										
Sabre Ford (Zephyr)	1.7 litre	4	1963/64	AUD 118F	F	RHIC	HS4	—	AUD 1126	—
				AUD 118R	R	LHIC	HS4	—	AUD 1126	—
Scimitar (In Line)	2.5 litre	6	1965/66	AUD 161F	F	RHIC	HS4	—	AUD 1228	—
				AUD 161C	C	RHIC	HS4	—	AUD 1228	—
				AUD 161R	R	LHIC	HS4	—	AUD 1228	—
Robin/Kitten 850	848cc	4	1975/	FZX 1027	—	RHIC	HS2	—	CUD 1002	—
Robin/Kitten 850	848cc	4	1976/	FZX 1275	—	RHIC	HS2	—	CUD 1017	—
RENAULT										
16T RH Drive	1665cc	4	1969/71	—	—	—	—	—	—	—
15/17 (U.S.A.)			1974/	—	—	—	—	—	—	—
RILEY										
One-Point-Five	1498cc	4	1957/64	AUC 864F	F	—	H4	AUD 1048	AUD 1035	AUD 1230
				AUC 864R	R	—	H4	AUD 1048	AUD 1035	AUD 1230
4/72 Saloon 1622cc	1622cc	4	1961/69	AUD 41F	F	—	HD4	AUD 1200	AUD 1231	AUD 1190
				AUD 41R	R	—	HD4	AUD 1200	AUD 1231	AUD 1190
Elf Mk II	998cc	4	1963/64	AUD 86	—	RHIC	HS2	AUD 1261	AUD 1227	AUD 1211
Elf Mk III	998cc	4	1968/69	AUD 298	—	RHIC	HS2	AUD 1261	AUD 1227	AUD 1211
Kestrel	1098cc	4	1965/66	AUD 69L	LH	RHIC	HS2	AUD 1144	AUD 1142	AUD 1225
				AUD 69R	RH	LHIC	HS2	AUD 1144	AUD 1142	AUD 1225
Kestrel	1275cc	4	1967/68	AUD 186	—	LHIC	HS4	AUD 1076	AUD 1528	AUD 1096
Kestrel Automatic	1275cc	4	1967/68	AUD 271	—	LHIC	HS4	AUD 1076	AUD 1528	AUD 1096
Kestrel Mk II	1275cc	4	1968	AUD 318L	LH	RHIC	HS2	AUD 1261	AUD 1149	AUD 1211
				AUD 318R	RH	LHIC	HS2	AUD 1261	AUD 1149	AUD 1211
Kestrel Mk II	1275cc	4	1968/69	AUD 344L	LH	RHIC	HS2	AUD 1261	AUD 1468	AUD 1211
				AUD 344R	RH	LHIC	HS2	AUD 1261	AUD 1468	AUD 1211
ROLLS-ROYCE										
B61 Power Unit	4887cc	6	1964/69	AUD 55F	F	LHIC	HS6	AUD 1117	AUD 1499	—
				AUD 55R	R	RHIC	HS6	AUD 1117	AUD 1499	—
B61 Power Unit	4887cc	6	1971	AUD 477F	F	LHIC	HS6	—	AUD 1117	—
				AUD 477R	R	RHIC	HS6	—	AUD 1117	—
B61 Power Unit	4887cc	6	1974/75	AUD 646F	F	LHIC	HS8	—	CUD 1107	—
				AUD 646R	R	RHIC	HS8	—	CUD 1107	—
B61 Power Unit	4887cc	6	1974/75	AUD 708F	F	LHIC	HS8	—	CUD 1129	—
				AUD 708R	R	RHIC	HS8	—	CUD 1129	—
Phantom V	6230cc	8	1969	AUD 384A	RH	—	HD8	—	AUD 1485	—
				AUD 384B	LH	—	HD8	—	AUD 1485	—
Phantom VI	6230cc	8	1971/72	AUD 474A	RH	—	HD8	—	CUD 1111	—
				AUD 474B	LH	—	HD8	—	CUD 1111	—
Phantom VI	6230cc	8	1971/72	AUD 446A	RH	—	HD8	—	AUD 1485	—
				AUD 446B	LH	—	HD8	—	AUD 1485	—
Phantom VI	6230cc	8	1973/	AUD 656A	RH	—	HD8	—	CUD 1152	—
				AUD 656B	LH	—	HD8	—	CUD 1152	—
S3 V8	6230cc	8	1963/64	AUD 54A	RH	—	HD8	—	AUD 1485	—
				AUD 54B	LH	—	HD8	—	AUD 1485	—
Silver Shadow	6230cc	8	1965/68	AUD 177A	RH	—	HD8	—	AUD 1517	—
				AUD 177B	LH	—	HD8	—	AUD 1517	—
Silver Shadow (U.S.A.)	6230cc	8	1968	AUD 269A	RH	—	HD8	—	AUD 1532	—
				AUD 269B	LH	—	HD8	—	AUD 1532	—
Silver Shadow (U.S.A.)	6750cc	8	1969	AUD 389A	RH	—	HD8	—	CUD 1104	—
				AUD 389B	LH	—	HD8	—	CUD 1104	—
Silver Shadow (U.S.A. and General)	6750cc	8	1969/71	AUD 387A	RH	—	HD8	—	CUD 1104	—
				AUD 387B	LH	—	HD8	—	CUD 1104	—
Silver Shadow (U.S.A. and General)	6750cc	8	1972	AUD 526A	RH	—	HD8	—	CUD 1104	—
				AUD 526B	LH	—	HD8	—	CUD 1104	—
Silver Shadow (Common Market and Europe)	6750cc	8	1973	AUD 526A	RH	—	HD8	—	CUD 1104	—
				AUD 526B	LH	—	HD8	—	CUD 1104	—
Silver Shadow/Corniche (U.S.A.)	6750cc	8	1973	AUD 574A	RH	—	HD8	—	CUD 1104	—
				AUD 574B	LH	—	HD8	—	CUD 1104	—
Silver Shadow (Japan)	6750cc	8	1973/	AUD 671A	RH	—	HD8	—	CUD 1146	—
				AUD 671B	LH	—	HD8	—	CUD 1146	—
Silver Shadow/Corniche (U.S.A.)	6750cc	8	1974	AUD 648A	RH	—	HD8	—	CUD 1149	—
				AUD 648B	LH	—	HD8	—	CUD 1149	—
Corniche	6750cc	8	1971	AUD 474A	RH	—	HD8	—	CUD 1111	—
				AUD 474B	LH	—	HD8	—	CUD 1111	—
Corniche (Home Market and Europe)	6750cc	8	1972/	AUD 530A	RH	—	HD8	—	CUD 1111	—
				AUD 530B	LH	—	HD8	—	CUD 1111	—
Silver Shadow/Corniche (U.S.A.)	6750cc	8	1974/	AUD 702A	RH	—	HD8	—	CUD 1162	—
				AUD 702B	LH	—	HD8	—	CUD 1162	—
Rolls Royce Silver Shadow (Sweden, Japan & Australia)	6750cc	8	1975	FZX 1026A	RH	—	HS8	—	NZX 8001	—
				FZX 1026B	LH	—	HS8	—	NZX 8001	—
Silver Shadow/Corniche	6750cc	8	1975/	FZX 1040A	RH	—	HD8	—	NZX 8004	—
				FZX 1040B	LH	—	HD8	—	NZX 8004	—

[1] Front F, Centre C, Rear R, Right Hand RH, Left Hand LH.   [2] Thermocarb gasket pack required in addition AUE 807.
[5] Air jet 0.116 in. diameter.

Spec. Repeated	Needle Guide	Needle Screw	Piston Spring	Damper	Jet	Needle and Seat	Float	Throttle Spindle	Throttle Disc	Gasket Pack	Pump OE	Pump Alt.
AUD 81	—	AUC 2057	AUC 1167	AUC 8102	AUC 8155	WZX 1101	WZX 1303	WZX 1216	WZX 1180	AUE 805	AUF 503	—
AUD 247	—	AUC 2057	AUC 1167	AUC 8102	AUC 8155	WZX 1101	WZX 1303	WZX 1216	WZX 1180	AUE 805	AUF 503/AUF 505 24volt	
AUD 201	—	AUC 2057	AUC 4826	AUC 8111	AUC 8156	WZX 1101	WZX 1303	WZX 1217	WZX 1376	AUE 806	AUF 503	—
AUD 118F	—	AUC 2057	AUC 4387	AUC 8103	AUD 9141	WZX 1100	WZX 1300	WZX 1312	WZX 1323	AUE 811	—	—
AUD 118R	—	AUC 2057	AUC 4387	AUC 8103	AUD 9142	WZX 1100	WZX 1300	WZX 1312	WZX 1323	AUE 811	—	—
AUD 161F	—	AUC 2057	AUC 4387	AUC 8114	AUD 9141	WZX 1100	WZX 1300	WZX 1312	WZX 1323	AUE 811	—	—
AUD 161C	—	AUC 2057	AUC 4387	AUC 8114	AUD 9142	WZX 1100	WZX 1300	WZX 1312	WZX 1323	AUE 811	—	—
AUD 161R	—	AUC 2057	AUC 4387	AUC 8114	AUD 9142	WZX 1100	WZX 1300	WZX 1312	WZX 1323	AUE 811	—	—
FZX 1027	AUD 4288	AUD 4250	AUD 4387	AUC 8103	AUD 9098	WZX 1100	WZX 1300	WZX 1310	WZX 1320	AUE 810	—	—
FZX 1275	AUD 4288	AUD 4250	AUD 4387	AUC 8103	AUD 9098	WZX 1100	WZX 1300	WZX 1310	WZX 1320	AUE 810	—	—
—	—	—	—	—	—	—	—	..—	—	—	AUF 219 AUF 307	AUF 223
AUC 864F	—	AUC 2057	AUC 4387	AUC 8102	AUC 8182	WZX 1100	WZX 1302	AUC 3242	WZX 1323	AUE 801	AUA 67	AUF 204
AUC 864R	—	AUC 2057	AUC 4387	AUC 8102	AUC 8182	WZX 1100	WZX 1302	AUC 3515	WZX 1323	AUE 801	—	—
AUD 41F	—	AUC 2057	AUC 4387	AUC 8114	AUC 8154	WZX 1100	WZX 1303	WZX 1215	WZX 1323	—	AUA 83	AUF 204
AUD 41R	—	AUC 2057	AUC 4387	AUC 8114	AUC 8154	WZX 1100	WZX 1303	WZX 1215	WZX 1323	—	—	—
AUD 86	—	AUC 2057	AUC 4387	AUC 8103	AUD 9098	WZX 1100	WZX 1300	WZX 1310	WZX 1320	AUE 810	AUA 83	AUF 201
AUD 298	—	AUC 2057	AUC 4387	AUC 8103	AUD 9098	WZX 1100	WZX 1300	WZX 1310	WZX 1320	AUE 810	AUF 214	—
AUD 69L	—	AUC 2057	AUC 4587	AUC 8103	AUD 9141	WZX 1100	WZX 1300	WZX 1310	WZX 1320	AUE 810	AUF 204	—
AUD 69R	—	AUC 2057	AUC 4587	AUC 8103	AUD 9142	WZX 1100	WZX 1300	WZX 1310	WZX 1320	AUE 810	—	—
AUD 186	—	AUC 2057	AUC 4387	AUC 8103	AUD 9451	WZX 1100	WZX 1300	WZX 1312	WZX 1324	AUE 811	AUF 207	AUF 204
AUD 271	—	AUC 2057	AUC 4387	AUC 8103	AUD 9451	WZX 1100	WZX 1300	WZX 1312	WZX 1324	AUE 811	AUF 207	AUF 204
AUD 318L	—	AUC 2057	AUC 4587	AUC 8103	AUD 9141	WZX 1100	WZX 1300	WZX 1310	WZX 1320	AUE 810	AUF 204	—
AUD 318R	—	AUC 2057	AUC 4587	AUC 8103	AUD 9142	WZX 1100	WZX 1300	WZX 1310	WZX 1320	AUE 810	—	—
AUD 344L	—	AUC 2057	AUC 4587	AUC 8103	AUD 9141	WZX 1100	WZX 1300	WZX 1310	WZX 1320	AUE 810	AUF 207	AUF 204
AUD 344R	—	AUC 2057	AUC 4587	AUC 8103	AUD 9142	WZX 1100	WZX 1300	WZX 1310	WZX 1320	AUE 810	—	—
AUD 55F	—	AUC 2057	AUC 1170	AUC 8102	AUD 9106	WZX 1101	WZX 1300	WZX 1311	WZX 1321	AUE 812	—	—
AUD 55R	—	AUC 2057	AUC 1170	AUC 8102	AUD 9105	WZX 1101	WZX 1300	WZX 1311	WZX 1321	AUE 812	—	—
AUD 477F	—	AUC 2057	AUC 1170	AUC 8102	AUD 9106	WZX 1101	WZX 1301	WZX 1311	WZX 1321	AUE 812	—	—
AUD 477R	—	AUC 2057	AUC 1170	AUC 8102	AUD 9105	WZX 1101	WZX 1301	WZX 1311	WZX 1321	AUE 812	—	—
AUD 646F	AUD 4288	AUD 4253	AUC 4826	AUC 8110	CUD 3176	WZX 1101	WZX 1300	WZX 1317	WZX 1373	AUE 813	—	—
AUD 646R	AUD 4288	AUD 4253	AUC 4826	AUC 8110	CUD 3177	WZX 1101	WZX 1300	WZX 1317	WZX 1373	AUE 813	—	—
AUD 708	AUD 4288	AUD 4253	AUC 4826	AUC 8110	CUD 3176	WZX 1101	WZX 1300	WZX 1317	WZX 1373	AUE 813	—	—
AUD 708	AUD 4288	AUD 4253	AUC 4826	AUC 8110	CUD 3177	WZX 1101	WZX 1300	WZX 1317	WZX 1373	AUE 813	—	—
AUD 384A	—	AUC 2057	AUC 4818	AUC 8111	AUD 9030	WZX 1102	WZX 1302	WZX 1202	WZX 1373	AUE 806	AUF 402	—
AUD 384B	—	AUC 2057	AUC 4818	AUC 8111	AUD 9030	WZX 1102	WZX 1302	WZX 1203	WZX 1373	AUE 806	—	—
AUD 474A	AUD 4288	AUD 4253	AUC 4818	AUC 8111	CUD 2637	WZX 1102	WZX 1302	WZX 1200	WZX 1373	AUE 806	AUF 402	—
AUD 474B	AUD 4288	AUD 4253	AUC 4818	AUC 8111	CUD 2637	WZX 1102	WZX 1302	WZX 1201	WZX 1373	AUE 806	—	—
AUD 446A	—	AUC 2057	AUC 4818	AUC 8111	AUD 9030	WZX 1102	WZX 1302	WZX 1202	WZX 1373	AUE 806	AUF 402	—
AUD 446B	—	AUC 2057	AUC 4818	AUC 8111	AUD 9030	WZX 1102	WZX 1302	WZX 1203	WZX 1373	AUE 806	—	—
AUD 656A	AUD 4288	AUD 4253	AUC 4818	AUC 8111	CUD 2637	WZX 1102	WZX 1302	WZX 1200	WZX 1373	AUE 806	AUF 402	—
AUD 656B	AUD 4288	AUD 4253	AUC 4818	AUC 8111	CUD 2637	WZX 1102	WZX 1302	WZX 1201	WZX 1373	AUE 806	—	—
AUD 54A	—	AUC 2057	AUC 4818	AUC 8111	AUD 9030	WZX 1102	WZX 1302	WZX 1218	WZX 1373	AUE 806	AUA 146	AUF 406
AUD 54B	—	AUC 2057	AUC 4818	AUC 8111	AUD 9030	WZX 1102	WZX 1302	WZX 1219	WZX 1373	AUE 806	—	—
AUD 177A	—	AUC 2057	AUC 4818	AUC 8111	AUD 9030	WZX 1102	WZX 1302	WZX 1202	WZX 1373	AUE 806	AUF 400	—
AUD 177B	—	AUC 2057	AUC 4818	AUC 8111	AUD 9030	WZX 1102	WZX 1302	WZX 1203	WZX 1373	AUE 806	—	—
AUD 269A	—	AUC 2057	AUC 4818	AUC 8111	AUD 9825	WZX 1102	WZX 1302	WZX 1202	WZX 1373	AUE 806	AUF 400	—
AUD 269B	—	AUC 2057	AUC 4818	AUC 8111	AUD 9825	WZX 1102	WZX 1302	WZX 1203	WZX 1373	AUE 806	—	—
AUD 389A	AUD 4288	AUD 4253	AUC 4818	AUC 8111	CUD 2637	WZX 1102	WZX 1302	WZX 1202	WZX 1373	AUE 806	AUF 402	—
AUD 389B	AUD 4288	AUD 4253	AUC 4818	AUC 8111	CUD 2637	WZX 1102	WZX 1302	WZX 1203	WZX 1373	AUE 806	—	—
AUD 387A	AUD 4288	AUD 4253	AUC 4818	AUC 8111	CUD 2637	WZX 1102	WZX 1302	WZX 1200	WZX 1373	AUE 806	AUF 402	—
AUD 387B	AUD 4288	AUD 4253	AUC 4818	AUC 8111	CUD 2637	WZX 1102	WZX 1302	WZX 1201	WZX 1373	AUE 806	—	—
AUD 526A	AUD 4288	AUD 4253	AUC 4818	AUC 8111	CUD 2637	WZX 1102	WZX 1302	WZX 1200	WZX 1373	AUE 806	AUF 402	—
AUD 526B	AUD 4288	AUD 4253	AUC 4818	AUC 8111	CUD 2637	WZX 1102	WZX 1302	WZX 1201	WZX 1373	AUE 806	—	—
AUD 526A	AUD 4288	AUD 4253	AUC 4818	AUC 8111	CUD 2637	WZX 1102	WZX 1302	WZX 1200	WZX 1373	AUE 806	AUF 402	—
AUD 526B	AUD 4288	AUD 4253	AUC 4818	AUC 8111	CUD 2637	WZX 1102	WZX 1302	WZX 1201	WZX 1373	AUE 806	—	—
AUD 574A	AUD 4288	AUD 4253	AUC 4818	AUC 8111	CUD 2637	WZX 1102	WZX 1302	WZX 1200	WZX 1373	AUE 806	AUF 402	—
AUD 574B	AUD 4288	AUD 4253	AUC 4818	AUC 8111	CUD 2637	WZX 1102	WZX 1302	WZX 1201	WZX 1373	AUE 806	—	—
AUD 671A	AUD 4288	AUD 4253	AUC 4818	AUC 8111	CUD 2637	WZX 1102	WZX 1302	WZX 1200	WZX 1373	AUE 806	AUF 402	—
AUD 671B	AUD 4288	AUD 4253	AUC 4818	AUC 8111	CUD 2637	WZX 1102	WZX 1302	WZX 1201	WZX 1373	AUE 806	—	—
AUD 648A	AUD 4288	AUD 4253	AUC 4818	AUC 8111	CUD 2637	WZX 1102	WZX 1302	WZX 1200	WZX 1373	AUE 806	AUF 402	—
AUD 648B	AUD 4288	AUD 4253	AUC 4818	AUC 8111	CUD 2637	WZX 1102	WZX 1302	WZX 1201	WZX 1373	AUE806	—	—
AUD 474A	AUD 4288	AUD 4253	AUC 4818	AUC 8111	CUD 2637	WZX 1102	WZX 1302	WZX 1200	WZX 1373	AUE 806	AUF 402	—
AUD 474B	AUD 4288	AUD 4253	AUC 4818	AUC 8111	CUD 2637	WZX 1102	WZX 1302	WZX 1201	WZX 1373	AUE 806	—	—
AUD 530A	AUD 4288	AUD 4253	AUC 4818	AUC 8111	CUD 2637	WZX 1102	WZX 1302	WZX 1200	WZX 1373	AUE 806	AUF 402	—
AUD 530B	AUD 4288	AUD 4253	AUC 4818	AUC 8111	CUD 2637	WZX 1102	WZX 1302	WZX 1201	WZX 1373	AUE 806	—	—
AUD 702A	AUD 4288	AUD 4253	AUC 4818	AUC 8111	CUD 2637	WZX 1102	WZX 1302	WZX 1308	WZX 1377	AUE 806	AUF 402	—
AUD 702B	AUD 4288	AUD 4253	AUC 4818	AUC 8111	CUD 2637	WZX 1102	WZX 1302	WZX 1309	WZX 1377	AUE 806	—	—
FZX 1026A	AUD 4288	AUD 4253	AUC 4818	AUC 8111	CUD 2637	WZX 1102	WZX 1302	WZX 1308	WZX 1377	AUE 806	AUF 414	—
FZX 1026B	AUD 4288	AUD 4253	AUC 4818	AUC 8111	CUD 2637	WZX 1102	WZX 1302	WZX 1309	WZX 1377	AUE 806	—	—
FZX 1040A	AUD 4288	AUD 4253	AUC 4818	AUC 8111	CUD 2637	WZX 1102	WZX 1303	WZX 1308	WZX 1373	AUE 806	AUF 414	—
FZX 1040B	AUD 4288	AUD 4253	AUC 4818	AUC 8111	CUD 2637	WZX 1102	WZX 1303	WZX 1309	WZX 1373	AUE 806	—	—

[3] AED Unit TZX 1002 supersedes AUH 308, 309, 310 and 317. (1 per installation).   [4] Service AED Unit AUH 300 (1 per installation).
[6] Air jet 0.102 in. diameter.   [7] Service AED Unit AUH 305 1 per installation Rover (U.S.A.) spec. only.

Model Details	Capacity	No. of Cyl.	Year	Spec.	[1] Position	Inter Connect	Type	Rich	Needle Std.	Weak
Silver Shadow V8	6750cc	8	1976/	FZX 1104A	F	LHIC	HIF7	—	NZX 8024	—
				FZX 1104B	R	LHIC	HIF7	—	NZX 8024	—
Rolls Royce V8 Shadow	6750cc	8	1976/	FZX 1141A	RH	—	HD8	—	NZX 8004	—
				FZX 1141B	LH	—	HD8	—	NZX 8004	—
Rolls Royce V8 (Australia)	6750cc	8	1976/	FZX 1116A	RH	—	HD8	—	NZX 8004	—
				FZX 1116B	LH	—	HD8	—	NZX 8004	—
ROVER										
3 litre Coupe P5	2995cc	6	1963/64	AUC 982	—	—	HD8[5]	—	AUD 1484	—
3 litre P5	2995cc	6	1963/64	AUD 114	—	—	HD8[5]	—	AUD 1484	—
3 litre	2995cc	6	1963/64	AUD 115	—	—	HD8[5]	—	AUD 1484	—
2000	1975cc	4	1963/64	AUC 968	—	RHIC	HS6	—	AUD 1491	—
2000	1975cc	4	1963/64	AUD 141	—	RHIC	HS6	—	AUD 1494	—
2000	1975cc	4	1965/68	AUD 211	—	RHIC	HS6	—	AUD 1491	—
2000	1975cc	4	1969/71	AUD 401	—	RHIC	HS6	—	AUD 1554	—
2000 (E.C.E.)	1975cc	4	1971	AUD 475	—	RHIC	HS6	—	CUD 1105	—
2000 TC	1975cc	4	1966	AUD 92F	F	—	HD8	—	AUD 1521	—
				AUD 92R	R	—	HD8	—	AUD 1521	—
2000 TC	1975cc	4	1967/68	AUD 264F	F	RHIC	HS8	—	AUD 1527	—
				AUD 264R	R	RHIC	HS8	—	AUD 1527	—
2000TC	1975cc	4	1969/71	AUD 330F	F	RHIC	HS8	—	AUD 1527	—
				AUD 330R	R	RHIC	HS8	—	AUD 1527	—
2000 TC	1975cc	4	1971/73	AUD 533F	F	RHIC	HS8	—	CUD 1011	—
				AUD 533R	R	RHIC	HS8	—	CUD 1011	—
2000 (U.S.A.)	1975cc	4	1967/68	AUD 267	—	RHIC	HS6	—	AUD 1494	—
2000 TC (U.S.A.)	1975cc	4	1967/68	AUD 254F	F	RHIC	HS8	—	AUD 1527	—
				AUD 254R	R	RHIC	HS8	—	AUD 1527	—
2000 TC (U.S.A.)	1975cc	4	1968	AUD 329F	F	RHIC	HS8	—	CUD 1001	—
				AUD 329R	R	RHIC	HS8	—	CUD 1001	—
2000 TC (U.S.A. and E.C.E)	1975cc	4	1969/75	AUD 411F	F	RHIC	HS8	—	CUD 1001	—
				AUD 411R	R	RHIC	HS8	—	CUD 1001	—
2200 SC	2204cc	4	1973/76	AUD 631	—	RHIC	HIF6	—	CUD 1144	—
2200 TC	2204cc	4	1973/76	AUD 632F	F	RHIC	HIF6	—	CUD 1145	—
				AUD 632R	R	LHIC	HIF6	—	CUD 1145	—
2300	2300cc	6	1976/	FZX 1130F	F	LHIC	HS6	—	NZX 8026	—
				FZX 1130R	R	RHIC	HS6	—	NZX 8026	—
2600	2600cc	6	1976/	FZX 1131F	F	LHIC	HS6	—	NZX 8027	—
				FZX 1131R	R	RHIC	HS6	—	NZX 8027	—
3.5 litre V8 P5	3528cc	8	1967/68	AUD 233L	LH	RHIC	HS6	—	AUD 1536	—
				AUD 233R	RH	LHIC	HS6	—	AUD 1536	—
3.5 litre V8 P5	3528cc	8	1968/69	AUD 270L	LH	RHIC	HS6AED[4]	—	AUD 1536	—
				AUD 270R	RH	LHIC	HS6	—	AUD 1536	—
3.5 litre V8 P6	3528cc	8	1968	AUD 313L	LH	RHIC	HS6	—	AUD 1539	—
				AUD 313R	RH	LHIC	HS6	—	AUD 1539	—
3500 V8 P6	3528cc	8	1968	AUD 350L	LH	RHIC	HS6AED[4]	—	AUD 1539	—
				AUD 350R	RH	LHIC	HS6	—	AUD 1539	—
3500S V8 P6 (U.S.A.)	3528cc	8	1969/70	AUD 312L	LH	RHIC	HS6AED[7]	—	CUD 1102	—
				AUD 312R	RH	LHIC	HS6	—	CUD 1102	—
3500S P6 (U.S.A.)	3528cc	8	1969/70	AUD 412L	LH	RHIC	HS6AED	—	CUD 1102	—
				AUD 412R	RH	LHIC	HS6	—	CUD 1102	—
3500 V8 P6	3528cc	8	1971/72	AUD 467L	LH	RHIC	HS6	—	CUD 1109	—
				AUD 467R	RH	LHIC	HS6	—	CUD 1109	—
3500 V8 P6 (E.C.E.)	3528cc	8	1972/73	AUD 408L	LH	RHIC	HIF6	—	CUD 1130	—
				AUD 408R	RH	LHIC	HIF6	—	CUD 1130	—
3500 V8 P6	3528cc	8	1972/73	AUD 521L	LH	RHIC	HIF6	—	CUD 1130	—
				AUD 521R	RH	LHIC	HIF6	—	CUD 1130	—
3500 V8 P6 (E.C.E.) and 3500S V8 P6 (E.C.E.)	3528cc	8	1973/	AUD 623L	LH	RHIC	HIF6	—	CUD 1143	—
				AUD 623R	RH	LHIC	HIF6	—	CUD 1143	—
3500 (Japan)	3528cc	8	1973/76	AUD 669L	LH	RHIC	HIF6	—	CUD 1143	—
				AUD 669R	RH	LHIC	HIF6	—	CUD 1143	—
3500 V8	3528cc	8	1976/	FZX 1270L	LH	LHIC	HIF6	—	CUD 1109	—
				FZX 1270R	RH	LHIC	HIF6	—	CUD 1109	—
3500	3528cc	8	1976/	AUD 664L	LH	RHIC	HIF6	—	CUD 1109	—
				AUD 664R	RH	LHIC	HIF6	—	CUD 1109	—
SUNBEAM										
Tiger		8	1964	—	—	—	—	—	—	—
TRIUMPH										
TR4A	2138cc	4	1965/66	AUD 209F	F	LHIC	HS6	AUD 1337	AUD 1362	AUD 1117
				AUD 209R	R	RHIC	HS6	AUD 1337	AUD 1362	AUD 1117
TR4A (U.S.A.)	2138cc	4	1968	AUD 284F	F	LHIC	HS6	—	AUD 1284	—
				AUD 284R	R	RHIC	HS6	—	AUD 1284	—
Spitfire Mk I and II	950cc	4	1962/66	AUC 983F	F	LHIC	HS2	AUD 1242	AUD 1478	AUD 1149
				AUC 983R	R	RHIC	HS2	AUD 1242	AUD 1478	AUD 1149
Spitfire Mk III	1296cc	4	1967/70	AUD 257F	F	LHIC	HS2	—	AUD 1526	—
				AUD 257R	R	RHIC	HS2	—	AUD 1526	—

[1] Front F, Centre C, Rear R, Right Hand RH, Left Hand LH.   [2] Thermocarb gasket pack required in addition AUE 807.
[5] Air jet 0.116 in. diameter.

Spec. Repeated	Needle Guide	Needle Screw	Piston Spring	Damper	Jet	Needle and Seat	Float	Throttle Spindle	Throttle Disc	Gasket Pack	Pump OE	Alt.
FZX 1104A	JZX 1039	AUD 4252	AUD 4355	CUD 2953	WZX 1456	WZX 1102	WZX 1401	WZX 1175	WZX 1189	WZX 1505	AUF 414	—
FZX 1104B	JZX 1039	AUD 4252	AUD 4355	CUD 2953	WZX 1456	WZX 1102	WZX 1401	WZX 1175	WZX 1189	WZX 1505	AUF 414	—
FZX 1141A	AUD 4288	AUD 4253	AUC 4818	AUC 8111	CUD 2637	WZX 1102	WZX 1302	WZX 1308	WZX 1373	AUE 806	AUF 414	—
FZX 1141B	AUD 4288	AUD 4253	AUC 4818	AUC 8111	CUD 2637	WZX 1102	WZX 1302	WZX 1309	WZX 1373	AUE 806	AUF 414	—
FZX 1116A	AUD 4288	AUD 4253	AUC 4818	AUC 8111	CUD 2637	WZX 1102	WZX 1302	WZX 1308	WZX 1377	AUE 806	AUF 414	—
FZX 1116B	AUD 4288	AUD 4253	AUC 4818	AUC 8111	CUD 2637	WZX 1102	WZX 1302	WZX 1309	WZX 1377	AUE 806	AUF 414	—
AUC 982	—	AUC 2057	AUC 4826	AUC 8111	AUC 8156	WZX 1101	WZX 1303	WZX 1217	WZX 1179	AUE 806	AUF 503	—
AUD 114	—	AUC 2057	AUC 4826	AUC 8111	AUC 8156	WZX 1101	WZX 1303	WZX 1196	WZX 1179	AUE 806	AUF 503	—
AUD 115	—	AUC 2057	AUC 4826	AUC 8111	AUC 8156	WZX 1101	WZX 1303	WZX 1196	WZX 1179	AUE 806	AUF 503	—
AUC 968	—	AUC 2057	AUC 1170	AUC 8103	AUD 9105	WZX 1101	WZX 1300	WZX 1315	WZX 1321	AUE 812	—	—
AUD 141	—	AUC 2057	AUC 1170	AUC 8103	AUD 9105	WZX 1101	WZX 1300	WZX 1315	WZX 1321	AUE 812	—	—
AUD 211	—	AUC 2057	AUC 1170	AUC 8103	AUD 9105	WZX 1101	WZX 1300	WZX 1315	WZX 1321	AUE 812	—	—
AUD 401	—	AUC 2057	AUC 1170	AUC 8103	AUD 9105	WZX 1101	WZX 1300	WZX 1311	WZX 1321	AUE 812	—	—
AUD 475	AUD 4288	AUD 4252	AUC 1170	AUC 8103	AUD 9105	WZX 1101	WZX 1300	WZX 1311	WZX 1321	AUE 812	—	—
AUD 92F	—	AUC 2057	AUC 2107	AUC 8119	AUC 8156	WZX 1101	WZX 1303	WZX 1195	AUD 2737	AUE 806	—	—
AUD 92R	—	AUC 2057	AUC 2107	AUC 8119	AUC 8156	WZX 1101	WZX 1303	WZX 1195	AUD 2737	AUE 806	—	—
AUD 264F	—	AUC 2057	AUC 2107	AUC 8119	AUD 9883	WZX 1102	WZX 1301	WZX 1318	WZX 1372	AUE 813	—	—
AUD 264R	—	AUC 2057	AUC 2107	AUC 8119	AUD 9883	WZX 1102	WZX 1301	WZX 1318	WZX 1372	AUE 813	—	—
AUD 330F	—	AUC 2057	AUC 2107	AUC 8119	CUD 2708	WZX 1102	WZX 1301	WZX 1318	WZX 1372	AUE 813	—	—
AUD 330R	—	AUC 2057	AUC 2107	AUC 8119	CUD 2708	WZX 1102	WZX 1301	WZX 1318	WZX 1372	AUE 813	—	—
AUD 535F	AUD 4288	AUD 4253	AUC 2107	AUC 8119	CUD 2708	WZX 1102	WZX 1301	WZX 1318	WZX 1372	AUE 813	—	—
AUD 533R	AUD 4288	AUD 4253	AUC 2107	AUC 8119	CUD 2708	WZX 1102	WZX 1301	WZX 1318	WZX 1372	AUE 813	—	—
AUD 267	—	AUC 2057	AUC 1170	AUC 8103	AUD 9105	WZX 1101	WZX 1300	WZX 1315	WZX 1326	AUE 812	—	—
AUD 254F	—	AUC 2057	AUC 2107	AUC 8119	AUD 9879	WZX 1102	WZX 1301	WZX 1318	WZX 1374	AUE 813	—	—
AUD 254R	—	AUC 2057	AUC 2107	AUC 8119	AUD 3879	WZX 1102	WZX 1301	WZX 1318	WZX 1374	AUE 813	—	—
AUD 329F	AUD 4288	AUD 4253	AUC 2107	AUC 8112	AUD 9971	WZX 1102	WZX 1301	WZX 1318	WZX 1374	AUE 813	—	—
AUD 329R	AUD 4288	AUD 4253	AUC 2107	AUC 8112	AUD 9971	WZX 1102	WZX 1301	WZX 1318	WZX 1374	AUE 813	—	—
AUD 411F	AUD 4287	AUD 4253	AUC 2107	AUC 8112	CUD 2709	WZX 1102	WZX 1301	WZX 1318	WZX 1374	AUE 813	—	—
AUD 411R	AUD 4287	AUD 4253	AUC 2107	AUC 8112	CUD 2709	WZX 1102	WZX 1301	WZX 1318	WZX 1374	AUE 813	—	—
AUD 631	AUD 4288	AUD 4252	AUC 1170	AUC 8103	WZX 1452	WZX 1101	WZX 1401	WZX 1170	WZX 1181	WZX 1505	—	—
AUD 632F	AUD 4288	AUD 4252	AUC 1167	CUD 4104	WZX 1452	WZX 1100	WZX 1401	WZX 1170	WZX 1181	WZX 1505	—	—
AUD 632R	AUD 4288	AUD 4252	AUC 1167	CUD 4104	WZX 1453	WZX 1100	WZX 1400	WZX 1170	WZX 1181	WZX 1505	—	—
FZX 1130F	JZX 1039	AUD 4252	AUD 4398	LZX 1287	LZX 1059	WZX 1100	WZX 1300	WZX 1311	WZX 1326	AUE 812	—	—
FZX 1130R	JZX 1039	AUD 4252	AUD 4398	LZX 1287	LZX 1058	WZX 1100	WZX 1300	WZX 1311	WZX 1326	AUE 812	—	—
FZX 1131F	JZX 1039	AUD 4252	AUD 4398	LZX 1287	LZX 1059	WZX 1100	WZX 1300	WZX 1311	WZX 1382	AUE 812	—	—
FZX 1131R	JZX 1039	AUD 4252	AUD 4398	LZX 1287	LZX 1058	WZX 1100	WZX 1300	WZX 1311	WZX 1382	AUE 812	—	—
AUD 233L	—	AUC 2057	AUC 1167	AUC 8103	AUD 9148	WZX 1102	WZX 1300	WZX 1311	WZX 1321	AUE 812	—	—
AUD 233R	—	AUC 2057	AUC 1167	AUC 8103	AUD 9149	WZX 1102	WZX 1300	WZX 1311	WZX 1321	AUE 812	—	—
AUD 270L	—	AUC 2057	AUC 1167	AUC 8103	AUD 9148	WZX 1102	WZX 1300	WZX 1311	WZX 1321	AUE 812	—	—
AUD 270R	—	AUC 2057	AUC 1167	AUC 8103	AUD 9149	WZX 1102	WZX 1300	WZX 1311	WZX 1321	AUE 812	—	—
AUD 313L	—	AUC 2057	AUC 1167	AUC 8103	AUD 9148	WZX 1102	WZX 1300	WZX 1311	WZX 1321	AUE 812	—	—
AUD 313R	—	AUC 2057	AUC 1167	AUC 8103	AUD 9149	WZX 1102	WZX 1300	WZX 1311	WZX 1321	AUE 812	—	—
AUD 350L	—	AUC 2057	AUC 1167	AUC 8103	AUD 9148	WZX 1102	WZX 1300	WZX 1311	WZX 1321	AUE 812	—	—
AUD 350R	—	AUC 2057	AUC 1167	AUC 8103	AUD 9149	WZX 1102	WZX 1300	WZX 1311	WZX 1321	AUE 812	—	—
AUD 312L	AUD 4288	AUD 4252	AUC 1167	AUC 8103	AUD 9148	WZX 1102	WZX 1300	WZX 1311	WZX 1327	AUE 812	—	—
AUD 312R	AUD 4288	AUD 4252	AUC 1167	AUC 8103	AUD 9149	WZX 1102	WZX 1300	WZX 1311	WZX 1327	AUE 812	—	—
AUD 412L	AUD 4288	AUD 4252	AUC 1167	AUC 8103	AUD 9148	WZX 1102	WZX 1300	WZX 1311	WZX 1327	AUE 812	—	—
AUD 412R	AUD 4288	AUD 4252	AUC 1167	AUC 8103	AUD 9149	WZX 1102	WZX 1300	WZX 1311	WZX 1327	AUE 812	—	—
AUD 467L	AUD 4288	AUD 4252	AUC 1167	AUC 8103	AUD 9148	WZX 1102	WZX 1300	WZX 1311	WZX 1321	AUE 812	—	—
AUD 467R	AUD 4288	AUD 4252	AUC 1167	AUC 8103	AUD 9149	WZX 1102	WZX 1300	WZX 1311	WZX 1321	AUE 812	—	—
AUD 408L	AUD 4287	AUD 4252	AUC 1167	AUC 8103	WZX 1452	WZX 1100	WZX 1401	WZX 1170	WZX 1326	WZX 1505	—	—
AUD 408R	AUD 4287	AUD 4252	AUC 1167	AUC 8103	WZX 1453	WZX 1100	WZX 1400	WZX 1170	WZX 1326	WZX 1505	—	—
AUD 521L	AUD 4287	AUD 4252	AUC 1167	AUC 8103	WZX 1452	WZX 1100	WZX 1401	WZX 1170	WZX 1321	WZX 1505	—	—
AUD 521R	AUD 4287	AUD 4252	AUC 1167	AUC 8103	WZX 1453	WZX 1100	WZX 1400	WZX 1170	WZX 1321	WZX 1505	—	—
AUD 623L	AUD 4287	AUD 4252	AUC 1167	AUC 8103	WZX 1452	WZX 1100	WZX 1401	WZX 1170	WZX 1326	WZX 1505	—	—
AUD 623R	AUD 4287	AUD 4252	AUC 1167	AUC 8103	WZX 1453	WZX 1100	WZX 1400	WZX 1170	WZX 1326	WZX 1505	—	—
AUD 669L	AUD 4288	AUD 4252	AUD 4398	CUD 2901	WZX 1452	WZX 1100	WZX 1401	WZX 1170	WZX 1326	WZX 1505	—	—
AUD 669R	AUD 4288	AUD 4252	AUD 4398	CUD 2901	WZX 1453	WZX 1100	WZX 1400	WZX 1170	WZX 1326	WZX 1505	—	—
FZX 1270L	AUD 4288	AUD 4252	AUD 4398	CUD 2901	WZX 1452	WZX 1100	WZX 1401	WZX 1170	WZX 1378	WZX 1505	—	—
FZX 1270R	AUD 4288	AUD 4252	AUD 4398	CUD 2901	WZX 1453	WZX 1100	WZX 1400	WZX 1170	WZX 1378	WZX 1505	—	—
AUD 664L	AUD 4288	AUD 4252	AUD 4398	CUD 2901	WZX 1452	WZX 1100	WZX 1401	WZX 1170	WZX 1378	WZX 1505	—	—
AUD 664R	AUD 4288	AUD 4252	AUD 4398	CUD 2901	WZX 1453	WZX 1100	WZX 1400	WZX 1170	WZX 1378	WZX 1505	—	—
—	—	—	—	—	—	—	—	—	—	AUF 301	—	
AUD 209F	—	AUC 2057	AUC 4387	AUC 8114	AUD 9148	WZX 1101	WZX 1300	WZX 1311	WZX 1321	AUE 812	—	—
AUD 209R	—	AUC 2057	AUC 4387	AUC 8114	AUD 9149	WZX 1101	WZX 1300	WZX 1311	WZX 1321	AUE 812	—	—
AUD 284F	—	AUC 2057	AUC 4387	AUC 8103	AUD 9142	WZX 1101	WZX 1300	WZX 1311	WZX 1326	AUE 812	—	—
AUD 284R	—	AUC 2057	AUC 4387	AUC 8103	AUD 9141	WZX 1101	WZX 1300	WZX 1311	WZX 1326	AUE 812	—	—
AUC 983F	—	AUC 2057	AUC 4387	AUC 8114	AUD 9104	WZX 1100	WZX 1300	WZX 1310	WZX 1320	AUE 810	—	—
AUC 983R	—	AUC 2057	AUC 4387	AUC 8114	AUD 9103	WZX 1100	WZX 1300	WZX 1310	WZX 1320	AUE 810	—	—
AUD 257F	—	AUC 2057	AUC 4387	AUC 8114	AUD 9104	WZX 1100	WZX 1300	WZX 1310	WZX 1320	AUE 810	—	—
AUD 257R	—	AUC 2057	AUC 4387	AUC 8114	AUD 9103	WZX 1100	WZX 1300	WZX 1310	WZX 1320	AUE 810	—	—

[3] AED Unit TZX 1002 supersedes AUH 308, 309, 310 and 317 (1 per installation).   [4] Service AED Unit AUH 300 (1 per installation).
[6] Air jet 0.102 in. diameter.   [7] Service AED Unit AUH 305 1 per installation Rover (U.S.A.) spec. only.

Model Details	Capacity	No. of Cyl.	Year	Spec.	[1] Position	Inter Connect	Type	Rich	Needle Std.	Weak
Spitfire Mk III (U.S.A.)	1296cc	4	1969	AUD 285F	F	LHIC	HS2	—	AUD 1531	—
				AUD 285R	R	RHIC	HS2	—	AUD 1531	—
Spitfire Mk III	1296cc	4	1967/68	AUD 275F	F	LHIC	HS2	—	AUD 1531	—
				AUD 275R	R	RHIC	HS2	—	AUD 1531	—
Spitfire Mk III (U.S.A.)	1296cc	4	1967/68	AUD 290F	F	LHIC	HS2	—	AUD 1531	—
				AUD 290R	R	RHIC	HS2	—	AUD 1531	—
Spitfire Mk IV	1296cc	4	1970/71	AUD 441F	F	LHIC	HS2	—	CUD 1012	—
				AUD 441R	R	RHIC	HS2	—	CUD 1012	—
Spitfire Mk IV (E.C.E.)	1296cc	4	1972	AUD 517F	F	LHIC	HS2	—	CUD 1012	—
				AUD 517R	R	RHIC	HS2	—	CUD 1012	—
Spitfire Mk IV	1296cc	4	1973	AUD 580F	F	LHIC	HS2	—	CUD 1012	—
				AUD 580R	R	RHIC	HS2	—	CUD 1012	—
Spitfire Mk V (E.C.E.)	1296cc	4	1973/	AUD 624F	F	LHIC	HS2	—	CUD 1012	—
				AUD 624R	R	RHIC	HS2	—	CUD 1012	—
Spitfire 1500 (E.C.E.)	1493cc	4	1974/76	AUD 665F	F	LHIC	HS4	—	CUD 1041	—
				AUD 665R	R	RHIC	HS4	—	CUD 1041	—
1300 TC	1296cc	4	1967/68	AUD 257F	F	LHIC	HS2	—	AUD 1526	—
				AUD 257R	R	RHIC	HS2	—	AUD 1526	—
Toledo	1296cc	4	1970/71	AUD 392	—	RHIC	HS4	—	CUD 1009	—
Toledo (E.C.E.)	1296cc	4	1972	AUD 515	—	RHIC	HS4	—	CUD 1020	—
Toledo	1296cc	4	1972/74	AUD 577	—	RHIC	HS4	—	CUD 1038	—
Toledo 1300	1296cc	4	1975	AUD 707	—	RHIC	HS4	—	CUD 1029	—
Toledo TS	1493cc	4	1974/76	AUD 665F	F	LHIC	HS4	—	CUD 1041	—
				AUD 665R	R	RHIC	HS4	—	CUD 1041	—
1500	1493cc	4	1970/71	AUD 392	—	RHIC	HS4	—	CUD 1009	—
1500 (E.C.E.)	1493cc	4	1972/73	AUD 516	—	RHIC	HS4	—	CUD 1009	—
1500	1493cc	4	1972/74	AUD 578	—	RHIC	HS4	—	CUD 1030	—
1500 TC (E.C.E.)	1493cc	4	1972/73	AUD 519F	F	LHIC	HS2	—	CUD 1021	—
				AUD 519R	R	RHIC	HS2	—	CUD 1021	—
1500 (E.C.E.)	1493cc	4	1973	AUD 579	—	RHIC	HS4	—	CUD 1030	—
1500 TC	1493cc	4	1973	AUD 582F	F	LHIC	HS2	—	CUD 1021	—
				AUD 582R	R	RHIC	HS2	—	CUD 1021	—
1500 TC (E.C.E.)	1493cc	4	1973/74	AUD 625F	F	LHIC	HS2	—	CUD 1021	—
				AUD 625R	R	RHIC	HS2	—	CUD 1021	—
1500 TC	1493cc	4 [2]	1974/76	AUD 665F	F	LHIC	HS4	—	CUD 1041	—
				AUD 665R	R	RHIC	HS4	—	CUD 1041	—
Dolomite 1300	1296cc	4	1976/	FZX 1269	—	RHIC	HS4	—	CUD 1029	—
1500 Dolomite	1493cc	4	1976/	FZX 1258F	F	LHIC	HS4	—	CUD 1041	—
				FZX 1258R	R	RHIC	HS4	—	CUD 1041	—
Dolomite (E.C.E.)	1854cc	4	1974/	AUD 603F	F	LHIC	HS4	—	CUD 1033	—
				AUD 603R	R	RHIC	HS4	—	CUD 1033	—
Dolomite	1854cc	4	1975	FZX 1005F	F	LHIC	HS4	—	CUD 1033	—
				FZX 1005R	R	RHIC	HS4	—	CUD 1033	—
Dolomite	1854cc	4	1976	FZX 1051F	F	LHIC	HS4	—	CUD 1033	—
				FZX 1051R	R	RHIC	HS4	—	CUD 1033	—
Dolomite	1854cc	4	1976/	FZX 1265F	F	LHIC	HS4	—	CUD 1033	—
				FZX 1265R	R	RHIC	HS4	—	CUD 1033	—
Dolomite Sprint	1998cc	4	1973/74	AUD 545F	F	LHIC	HS6	—	CUD 1141	—
				AUD 545R	R	RHIC	HS6	—	CUD 1141	—
Dolomite Sprint (E.C.E.)	1998cc	4	1974	AUD 661F	F	LHIC	HS6	—	CUD 1159	—
				AUD 661R	R	RHIC	HS6	—	CUD 1159	—
Triumph Sprint	1998cc	4	1975/76	AUD 680F	F	LHIC	HS6	—	CUD 1159	—
				AUD 680R	R	RHIC	HS6	—	CUD 1159	—
Triumph Sprint	1998cc	4	1976/	AUD 663F	F	LHIC	HS6	—	NZX 8015	—
				AUD 663R	R	RHIC	HS6	—	NZX 8015	—
TR7	1998cc	4	1974/76	AUD 634F	F	LHIC	HS6	—	NZX 8012	—
				AUD 634R	R	RHIC	HS6	—	NZX 8012	—
TR7	1998cc	4	1976/	FZX 1242F	F	LHIC	HS6	—	NZX 8012	—
				FZX 1242R	R	RHIC	HS6	—	NZX 8012	—
Sprint and TR7 (E.C.E.)	1998cc	4	1976/	FZX 1257F	F	LHIC	HS6	—	NZX 8015	—
				FZX 1257R	R	RHIC	HS6	—	NZX 8015	—
2000	1998cc	6	1974/5	AUD 604F	F	LHIC	HS4	—	CUD 1034	—
				AUD 604R	R	RHIC	HS4	—	CUD 1034	—
2000	1998cc	6	1975/76	AUD 676F	F	LHIC	HS6	—	CUD 1170	—
				AUD 676R	R	RHIC	HS6	—	CUD 1170	—
2000	1998cc	6	1976/	FZX 1264F	F	LHIC	HS6	—	CUD 1170	—
				FZX 1264R	R	RHIC	HS6	—	CUD 1170	—
2500 TC	2498cc	6	1974/5	AUD 607F	F	LHIC	HS4	—	CUD 1042	—
				AUD 607R	R	RHIC	HS4	—	CUD 1042	—
2500 TC	2498cc	6	1975/	AUD 678F	F	LHIC	HS6	—	NZX 8002	—
				AUD 678R	R	RHIC	HS6	—	NZX 8002	—[3]
2500 (Australia)	2498cc	6	1975	FZX 1070F	F	LHIC	HS6	—	NZX 8002	—
				FZX 1070R	R	RHIC	HS6	—	NZX 8002	—
2.5	2498cc	6	1976	FZX 1105F	F	LHIC	HS6	—	NZX 8019	—
				FZX 1105R	R	RHIC	HS6	—	NZX 8019	—
2500	2498cc	6	1976/	FZX 1263F	F	LHIC	HS6	—	NZX 8002	—
				FZX 1263R	R	RHIC	HS6	—	NZX 8002	—
Stag V8	2997cc	8	1970/74	—	—	—	—	—	—	—

UNIVERSAL POWER DRIVES

Model Details	Capacity	No. of Cyl.	Year	Spec.	[1] Position	Inter Connect	Type	Rich	Needle Std.	Weak
Unipower	998cc	4	—	AUD 104L	LH	RHIC	HS2	AUD 1261	AUD 1468	AUD 1211
				AUD 104R	RH	LHIC	HS2	AUD 1261	AUD 1468	AUD 1211

[1] Front F, Centre C, Rear R, Right Hand RH, Left Hand LH.   [2] Thermocarb gasket pack required in addition AUE 807.
[3] Air jet 0.116 in. diameter.

Spec. Repeated	Needle Guide	Needle Screw	Piston Spring	Damper	Jet	Needle and Seat	Float	Throttle Spindle	Throttle Disc	Gasket Pack	OE	Pump Alt.
AUD 285F		AUC 2057	AUC 4387	AUC 8103	AUD 9889	WZX 1100	WZX 1300	WZX 1310	WZX 1383	AUE 810	—	—
AUD 285R		AUC 2057	AUC 4387	AUC 8103	AUD 9888	WZX 1100	WZX 1300	WZX 1310	WZX 1383	AUE 810	—	—
AUD 275F		AUC 2057	AUC 4387	AUC 8103	AUD 9104	WZX 1100	WZX 1300	WZX 1310	WZX 1320	AUE 810	—	—
AUD 275R		AUC 2057	AUC 4387	AUC 8103	AUD 9103	WZX 1100	WZX 1300	WZX 1310	WZX 1383	AUE 810	—	—
AUD 290F		AUC 2057	AUC 4387	AUC 8103	AUD 9104	WZX 1100	WZX 1300	WZX 1310	WZX 1383	AUE 810	—	—
AUD 290R		AUC 2057	AUC 4387	AUC 8103	AUD 9103	WZX 1100	WZX 1300	WZX 1310	WZX 1320	AUE 810	—	—
AUD 441F	AUD 4288	AUD 4250	AUC 4387	AUC 8114	AUD 9104	WZX 1100	WZX 1300	WZX 1310	WZX 1383	AUE 810	—	—
AUD 441R	AUD 4288	AUD 4250	AUC 4387	AUC 8114	AUD 9103	WZX 1100	WZX 1300	WZX 1310	WZX 1320	AUE 810	—	—
AUD 517F	AUD 4288	AUD 4250	AUC 4387	AUC 8114	AUD 9104	WZX 1100	WZX 1300	WZX 1310	WZX 1383	AUE 810	—	—
AUD 517R	AUD 4288	AUD 4250	AUC 4387	AUC 8114	AUD 9103	WZX 1100	WZX 1300	WZX 1310	WZX 1383	AUE 810	—	—
AUD 580F	AUD 4288	AUD 4250	AUC 4387	AUC 8114	AUD 9104	WZX 1100	WZX 1300	WZX 1310	WZX 1383	AUE 810	—	—
AUD 580R	AUD 4288	AUD 4250	AUC 4387	AUC 8114	AUD 9103	WZX 1100	WZX 1300	WZX 1310	WZX 1383	AUE 810	—	—
AUD 624F	AUD 4288	AUD 4250	AUC 4387	AUC 8114	AUD 9104	WZX 1100	WZX 1300	WZX 1310	WZX 1322	AUE 810	—	—
AUD 624R	AUD 4288	AUD 4250	AUC 4387	AUC 8114	AUD 9103	WZX 1100	WZX 1300	WZX 1310	WZX 1322	AUE 810	—	—
AUD 665F	AUD 4288	AUD 4251	AUC 4387	AUC 8114	AUD 9451	WZX 1100	WZX 1300	WZX 1312	WZX 1385	AUE 811	—	—
AUD 665R	AUD 4288	AUD 4251	AUC 4387	AUC 8114	AUD 9450	WZX 1100	WZX 1300	WZX 1312	WZX 1385	AUE 811	—	—
AUD 257F	—	AUC 2057	AUC 4387	AUC 8114	AUD 9104	WZX 1100	WZX 1300	WZX 1310	WZX 1320	AUE 810	—	—
AUD 257R	—	AUC 2057	AUC 4387	AUC 8114	AUD 9103	WZX 1100	WZX 1300	WZX 1310	WZX 1320	AUE 810	—	—
AUD 392	AUD 4288	AUD 4251	AUC 4387	CUD 4103	AUD 9596	WZX 1100	WZX 1300	WZX 1312	WZX 1323	AUE 811	—	—
AUD 515	AUD 4288	AUD 4251	AUC 4387	CUD 4103	AUD 9596	WZX 1100	WZX 1300	WZX 1312	WZX 1323	AUE 811	—	—
AUD 577	AUD 4288	AUD 4251	AUC 4387	CUD 4103	AUD 9596	WZX 1100	WZX 1300	WZX 1312	WZX 1323	AUE 811	—	—
AUD 707	AUD 4288	AUD 4251	AUC 4387	CUD 4103	AUD 9596	WZX 1100	WZX 1300	WZX 1312	WZX 1385	AUE 811	—	—
AUD 665F	AUD 4288	AUD 4251	AUC 4387	AUC 8114	AUD 9451	WZX 1100	WZX 1300	WZX 1312	WZX 1385	AUE 811	—	—
AUD 665R	AUD 4288	AUD 4251	AUC 4387	AUC 8114	AUD 9450	WZX 1100	WZX 1300	WZX 1312	WZX 1385	AUE 811	—	—
AUD 392	AUD 4288	AUD 4251	AUC 4387	CUD 4103	AUD 9596	WZX 1100	WZX 1300	WZX 1312	WZX 1323	AUE 811	—	—
AUD 516	AUD 4288	AUD 4251	AUC 4387	CUD 4103	AUD 9596	WZX 1100	WZX 1300	WZX 1312	WZX 1323	AUE 811	—	—
AUD 578	AUD 4288	AUD 4251	AUC 4387	CUD 4103	AUD 9596	WZX 1100	WZX 1300	WZX 1312	WZX 1323	AUE 811	—	—
AUD 519F	AUD 4288	AUD 4251	AUC 4387	AUC 8114	AUD 9104	WZX 1100	WZX 1300	WZX 1310	WZX 1383	AUE 810	—	—
AUD 519R	AUD 4288	AUD 4251	AUC 4387	AUC 8114	AUD 9103	WZX 1100	WZX 1300	WZX 1310	WZX 1383	AUE 810	—	—
AUD 579	AUD 4288	AUD 4251	AUC 4387	CUD 4103	AUD 9596	WZX 1100	WZX 1300	WZX 1312	WZX 1323	AUE 811	—	—
AUD 582F	AUD 4288	AUD 4250	AUC 4387	AUC 8114	AUD 9104	WZX 1100	WZX 1300	WZX 1310	WZX 1383	AUE 810	—	—
AUD 582R	AUD 4288	AUD 4250	AUC 4387	AUC 8114	AUD 9103	WZX 1100	WZX 1300	WZX 1310	WZX 1383	AUE 810	—	—
AUD 625F	AUD 4288	AUD 4250	AUC 4387	AUC 8114	AUD 9104	WZX 1100	WZX 1300	WZX 1310	WZX 1322	AUE 810	—	—
AUD 625R	AUD 4288	AUD 4250	AUC 4387	AUC 8114	AUD 9103	WZX 1100	WZX 1300	WZX 1310	WZX 1322	AUE 810	—	—
AUD 665F	AUD 4288	AUD 4250	AUC 4387	AUC 8114	AUD 9451	WZX 1100	WZX 1300	WZX 1312	WZX 1385	AUE 811	—	—
AUD 665R	AUD 4288	AUD 4250	AUC 4387	AUC 8114	AUD 9450	WZX 1100	WZX 1300	WZX 1312	WZX 1385	AUE 811	—	—
FZX 1269	AUD 4288	AUD 4251	AUC 4387	CUD 4103	LZX 1112	WZX 1100	WZX 1300	WZX 1312	WZX 1385	AUE 811	—	—
FZX 1258F	AUD 4288	AUD 4251	AUC 4387	AUC 8114	LZX 1113	WZX 1100	WZX 1300	WZX 1312	WZX 1385	AUE 811	—	—
FZX 1258R	AUD 4288	AUD 4251	AUC 4387	AUC 8114	LZX 1112	WZX 1100	WZX 1300	WZX 1312	WZX 1385	AUE 811	—	—
AUD 603F	AUD 4288	AUD 4251	AUC 4387	AUC 8114	AUD 9451	WZX 1100	WZX 1300	WZX 1312	WZX 1323	AUE 811	—	—
AUD 603R	AUD 4288	AUD 4251	AUC 4387	AUC 8114	AUD 9450	WZX 1100	WZX 1300	WZX 1312	WZX 1323	AUE 811	—	—
FZX 1005F	AUD 4288	AUD 4251	AUC 4387	AUC 8114	AUD 9451	WZX 1100	WZX 1300	WZX 1312	WZX 1385	AUE 811	—	—
FZX 1005R	AUD 4288	AUD 4251	AUC 4387	AUC 8114	AUD 9450	WZX 1100	WZX 1300	WZX 1312	WZX 1385	AUE 811	—	—
FZX 1061F	AUD 4288	AUD 4251	AUC 4387	AUC 8103	AUD 9451	WZX 1100	WZX 1300	WZX 1312	WZX 1385	AUE 811	—	—
FZX 1051R	AUD 4288	AUD 4251	AUC 4387	AUC 8103	AUD 9450	WZX 1100	WZX 1300	WZX 1312	WZX 1385	AUE 811	—	—
FZX 1265F	AUD 4288	AUD 4251	AUC 4387	AUC 8103	LZX 1113	WZX 1100	WZX 1300	WZX 1312	WZX 1385	AUE 811	—	—
FZX 1265R	AUD 4288	AUD 4251	AUC 4387	AUC 8103	LZX 1112	WZX 1100	WZX 1300	WZX 1312	WZX 1385	AUE 811	—	—
AUD 545F	AUD 4288	AUD 4252	AUC 1167	CUD 4108	AUD 9106	WZX 1100	WZX 1300	WZX 1311	WZX 1321	AUE 812	—	—
AUD 545R	AUD 4288	AUD 4252	AUC 1167	CUD 4108	AUD 9105	WZX 1100	WZX 1300	WZX 1311	WZX 1321	AUE 812	—	—
AUD 661F	AUD 4288	AUD 4252	AUC 1167	CUD 4108	AUD 9106	WZX 1100	WZX 1300	WZX 1311	WZX 1321	AUE 812	—	—
AUD 661R	AUD 4288	AUD 4252	AUC 1167	CUD 4108	AUD 9105	WZX 1100	WZX 1300	WZX 1311	WZX 1321	AUE 812	—	—
AUD 680F	AUD 4288	AUD 4252	AUC 1167	AUC 8114	WZX 1454	WZX 1100	WZX 1300	WZX 1170	WZX 1329	AUE 812	—	—
AUD 680R	AUD 4288	AUD 4252	AUC 1167	AUC 8114	WZX 1455	WZX 1100	WZX 1300	WZX 1170	WZX 1329	AUE 812	—	—
AUD 663F	AUD 4288	AUD 4252	AUC 1167	CUD 4108	AUD 9106	WZX 1100	WZX 1300	WZX 1311	WZX 1326	AUE 812	—	—
AUD 663R	AUD 4288	AUD 4252	AUC 1167	CUD 4108	AUD 9105	WZX 1100	WZX 1300	WZX 1311	WZX 1326	AUE 812	—	—
AUD 634F	AUD 4288	AUD 4252	AUC 4387	AUC 8103	AUD 9106	WZX 1100	WZX 1300	WZX 1311	WZX 1386	AUE 812	—	—
AUD 634R	AUD 4288	AUD 4252	AUC 4387	AUC 8103	AUD 9105	WZX 1100	WZX 1300	WZX 1311	WZX 1386	AUE 812	—	—
FZX 1242F	AUD 4288	AUD 4252	AUC 4387	AUC 8103	LZX 1121	WZX 1100	WZX 1300	WZX 1311	WZX 1386	AUE 812	—	—
FZX 1242R	AUD 4288	AUD 4252	AUC 4387	AUC 8103	LZX 1120	WZX 1100	WZX 1300	WZX 1311	WZX 1386	AUE 812	—	—
FZX 1257F	AUD 4288	AUD 4252	AUC 1167	CUD 4108	LZX 1121	WZX 1100	WZX 1300	WZX 1311	WZX 1326	AUE 812	—	—
FZX 1257R	AUD 4288	AUD 4252	AUC 1167	CUD 4108	LZX 1120	WZX 1100	WZX 1300	WZX 1311	WZX 1326	AUE 812	—	—
AUD 604F	AUD 4288	AUD 4251	AUC 1167	AUC 8103	AUD 9451	WZX 1100	WZX 1300	WZX 1312	WZX 1323	AUE 811	—	—
AUD 604R	AUD 4288	AUD 4251	AUC 1167	AUC 8103	AUD 9450	WZX 1100	WZX 1300	WZX 1312	WZX 1323	AUE 811	—	—
AUD 676F	AUD 4288	AUD 4252	AUC 1167	AUC 8103	AUD 9106	WZX 1100	WZX 1300	WZX 1311	WZX 1382	AUE 812	—	—
AUD 676R	AUD 4288	AUD 4252	AUC 1167	AUC 8103	AUD 9105	WZX 1100	WZX 1300	WZX 1311	WZX 1382	AUE 812	—	—
FZX 1264F	AUD 4288	AUD 4252	AUC 1167	AUC 8103	LZX 1121	WZX 1100	WZX 1300	WZX 1311	WZX 1382	AUE 812	—	—
FZX 1264R	AUD 4288	AUD 4252	AUC 1167	AUC 8103	LZX 1120	WZX 1100	WZX 1300	WZX 1311	WZX 1382	AUE 812	—	—
AUD 607F	AUD 4288	AUD 4251	AUC 1167	AUC 8103	AUD 9451	WZX 1100	WZX 1300	WZX 1312	WZX 1323	AUE 811	—	—
AUD 607R	AUD 4288	AUD 4251	AUC 1167	AUC 8103	AUD 9450	WZX 1100	WZX 1300	WZX 1312	WZX 1323	AUE 811	—	—
AUD 678F	AUD 4288	AUD 4252	AUC 1167	AUC 8103	AUD 9106	WZX 1100	WZX 1300	WZX 1311	WZX 1382	AUE 812	—	—
AUD 678R	AUD 4288	AUD 4252	AUC 1167	AUC 8103	AUD 9105	WZX 1100	WZX 1300	WZX 1311	WZX 1382	AUE 812	—	—
FZX 1263F	AUD 4288	AUD 4252	AUC 1167	AUC 8103	LZX 1121	WZX 1100	WZX 1300	WZX 1311	WZX 1386	AUE 812	—	—
FZX 1263R	AUD 4288	AUD 4252	AUC 1167	AUC 8103	LZX 1120	WZX 1100	WZX 1300	WZX 1311	WZX 1386	AUE 812	—	—
FZX 1070F	AUD 4288	AUD 4252	AUC 1167	AUC 8103	AUD 9106	WZX 1100	WZX 1300	WZX 1311	WZX 1382	AUE 812	—	—
FZX 1070R	AUD 4288	AUD 4252	AUC 1167	AUC 8103	AUD 9105	WZX 1100	WZX 1300	WZX 1311	WZX 1382	AUE 812	—	—
FZX 1105F	JZX 1039	AUD 4252	AUD 4398	CUD 2904	LZX 1059	WZX 1100	WZX 1300	WZX 1311	WZX 1379	AUE 812	—	—
FZX 1105R	JZX 1039	AUD 4252	AUD 4398	CUD 2904	LZX 1058	WZX 1100	WZX 1300	WZX 1311	WZX 1379	AUE 812	—	—
—	—	—	—	—	—	—	—	—	—	—	AUF 306	AUF 303
AUD 104L	—	AUC 2057	AUC 4587	AUC 8103	AUD 9141	WZX 1100	WZX 1300	WZX 1310	WZX 1320	AUE 810	—	—
AUD 104R	—	AUC 2057	AUC 4587	AUC 8103	AUD 9142	WZX 1100	WZX 1300	WZX 1310	WZX 1320	AUE 810	—	—

[3] AED Unit TZX 1002 supersedes AUH 308, 309, 310 and 317 (1 per installation). [4] Service AED Unit AUH 300 (1 per installation).
[6] Air Jet 0.102 in. diameter.   [7] Service AED Unit AUH 305 1 per installation Rover (U.S.A.) spec. only.

Model Details	Capacity	No. of Cyl.	Year	Spec.	Position	Inter Connect	Type	Rich	Needle Std.	Weak
VANDEN PLAS										
Princess 4 litre DM4		6	1956/64	—	—	—	—	—	—	—
Princess 4 litre R	3909cc	6	1964	AUD 97F	F	LHIC	HS8	—	AUD 1493	—
				AUD 97R	R	RHIC	HS8	—	AUD 1493	—
Princess 4 litre R	3909cc	6	1965/66	AUD 215F	F	LHIC	HS8	—	AUD 1493	—
				AUD 215R	R	RHIC	HS8	—	AUD 1493	—
Princess 4 litre R	3909cc	6	1964/66	AUD 418F	F	LHIC	HS8	—	AUD 1493	—
(Service Replacement)				AUD 418R	R	RHIC	HS8	—	AUD 1493	—
Princess 1100	1098cc	4	1964	AUD 69L	LH	RHIC	HS2	AUD 1144	AUD 1142	AUD 1225
				AUD 69R	RH	RHIC	HS2	AUD 1144	AUD 1142	AUD 1225
Princess 1300	1275cc	4	1967/68	AUD 186	—	LHIC	HS4	AUD 1076	AUD 1528	AUD 1096
Princess Automatic	1275cc	4	1967/68	AUD 271	—	LHIC	HS4	AUD 1076	AUD 1528	AUD 1096
Princess 1300	1275cc	4	1968/69	AUD 318L	LH	RHIC	HS2	AUD 1261	AUD 1149	AUD 1211
				AUD 318R	RH	LHIC	HS2	AUD 1261	AUD 1149	AUD 1211
Princess 1300	1275cc	4	1969/71	AUD 344L	LH	RHIC	HS2	AUD 1261	AUD 1468	AUD 1211
				AUD 344R	RH	LHIC	HS2	AUD 1261	AUD 1468	AUD 1211
Princess 1300	1275cc	4	1971/	AUD 431L	LH	RHIC	HS2	AUD 1261	AUD 1468	AUD 1211
				AUD 431R	RH	LHIC	HS2	AUD 1261	AUD 1468	AUD 1211
Princess 1300 (E.C.E.)	1275cc	4	1971/72	AUD 454L	LH	RHIC	HS2	—	CUD 1013	—
				AUD 454R	RH	LHIC	HS2	—	CUD 1013	—
Princess 1300 (E.C.E.)	1275cc	4	1971/72	AUD 496L	LH	RHIC	HS2	—	CUD 1013	—
				AUD 496R	RH	LHIC	HS2	—	CUD 1013	—
Princess 1500	1485cc	4	1974/75	AUD 628	—	RHIC	HS6	—	CUD 1116	—
VOLVO										
B18B Snow Weasel (Pancake Filter)	1788cc	4	1965/66	AUD 95F	F	RHIC	HS6	—	AUD 1490	—
				AUD 95R	R	LHIC	HS6	—	AUD 1490	—
B18B Snow Weasel	1788cc	4	1967	AUD 277F	F	RHIC	HS6	—	AUD 1490	—
				AUD 277R	R	LHIC	HS6	—	AUD 1490	—
Snow Weasel	1788cc	4	1976/	FZX 1238	F	RHIC	HS6	—	AUD 1490	—
				FZX 1238	R	LHIC	HS6	—	AUD 1490	—
B18B P1800	1788cc	4	1963/65	AUD 94F	F	RHIC	HS6	—	AUD 1490	—
				AUD 94R	R	LHIC	HS6	—	AUD 1490	—
B18B 1800S (Pancake Filter)	1788cc	4	1965/66	AUD 193F	F	RHIC	HS6	—	AUD 1501	—
				AUD 193R	R	LHIC	HS6	—	AUD 1501	—
B18B 1800S (Silencer, Paper Element)	1788cc	4	1965/66	AUD 204F	F	RHIC	HS6	—	AUD 1518	—
				AUD 204R	R	LHIC	HS6	—	AUD 1518	—
B18B 144S (Pancake Filter)	1788cc	4	1967/68	AUD 230F	F	RHIC	HS6	—	AUD 1501	—
				AUD 230R	R	LHIC	HS6	—	AUD 1501	—
B18B 144 (Silencer Filter)	1788cc	4	1967/68	AUD 231F	F	RHIC	HS6	—	AUD 1518	—
				AUD 231R	R	LHIC	HS6	—	AUD 1518	—
B18B 144	1788cc	4	1968	AUD 305F	F	RHIC	HS6	—	CUD 1538	—
				AUD 305R	R	LHIC	HS6	—	CUD 1538	—
B18B 144 (U.S.A.)	1788cc	4	1967/68	AUD 252F	F	RHIC	HS6	—	AUD 1525	—
				AUD 252R	R	LHIC	HS6	—	AUD 1525	—
B18B 144 (U.S.A.)	1788cc	4	1968	AUD 331F	F	RHIC	HS6	—	CUD 1538	—
				AUD 331R	R	LHIC	HS6	—	CUD 1538	—
B18D P544 and P122S (Pancake Filter)	1788cc	4	1965/66	AUD 94F	F	RHIC	HS6	—	AUD 1490	—
				AUD 94R	R	LHIC	HS6	—	AUD 1490	—
B18D P544 and P122S (Oil Bath Filter)	1788cc	4	1965/66	AUD 200F	F	RHIC	HS6	—	AUD 1502	—
				AUD 200R	R	LHIC	HS6	—	AUD 1502	—
B18D (Silencer Filter)	1788cc	4	1966/67	AUD 202F	F	RHIC	HS6	—	AUD 1519	—
				AUD 202R	R	LHIC	HS6	—	AUD 1519	—
B18D 144 (Pancake Filter)	1788cc	4	1967/68	AUD 232F	F	RHIC	HS6	—	AUD 1328	—
				AUD 232R	R	LHIC	HS6	—	AUD 1328	—
B20A 142/144	1990cc	4	1969/70	AUD 403	—	LHIC	HS6	—	CUD 1107	—
B20B 144S	1990cc	4	1969/70	AUD 331F	F	RHIC	HS6	—	CUD 1538	—
				AUD 331R	R	LHIC	HS6	—	CUD 1538	—
B20B 144 (U.S.A.)	1990cc	4	1971	AUD 388F	F	LHIC	HIF6	—	CUD 1110	—
				AUD 388R	R	RHIC	HIF6	—	CUD 1110	—
B20B 144 (LHD)	1990cc	4	1971/72	AUD 499F	F	LHIC	HIF6	—	CUD 1125	—
				AUD 499R	R	RHIC	HIF6	—	CUD 1125	—
B20B 144 Automatic (LHD)	1990cc	4	1971/72	AUD 511F	F	LHIC	HIF6	—	CUD 1125	—
				AUD 511R	R	RHIC	HIF6	—	CUD 1125	—
B20D 144 (LHD)	1990cc	4	1971	AUD 433F	F	LHIC	HIF6	—	CUD 1110	—
				AUD 433R	R	RHIC	HIF6	—	CUD 1110	—
B20D 144 (LHD)	1990cc	4	1972	AUD 522F	F	LHIC	HIF6	—	CUD 1147	—
				AUD 522R	R	RHIC	HIF6	—	CUD 1147	—
B20B (LHD)	1990cc	4	1972/73	AUD 599F	F	LHIC	HIF6	—	CUD 1125	—
				AUD 599R	R	RHIC	HIF6	—	CUD 1125	—
B20B 144 Automatic (LHD)	1990cc	4	1972/73	AUD 600F	F	LHIC	HIF6	—	CUD 1125	—
				AUD 600R	R	RHIC	HIF6	—	CUD 1125	—
B20B 144 (Canada)	1090cc	4	1973/74	AUD 666F	F	LHIC	HIF6	—	CUD 1125	—
				AUD 655R	R	RHIC	HIF6	—	CUD 1125	—
B20B 144 Automatic (Canada)	1990cc	4	1973/74	AUD 677F	F	LHIC	HIF6	—	CUD 1125	—
				AUD 655R	R	RHIC	HIF6	—	CUD 1125	—
B20A 144 (LHD)	1990cc	4	1974	AUD 466	—	LHIC	HIF6	—	CUD 1156	—
B20A 144 (LHD)	1990cc	4	1974/	AUD 699	—	LHIC	HIF6	—	CUD 1156	—
B20A	1990cc	4	1975/	FZX 1055	—	LHIC	HIF6	—	NZX 8007	—
B21A (Sweden)	2127cc	4	1975/	FZX 1056	—	RHIC	HIF6	—	NZX 8009	—

[1] Front F, Centre C, Rear R, Right Hand RH, Left Hand LH.
[2] Thermocarb gasket pack required in addition AUE 807.
[3] Air jet 0.116 in. diameter.

Spec. Repeated	Needle Guide	Needle Screw	Piston Spring	Damper	Jet	Needle and Seat	Float	Throttle Spindle	Throttle Disc	Gasket Pack	Pump OE	Pump Alt.
											AUA 165	AZX 1301
AUD 97F	—	AUC 2057	AUC 4818	AUC 8102	AUD 9480	WZX 1101	WZX 1300	WZX 1317	WZX 1373	AUE 813	AUF 400	—
AUD 97R	—	AUC 2057	AUC 4818	AUC 8102	AUD 9481	WZX 1101	WZX 1300	WZX 1317	WZX 1373	AUE 813	—	—
AUD 215F	—	AUC 2057	AUC 4818	AUC 8102	AUD 9480	WZX 1101	WZX 1300	WZX 1317	WZX 1309	AUE 813	AUF 400	—
AUD 215R	—	AUC 2057	AUC 4818	AUC 8102	AUD 9481	WZX 1101	WZX 1300	WZX 1317	WZX 1309	AUE 813	—	—
AUD 418F	—	AUC 2057	AUC 4818	AUC 8102	CUD 2697	WZX 1101	WZX 1300	WZX 1317	WZX 1309	AUE 813	AUF 400	—
AUD 418R	—	AUC 2057	AUC 4818	AUC 8102	CUD 2698	WZX 1101	WZX 1300	WZX 1317	WZX 1309	AUE 813	—	—
AUD 69L	—	AUC 2057	AUC 4587	AUC 8103	AUD 9141	WZX 1100	WZX 1300	WZX 1310	WZX 1320	AUE 810	AUF 207	AUF 204
AUD 69R	—	AUC 2057	AUC 4587	AUC 8103	AUD 9142	WZX 1100	WZX 1300	WZX 1310	WZX 1320	AUE 810	—	—
AUD 186	—	AUC 2057	AUC 4387	AUC 8103	AUD 9451	WZX 1100	WZX 1300	WZX 1312	WZX 1324	AUE 811	AUF 207	AUF 204
AUD 271	—	AUC 2057	AUC 4387	AUC 8103	AUD 9451	WZX 1100	WZX 1300	WZX 1312	WZX 1324	AUE 811	AUF 207	AUF 204
AUD 318L	—	AUC 2057	AUC 4587	AUC 8103	AUD 9141	WZX 1100	WZX 1300	WZX 1310	WZX 1320	AUE 810	AUF 207	AUF 204
AUD 318R	—	AUC 2057	AUC 4587	AUC 8103	AUD 9142	WZX 1100	WZX 1300	WZX 1310	WZX 1320	AUE 810	—	—
AUD 344L	—	AUC 2057	AUC 4587	AUC 8103	AUD 9141	WZX 1100	WZX 1300	WZX 1310	WZX 1320	AUE 810	AUF 207	AUF 204
AUD 344R	—	AUC 2057	AUC 4587	AUC 8103	AUD 9142	WZX 1100	WZX 1300	WZX 1310	WZX 1320	AUE 810	—	—
AUD 431L	—	AUC 2057	AUC 4587	AUC 8103	AUD 9141	WZX 1100	WZX 1300	WZX 1310	WZX 1320	AUE 810	AUF 207	AUF 204
AUD 431R	—	AUC 2057	AUC 4587	AUC 8103	AUD 9142	WZX 1100	WZX 1300	WZX 1310	WZX 1320	AUE 810	—	—
AUD 454L	AUD 4288	AUD 4250	AUC 4587	AUC 8103	AUD 9141	WZX 1100	WZX 1300	WZX 1310	WZX 1380	AUE 810	AUF 207	AUF 204
AUD 454R	AUD 4288	AUD 4250	AUC 4587	AUC 8103	AUD 9142	WZX 1100	WZX 1300	WZX 1310	WZX 1380	AUE 810	—	—
AUD 496L	AUD 4288	AUD 4250	AUC 4587	AUC 8103	AUD 9141	WZX 1100	WZX 1300	WZX 1310	WZX 1380	AUE 810	AUF 207	AUF 204
AUD 496R	AUD 4288	AUD 4250	AUC 4587	AUC 8103	AUD 9142	WZX 1100	WZX 1300	WZX 1310	WZX 1380	AUE 810	—	—
AUD 628	AUD 4288	AUD 4252	AUC 4387	AUC 8103	AUD 9105	WZX 1100	WZX 1300	WZX 1311	WZX 1321	AUE 812	AUF 809	—
AUD 95F	—	AUC 2057	AUC 4387	AUC 8103	AUD 9148	WZX 1100	WZX 1300	WZX 1311	WZX 1321	AUE 812	—	—
AUD 95R	—	AUC 2057	AUC 4387	AUC 8103	AUD 9149	WZX 1100	WZX 1300	WZX 1311	WZX 1321	AUE 812	—	—
AUD 277F	—	AUC 2057	AUC 4387	AUC 8103	AUD 9148	WZX 1100	WZX 1300	WZX 1311	WZX 1321	AUE 812	—	—
AUD 277R	—	AUC 2057	AUC 4387	AUC 8103	AUD 9149	WZX 1100	WZX 1300	WZX 1311	WZX 1321	AUE 812	—	—
FZX 1238F	—	AUC 2057	AUC 4387	AUC 8103	AUD 9148	WZX 1101	WZX 1304	WZX 1176	WZX 1321	AUE 812	—	—
FZX 1238R	—	AUC 2057	AUC 4387	AUC 8103	AUD 9149	WZX 1101	WZX 1304	WZX 1176	WZX 1321	AUE 812	—	—
AUD 94F	—	AUC 2057	AUC 4387	AUC 8103	AUD 9148	WZX 1100	WZX 1300	WZX 1311	WZX 1321	AUE 812	—	—
AUD 94R	—	AUC 2057	AUC 4387	AUC 8103	AUD 9149	WZX 1100	WZX 1300	WZX 1311	WZX 1321	AUE 812	—	—
AUD 193F	—	AUC 2057	AUC 4387	AUC 8103	AUD 9105	WZX 1100	WZX 1300	WZX 1311	WZX 1321	AUE 812	—	—
AUD 193R	—	AUC 2057	AUC 4387	AUC 8103	AUD 9106	WZX 1100	WZX 1300	WZX 1311	WZX 1321	AUE 812	—	—
AUD 204F	—	AUC 2057	AUC 4387	AUC 8103	AUD 9148	WZX 1100	WZX 1300	WZX 1311	WZX 1321	AUE 812	—	—
AUD 204R	—	AUC 2057	AUC 4387	AUC 8103	AUD 9149	WZX 1100	WZX 1300	WZX 1311	WZX 1321	AUE 812	—	—
AUD 230F	—	AUC 2057	AUC 4387	AUC 8103	AUD 9148	WZX 1100	WZX 1300	WZX 1311	WZX 1321	AUE 812	—	—
AUD 230R	—	AUC 2057	AUC 4387	AUC 8103	AUD 9149	WZX 1100	WZX 1300	WZX 1311	WZX 1321	AUE 812	—	—
AUD 231F	—	AUC 2057	AUC 4387	AUC 8103	AUD 9148	WZX 1100	WZX 1300	WZX 1311	WZX 1321	AUE 812	—	—
AUD 231R	—	AUC 2057	AUC 4387	AUC 8103	AUD 9149	WZX 1100	WZX 1300	WZX 1311	WZX 1321	AUE 812	—	—
AUD 305F	AUD 4290	AUD 4252	AUC 4387	AUC 8108	AUD 9148	WZX 1100	WZX 1300	WZX 1311	WZX 1381	AUE 812	—	—
AUD 305R	AUD 4290	AUD 4252	AUC 4387	AUC 8108	AUD 9149	WZX 1100	WZX 1300	WZX 1311	WZX 1381	AUE 812	—	—
AUD 252F	—	AUC 2057	AUC 4387	AUC 8108	AUD 9148	WZX 1100	WZX 1300	WZX 1311	WZX 1186	AUE 812	—	—
AUD 252R	—	AUC 2057	AUC 4387	AUC 8108	AUD 9149	WZX 1100	WZX 1300	WZX 1311	WZX 1186	AUE 812	—	—
AUD 331F	AUD 4288	AUD 4252	AUC 4387	AUC 8103	AUD 9148	WZX 1101	WZX 1300	WZX 1311	WZX 1381	AUE 812	—	—
AUD 331R	AUD 4288	AUD 4252	AUC 4387	AUC 8103	AUD 9149	WZX 1101	WZX 1300	WZX 1311	WZX 1381	AUE 812	—	—
AUD 94F	—	AUC 2057	AUC 4387	AUC 8103	AUD 9148	WZX 1101	WZX 1300	WZX 1311	WZX 1321	AUE 812	—	—
AUD 94R	—	AUC 2057	AUC 4387	AUC 8103	AUD 9149	WZX 1101	WZX 1300	WZX 1311	WZX 1321	AUE 812	—	—
AUD 200F	—	AUC 2057	AUC 4387	AUC 8103	AUD 9148	WZX 1101	WZX 1300	WZX 1311	WZX 1321	AUE 812	—	—
AUD 200R	—	AUC 2057	AUC 4387	AUC 8103	AUD 9149	WZX 1101	WZX 1300	WZX 1311	WZX 1321	AUE 812	—	—
AUD 202F	—	AUC 2057	AUC 4387	AUC 8103	AUD 9148	WZX 1101	WZX 1300	WZX 1311	WZX 1321	AUE 812	—	—
AUD 202R	—	AUC 2057	AUC 4387	AUC 8103	AUD 9149	WZX 1101	WZX 1300	WZX 1311	WZX 1321	AUE 812	—	—
AUD 232F	—	AUC 2057	AUC 4387	AUC 8103	AUD 9148	WZX 1101	WZX 1300	WZX 1311	WZX 1321	AUE 812	—	—
AUD 232R	—	AUC 2057	AUC 4387	AUC 8103	AUD 9149	WZX 1101	WZX 1300	WZX 1311	WZX 1321	AUE 812	—	—
AUD 403	AUD 4290	AUD 4252	AUC 1170	AUC 8103	AUD 9149	WZX 1101	WZX 1300	WZX 1191	WZX 1183	AUE 812	—	—
AUD 331F	AUD 4288	AUD 4252	AUC 4387	AUC 8103	AUD 9148	WZX 1101	WZX 1300	WZX 1311	WZX 1381	AUE 812	—	—
AUD 331R	AUD 4288	AUD 4252	AUC 4387	AUC 8103	AUD 9149	WZX 1101	WZX 1300	WZX 1311	WZX 1381	AUE 812	—	—
AUD 388F	AUD 4290	AUD 4252	AUC 4387	AUC 8103	WZX 1453	WZX 1100	WZX 1400	WZX 1172	WZX 1185	WZX 1505	—	—
AUD 388R	AUD 4290	AUD 4252	AUC 4387	AUC 8103	WZX 1452	WZX 1100	WZX 1401	WZX 1172	WZX 1185	WZX 1505	—	—
AUD 499F	AUD 4290	AUD 4252	AUC 4387	AUC 8103	WZX 1453	WZX 1100	WZX 1400	WZX 1172	WZX 1184	WZX 1505	—	—
AUD 499R	AUD 4290	AUD 4252	AUC 4387	AUC 8103	WZX 1452	WZX 1100	WZX 1401	WZX 1172	WZX 1184	WZX 1505	—	—
AUD 511F	AUD 4290	AUD 4252	AUC 4387	AUC 8103	WZX 1453	WZX 1100	WZX 1400	WZX 1172	WZX 1182	WZX 1505	*	—
AUD 511R	AUD 4290	AUD 4252	AUC 4387	AUC 8103	WZX 1452	WZX 1100	WZX 1401	WZX 1172	WZX 1182	WZX 1505	—	—
AUD 433F	AUD 4290	AUD 4252	AUC 4387	AUC 8103	WZX 1453	WZX 1100	WZX 1400	WZX 1172	WZX 1183	WZX 1505	—	—
AUD 433R	AUD 4290	AUD 4252	AUC 4387	AUC 8103	WZX 1452	WZX 1100	WZX 1401	WZX 1172	WZX 1183	WZX 1505	—	—
AUD 522F	AUD 4290	AUD 4252	AUC 4387	AUC 8103	WZX 1453	WZX 1100	WZX 1400	WZX 1172	WZX 1183	WZX 1505	—	—
AUD 522R	AUD 4290	AUD 4252	AUC 4387	AUC 8103	WZX 1452	WZX 1100	WZX 1401	WZX 1172	WZX 1183	WZX 1505	—	—
AUD 599F	AUD 4290	AUD 4252	AUC 4387	AUC 8103	WZX 1453	WZX 1100	WZX 1400	WZX 1172	WZX 1184	WZX 1505	—	—
AUD 599R	AUD 4290	AUD 4252	AUC 4387	AUC 8103	WZX 1452	WZX 1100	WZX 1401	WZX 1172	WZX 1184	WZX 1505	—	—
AUD 600F	AUD 4290	AUD 4252	AUC 4387	AUC 8103	WZX 1453	WZX 1100	WZX 1400	WZX 1172	WZX 1184	WZX 1505	—	—
AUD 600R	AUD 4290	AUD 4252	AUC 4387	AUC 8103	WZX 1452	WZX 1100	WZX 1401	WZX 1172	WZX 1184	WZX 1505	—	—
AUD 666F	AUD 4290	AUD 4252	AUC 4387	AUC 8103	WZX 1453	WZX 1100	WZX 1400	WZX 1192	WZX 1184	WZX 1505	—	—
AUD 655R	AUD 4290	AUD 4252	AUC 4387	AUC 8103	WZX 1452	WZX 1100	WZX 1401	WZX 1192	WZX 1184	WZX 1505	—	—
AUD 677F	AUD 4290	AUD 4252	AUC 4387	AUC 8103	WZX 1453	WZX 1100	WZX 1400	WZX 1192	WZX 1184	WZX 1505	—	—
AUD 655R	AUD 4290	AUD 4252	AUC 4387	AUC 8103	WZX 1452	WZX 1100	WZX 1401	WZX 1192	WZX 1184	WZX 1505	—	—
AUD 466	AUD 4290	AUD 4252	AUC 1170	AUC 8103	WZX 1453	WZX 1100	WZX 1400	WZX 1194	WZX 1183	WZX 1505	—	—
AUD 699	AUD 4290	AUD 4252	AUC 1170	AUC 8103	WZX 1453	WZX 1100	WZX 1400	WZX 1193	WZX 1183	WZX 1505	—	—
FZX 1055	JZX 1038	AUD 4252	AUC 1170	AUC 8103	WZX 1453	WZX 1100	WZX 1400	WZX 1499	WZX 1183	WZX 1505	—	—
FZX 1056	JZX 1038	AUD 4252	AUC 1170	AUC 8103	WZX 1452	WZX 1100	WZX 1401	WZX 1307	WZX 1186	WZX 1505	—	—

[3] AED Unit TZX 1002 supersedes AUH 308, 309, 310 and 317 (1 per installation).   [4] Service AED Unit AUH 300 (1 per installation).
[6] Air jet 0.102 in. diameter.   [7] Service AED Unit AUH 305 1 per installation Rover (U.S.A.) spec. only.

Model Details	Capacity	No. of Cyl.	Year	Spec.	Position[1]	Inter Connect	Type	Rich	Needle Std.	Weak
B21A (Australia)	2127cc	4	1975	FZX 1057	—	RHIC	HIF6	—	NZX 8009	—
B21A	2127cc	4	1976/	FZX 1259	—	RHIC	HIF6	—	NZX 8009	—
B21A (Canada)	2127cc	4	1976/	FZX 1267	—	RHIC	HIF6	—	NZX 8009	—
B27A	2664cc	6	1975	FZX 1059	—	RHIC	HIF6	—	NZX 8010	—
B27A	2664cc	6	1976 /	FZX 1205	—	RHIC	HIF6	—	NZX 8010	—
WOLSELEY										
1500	1485cc	4	1962/64	AUC 979	—	RHIC	HS2	AUD 1261	AUD 1468	AUD 1211
Hornet Mk I & Mk II	998cc	4	1963/68	AUD 86	—	RHIC	HS2	AUD 1261	AUD 1227	AUD 1211
Hornet Mk III	998cc	4	1968/69	AUD 298	—	RHIC	HS2	AUD 1261	AUD 1227	AUD 1211
1100	1098cc	4	1965/66	AUD 69L	LH	RHIC	HS2	AUD 1144	AUD 1142	AUD 1225
				AUD 69R	RH	LHIC	HS2	AUD 1144	AUD 1142	AUD 1225
6/110	2912cc	6	1967	AUD 240F	F	—	H4	AUD 1002	AUD 1048	AUD 1230
				AUD 240R	R	—	H4	AUD 1002	AUD 1048	AUD 1230
1300	1275cc	4	1967/68	AUD 186	—	LHIC	HS4	AUD 1076	AUD 1528	AUD 1096
1300 Automatic	1275cc	4	1967/68	AUD 271	—	LHIC	HS4	AUD 1076	AUD 1528	AUD 1096
1300	1275cc	4	1968/69	AUD 318L	LH	RHIC	HS2	AUD 1261	AUD 1149	AUD 1211
				AUD 318R	RH	LHIC	HS2	AUD 1261	AUD 1149	AUD 1211
1300 Mk II	1275cc	4	1969/71	AUD 344L	LH	RHIC	HS2	AUD 1261	AUD 1468	AUD 1211
				AUD 344R	RH	LHIC	HS2	AUD 1261	AUD 1468	AUD 1211
1300 Mk II	1275cc	4	1971/75	AUD 431L	LH	RHIC	HS2	AUD 1261	AUD 1468	AUD 1211
				AUD 431R	RH	LHIC	HS2	AUD 1261	AUD 1468	AUD 1211
1300 Mk II	1275cc	4	1971/74	AUD 454L	LH	RHIC	HS2	—	CUD 1013	—
				AUD 454R	RH	LHIC	HS2	—	CUD 1013	—
1300 Mk II	1275cc	4	1971/74	AUD 496L	LH	RHIC	HS2	—	CUD 1013	—
				AUD 496R	RH	LHIC	HS2	—	CUD 1013	—
18/85 Automatic	1798cc	4	1967	AUD 273	—	RHIC	HS6	AUD 1337	AUD 1362	AUD 1117
18/85 Mk II Automatic	1798cc	4	1969/71	AUD 291	—	RHIC	HS6	AUD 1317	AUD 1490	AUD 1117
18/85 Mk II 'S'	1798cc	4	1969/71	AUD 171L	LH	RHIC	HS6	AUD 1099	AUD 1469	AUD 1117
				AUD 171R	RH	LHIC	HS6	AUD 1099	AUD 1469	AUD 1117
Six	2227cc	6	1972/74	AUD 409F	LH	LHIC	HS6	—	CUD 1127	—
				AUD 409R	RH	LHIC	HS6	—	CUD 1127	—
Six (E.C.E.)	2227cc	6	1972/75	AUD 546F	LH	RHIC	HIF6	—	CUD 1136	—
				AUD 546R	RH	LHIC	HIF6	—	CUD 1136	—
Six Automatic (E.C.E.)	2227cc	6	1972/75	AUD 581F	LH	RHIC	HIF6	—	CUD 1136	—
				AUD 581R	RH	LHIC	HIF6	—	CUD 1136	—

[1] Front F, Centre C, Rear R, Right Hand RH, Left Hand LH.
[2] Thermocarb gasket pack required in addition AUE 807.
[3] Air jet 0.116 in. diameter.

Spec. Repeated	Needle Guide	Needle Screw	Piston Spring	Damper	Jet	Needle and Seat	Float	Throttle Spindle	Throttle Disc	Gasket Pack	OE	Pump Alt.
FZX 1057	JZX 1038	AUD 4252	AUC 1170	AUC 8103	WZX 1452	WZX 1100	WZX 1401	WZX 1307	WZX 1186	WZX 1505	—	—
FZX 1259	JZX 1038	AUD 4252	AUC 1170	AUC 8103	WZX 1452	WZX 1100	WZX 1401	WZX 1305	WZX 1186	WZX 1505	—	—
FZX 1267	JZX 1038	AUD 4252	JZX 1088	LZX 1287	WZX 1452	WZX 1100	WZX 1401	WZX 1305	WZX 1186	WZX 1505	—	—
FZX 1059	JZX 1038	AUD 4252	JZX 1088	CUD 2910	WZX 1452	WZX 1101	WZX 1401	WZX 1307	WZX 1187	WZX 1505	—	—
FZX 1205	JZX 1038	AUD 4252	JZX 1088	CUD 2900	WZX 1452	WZX 1101	WZX 1401	WZX 1305	WZX 1187	WZX 1505	—	—
AUC 979	—	AUC 2057	AUC 4387	AUC 8103	AUD 9098	WZX 1101	WZX 1300	WZX 1310	WZX 1320	AUE 810	AUB 83	AUF 204
AUD 86	—	AUC 2057	AUC 4387	AUC 8103	AUD 9098	WZX 1100	WZX 1300	WZX 1310	WZX 1320	AUE 810	AUB 83	AUF 204
AUD 298	—	AUC 2057	AUC 4387	AUC 8103	AUD 9098	WZX 1100	WZX 1300	WZX 1310	WZX 1320	AUE 810	AUF 214	—
AUD 69L	—	AUC 2057	AUC 4587	AUC 8103	AUD 9141	WZX 1100	WZX 1300	WZX 1310	WZX 1320	AUE 810	AUF 204	—
AUD 69R	—	AUC 2057	AUC 4587	AUC 8103	AUD 9142	WZX 1100	WZX 1300	WZX 1310	WZX 1320	AUE 810	—	—
AUD 240F	—	AUC 2057	AUC 1167	AUC 8102	WZX 1595	WZX 1100	WZX 1303	WZX 1590	WZX 1592	AUE 801	AUF 208	AUF 204
AUD 240R	—	AUC 2057	AUC 1167	AUC 8102	WZX 1595	WZX 1100	WZX 1303	WZX 1590	WZX 1592	AUE 801	—	—
AUD 186	—	AUC 2057	AUC 4387	AUC 8103	AUD 9451	WZX 1100	WZX 1300	WZX 1312	WZX 1324	AUE 811	AUF 207	AUF 204
AUD 271	—	AUC 2057	AUC 4387	AUC 8103	AUD 9451	WZX 1100	WZX 1300	WZX 1312	WZX 1324	AUE 811	AUF 207	AUF 204
AUD 318L	—	AUC 2057	AUC 4587	AUC 8103	AUD 9141	WZX 1100	WZX 1300	WZX 1310	WZX 1320	AUE 810	AUF 207	AUF 204
AUD 318R	—	AUC 2057	AUC 4587	AUC 8103	AUD 9142	WZX 1100	WZX 1300	WZX 1310	WZX 1320	AUE 810	—	—
AUD 344L	—	AUC 2057	AUC 4587	AUC 8103	AUD 9141	WZX 1100	WZX 1300	WZX 1310	WZX 1320	AUE 810	AUF 207	AUF 204
AUD 344R	—	AUC 2057	AUC 4587	AUC 8103	AUD 9142	WZX 1100	WZX 1300	WZX 1310	WZX 1320	AUE 810	—	—
AUD 431L	—	AUC 2057	AUC 4587	AUC 8103	AUD 9141	WZX 1100	WZX 1300	WZX 1310	WZX 1320	AUE 810	AUF 207	AUF 204
AUD 431R	—	AUC 2057	AUC 4587	AUC 8103	AUD 9142	WZX 1100	WZX 1300	WZX 1310	WZX 1320	AUE 810	—	—
AUD 454L	AUD 4288	AUD 4250	AUC 4587	AUC 8103	AUD 9141	WZX 1100	WZX 1300	WZX 1310	WZX 1380	AUE 810	AUF 207	AUF 204
AUD 454R	AUD 4288	AUD 4250	AUC 4587	AUC 8103	AUD 9142	WZX 1100	WZX 1300	WZX 1310	WZX 1380	AUE 810	—	—
AUD 496L	AUD 4288	AUD 4250	AUC 4587	AUC 8103	AUD 9141	WZX 1100	WZX 1300	WZX 1310	WZX 1380	AUE 810	AUF 207	AUF 204
AUD 496R	AUD 4288	AUD 4250	AUC 4587	AUC 8103	AUD 9142	WZX 1100	WZX 1300	WZX 1310	WZX 1380	AUE 810	—	—
AUD 273	—	AUC 2057	AUC 1167	AUC 8103	AUD 9148	WZX 1101	WZX 1300	WZX 1311	WZX 1321	AUE 812	AUF 209	AUF 201
AUD 291	—	AUC 2057	AUC 1167	AUC 8103	AUD 9148	WZX 1100	WZX 1300	WZX 1311	WZX 1321	AUE 812	AUF 704	AUF 803
AUD 171L	—	AUC 2057	AUC 4387	AUC 8103	AUD 9148	WZX 1101	WZX 1300	WZX 1311	WZX 1321	AUE 812	AUF 704	AUF 803
AUD 171R	—	AUC 2057	AUC 4387	AUC 8103	AUD 9149	WZX 1101	WZX 1300	WZX 1311	WZX 1321	AUE 812	AUF 222 or	—
AUD 409F	AUD 4288	AUD 4252	AUC 4387	AUC 8103	AUD 9106	WZX 1101	WZX 1300	WZX 1314	WZX 1321	AUE 812	AUF 305	—
AUD 409R	AUD 4288	AUD 4252	AUC 4387	AUC 8103	AUD 9106	WZX 1101	WZX 1300	WZX 1314	WZX 1326	WZX 1505	AUF 305	AZX 1304
AUD 546F	AUD 4288	AUD 4252	AUC 4387	CUD 2901	WZX 1453	WZX 1102	WZX 1400	WZX 1170	WZX 1326	WZX 1505	—	—
AUD 546R	AUD 4288	AUD 4252	AUC 4387	CUD 2901	WZX 1453	WZX 1102	WZX 1400	WZX 1170	WZX 1326	WZX 1505	AUF 305	AZX 1304
AUD 581F	AUD 4288	AUD 4252	AUC 4387	CUD 2901	WZX 1452	WZX 1102	WZX 1401	WZX 1170	WZX 1326	WZX 1505	AUF 305	AZX 1304
AUD 581R	AUD 4288	AUD 4252	AUC 4387	CUD 2901	WZX 1453	WZX 1102	WZX 1400	WZX 1170	WZX 1326	WZX 1505	—	—

[3] AED Unit TZX 1002 supersedes AUH 308, 309, 310 and 317.(1 per installation). [4] Service AED Unit AUH 300 (1 per installation).
[5] Air jet 0.102 in. diameter.   [7] Service AED Unit AUH 305 1 per installation Rover (U.S.A.) spec. only.

Appendix 2 Jet Identification

1. H TYPE JETS

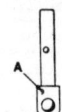

Carburetter Jet   Thermo Jet

A. Jet Size: 9=0·090"   1=0·10"   125=0·125"

2. HD TYPE JETS

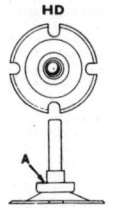

Normal HD Jet   Rolls Royce

A. Jet Size: 9=0·090"   1=0·10"   125=0·125"

3. HS JETS

A. Early HS2.
B. Intermediate HS2.
C. Latest HS2.
D. HS8.

1. Brass
2. Plastic
3a. 0·090" Jet (No groove)
3b. 0·10" Jet (One groove)
3c. 0·125" Jet (Two grooves)
4. Brass inner tube
5. Rubber Washer
6. Brass Washer.
7. Identification Sleeves
8. Black Plastic Semi downdraught
9. Red plastic Horizontal.
10. Moulded swan neck (HS8)

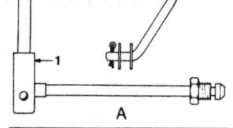
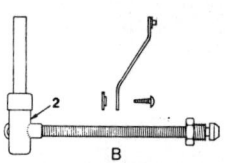
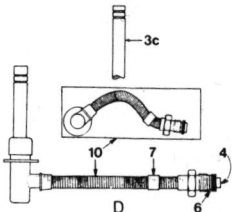

NOTE
For further details of applications and detailed specifications of HS Jets, see following pages.

4. HIF JETS

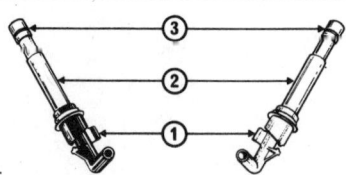

Right Hand Interconnection Carbs.

1. Jet Head—Black
2. Jet Assy.
3. Without Groove—0·090"
    With Groove—0·10"

Left Hand Interconnection Carbs.

1. Jet Head—White.
2. Jet Assy.
3. Without Groove—0·090"
    With Groove—0·10"

Appendix 3

JET NEEDLE IDENTIFICATION & CROSS REFERENCE CHART

Jet needles are identified by letters and/or numbers marked on their shank, e.g. AAK; OA7; 35. The preferred part number annotation however is a three letter – four numeral system, e.g. CUD 1009; AUD1277, and this system is adopted in the Carburetter Specifications Appendix I.

The appropriate needle part number for ordering may be found by looking through the cross reference chart.

(Lack of space prevents the preferred marking being used on the needle shank.)

HS Jet Identification Information

Float Chamber Angle	Carb Type	Interconnection[2]	Jet Part No.	Sleeve Colours (i)	Sleeve Colours (ii)	Jet Size	Jet Head	Type	Replaced by
30°	HS 2	RH	AUC 8212			·09"	Brass	A	AUD 9098 see AUE 389
30°	HS 2	RH	AUC 8780	White		·09"	Black	B	AUD 9098
30°	HS 2	LH	AUC 8781	Black		·09"	Black	B	AUD 9102
30°	HS 4	RH	AUC 8782	Red		·09"	Black	B	AUD 9098
30°	HS 4	LH	AUC 8783	Blue		·09"	Black	B	AUD 9102
30°	HS 6	RH	AUC 8784	Yellow		·10"	Black	B	AUD 9148
30°	HS 6	LH	AUC 8785	Orange		·10"	Black	B	AUD 9149
H	HS 2	RH	AUD 9028	Grey		·09"	Red	B	AUD 9103
H	HS 2	LH	AUD 9029	Brown		·09"	Red	B	AUD 9104
20°	HS 2	RH	AUD 9072	Green		·09"	Black	B	AUD 9141
20°	HS 2	LH	AUD 9073	Pink		·09"	Black	B	AUD 9142
30°	HS 2	RH	AUD 9098		White	·09"	Black	C	
30°	HS 2	LH	AUD 9102	Black		·09"	Black	C	
H	HS 2	RH	AUD 9103	Black	Grey	·09"	Red	C	
H	HS 2	LH	AUD 9104	Black	Brown	·09"	Red	C	
H	HS 6	RH	AUD 9105		Yellow	·10"	Red	C	
H	HS 6	LH	AUD 9106		Orange	·10"	Red	C	
20°	HS 2	RH	AUD 9141		Green	·09"	Black	C	
20°	HS 2	LH	AUD 9142		Pink	·09"	Black	C	
30°	HS 6	RH	AUD 9148		Yellow	·10"	Black	C	
30°	HS 6	LH	AUD 9149		Orange	·10"	Black	C	
30°	HS 4	RH	AUD 9150	Black	Red	·09"	Black	C	AUD 9098
30°	HS 4	LH	AUD 9151	Black	Blue	·09"	Black	C	AUD 9102
30°	HS 6	RH	AUD 9268	White	Yellow	·10"	Black	C	
30°	HS 6	LH	AUD 9269	White	Orange	·10"	Black	C	
H	HS 6	RH	AUD 9286	White	Yellow	·10"	Red	C	
H	HS 6	LH	AUD 9287	White	Orange	·10"	Red	C	
H	HS 6	RH	AUD 9419	Red		·125"	Black	C	
H	HS 6	LH	AUD 9487	Blue		·125"	Black	C	
H	HS 4	RH	AUD 9450	White		·09"	Red	C	
H	HS 4	LH	AUD 9451	Black		·09"	Red	C	
H	HS 6	RH	AUD 9596	Grey		·09"	Red	C	
H	HS 6	LH	AUD 9597	Brown		·09"	Red	C	
30°	HS 6	RH	AUD 9598	White		·09"	Black	C	AUD 9098
30°	HS 6	LH	AUD 9599	Black		·09"	Black	C	AUD 9102
30°	HS 6	RH	AUD 9778	Yellow	Pink	·10"	Black	C	AUD 9148
30°	HS 6	LH	AUD 9779	Orange	Pink	·10"	Black	C	AUD 9149
20°	HS 2	RH	AUD 9860	Green	Grey	·09"	Black	C	AUD 9141
20°	HS 2	LH	AUD 9861	Pink	Grey	·09"	Black	C	AUD 9142
H	HS 6	RH	AUD 9872	White	Blue	·10"	Red	C	AUD 9105
H	HS 6	LH	AUD 9873	Blue	Pink	·10"	Red	C	AUD 9106
H	HS 2	RH	AUD 9888	White	Brown	·09"	Red	C	AUD 9103
H	HS 2	LH	AUD 9889	Blue	Brown	·09"	Red	C	AUD 9104
H	HS 4	RH	AUD 9893	Yellow	Brown	·09"	Red	C	AUD 9450
H	HS 4	LH	AUD 9894	Orange	Brown	·09"	Red	C	AUD 9451
H	HS 8	LH	AUD 9798	Green		·09"	White	D	
H	HS 8	RH	AUD 9799	Grey		·09"	White	D	
H	HS 8	LH	AUD 9800	Pink		·10"	White	D	
H	HS 8	RH	AUD 9801	Yellow		·10"	White	D	
H	HS 8	LH	AUD 9802	Blue		·125"	White	D	
H	HS 8	RH	AUD 9803	Brown		·125"	White	D	
H	HS 8	LH	AUD 9814	Red	Blue	·09"	White	D	
H	HS 8	RH	AUD 9815	Red	Pink	·09"	White	D	
H	HS 8	LH	AUD 9480	White		·125"	Black	D	
H	HS 8	RH	AUD 9481	Black		·125"	Black	D	
H	HS 6	LH	AUD 9482	Black	Red	·125"	Black	D	
H	HS 6	RH	AUD 9483	White	Red	·125"	Black	D	
H	HS 8	LH	AUD 9665	White	Black	·09"	Black	D	
H	HS 8	RH	AUD 9666	Red	Black	·09"	Black	D	
H	HS 8	LH	AUD 9667	Red		·10"	Black	D	
H	HS 8	RH	AUD 9668	Red	White	·10"	Black	D	
H	HS 8	LH	AUD 9297			·09"	Black	D	AUD 9480
H	HS 8	RH	AUD 9391			·09"	Black	D	AUD 9481
H	HS 8	LH	AUD 9878	White	Grey	·09"	Black	D	
H	HS 8	RH	AUD 9879	White	Orange	·09"	Black	D	
H	HS 8	LH	AUD 9882	Black	Grey	·09"	Black	D	
H	HS 8	RH	AUD 9883	Black	Orange	·09"	Black	D	
H	HS 8	LH	AUD 9971	Blue		·09"	Black	D	
H	HS 8	RH	AUD 9972	Yellow		·09"	Black	D	
H	HS 8	LH	AUD 9973	Green		·09"	Black	D	
H	HS 8	RH	AUD 9974	Pink		·09"	Black	D	
M	HS 8	LH	CUB 2691	Red	Grey	·10"	Black	D	
H	HS 8	RH	CUD 2692	Pink	Grey	·10"	Black	D	
H	HS 8	LH	CUD 2697	Orange	Grey	·125"	Black	D	
H	HS 8	RH	CUD 2698	Green	Grey	·125"	Black	D	
H	HS 8	LH	CUD 2706	Orange	Green	·125"	Black	D	
H	HS 8	RH	CUD 2707	Orange	Pink	·125"	Black	D	
H	HS 8	LH	CUD 2708	White	Blue	·09"	Black	D	
H	HS 8	RH	CUD 2709	White	Yellow	·09"	Black	D	
H	HS 8	LH	CUD 2747	Red	Blue	·09"	Black	D	
H	HS 8	LH	CUD 2749	White	Green	·09"	Black	D	
H	HS 8	RH	CUD 2752	Yellow	Grey	·10"	Black	D	
H	HS 8	LH	CUD 2753	Blue	Grey	·10"	Black	D	
H	HS 4C	R.LH	CUD 3178[1]	Red		·09"	White	D	
H	HS 8	RH	CUD 3176	White	Red	·125"	Black	D	
H	HS 8	LH	CUD 3177	White	Pink	·125"	Black	D	

[1] Straight jet feed tube—not preformed.
[2] Right hand Interconnection normally has a left hand float chamber.

Jet Needle Cross Reference Chart.
Part No. (Three Alpha Four Numeric) To Jet Needle Identification

Part Number	Needle Marking	Part Number	Needle Marking	Part Number	Needle Marking	Part Number	Needle Marking
AUD1000	1	AUD1087	BM2	AUD1174	E2	AUD1261	M
AUD1001	2	AUD1088	BM4	AUD1175	E21	AUD1262	MA
AUD1002	3	AUD1089	BM6	AUD1176	E3	AUD1263	MO
AUD1003	4	AUD1090	BM8	AUD1177	E31	AUD1264	MW
AUD1004	5	AUD1091	C	AUD1178	E4	AUD1265	MME
AUD1005	6	AUD1092	CB	AUD1179	EX1	AUD1266	MOW
AUD1006	7	AUD1093	CC	AUD1180	FA	AUD1267	M1
AUD1007	20	AUD1094	CD	AUD1181	FB	AUD1268	M2
AUD1008	21	AUD1095	CE	AUD1182	FC	AUD1269	M5
AUD1009	24	AUD1096	CF	AUD1183	FD	AUD1270	M6
AUD1010	24A	AUD1097	CG	AUD1184	FE	AUD1271	M7
AUD1011	24B	AUD1098	CH	AUD1185	FF	AUD1272	M8
AUD1012	25	AUD1099	CI	AUD1186	FG	AUD1273	M9
AUD1013	35	AUD1100	CJ	AUD1187	FH	AUD1274	O1
AUD1014	45	AUD1101	CK	AUD1188	FI	AUD1275	O7
AUD1015	50	AUD1102	CL	AUD1189	FJ	AUD1276	OA6
AUD1016	53	AUD1103	CM	AUD1190	FK	AUD1277	OA7
AUD1017	55	AUD1104	CN	AUD1191	FL	AUD1278	OA8
AUD1018	58	AUD1105	CO	AUD1192	FM	AUD1279	PJ
AUD1019	59	AUD1106	CP	AUD1193	FN	AUD1280	P4
AUD1020	60	AUD1107	CQ	AUD1194	FO	AUD1261	P6
AUD1021	61	AUD1108	CR	AUD1195	FP	AUD1282	P61
AUD1022	62	AUD1109	CS	AUD1196	FQ	AUD1283	QA
AUD1023	69	AUD1110	CT	AUD1197	FR	AUD1284	QW
AUD1024	70	AUD1111	CU	AUD1198	FS	AUD1285	RA
AUD1025	74	AUD1112	CV	AUD1199	FT	AUD1286	RB
AUD1026	75	AUD1113	CW	AUD1200	FU	AUD1287	RC
AUD1027	76	AUD1114	CX	AUD1201	FV	AUD1288	RD
AUD1028	78	AUD1115	CY	AUD1202	FW	AUD1289	RF
AUD1029	79	AUD1116	CZ	AUD1203	FY	AUD1290	RG
AUD1030	80	AUD1117	CIW	AUD1204	FZ	AUD1291	RH
AUD1031	81	AUD1118	CP4	AUD1205	GA	AUD1292	RJ
AUD1032	AA	AUD1119	CS1	AUD1206	GB	AUD1293	RK
AUD1033	AB	AUD1120	CS2	AUD1207	GC	AUD1294	RL
AUD1034	AC	AUD1121	DA	AUD1208	GD	AUD1295	RO
AUD1035	AD	AUD1122	DC	AUD1209	GE	AUD1296	RP
AUD1036	AE	AUD1123	DE	AUD1210	GF	AUD1297	RS
AUD1037	AF	AUD1124	DF	AUD1211	GG	AUD1298	RU
AUD1038	AG	AUD1125	DG	AUD1212	GH	AUD1299	RV
AUD1039	AH	AUD1126	DH	AUD1213	GI	AUD1300	RLB
AUD1040	AI	AUD1127	DJ	AUD1214	GJ	AUD1301	RLS
AUD1041	AJ	AUD1128	DK	AUD1215	GK	AUD1302	R3
AUD1042	AK	AUD1129	DM	AUD1216	GL	AUD1303	R6
AUD1043	AL	AUD1130	DN	AUD1217	GM	AUD1304	R32
AUD1044	AM	AUD1131	DP	AUD1218	GN	AUD1305	RM
AUD1045	AO	AUD1132	DQ	AUD1219	GO	AUD1306	RMO
AUD1046	AP	AUD1133	DR	AUD1220	GP	AUD1307	RM1
AUD1047	AQ	AUD1134	DS	AUD1221	GR	AUD1308	RM2
AUD1048	AR	AUD1135	DT	AUD1222	GS	AUD1309	RM3
AUD1049	AS	AUD1136	DU	AUD1223	GT	AUD1310	RM4
AUD1050	AT	AUD1137	DV	AUD1224	GU	AUD1311	RM5
AUD1051	AU	AUD1138	DW	AUD1225	GV	AUD1312	RM6
AUD1052	AV	AUD1139	DY	AUD1226	GW	AUD1313	RM7
AUD1053	AW	AUD1140	D1	AUD1227	GX	AUD1314	RM8
AUD1054	AX	AUD1141	D2	AUD1228	GER	AUD1315	RM9
AUD1055	AY	AUD1142	D3	AUD1229	G2	AUD1316	S
AUD1056	AZ	AUD1143	D4	AUD1230	HA	AUD1317	SA
AUD1057	AC2	AUD1144	D6	AUD1231	HB	AUD1318	SB
AUD1058	AH1	AUD1145	D7	AUD1232	HC	AUD1319	SC
AUD1059	AH2	AUD1146	D8	AUD1233	HD	AUD1320	SD
AUD1060	A5	AUD1147	D9	AUD1234	HE	AUD1321	SE
AUD1061	A9	AUD1148	EA	AUD1235	HF	AUD1322	SF
AUD1062	BA	AUD1149	EB	AUD1236	HV2	AUD1323	SG
AUD1063	BC	AUD1150	EC	AUD1237	HV3	AUD1324	SH
AUD1064	BD	AUD1151	ED	AUD1238	HV4	AUD1325	SJ
AUD1065	BE	AUD1152	EE	AUD1239	H1	AUD1326	SK
AUD1066	BF	AUD1153	EF	AUD1240	H2	AUD1327	SL
AUD1067	BG	AUD1154	EG	AUD1241	H4	AUD1328	SM
AUD1068	BH	AUD1155	EH	AUD1242	H6	AUD1329	SN
AUD1069	BI	AUD1156	EI	AUD1243	JM	AUD1330	SO
AUD1070	BJ	AUD1157	EJ	AUD1244	K	AUD1331	SP
AUD1071	BK	AUD1158	EK	AUD1245	KI	AUD1332	SQ
AUD1072	BL	AUD1159	EL	AUD1246	KT	AUD1333	SR
AUD1073	BM	AUD1160	EM	AUD1247	KW	AUD1334	SS
AUD1074	BN	AUD1161	EN	AUD1248	KTA	AUD1335	ST
AUD1075	BP	AUD1162	EO	AUD1249	KWR	AUD1336	SV
AUD1076	BQ	AUD1163	EP	AUD1250	KW1	AUD1337	SW
AUD1077	BR	AUD1164	EQ	AUD1251	KW2	AUD1338	SY
AUD1078	BS	AUD1165	ER	AUD1252	L	AUD1339	SZ
AUD1079	BT	AUD1166	ES	AUD1253	LS	AUD1340	S4
AUD1080	BU	AUD1167	ET	AUD1254	LB1	AUD1341	S5
AUD1081	BV	AUD1168	EU	AUD1255	LB2	AUD1342	S6
AUD1082	BW	AUD1169	EV	AUD1256	LBA	AUD1343	TA
AUD1083	BX	AUD1170	EW	AUD1257	LFN	AUD1344	T8
AUD1084	BY	AUD1171	EX	AUD1258	LSI	AUD1345	TC
AUD1085	BZ	AUD1172	EY	AUD1259	L11	AUD1346	TD
AUD1086	BX1	AUD1173	EZ	AUD1260	L12	AUD1347	TE

Jet Needle Cross Reference Chart.
Part No. (Three Alpha Four Numeric) To Jet Needle Identification

Part Number	Needle Marking	Part Number	Needle Marking	Part Number	Needle Marking	Part Number	Needle Marking
AUD1348	TF	AUD1435	XG	AUD1522	DL	CUD1053	ACF
AUD1349	TG	AUD1436	XH	AUD1523	DB	CUD1054	ACG
AUD1350	TH	AUD1437	XI	AUD1524	NA	CUD1055	ACH
AUD1351	TJ	AUD1438	XJ	AUD1525	DX	CUD1056	ACJ
AUD1352	TK	AUD1439	XK	AUD1526	BO	CUD1057	ACK
AUD1353	TL	AUD1440	XL	AUD1527	AAA	CUD1058	ACL
AUD1354	TM	AUD1441	XM	AUD1528	DZ	CUD1059	ACM
AUD1355	TN	AUD1442	XN	AUD1529	KK	CUD1100	BAA
AUD1356	TO	AUD1443	XO	AUD1530	FX	CUD1101	BAB
AUD1357	TP	AUD1444	XQ	AUD1531	DD	CUD1102	BAC
AUD1358	TR	AUD1445	XR	AUD1532	UVU	CUD1103	BAD
AUD1359	TS	AUD1446	XS	AUD1533	BB2	CUD1104	BAE
AUD1360	TT	AUD1447	XT	AUD1534	BB3	CUD1105	BAF
AUD1361	TU	AUD1448	XU	AUD1535	BB4	CUD1106	BAG
AUD1362	TW	AUD1449	XV	AUD1536	KL	CUD1107	BAH
AUD1363	TX	AUD1450	XW	AUD1537	KM	CUD1108	BAJ
AUD1364	UA	AUD1451	XX	AUD1539	KO	CUD1109	BAK
AUD1365	UB	AUD1452	XY	AUD1541	KP	CUD1110	BAL
AUD1366	UC	AUD1453	XZ	AUD1548	UVV	CUD1111	BAM
AUD1367	UD	AUD1454	YA	AUD1549	UVW	CUD1112	BAN
AUD1368	UE	AUD1455	YB	AUD1550	KQ	CUD1113	BAP
AUD1369	UF	AUD1456	YC	AUD1552	KR	CUD1114	BAQ
AUD1370	UH	AUD1457	YD	AUD1553	KS	CUD1115	BAR
AUD1371	UJ	AUD1458	YE	AUD1554	KU	CUD1116	BAS
AUD1372	UK	AUD1459	ZA	AUD1583	KV	CUD1117	BAT
AUD1373	UVA	AUD1460	ZB	AUD1586	UVX	CUD1118	BAU
AUD1374	UVB	AUD1461	ZC	AUD1644	KX	CUD1119	BAV
AUD1375	UVC	AUD1462	ZD	AUD1681	NB	CUD1120	BAW
AUD1376	UVD	AUD1463	ZE	AUD1682	KY	CUD1121	BAX
AUD1377	UVE	AUD1464	ZF	AUD1683	KZ	CUD1122	BAY
AUD1378	UVF	AUD1465	ZG	AUD1684	HH	CUD1123	BAZ
AUD1379	UVG	AUD1466	UL	AUD1685	HI	CUD1124	BBA
AUD1380	UVH	AUD1467	UM	AUD1686	HJ	CUD1125	BBB
AUD1381	UVI	AUD1468	GY	AUD1687	HK	CUD1126	BBC
AUD1382	UVJ	AUD1469	TZ	CUD1000	AAA	CUD1127	BBD
AUD1383	UVK	AUD1470	KA	CUD1001	AAB	CUD1128	BBE
AUD1384	UVL	AUD1471	TY	CUD1002	AAC	CUD1129	BBF
AUD1385	UVM	AUD1472	UO	CUD1003	AAD	CUD1130	BBG
AUD1386	UVN	AUD1473	GZ	CUD1004	AAE	CUD1131	BBH
AUD1387	UVO	AUD1474	UN	CUD1005	AAF	CUD1132	BBJ
AUD1388	UVP	AUD1475	SU	CUD1006	AAG	CUD1133	BBK
AUD1389	UVR	AUD1476	SX	CUD1007	AAH	CUD1134	BBL
AUD1390	UVT	AUD1477	KB	CUD1008	AAJ	CUD1135	BBM
AUD1391	VA	AUD1478	AN	CUD1009	AAK	CUD1136	BBN
AUD1392	VB	AUD1479	BB	CUD1010	AAL	CUD1137	BBP
AUD1393	VC	AUD1480	CA	CUD1011	AAM	CUD1138	BBQ
AUD1394	VD	AUD1481	UG	CUD1012	AAN	CUD1139	BBR
AUD1395	VE	AUD1482	UP	CUD1013	AAP	CUD1140	BBS
AUD1396	VF	AUD1483	MB	CUD1014	AAQ	CUD1141	BBT
AUD1397	VG	AUD1484	UR	CUD1015	AAR	CUD1142	BBU
AUD1398	VH	AUD1485	US	CUD1016	AAS	CUD1143	BBV
AUD1399	VI	AUD1486	UT	CUD1017	AAT	CUD1144	BBW
AUD1400	VJ	AUD1487	RE	CUD1018	AAU	CUD1145	BBX
AUD1401	VK	AUD1488	RI	CUD1019	AAV	CUD1146	BBY
AUD1402	VL	AUD1489	MC	CUD1020	AAW	CUD1147	BBZ
AUD1403	VM	AUD1490	ZH	CUD1021	AAX	CUD1148	BCA
AUD1404	VN	AUD1491	RN	CUD1022	AAY	CUD1149	BCB
AUD1405	VO	AUD1492	UU	CUD1023	AAZ	CUD1150	BCC
AUD1406	VP	AUD1493	UV	CUD1024	ABA	CUD1151	BCD
AUD1407	VR	AUD1494	RR	CUD1025	ABB	CUD1152	BCE
AUD1408	VS	AUD1495	KH	CUD1026	ABC	CUD1153	BCF
AUD1409	VT	AUD1496	HG	CUD1027	ABD	CUD1154	BCG
AUD1410	V2	AUD1497	UW	CUD1028	ABE	CUD1155	BCH
AUD1411	V3	AUD1498	UX	CUD1029	ABF	CUD1156	BCJ
AUD1412	WX	AUD1499	TV	CUD1030	ABG	CUD1157	BCK
AUD1413	WX1	AUD1500	KC	CUD1031	ABH	CUD1158	BCL
AUD1414	WO2	AUD1501	KD	CUD1032	ABJ	CUD1159	BCM
AUD1415	WO3	AUD1502	KE	CUD1033	ABK	CUD1160	BCN
AUD1416	WO4	AUD1503	UY	CUD1034	ABL	CUD1161	BCP
AUD1417	W3	AUD1504	UO1	CUD1035	ABM	CUD1162	BCQ
AUD1418	WA	AUD1505	U25	CUD1036	ABN	CUD1163	BCR
AUD1419	WB	AUD1506	U35	CUD1037	ABP	CUD1164	BCS
AUD1420	WC	AUD1507	U45	CUD1038	ABQ	CUD1165	BCT
AUD1421	WD	AUD1508	U50	CUD1039	ABR	CUD1166	BCU
AUD1422	WE	AUD1509	U59	CUD1040	ABS	CUD1167	BCV
AUD1423	WF	AUD1510	U60	CUD1041	ABT	CUD1168	BCW
AUD1424	WG	AUD1511	U70	CUD1042	ABU	CUD1169	BCX
AUD1425	WH	AUD1512	U74	CUD1043	ABV	CUD1170	BCY
AUD1426	WI	AUD1513	U75	CUD1044	ABW	CUD1171	BCZ
AUD1427	WJ	AUD1514	U76	CUD1045	ABX	CUD1200	CAA
AUD1428	WM	AUD1515	U78	CUD1046	ABY	CUD1201	CAB
AUD1429	WN	AUD1516	U79	CUD1047	ABZ	CUD1202	CAC
AUD1430	XB	AUD1517	UZ	CUD1048	ACA	CUD1203	CAD
AUD1431	XC	AUD1518	KF	CUD1049	ACB	CUD1204	CAE
AUD1432	XD	AUD1519	KG	CUD1050	ACC	CUD1205	CAF
AUD1433	XE	AUD1520	KJ	CUD1051	ACD	CUD1206	CAG
AUD1434	XF	AUD1521	UI	CUD1052	ACE	CUD1207	CAH

Jet Needle Cross Reference Chart.
Part No. (Three Alpha Four Numeric) To Jet Needle Identification

Part Number	Needle Marking	Part Number	Needle Marking	Part Number	Needle Marking	Part Number	Needle Marking
CUD1208	CAJ	NZX4071	AFY				
CUD1209	CAK	NZX4072	AFZ				
CUD1210	CAL	NZX8001	BDA				
CUD1211	CAM	NZX8002	BDB				
CUD1212	CAN	NZX8003	BDC				
CUD1213	CAP	NZX8004	BDD				
CUD1214	CAQ	NZX8005	BDE				
CUD1215	CAR	NZX8006	BDF				
CUD1216	CAS	NZX8007	BDG				
CUD1217	CAT	NZX8008	BDH				
CUD1218	CAU	NZX8009	BDJ				
CUD1219	CAV	NZX8010	BDK				
CUD1220	CAW	NZX8011	BDL				
CUD1221	CAX	NZX8012	BDM				
CUD1222	CAY	NZX8013	BDN				
CUD1223	CAZ	NZX8014	BDP				
CUD1538	KN	NZX8015	BDQ				
NZX4001	ADA	NZX8016	BDR				
NZX4002	ADB	NZX8017	BDS				
NZX4003	ADC	NZX8018	BDT				
NZX4004	ADD	NZX8019	BDU				
NZX4005	ADE	NZX8020	BDV				
NZX4006	ADF	NZX8021	BDW				
NZX4007	ADG	NZX8022	BDX				
NZX4008	ADH	NZX8023	BDY				
NZX4009	ADJ	NZX8024	BDZ				
NZX4010	ADK	NZX8025	BEA				
NZX4011	ADL	NZX8026	BEB				
NZX4012	ADM	NZX8027	BEC				
NZX4013	ADN	NZX8028	BED				
NZX4014	ADP	NZX8029	BEE				
NZX4015	ADQ	NZX8030	BEF				
NZX4016	ADR	NZX8031	BEG				
NZX4017	ADS	NZX8032	BEH				
NZX4018	ADT	NZX8033	BEJ				
NZX4019	ADU	NZX8034	BEK				
NZX4020	ADV	NZX8035	BEL				
NZX4021	ADW	NZX8036	BEM				
NZX4022	ADX	NZX8037	BEN				
NZX4023	ADY	NZX8038	BEP				
NZX4024	ADZ	NZX8039	BEQ				
NZX4025	AEA	NZX8040	BER				
NZX4026	AEB	NZX8041	BES				
NZX4027	AEC	NZX8042	BET				
NZX4028	AED	NZX8043	BEU				
NZX4029	AEE	NZX8044	BEV				
NZX4030	AEF	NZX8045	BEW				
NZX4031	AEG	NZX8046	BEX				
NZX4032	AEH	NZX8047	BEY				
NZX4033	AEJ	NZX8048	BEZ				
NZX4034	AEK	NZX8049	BFA				
NZX4035	AEL	NZX8050	BFB				
NZX4036	AEM	NZX8051	BFC				
NZX4037	AEN	NZX8052	BFD				
NZX4038	AEP	NZX8053	BFE				
NZX4039	AEQ	NZX8054	BFF				
NZX4040	AER	NZX8055	BFG				
NZX4041	AES	NZX8056	BFH				
NZX4042	AET	NZX8057	BFJ				
NZX4043	AEU	NZX8058	BFK				
NZX4044	AEV	NZX8059	BFL				
NZX4045	AEW	NZX8060	BFM				
NZX4046	AEX	NZX8061	BFN				
NZX4047	AEY	NZX8062	BFP				
NZX4048	AEZ	NZX8063	BFQ				
NZX4049	AFA	NZX8064	BFR				
NZX4050	AFB	NZX8065	BFS				
NZX4051	AFC	NZX8066	BFT				
NZX4052	AFD	NZX8067	BFU				
NZX4053	AFE	NZX8068	BFV				
NZX4054	AFF	NZX8069	BFW				
NZX4055	AFG	NZX8070	BFX				
NZX4056	AFH	NZX8071	BFY				
NZX4057	AFJ	NZX8072	BFZ				
NZX4058	AFK						
NZX4059	AFL						
NZX4060	AFM						
NZX4061	AFN						
NZX4062	AFP						
NZX4063	AFQ						
NZX4064	AFR						
NZX4065	AFS						
NZX4066	AFT						
NZX4067	AFU						
NZX4068	AFV						
NZX4069	AFW						
NZX4070	AFX						

Appendix 4

THE GUNSON'S COLORTUNE DEVICE

After a satisfactory check on engine mechanical and electrical components and carburetter(s) the final adjustments in engine tuning are to carburetter mixture strength and idling speed setting. On variable orifice carburetters (such as SU types) this setting is most important as the single jet/needle combination controls the mixture strength throughout the entire engine speed range.

Combustion performance is generally assessed by overall exhaust gas analysis from which the air/fuel ratio can be determined; this is done commercially by the use of specialised electronic diagnostic equipment. The overall result however does not tell us how well or otherwise each cylinder is performing; this the Colortune, in a qualitative manner, can tell us, so enabling the corrective action required to obtain optimum combustion performance to be reduced.

In operation, the Colortune replaces the normal engine spark plug; if you can change a plug, you can use a Colortune 500 — it is as simple as that!

Gunson's Colortune 500

The Gunson's Colortune 500 is a test spark plug with a flame resistant glass top that enables the combustion flame to be observed and its application depends on the fact that different air/petrol mixtures burn with different colours. The colours seen through a Colortune depend entirely on the nature of the mixture in the cylinder being viewed. This mixture depends on the proportion of fuel added to the air being drawn through the carburetter, and the presence, if any, of oil in the cylinder.

One of seven types of flame will be seen through a Colortune according to the combustion condition, as indicated below:-

	Flame type	Combustion Condition Indicated
1.	Orange	Rich mixture
2.	Bunsen blue	Correct Mixture
3.	Whitish blue	Weak mixture
4.	No flame, or intermittent flame	Could indicate a faulty spark or mixture too weak to ignite
5.	Intermittent bright white flashes	
6.	Bunsen blue with a purple tinge	Indicates presence of oil burning in a correctly proportioned mixture
7.	Bunsen blue with a purple tinge	Indicates the correctly proportioned mixture in a two-stroke motor running on a petrol/oil mix.

(Colour 6/7 could also result from the presence of Upper Cylinder Lubricant in the mixture)

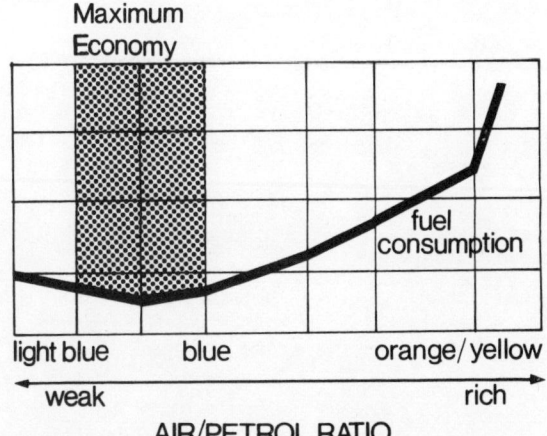

FUEL CONSUMPTION RELATIONSHIP TO AIR/PETROL RATIO AND FLAME COLOUR

Fault Finding System

The Colortune kit may be obtained in single plug or four plug form. The standard Colortune 500 has a 14 mm thread to correspond with standard spark plug sizes; simple conversion kits adapt to 18 mm taper, 12 mm or 10 mm sizes.

A comprehensive Engine Diagnosis Chart is provided giving a progressive test sequence indicating carburetter and engine conditions appropriate to the flame type observed and from which the necessary corrective action may be rapidly deduced.

Fault Indications

Flame colour change has been shown responsive to as small an amount of jet adjustment as one-twelfth of a turn. With such sensitivity it is not surprising that a wide range of carburetter and engine faults can be detected, as the following table shows.

Gunson's Colortune 500. Fault Diagnosis.

Carburetter Condition

Float level too low.

Carburetters not balanced.

Incorrect, worn, or dirty components.

Float level too high.

Dry dashpot cylinder.

Acceleration enrichment device not operating correctly.

Worn, dirty or incorrect jets or needles.

Inoperative choke.

All jets or enrichment devices faulty.

Jet not returning completely.

Dirty enrichment device.

Automatic choke faulty.

Major air leak within carburetter(s).

Engine Condition

Ignition fault.

Air leak on engine side of butterfly.

Bad manifold design.

Choke control or linkage sticking.

Insufficient warm-up.

Oil being burnt in affected cylinders.

Air leak on carburetter side of butterfly.

Petrol Saving

Controlled tests conducted on a sample of cars (two of which had just been serviced) before and after tune-up by Colortune 500 procedure, indicated fuel consumption improvements in the range 4% to 17%. The test circuit was mainly town driving, speed restricted roads. Very little difference in engine response was noted after 'Colortune' adjustments, thus indicating the sensitivity of the adjustment and the potential for probable improvement with any engine having incorrectly set carburation although apparently operating satisfactorily.

Inquiries to:
Gunson's Colorplugs Ltd.
66 Royal Mint Street
London E1 8LG, England.
Tel: 01-480 7561